T5-BBF-965

GREGORY OF NAZIANZUS

Gregory of Nazianzus, a complex and colorful figure in a crucial age (fourth century AD) when it was permissible for the first time to be a public Christian intellectual, was well placed to become one of the outstanding defenders and formulators of Church doctrine.

A gifted and skilled rhetorician, poet, and orator and a profound theologian, Gregory was ordained a bishop and served for almost two years as head of the orthodox Christian community in Constantinople, where he played a crucial role in formulating the classical doctrines of the Trinity and the person of Christ. Under fire from opponents in the Church, the enigmatic Gregory eventually retreated into a quiet life of study and simple asceticism in his native Cappadocia, concentrating there on bringing the broad canon of his own writings to their present form.

The body of his works, including poetry, letters, sermons, and lectures on religious themes and written with the precision and elegance found in classical Greek literature, was recognized in the Byzantine age as equal in quality to the achievements of the greatest Greek writers.

A collection of new translations of a selection of these works, with an extensive introduction to Gregory's life, thought, and writings, *Gregory of Nazianzus* presents to us a vivid portrait of a fascinating character who deserves to be regarded as one of the Christian tradition's outstanding theologians and as the first true Christian humanist.

Brian E. Daley, S.J., is the Catherine F. Huisking Professor of Theology at the University of Notre Dame. A student of the theology of the Church Fathers, he has been a member of the North American Roman Catholic-Orthodox dialogue for over 25 years. His publications include *The Hope of the Early Church* (1991).

THE EARLY CHURCH FATHERS

Edited by Carol Harrison
University of Durham

The Greek and Latin fathers of the Church are central to the creation of Christian doctrine, yet often unapproachable because of the sheer volume of their writing and the relative paucity of accessible translations. This series makes available translations of key selected texts by the major Fathers to all students of the Early Church

CYRIL OF JERUSALEM
Edward Yarnold, S.J.

EARLY CHRISTIAN LATIN POETS
Caroline White

CYRIL OF ALEXANDRIA
Norman Russell

MAXIMUS THE CONFESSOR
Andrew Louth

IRENAEUS OF LYONS
Robert M. Grant

AMBROSE
Boniface Ramsey, O.P.

ORIGEN
Joseph W. Trigg

GREGORY OF NYSSA
Anthony Meredith, S.J.

JOHN CHRYSOSTOM
Wendy Mayer and Pauline Allen

JEROME
Stefan Rebenich

TERTULLIAN
Geoffrey Dunn

ATHANASIUS
Khaled Anatolios

SEVERUS OF ANTIOCH
Pauline Allen and C.T.R. Hayward

GREGORY THE GREAT
John Moorhead

GREGORY OF NAZIANZUS
Brian E. Daley, S.J.

GREGORY OF NAZIANZUS

Brian E. Daley, S.J.

Routledge
Taylor & Francis Group
LONDON AND NEW YORK

BR
65
.G82
E5
2006

First published 2006
by Routledge
2 Park Square, Milton Park, Abingdon, Oxfordshire OX14 4RN

Simultaneously published in the USA and Canada
by Routledge
270 Madison Ave, New York, NY 10016

Routledge is an imprint of the Taylor & Francis Group

© 2006 Brian E. Daley, S.J.

Typeset in Garamond by
HWA Text and Data Management, Tunbridge Wells
Printed and bound in Great Britain by
TJ International Ltd, Padstow, Cornwall

All rights reserved. No part of this book may be reprinted or
reproduced or utilised in any form or by any electronic, mechanical, or
other means, now known or hereafter invented, including
photocopying and recording, or in any information storage or retrieval
system, without permission in writing from the publishers.

British Library Cataloguing-in-Publication Data
A catalogue record for this book is available from the British Library

Library of Congress Cataloging-in-Publication Data
A catalog record for this book has been requested

ISBN10: 0–415–12180–9 (hbk)
ISBN10: 0–415–12181–7 (pbk)

ISBN13: 978–0–415–12180–4 (hbk)
ISBN13: 978–0–415–12181–7 (pbk)

JKM Library
1100 East 55th Street
Chicago, IL 60615

For John W. O'Malley, S.J.,
another Christian humanist

To Gregory the Theologian
(before an icon of the "Three Hierarchs")
Father, what has this pensive face of yours to say?
Perhaps you feel constrained to tell me something new,
But cannot find new words! For what to us seems strange,
Your sermons have already clarified for me.

Michael Psellos (1018–after 1081)
(PG 122.909 A3–7)

CONTENTS

ACKNOWLEDGEMENTS

A completed book always bears the traces of many hands. Although I take full responsibility for all the shortcomings and inaccuracies from which this book may suffer, I also express my profound gratitude to the many people who helped it on the long journey from conception to birth: to Dr. Carol Harrison, of the University of Durham, the general editor of *The Early Church Fathers*, for her patience and kind encouragement, and for her many helpful suggestions on how to improve the final draft; to her colleagues at Routledge, particularly Dr. Richard Stoneman, for showing continuing interest in the book's progress, without ever exerting pressure; to the staff of the Center of Theological Inquiry, in Princeton, NJ, and to my fellow resident members there in 2004–2005, for offering me a setting of warm colleagueship in which to bring the project to completion; to Ms. Kate Skrebutenas and the rest of the staff at the library of the Princeton Theological Seminary, for friendly help in the midst of unparalleled library resources; to my student and assistant, Mr. Scott Moringiello, of the University of Notre Dame, for his lively interest and perceptive comments; and to my friend, colleague, and former student, Professor Christopher Beeley, of Yale Divinity School, for his enthusiasm, careful critique, and unfailing scholarly help during all the years both of us were puzzling over Gregory of Nazianzus together and for saving the book's final version from many errors of fact and judgment. I hope the Cappadocian Saint, in a mood of unusual geniality, smiles on us all and that he is pleased with the result—despite the barbarity of our speech!

1

INTRODUCTION

By almost any criterion, St. Gregory of Nazianzus is a complex figure. Like a number of the most influential of those early Christian writers whom we call "Fathers of the Church," he lived in an age—the last three quarters of the fourth century—in which it was, for the first time, legally and socially permissible to be a public Christian intellectual. The body of works that he left us spans the entire range of Greek literary forms but deals almost exclusively with Christian themes: 44 highly elaborate "orations," including sermons for liturgical solemnities, panegyrics on great figures of the Christian past, funeral orations for friends and family members, polemics against his enemies, treatises on doctrine, and personal apologiae for his own life and ministry; 249 letters, on a variety of subjects, some familiar in tone, some dealing with business matters, some ornate and courtly, but all written with the terseness and elegance that classical antiquity expected in the letters of a trained writer; and some 17,000 lines of poetry, including solemn hymns in Homeric language and style, extended narratives of the "epic" of his own life, didactic expositions on classical and Christian virtue, personal prayers, epitaphs for friends, and wry personal comments on illness, aging, and human foibles.

Gregory's literary ability was regarded so highly by the learned connoisseurs of medieval Byzantium that they ranked him with the great stylists of classical poetry and prose. The eleventh-century scholar Michael Psellos, for instance, speaks of his own hope to write a rhetorical treatise some day, using Gregory as sole model, "since in ideas he surpasses Demosthenes, in quality of prose Plato, and so is superior to both of them, and bears first prize against all comers."[1] Desiderius Erasmus, in the sixteenth-century West, was first impressed by Gregory's Greek style and only later discovered his importance as a defender and formulator of Trinitarian orthodoxy.[2] Yet, in the Greek Christian theological tradition, since the early fifth century, Gregory is generally known as "the Theologian": along with John the Evangelist and the tenth- and eleventh-century spiritual writer Symeon "the New Theologian,"[3] one of only three to bear that epithet by general consensus. All were thought to be exemplary in their ability to speak of God in Christian terms, to develop a vocabulary and a set of concepts for thinking about the reality of God's saving and transforming presence in human history. Of the three figures, Gregory is the only "theologian" to claim eminence on both literary and strictly religious grounds—to write works of theology that are also deliberately constructed as works of art. No wonder that he was, as Jacques Noret has argued, "the most cited author, after the Bible, in Byzantine ecclesiastical literature."[4]

And Gregory is not only a complex figure in terms of his work. Living in an age in which personal self-disclosure was becoming a new literary form, he has a great deal to tell us about his own life, his feelings, and his judgments; yet, he remains always something of an enigma, hiding as much as he reveals about himself through the literary conventions and allusions in which he recounts his experiences. Like Augustine, his younger contemporary, Gregory shows in his writings the high value he places on friendship and family; yet, he often appears in these same works as a troublesome son and a difficult friend: suspicious, oversensitive, self-pitying, demanding, dark in his views of humanity and the world. The older son of a local bishop in rural Cappadocia, Gregory was involved in pastoral leadership from the beginning of his adult life, was ordained bishop of a small Cappadocian hamlet in 372, and found himself unexpectedly at the head of the pro-Nicene community in Constantinople during the first year of the reign of the Emperor Theodosius, in the autumn of 379. His orations and letters show him—again like Augustine—as an active, energetic pastor, deeply engaged in theological controversy, ecclesiastical politics, liturgical leadership, and the care of the poor. Yet, he frequently portrays himself as a hermit out of his proper place, an ailing contemplative forced into action, a pacific loner ill-suited to the conflicts of public administration, a rustic permanently ill at ease amid the sophistication of the Eastern capital. His early retirement from office as bishop of Constantinople was the fulfillment of his dreams, Gregory assures us; yet, his accounts of the events that forced him to retire are clearly tinged with anger and regret. In reading his works, we must thread our way carefully through the details of Gregory's emotional, dramatic, often self-justifying presentation of himself, to try to discover the man, the priest, the theologian, as others in his day might have known him. Like few other figures from Christian antiquity, Gregory of Nazianzus embodies for us both the challenge and the allure of coming to recognize faith, culture, and distinctive human traits embodied in the literary production of a single person: a giant in the developing tradition of Christian reflection on the "mixing" of the human and the divine; a man full of human learning, frailty, and passion and enlivened by an unshakeable faith in the nearness of God.

GREGORY THE MAN

Gregory was born into a family of landed gentry on a country estate called *Karbala*, near Arianzus, a village in the hilly center of the Roman province of Cappadocia, sometime between 326 and 330.[5] His father, also named Gregory, had been raised in what seems to have been a Judaeo-Christian sect called the *Hypsistarii*, the servants of the Most High God;[6] his mother, Nonna, came from a wealthy local Christian family and was the sister of Amphilochius the Elder, a respected lawyer and man of letters and a friend of the noted pagan rhetoricians Libanius and Themistius.[7] Gregory the Elder had become a Christian shortly after marrying Nonna, thanks to her good example and strong persuasion;[8] shortly afterward, probably in 329, he was chosen—50 years old and still a layman—to be bishop of Nazianzus, a small town some eight miles to the northwest of the villa at Karbala, where Nonna's family seem to have owned property.[9] Gregory's father built a church for the faithful of Nazianzus and clearly took his pastoral responsibilities there very seriously throughout his life. Gregory's own efforts in Oration 16 to defend his father's Nicene orthodoxy render clear, however, that the elder Gregory was not always well versed on current theological debates.[10]

Although Nonna and Gregory the Elder seem to have remained childless for a number of years, they eventually had three children: Gorgonia, who seems to have been the eldest, Gregory, and Caesarius. Gregory tells us that before his birth, his mother prayed earnestly to have a son, like several mothers of Old Testament prophets; having been shown in a dream that her prayers would be answered, she dedicated Gregory to God's service as soon as he was born, a promise he regarded as the origin of his vocation.[11] His sister Gorgonia, whose holy and ascetic life Gregory portrays in her funeral oration, eventually married a senior military officer named Alypius, who also became a Christian shortly before his death. They had at least three daughters[12] and lived near Iconium in Lycaonia, the next province to the southwest, where Nonna's family seems also to have had connections.[13] Caesarius, the youngest child, studied philosophy and the natural sciences in Alexandria as a young man and became a physician; after completing his studies, he settled in Constantinople, developed a successful medical practice, and eventually became senior doctor (ἀρχιατρός) at the imperial court and a wealthy man.[14] During the brief reign of the "apostate" Emperor Julian (361–363), Caesarius remained in his official post, despite his older brother's fears that he stood in danger of being pressured to abandon his Christian faith.[15] Obviously a rising star in the ranks of the civil service, Caesarius became the chief financial officer of the province of Bithynia in 368, where he lived through the disastrous earthquake of October 11 of that year.[16] Soon after that event, Caesarius died, still unmarried and in his mid-30s. His death was an event that seems to have been an enormous shock to his older brother: Gregory later wrote, "I died to the world and the world to me, and I have become a living corpse, as devoid of strength as a dreamer. Since that day my life is elsewhere …"[17]

Gregory's life took an even more intellectual turn than that of his younger brother. After the usual elementary studies in Nazianzus and several months under the instruction of their uncle Amphilochius at Iconium, Gregory and Caesarius were sent—probably for most of 346—to a school of grammar and rhetoric in Caesaraea, the provincial capital. These linguistic and literary studies had been, for almost a millennium, the core of Greek and Roman education: young men, for whom alone such formal education was normally possible, were set to study the classics, with the object not only of acquiring the habits of correct speaking and writing, of idiom and orthography and punctuation, but of learning to judge literary eloquence, to cultivate taste, and eventually to become "eloquent" in the complex discourse of Hellenic culture: capable of moving and persuading their peers, of forging the social ties and conventions that alone preserved the fabric of the political body.[18] For the two young brothers, expected to take their place as members of an educated Christian elite in the empire of Constantine's descendants, education necessarily meant both absorbing the heritage of Greek literary and philosophical culture and deepening their own intellectual identification with the Church's tradition of faith: a hybridization of humanism and theology that was only in its beginning stages but that was to be the central preoccupation, in a variety of ways, of Gregory's future life.

After the two brothers had spent perhaps a year in the provincial capital, their parents decided to send them still further afield for cultural formation. The first stop was another Caesaraea, "maritime Caesaraea" in Palestine, which John McGuckin has called "the closest thing in the fourth century to a Christian university town."[19] In that metropolitan city of the Roman province of Palestine,[20] long associated with Origen's exegetical school and library, and with the continuation of the tradition of Origenist learning under Bishop Eusebius, who had died only a few years before their arrival, all the passion and exegetical subtlety of the mid–fourth century debates on the nature of Christ's divinity were doubtless running at high tide.

Aside from some comments in his funeral oration on Caesarius,[21] however, Gregory tells us little about his stay in Origen's city; he seems to have spent time learning rhetoric from the noted stylist Thespesios, for whom he later wrote a graceful epitaph.[22] Very probably, though, he first made the acquaintance here of Origen's exegetical and theological works, which would later have a powerful influence on the theology and scriptural interpretation of all three Cappadocian Fathers.

By the end of 348, Gregory and Caesarius moved on again to the great metropolis of Alexandria, the intellectual heart of the Hellenistic world for both literary and scientific studies—hence, a magnet for the scientifically inclined Caesarius—and as the center of the continuing Origenist tradition of exegesis, represented by the lay scholar Didymus the Blind. In Didymus, if he ever actually met him, Gregory would have found not only a representative of Origen's intellectual legacy but a supporter, unlike most fourth-century Origenists, of the theology framed in the creed of Nicaea, just coming to be taken with full seriousness as a normative expression of apostolic faith. At the same time, Didymus was not an Apollinarian and insisted (like Origen) on the central role of a human soul in the constitution of Christ, the incarnate Son of God.[23] Possibly Gregory and Caesarius too may have met or heard Athanasius the bishop, then resident in Alexandria after returning from his second exile, in the West in 346. Gregory's encomium on Athanasius (Or 21), written shortly after he himself became Nicene bishop of Constantinople in 379, shows no sign of personal contact; still, in offering Athanasius as a model for an orthodox pastor, the work could well hint at an early, distant impression that had been made on Gregory's mind.

Toward the end of 348,[24] Gregory made up his mind to move on to Athens to continue his studies, leaving Caesarius behind in Alexandria.[25] In his poem *On his own Life*, Gregory describes it as an impulsive decision,[26] and his choice to cross the eastern Mediterranean by boat at the beginning of winter was, as it turned out, imprudent as well. The poem describes in epic style a serious storm south of Cyprus, lasting almost three weeks, in which the little ship lost its water cistern overboard and would probably have foundered if it had not been joined by a Phoenician merchantman, whose crew lashed the two ships together to give them a stability that saved them.[27] Gregory recalls his own anguish and fear for his life and tells us that the prospect of dying unbaptized made the danger of shipwreck all the more terrifying for him:

> All of us feared a common death, but more terrifying for me was the hidden death. Those murderous waters were keeping me away from the purifying waters which divinize us. That was my lament

and my misfortune. For this I kept sending up cries and stretching out my hands, and my cries overcame the pounding of the waves.[28]

In dramatic terms, Gregory describes turning to God as his only hope and consecrating himself personally to God for the future, if he should survive, as his mother had consecrated him before his birth:

> Despairing of all hope here below, I turned to you, my life, my breath, my light, my strength, my salvation, the source of terror and affliction, but the benign healer, too, ever weaving good into the dark pattern … Yours, I said, I have been formerly; yours am I now. Please accept me for a second time, the possession of your honored servants, the gift of land and sea, dedicated by the prayers of my mother and by this unparalleled crisis. If I escape a double danger, I shall live for you …[29]

It was a promise not only to seek baptism but to focus his future completely on God's service.

Despite this resolution in a moment of crisis, it is uncertain just when Gregory was actually baptized; following a custom he himself would decry in Oration 40, he may well have delayed his decision for almost another decade.[30] In Athens, whether by prearrangement or by chance, he was soon joined by his fellow Cappadocian, Basil of Caesaraea, who was the son of a teacher of rhetoric in the provincial capital and whom Gregory and Caesarius may well have known from their earlier studies. Gregory and Basil shared lodgings, heard lectures, and engaged in academic exercises together in an atmosphere charged with passion for ideas and linguistic elegance;[31] in Athens, they developed a deep friendship that was to last through repeated crises and misunderstandings until Basil's death thirty years later.[32] Although no longer a city of great political importance, Athens enjoyed the prestige of being the Hellenic world's traditional intellectual center.[33] The focus of Basil's and Gregory's studies would largely have been a continuation of their advanced rhetorical training; at least thirty "sophists" were practicing in Athens at the time, including, as one of the most renowned, the Christian Prohairesios.[34] But a cultured gentleman of the time was expected to have a smattering of knowledge on a great many subjects—geography, history, natural science and, above all, the tradition of Greek philosophy—most of them learned from handbooks compressing a great deal of information into a schematic form.[35] Neoplatonic philosophy, a highly religious, mystical, and sacramental reading of the Platonic understanding of reality, was taught at that time in Athens by Priscus, a disciple of Iamblichus, and he probably also had an influence on the young Cappadocian friends. The future emperor Julian, a nephew of Constantine who had not yet formally abandoned the Christian faith, heard Priscus's Athenian lectures while Gregory and Basil were students there and found in the Neoplatonic system a religious alternative to Christian monotheism that to him appeared more intellectually profound and more respectful of the religious underpinnings of Greek literature and civic life than the faith in which he had been baptized.

For Basil and Gregory, conversely, the intellectual richness of Athenian culture seems, by Gregory's account, at least, only to have moved them to penetrate deeper the Christian narrative of creation and salvation and to search for a new synthesis of faith and philosophical reflection consistent with their upbringing. Gregory later stresses in his funeral panegyric for Basil that the deep friendship that developed between them in their student days was based on their shared commitment to pursue a life of virtue centered on Scriptural teaching rather than to seek academic prestige:

> The sole business of both of us was virtue, and living for the hopes to come, having retired from this world, before our actual departure hence. With a view to this were directed all our life and actions, under the guidance of the commandment, as we sharpened upon each other our weapons of virtue.[36]

This experience of the sometimes hostile, sometimes fruitful contact between Christian doctrine and practice and classical culture, in its most idealistic and rarefied form, was to remain a constant source of energy and tension for the two Cappadocians, as for so many of their Christian contemporaries.

As Gregory himself tells us, Basil was the first to decide to return home to Cappadocia, probably early in 356; Gregory claims to have been persuaded by fellow students to remain in Athens a while longer and accuses Basil of "betrayal" for having joined in that urging while he himself was preparing to depart.[37] A short while later, however, Gregory returned to Cappadocia himself, after ten years abroad in pursuit of learning and wisdom: now, as he tells us, "almost in his thirtieth year."[38] He went by way of Constantinople, the imperial capital of the East and there, by accident, met his brother Caesarius, who had himself recently arrived from Alexandria and who had already made important political and social contacts that were to be the foundation of his later career.[39] Both brothers, according to Gregory's later account, were being drawn home by God in answer to the prayers of their mother, who earnestly hoped to see them together before she died.[40] By the time of his arrival, Gregory makes clear, he was already committed to leading a life of asceticism, which would predictably have included celibacy, a simple lifestyle, and the focusing of his energies on study and prayer.[41]

According to his seventh-century biographer, Gregory the Presbyter, it was only on his return to Nazianzus that Gregory was baptized, "sealing" his commitment to a fully Christian form of life by sacramental initiation.[42] Whether he was baptized then or had been baptized earlier in Athens, as Gregory settled back into the life of family and village, he began to experience a tension that was to torture him until the last few years of his life: the tension between contemplation and pastoral action, between the quiet, scholarly life of an ascetical but comfortable Christian gentleman and the assumption of responsibility for leadership in the turbulent Church of Asia Minor in the mid-fourth century—a level of responsibility commensurate with his education and family connections.[43] A letter written fairly soon after his return to Cappadocia[44] shows him tutoring a young man named Evagrius in the "art of words": in grammar or rhetoric. Basil had by now withdrawn to his family's estate in the mountains of Pontus, in northern Asia Minor; several other letters from this time[45] express Gregory's strong desire to accept his friend's repeated invitation to join him there, along with Basil's mother and older sister Macrina, in a life of austere, intellectually focused withdrawal: the combination of ascetic self-control and concentration on the things of mind and spirit that was known in this period by the simple, comprehensive label "philosophy."[46] One brief note to Basil, probably from the late 350s, expresses Gregory's dilemma and his proposed solution:

> I confess, I have not kept my promise to join you and to share with you the philosophic life, although I committed myself to it during our Athenian years, and our friendship and common life there. I have not willingly failed to keep my word, but one law has trumped another: the law that commands us to care for our parents has overcome the law of companionship and oneness of mind. But I will not fail my promise altogether, if you are willing to accept this proposal: some of the time we will spend with you, if you agree at other times to be with us, so that we may share everything, and respect the demands of friendship equally. This is the way I will succeed both in not offending them and in having your company![47]

It is during visits to Basil's family retreat, in the late 350s and early 360s, that the two friends are traditionally thought to have put together their own anthology of selections from Origen's Scriptural commentaries and writings on hermeneutics, known as the *Philokalia Origenis*.[48] Although it is not certain that Basil and Gregory actually were the compilers of this ancient collection, Gregory did apparently know and use it or something very much like it;[49] in any case, the study of Origen was very likely a substantial component of his study at this time of his life.

In the years after his return to Cappadocia, Gregory seems also to have felt a certain amount of pressure from his father to join in the pastoral care of the Church at Nazianzus. If the elder Gregory was indeed older than fifty at the time of his son's birth, he must now have been in his mid-eighties and clearly in need of assistance in preaching and administration. As Gregory relates in several of his works, his father eventually forced him to be ordained as presbyter, a senior member of what was probably a very small body of local clergy, apparently during the Christmas festival in December 361 or January 362:

> He exerted pressure to raise me to an auxiliary throne, so that he might constrain me by the bonds of the Spirit and pay me the highest honor in his power. Why he did so I cannot say. Perhaps he was moved by fatherly affection, which when combined with power is a considerable force.[50]

Gregory's immediate reaction seems to have been panic or at least severe reluctance to take on his new duties, and he fled to Basil's retreat in the foggy northern mountains yet again:

> Like an ox stricken by the gadfly, I made for Pontus, anxious to have the most godly of my friends as medicine for my agitation. For there, hidden in that cloud, like one of the sages of old, practicing union with God, was Basil, who is now with the angels. With him I soothed my agony of spirit.[51]

By Easter, however, he was back at his father's side and, in the days that followed, probably delivered the core of one of his most famous and influential orations, *In Defense of his Flight*: actually an essay on the theological significance and spiritual challenges of Church ministry.[52]

We know little in detail of the next ten years of Gregory's life. Undoubtedly they were years in which he struggled to keep to the "middle way" combining pastoral activity and intermittent ascetical withdrawal, which he claimed to have chosen as his life's direction.[53] Undoubtedly, too, these were the years in which Gregory's activity as a preacher came to be a central occupation, bringing into a single focus his intense engagement with Scripture and the earlier tradition of its interpretation and his world-class training in the art of eloquence. It is probably from this time, for instance, that both his two orations of invective *Against Julian* appear[54] in addition to his funeral oration for his brother Caesarius[55] and probably that for his sister Gorgonia.[56] It also seems likely that his long, moving oration *On Loving the Poor*, the early Church's most theologically profound reflection on the Christian obligation to social justice, comes from the years between 369 and 372.[57]

Gregory's friend Basil had persisted more single-mindedly for some years in pursuing the life of retirement; by 360, however, he had been drawn into the debates and infighting of the post-Nicene struggle and, in 364, he was ordained a presbyter by Eusebius, the new metropolitan bishop of his native city, Cappadocian Caesaraea. Although his relationship with Eusebius had ups and downs, Basil dedicated himself seriously to reforming the pastoral life of Caesaraea, promoting a new form of ascetic community life that would be led not in withdrawal, or *anachoresis*, but within the city, its energies focused not only on productive labor but on care for the poor, the sick, and the traveler. In 370, on Eusebius's death, Basil recognized that the Church in Asia Minor was at a critical juncture; the Emperor Valens, in hopes of promoting a theological consensus in the Eastern Empire on the lingering questions raised by Nicaea and its critics, was making strong efforts to support the opponents of Athanasius and those—seemingly on one extreme of the Christian theological spectrum—who spoke of the Son as "of the same substance" as the Father. Having come gradually to accept this "homoousian" position himself (with some nuances) as a central element of orthodoxy and encouraged by his success as a monastic reformer and pastoral innovator, Basil seems to have let go of whatever attractions he still cherished for a life of retirement. He campaigned successfully to be elected Eusebius's successor and immediately took steps to affirm his own position of leadership throughout the Churches of Asia Minor by staking out the ecclesiastical and theological opposition to the imperial policy.

Early in 372, Valens announced that he was dividing the civil province of Cappadocia, whose capital city was Caesaraea, into two parts, with Tyana on the main road south toward Antioch as the capital of the new province of Cappadocia Secunda. Anthimus, bishop of Tyana, a supporter of Valens's religious and political aims, clearly saw his opportunity for checking the influence of the bishop of Caesaraea. On his part, Basil was not willing simply to accept the assumption that ecclesiastical reorganization must follow civil division and continued to regard the territory that had been under Eusebius's supervision as subject to his own metropolitan primacy.[58] However, he also realized that it was crucial to fill his own province with suffragan bishops who would support him in synodal debates. Shortly before Easter of 372, he pressed both his own younger brother

Gregory and Gregory of Nazianzus to be ordained bishops for what apparently were newly created sees. With the urging of his own father, whom Basil had co-opted to support his plan, Gregory of Nazianzus became bishop of Sasima, a small village at an important crossroads near the border of the two Cappadocian provinces, while Basil's brother Gregory became bishop of Nyssa, at the northwestern edge of Cappadocia Prima. When the region of Lycaonia, across the Taurus Mountains to the south, was also removed from Cappadocia and made a separate Roman province in 373, Basil ordained Gregory's cousin Amphilochius the Younger,[59] himself a well-educated ascetic with theological commitments similar to his Cappadocian friends, as bishop of Iconium, the new province's capital. Suddenly, a number of Basil's friends were swept into a dangerous and unfamiliar game.

Gregory Nazianzen's reaction to Basil's gesture of ecclesiastical patronage, when he had time to reflect on it further, was typically complex and largely resentful. On the one hand, he does genuinely seem to have regretted the loss of contemplative leisure that resulted from his new involvement in Church politics during a time of transition and to have seen this forced extraction from the quiet life as a betrayal of friendship. He also clearly resented being made head of a tiny Church with no previous tradition of faith, no cultural attractions, and no political importance besides its position on a major road through the mountains. Gregory may well have expected, as John McGuckin suggests,[60] that Basil really intended to involve him more directly in the affairs of the provincial capital as a regular advisor and spokesman; much of his disappointment, then, may also have come from the realization that his services would amount to little more than being bishop of a place hardly worthy of his family and education, let alone worth his loss of solitude.

Gregory's resentment comes to expression with satiric force in his poem *On his own Life*:

> Midway along the high road through Cappadocia, where the road divides into three, there's a stopping place. It's without water or vegetation, not quite civilized, a thoroughly deplorable and cramped little village. There's dust all around the place, the din of wagons, laments, groans, tax officials, implements of torture, and public stocks. The population consists of casuals and vagrants. Such was my church of Sasima. He who was surrounded by fifty *chorepiscopi* was so magnanimous as to make me incumbent here![61]

His response to the perceived betrayal, in fact, was passive resistance: Gregory apparently never took up residence in Sasima[62] and ostentatiously refused to engage himself either in the affairs of the district where it was located or in Basil's ecclesio-political struggles. So he writes defiantly to Basil, apparently shortly after his episcopal ordination:

> You reproach us with inactivity and laziness, because we have not taken possession of your Sasima, and are not making motions of a duly episcopal kind or helping arm all of you for your struggles, like some scrap of food thrown in the midst of the dogs! For me, the main form of action is inaction. And to let you know one of my good qualities: I am so ambitious about my inactivity as to think it should be a law for anybody aspiring to magnanimity in this whole affair. So much so, that if everyone were to imitate us, there would be no dispute among the Churches, nor would the faith be swept away in the flood by becoming the weapon of each one's private ambitions![63]

More clearly than in most of his writings, Gregory here makes it clear that he feels he is being used simply as a tool for the advancement of Basil's personal ambitions.

As he had done after presbyteral ordination ten years before, Gregory expressed his resistance to office by "fleeing" once again to contemplative solitude: "Once more the goad struck me: I became a fugitive again, making for the mountain in search of my pet luxury, that beloved mode of life."[64] And once again, a strong sense of filial duty forced him to cut short his retreat. According to his poem *On his own Life*,[65] Gregory's aging father again begged him to return to Nazianzus and share in his pastoral duties, this time as assistant bishop, probably with an eye to becoming his father's successor. Gregory gave in to his wishes and returned to be with his parents, apparently with enthusiastic support from some members of the local congregation.[66] The elder Gregory died not long afterward, at the age of almost a hundred, probably in the spring of 374; and was followed by his wife Nonna a few months later.[67] Gregory found himself acting as bishop of Nazianzus by default: never canonically installed in his father's place, yet unable to persuade the other bishops of the provincial synod to sympathize with his desire for solitude and to appoint a regular successor.[68] It was probably during this period as acting bishop in what had been his father's church that Gregory preached his celebrated sermon for "New Sunday" (Oration 44), at the annual dedication festival of the shrine of St. Mamas in Caesaraea, an oration that seems to allude to the presence of his imperious friend Basil in the congregation.[69] Shortly after his father's death, also, he seems to have given Oration 19, an exhortation to Christian behavior aimed both at the people of Nazianzus and at the newly appointed tax-collector, another Julian, who had recently been assigned to the district.

However, pastoral responsibility, especially in his home town, never sat easily with Gregory. So he fled yet again, probably early in 375: this time taking refuge in the women's monastic community in Seleucia, the region on the Mediterranean coast south of Cappadocia. The convent was dedicated to St. Thecla, the early martyr associated with Paul and with the city of Iconium, not far away to the northwest, where his sister Gorgonia had lived and his cousin Amphilochius was now bishop.[70] Here, in a well-traveled part of Asia Minor fairly close to the busy cultural and ecclesiastical center of Antioch, yet secure enough from everyday Church administration and the political tensions of Cappadocia to let him concentrate on his reading and writing, Gregory remained based, as he says, for "quite a considerable time,"[71] probably until the summer or early autumn of 379. The fact that we know relatively little about his activities at this period suggests it was one of the happier times of his life.

During these years of quiet, Gregory undoubtedly came into more direct contact than he had previously experienced with the theological controversies brewing in and around the Church of Antioch. The debate over the status of the Son of God, in his relationship to the Father, which preoccupied the whole Church since the time of Constantine, had split the Church at Antioch into three rival communities, each with its own bishop. An "Arian" or "Homoean" community, true to the official imperial policy, rejected the creedal formula of Nicaea altogether and confessed that the Son is simply "like" the Father. A strongly pro-Nicene or "Homoousian" community, led by Bishop Paulinus and supported by the bishops of Rome and by Athanasius of Alexandria until his death in 373, held a strict substantial unity of Son and Father. And a more moderate pro-Nicene group, led by Bishop Melitius and supported by Basil and most of the other bishops of Asia Minor, sought for ways of harmonizing the Nicene formula, and its confession of the ontological divinity of the Son, with a parallel emphasis of the permanent distinction of Son from Father.

Although we do not have details of Gregory's contact with these groups in Antioch, his friendship with Melitius in the early 380s suggests he may already have been involved sympathetically with his faction during his years on the Seleucian coast.

These were also the years in which Apollinarius of Laodicaea—a highly talented writer from the Antiochene world, the pioneer of a new movement to create a Christian Hellenic literature, but also an ambitious ecclesiastical entrepreneur—advanced his view of Christ as the embodiment, in a perfect, "heavenly" human form, of the eternal Logos: as the "mind of God" who has become in Jesus what the created mind is in each of us.[72] Whereas Apollinarius actively promoted this understanding of the person of Christ among the bishops of Syria and southern Asia Minor as an answer to Arianism in the 360s and 370s, other Antiochenes, especially the exegete-bishop Diodore of Tarsus, drew attention to the potential dangers of such a view. Gregory himself was to emerge, in the period after 379, as the leading voice in articulating what would become the Church's classical core of doctrine: both the doctrine of an irreducible Trinity of consubstantial persons in God (essentially, the position of Melitius and his followers) and that of a Christ who, as the divine Savior, is personally Son of God yet complete in every aspect of his assumed humanity—"for what has not been assumed has not been healed."[73]

On August 9, 378, the emperor Valens was killed at Adrianople, northwest of Constantinople in Thrace, along with two-thirds of his army. He was attempting (unsuccessfully) to quell an uprising by Goths who had been allowed to settle within the Empire's borders. The Spanish general Theodosius, headquartered at Thessalonica nearby, crushed the Gothic forces when they moved further south and was himself acclaimed by the armies as emperor of the East on January 19, 379. The succession was laden with importance for the struggling parties within the Eastern Church. A devout Christian himself and an unequivocal supporter of the Nicene confession, Theodosius put an end to his predecessor's efforts to find a middle position between the supporters of Nicaea and the representatives of various forms of what the Nicenes labeled *Arianism*: those who held the Son of God to be in some sense a "created" being. Sensing that major changes were on the way, pro-Nicene Christians in Antioch and Asia Minor began actively searching for a learned and eloquent leader for the Nicene community (then in the minority) in the capital: an episcopal position that had not been filled since the exile of bishop Evagrius around 370. The officially recognized bishop of Constantinople at the time of Valens's death was Demophilus, who, with most of his clergy, continued to profess the Homoean or moderately Arian understanding of Christ, which had been made the Empire's official doctrine by Constantius in 359. A variety of Gregory's friends and colleagues in the Antiochene region, perhaps encouraged by Basil himself in the months before his death on January 1, 379,[74] apparently put pressure on Gregory once again to become involved in Church administration, this time in no less a place than the imperial capital. Though it was too early to have him canonically recognized as bishop, he could serve Nicene sympathizers there as an experienced pastor and preacher, capable of forming a new intellectual consensus opposed to the Arian and Apollinarian trends. As Gregory put it:

> As God would have it (for people thought me prominent in career and eloquence, though I had always lived a provincial life) at the instance of many pastors and their flocks, the grace of the Spirit sent me to these as helper for the people and support of orthodoxy.[75]

A synod of bishops from all over the Greek East, almost identical in membership to the council of Constantinople of June, 381, was called together by Melitius at Antioch in the autumn of 379 in hopes of ending the schism in that city and forming a new, moderately pro-Nicene theological front. This gathering, as McGuckin suggests, may well have convinced Gregory to take the call to Constantinople, open-ended as it was.[76] Gregory's first cousin Theodosia, the sister of Amphilochius of Iconium and Nonna's niece, had married a prominent senator named Ablabius and had a large villa in the capital. A Nicene herself, she was able to offer him both a suitable place to live and a hall on her property in which to gather the faithful, and which Gregory would name "Anastasia": "place of resurrection."[77] The opportunity seemed too inviting to resist, and Gregory took on this new challenge sometime in the early autumn of 379.[78]

During the next eighteen to twenty months, Gregory found himself facing considerable opposition. During the Easter celebrations in his first year in the city (380), he and his Nicene congregation were pelted with stones by a crowd of anti-Nicene monks who had broken into the Anastasia.[79] He was also enormously busy. He had been brought to the capital of the Eastern Empire because of his unique combination of learning, eloquence, and unrelenting commitment to Nicene orthodoxy, which was now coming to be viewed with new sophistication and new complexity through the Cappadocian lens. Much of his work, clearly, was public speaking: delivering the festal homilies, theological lectures, and polemical challenges that he edited after his retirement into the elaborate, highly finished "orations" (Greek: λόγοι) that, along with some earlier and a few later pieces, form the center of his literary legacy. With the exception of Oration 35, which is now generally recognized to be spurious, numbers 20 to 42 of Gregory's corpus of 45 (or 44) orations can be dated to his time as pastor of the Nicene community in Constantinople. They are mainly expressions of his struggle to articulate with all the linguistic and philosophical brilliance he could muster a rationale for what was to become the new, imperially endorsed orthodoxy.

Reconstructing the chronology of Gregory's preaching from this period is a speculative enterprise. John McGuckin, whose suggestions we generally follow here, offers a somewhat more compressed schedule than the usual one for Gregory's oratorical activity in the capital. McGuckin's hypothesis that Gregory arrived in the capital in the early autumn of 379 requires a later start for his series of addresses there than that assumed, for example, by Paul Gallay.[80]

However we attempt to date them, Gregory's orations from this busy time took a number of literary forms. Two of them, for example, were formal commemorations of the lives of distinguished heroes of the Church's past: Oration 24, on St. Cyprian (probably given on October 2, 379, shortly after Gregory's arrival),[81] and Oration 21, on St. Athanasius (given probably on May 2, 380). Though Gregory's knowledge of Cyprian's life and work was sketchy at best, Athanasius was a figure of more immediate relevance to the political and theological debates of his time, and his panegyric was a complimentary gesture toward the Church of Alexandria. It further embodied a distancing of himself from the former rival claimant to Athanasius's see—his countryman George of Cappadocia (356–361)—and a clear, if not particularly elaborate, affirmation of Athanasius's Nicene theology.

Other works were salvos fired off in his continued skirmishing with the opponents of Nicaea: Orations 23 and 33, complaining of the arrogant tactics and spurious arguments of the various Arian groups in the city, were given probably in the late spring of 380 as Gregory worked hard to build up a Nicene consensus that would win support both from the Melitians in Antioch and from the Alexandrians. Still other addresses were aimed at damping the fires of controversy, expressing what seems to have been Gregory's instinct for avoiding conflict wherever possible. Oration 22, *On Peace*, urging the various factions in Antioch to continue the process of reconciliation and mutual understanding, was composed probably shortly after Gregory's arrival in the capital in September, 379. Oration 32, *On Moderation in Theological Argument*, seems to have been delivered the following winter and drew on the classical ideal of the "golden mean" to reinforce the Gospel ideal of reconciliation among enemies.

Gregory's most celebrated writings from the years in Constantinople, however, are his positive expositions of the synthetic position on God, Jesus, and the Holy Spirit, fully elaborated for the first time by the Cappadocians; this position was to become the classical Trinitarian doctrine of both Eastern and Western Christianity. His first effort in this direction, probably composed also in the early autumn of 379, is Oration 20, which in most manuscripts is given the somewhat puzzling title *On Theology and the Appointment of Bishops*. As we will see later, it is a brief exposition of the same Christian conception of the divine reality that he will develop at much greater length in the "Five Theological Orations," probably written the following summer. The simplest way to understand its traditional title, as well as Gregory's rather obscure allusion to candidates for ecclesiastical office at the end of Chapter 1, is to suppose that this was intended to be the new bishop's personal manifesto on the Trinity. It could be read as a description of the kind of Nicene faith that ought to be the norm for anyone appointed to Church office under a pro-Nicene emperor, and an inaugural profession of Gregory's own orthodoxy, addressed to the faithful in Constantinople and the bishops of the other Churches with whom he hoped his Church would be in communion.[82]

The "Five Theological Orations" (Orations 27–31), probably composed during the summer of 380, are Gregory's best-known works. They are five essays on the nature and content of Christian *theologia*, which together form a subtle and perennially suggestive summary of classical Greek Patristic thought on the requirements for speaking meaningfully about the divine reality in a way that is legitimately derived from the Christian Scriptures. Original, daring, experimental in places, yet always powerful as an appeal to the spirit of worship and adoration at the heart of theological argument, these discourses are anything but the glib, derivative summary of other people's ideas that they have sometimes been judged to be. In them, above all his other works, Gregory won for himself his title *Theologian*. These writings remain early Christianity's classic and most comprehensive expression of the late fourth century's new consciousness of God, as three "hypostases," three irreducibly individual and inseparably related poles of being, who form together—precisely in their relatedness—the single, ineffable, ontologically foundational "substance" Christians adore as ultimate and immediate reality.

Very likely in the summer of 380 as well, Gregory became the victim of a strange personal conspiracy that disappointed and wounded him deeply, a conspiracy that may have been engineered from afar by high officials in the Church of Alexandria but was carried out by a bizarre character known as Maximus "the Cynic."[83] Maximus seems to have arrived in the capital from his native Alexandria early in 380, presenting himself as a traveling Christian philosopher of the "Cynic" school: deliberately unconventional in dress, flamboyant in demeanor, yet also, according to the historian Sozomen, "zealously attached to the Nicene doctrine."[84] Gregory depicts him with the help of hindsight as an oversized and effeminate poseur who became most widely known in Constantinople for his abundant mane of bleached curls and his facial make-up.[85] Gregory suggests that Maximus's ability as a Christian preacher was dubious[86] and that his original absence from Alexandria was due to some kind of misbehavior;[87] Gregory himself, however, clearly was taken in by Maximus when he first appeared in the capital claiming to be a loyal supporter. He tells the tale with bitter irony in his poem *On his own Life*:

Like a true professional in the art of fraud, he didn't use outside help, he used myself to stage the whole business … Consider, for instance, his subtlety in manipulating this matter. You will recognize another Egyptian Proteus! He joins the group of the well-disposed, those altogether loyal to me. Was there anyone who shared my roof, my table, my teaching, my plans as Maximus did? It was little wonder: he kept barking, like the great dog he was, against my enemies, and was an eager admirer of my sermons.[88]

As Gregory was to discover, Maximus's real ambition in joining his entourage was to unseat the Cappadocian from his still-uncanonical episcopal throne and to become bishop of Constantinople himself. The Church in Alexandria, whose bishop, Peter, had warmly welcomed Gregory, a fellow Nicene, by letters of recognition when he first arrived in the capital,[89] may have had a hand in encouraging Maximus's intrigue. Oration 34, which McGuckin plausibly dates to late May 380, is Gregory's speech of welcome to a delegation of Alexandrians who have arrived on the first grain ships of the spring: possibly that same party of notables and seeming well-wishers whom he later likened to the Israelite spies led by Joshua and Caleb to survey the Promised Land.[90] In any case, Gregory was still positively impressed by Maximus at the end of summer, 380; that is the only explanation for Oration 25, a fulsome discourse of praise for Maximus, called here by the somewhat mysterious code-name "Hero,"[91] as an eloquent defender of the Nicene faith, an admirable ascetic, and an example of philosophic moderation. At the beginning of the oration, Gregory even invites the wandering philosopher to come up from the congregation and stand at his side, a gesture that some may have read as encouraging Maximus to expect some active share in the pastoral leadership of Gregory's Church. Both Gregory and his congregation, however, were soon to see him in a different light.

According to Gregory's poem *On his own Life*, Maximus soon began to use bribes to increase his influence among the leaders in Constantinople. A priest who had come from the island of Thasos to purchase marble tiles for his church was persuaded by Maximus to use his funds instead to build up a clientele for the Egyptian philosopher. Shortly thereafter, another delegation arrived from Alexandria, this time a group of bishops who had been commissioned by Patriarch Peter to ordain Maximus bishop on the spot, presumably in the hope that he could then be recognized as the legitimate Nicene head of the Church in the capital.[92] Probably in September 380, at a time when Gregory himself was confined to his quarters by one of his recurring bouts of illness, Maximus and his clerical sponsors entered a Church building (presumably the basilica of the Holy Apostles, the city's cathedral Church) late at night with the help of some Alexandrian sailors.[93] Without Gregory's permission or local cooperation, they began to celebrate a liturgy of ordination. Just at dawn, however, someone aroused the clergy and police, and Maximus's party was forced to leave the basilica without completing the ceremony, retiring to the nearby house of a flute-player, a profession redolent of associations with erotic banquets. In the end, Gregory observes with bitter delight, the only valuable achievement of the rump liturgy was to clip off the ordinand's blond curls![94]

Maximus then quietly disappeared from the capital, returning first to Alexandria to try to build support for his project there, then going to Thessalonike to visit Theodosius, finally traveling west to persuade the Italian bishops, by presenting them with a treatise he had written against the Arians, that he was the legitimate new orthodox bishop of Constantinople. Even a year later, in September 381, Ambrose of Milan and Damasus of Rome were willing to support Maximus in his claims, probably in the understanding that he had the support both of the bishop of Alexandria and the Emperor.[95] Public opinion in Constantinople turned violently against the impostor, however; "bitter accusations flooded in," Gregory later wrote, "about his manner of life ... From every source different details were brought up by different people, all of which fitted in with his great coup d'état,"[96] and all of which also raised questions about Gregory's own lack of judgment. Gregory seems first to have coped with the shock of these scandalous events by his habitual strategy of flight. He left the city for a while in a combined fall vacation and spiritual retreat, cultivating again for himself the "philosophic" life that seemed to have been lost in the hubbub. In Oration 26, delivered shortly after his return to the capital several weeks later, Gregory invites his congregation to join him in a mutual "accounting" for their recent behavior; he praises them for their faithful support and develops a powerful image of himself as the single-minded, other-worldly, somewhat naïve ascetic he had always attempted to be.

Gregory's remaining orations in Constantinople, however, soon took on a more official and liturgical character. After defeating the rebellious Goths, Theodosius entered the city in triumph on November 24, 380 and promptly took steps to stabilize the political and religious situation. He apparently first offered to allow Demophilus, the anti-Nicene bishop previously sponsored by Valens, to continue in his post uncontested if he would change his theological position and subscribe to the Nicene confession.[97] When Demophilus refused, the Emperor sent him and many of his clergy into exile and immediately made the symbolic gesture of inviting Gregory to join him in a solemn procession as he claimed official control of the basilica of the Holy Apostles. Although Gregory admits to having had doubts about Theodosius's readiness to enforce his Nicene faith as the imperial norm, the Emperor greatly surprised and delighted him as the procession began by promising to commit the care of the Church in the capital to his hands.[98] Gregory describes the ensuing scene dramatically in his poem *On his own Life*:

> Armed forces, drawn up in the various aisles, invested the church. An agitated mob confronted them, like the sand of the sea, or snow, or storm-tossed waves. Their mood veered between hostility and entreaty; hostility towards me but entreaty where the civil power was concerned. Every place was crowded, the streets, the arenas, the piazzas. Men and women, children and old folk, craned down from second and third stories. Struggles, groans, tears and grumblings gave the impression of a town being sacked by force. And the noble leader was myself, sickly and decrepit, the breath scarcely left in my carcass, marching between general and army, my eyes raised to heaven. Hope sustained me as we wound our way, until finally I stood in the church, I know not how.[99]

As the sun unexpectedly burst through an overcast sky, filling the church with light, Gregory continues, the mood of the crowd seems to have become sunny toward him as well, and a general outcry began, urging the new Emperor to enthrone Gregory as canonical bishop of Constantinople there and then. Through a spokesman, however, Gregory deflected the proposal, pointing out that the present occasion was meant to celebrate the Emperor's arrival in the city and that the "greater issue" of leadership in the Church would be better decided later on.[100]

Although Gregory was now clearly at the center of the ecclesiastical stage in the imperial city, he apparently refused to adopt a strategy of forcefully expelling the remnants of opposition to the Nicene confession or clearing the city of personal enemies. From his later narrative perspective, Gregory makes it clear that his motive was religious, rather than political or self-interested:

> The question was whether by a flagrant use of power and opportunity to push, drive, plunder and devastate; or to heal with the medicine of salvation. The latter course had two notable advantages: people could be made moderate by the use of moderation, and I was in a position to win glory and affection for myself. It was the right procedure naturally, the one I propose always and openly to follow … Everyone courts the majesty of

those in power, particularly those with confidential positions, people who are devoid of manhood except where money is concerned ... I was alone in choosing to be loved rather than hated. I won respect by keeping to myself, and devoting myself for the most part to God and the pursuit of perfection. The doors of the mighty I left to others.[101]

One moving instance of this deliberately conciliatory approach that Gregory describes in the same poem in some detail was his behavior toward a would-be assassin. At some time after Theodosius's entry, presumably while Gregory was again confined to his quarters by illness, a crowd of the faithful entered his apartment, leading a rather disheveled-looking young man who was clearly in emotional distress. The young man fell at Gregory's feet sobbing while most of the crowd withdrew. After some anxious questioning, Gregory discovered that the man had been plotting to kill him—probably at the urging or bribery of one of the groups that resisted his accession—but had seen the error of the plan just in time, and now confessed it all. Gregory's reaction was simply to be forgiving:

> I was utterly broken by these words, and hastened to say something that would obliterate all unpleasantness. 'God save you. For me, who have been delivered, to be kind to my attacker is but a little thing. Your courage has made you mine. See to it that you become a credit both to me and to God.' The city—for you can't keep good hidden—was immediately mollified by my reaction, just like iron by the action of fire.[102]

The next months were full of new complications. Gregory tells us that he soon discovered all financial records for the Church of Constantinople were missing, so that he had no way of telling how much of the ecclesiastical funds had been plundered by his predecessors.[103] He seems to have adopted a fatalistic attitude to the disappearance of the money and says he devoted himself to the more spiritual side of his office: to caring for the poor, to supporting ascetics, and to preaching and liturgy.[104]

One of his first sermons as all-but-canonical bishop of the capital seems to have been Oration 36, presenting himself and his priorities to Theodosius and his court, delivered, as McGuckin suggests, on the Sunday after his installation, either on November 29 or December 7, 380.[105] Within the next few weeks, he seems also to have given Oration 37, his only extant discourse directly based on a single Scriptural passage; in it, Gregory discusses Christian marriage and Christian chastity in the context of Jesus' words in Matthew 19.1–9, against the background of his now-familiar

theological vision of the Trinity and the person of Christ. At the great
celebration of the birth and manifestation of Christ (possibly beginning
on December 25, as the Western Church had practiced for decades, or
possibly still concentrated in a three-day festival centered on January 6) he
delivered a trilogy of sermons on the Christian Mystery of salvation,
presumably in the official bishop's Church of the Holy Apostles. The trilogy
has come down to us as Orations 38–40: *On the Theophany* or the revelation
of God in the world (Or. 38); *On the Holy Lights* (Or. 39), dealing with
the Mystery of God's reconciliation with a fallen humanity and centered
on the baptism of Jesus; and *On Baptism* (Or. 40), exhorting the faithful
to participate in the saving Mystery without delay by coming forward to
enroll for baptism themselves.[106] All these sermons present a powerful,
Biblically based narrative of the fall and redemption that expresses, on a
broad and detailed canvas, Gregory's understanding of Christian orthodoxy
in contrast to classical paganism and the various forms of Arian and
Apollinarian Christianity then current. Taken together, they offer a
comprehensive view of the Christian Gospel of salvation and renewal,
through Christ and in the Church, that has rarely been equaled for the
richness of its theological imagination.

Theodosius faced a number of Church questions after his entry into
the Eastern capital. Shortly after taking possession of the city, he issued an
invitation convening a council of Eastern bishops in the city for the coming
May: In membership and agenda, it would be largely a continuation of
Melitius's council in Antioch of September 379, but now it was to be
formally sponsored by the Emperor.[107] On January 10, Theodosius also
issued a decree prohibiting both the hard-line, Eunomian Arians and the
modalist Photinians from using churches in the city, and depriving the
more moderate followers of Demophilus, Gregory's anti-Nicene predecessor,
of their clerical privileges.[108] The way seemed clear for the official
recognition of Gregory by Emperor and Council as undisputed bishop of
Constantinople and (by implication) as theological spokesman for Eastern
Christendom; the decree also seemed to promise an opportunity for a
reaffirmation of the Nicene creed and an extension of its confession of the
Son's consubstantiality with the Father to include the Holy Spirit as well.

In the event, things were not quite so simple. When the 150 invited
Greek bishops (drawn mainly from Asia Minor and Syria but including a
vocal delegation from Egypt) assembled for deliberations in late May under
the presidency of the aged Melitius of Antioch, they apparently did reaffirm
the faith of Nicaea in a formula of some kind but seem to have spoken of
the status and activity of the Holy Spirit in terms that stopped just short
of calling him "God" or confessing (as Gregory had not feared to do in the
"Theological Orations") that the Spirit is *homoousion* with Father and

Son.[109] A few weeks after the Council's opening, Melitius died suddenly, and Gregory himself took the chair. By his own testimony, Gregory found his new position desperately uncomfortable. He describes the situation, in typically dramatic and ironic terms, in his poem *On his own Life*:

> I thought, in my vain imaginings, that once I had control of this throne (outward show carries great weight) I could act like a chorus leader between two choruses. Putting the two groups chorus-fashion, one on this side of me, the other on that, I could blend them with myself and thus weld into a unity what had been so badly divided. The division certainly ran deep ... The leaders and teachers of the people, donors of the Spirit, whose doctrine of salvation is poured forth from high thrones, who constantly with booming voices preach peace to everyone publicly in churches, raged bitterly against one another. And as they clamored, gathered support, accused and were accused, jumped from their seats beside themselves, appropriated to their side anyone they could get to first in a furious struggle for power and control (I have no words really to stigmatize such goings-on), they burst the whole universe apart.[110]

Gregory's support undoubtedly was centered in the delegations from central Asia Minor and the region around Antioch; the bishops from Egypt, who had encouraged him on his arrival in the capital two years earlier, had since then conspired to put Maximus in his place and by now were clearly the core of his opposition. They seem to have received moral support from Pope Damasus and the West, although no Latin bishops attended the Council as voting members. From the perspective of the mid-fifth century, the historian Sozomen describes the Council's discussion of the succession at Constantinople in typically sober terms. After the discussion of the central theological issues and after the "Macedonians," who refused to acknowledge the full divine personhood of the Holy Spirit, had withdrawn,

> the bishops who remained at Constantinople now turned their attention to the election of a prelate to the see of that city. It is said that the Emperor, from profound admiration of the sanctity and eloquence of Gregory, judged that he was worthy of this bishopric and that, from reverence for his virtue, the greater number of the Synod was of the same opinion. Gregory at first consented to accept the presidency of the church of Constantinople; but afterwards, on ascertaining that some of the

bishops, particularly those of Egypt, objected to the election, he withdrew his consent … He surrendered his appointment to the bishops when it was required of him, and never complained of his many labors, or of the dangers he had incurred in the suppression of heresies. [111]

Sozomen hints at the canonical grounds on which Gregory's succession to the see of Constantinople was being contested: he was already bishop of Sasima and had also been acting as bishop of Nazianzus after his father's death;[112] the canons of Nicaea forbade the transfer of bishops from one see to another, a prohibition already more honored in the breach than in the observance, but one that still offered a legal excuse for objection. Sozomen continues:

> Had he retained possession of the bishopric of Constantinople, it would have been no detriment to the interests of any individual, as another bishop had been appointed in his stead at Nazianzus. But the council, in strict obedience to the laws of the fathers and ecclesiastical order, withdrew from him, with his own acquiescence, the deposit which had been confided to him, without making an exception in favor of so eminent a man. The emperor and the priests therefore proceeded to the election of another bishop …[113]

The Council of Constantinople adjourned on July 9, 381; its decrees were formally received by the Emperor on July 30. At some point before its end, Gregory seems to have given his valedictory, although Jean Bernardi has made a convincing case that Oration 42, his powerful "Farewell Address," cannot have been delivered in its present form to any conceivable gathering in Constantinople at that time.[114] As Gregory tells the story, Theodosius only reluctantly agreed to his resignation and sealed his approval with applause; the local clergy and congregation, whom he had led in the days before Theodosius's accession, tried energetically to persuade him to stay. However, Gregory, who had always depicted himself in pathetic terms—a sick, poor, elderly figure; a loner; an awkward foreigner; a stumbling academic; an ascetical practitioner of Christian "philosophy"; as someone who hated conflict and had only contempt for political infighting, who pursued peace through a policy of Christian forgiveness but who was regarded by many as indecisive and overly tolerant toward his opposition—now resolutely insisted on retiring from public life for good. Sometime in late summer, 381 (although the time of his departure from the capital is uncertain), he returned to his family estate at Karbala in Cappadocia, where he remained resident until his death, probably around 390.

On the last day of that fateful year, December 31, 381, Gregory seems to have made his will,[115] witnessed by a number of neighboring bishops, including his cousin Amphilochius of Iconium. In it, he left substantial gifts to a few faithful friends and supporters, including his deacon and intellectual assistant from his time in Constantinople, the theologian and spiritual writer Evagrius of Pontus. All the rest he put at the disposal of the poor in Nazianzus. Yet in his will, Gregory continued to style himself as "bishop of the Catholic Church at Constantinople," the only ecclesiastical office to which he had ever seriously dedicated his energies, even though it had never formally been his. Homecoming seems to have remained for him a bitter-sweet time of forced exile, both the fulfillment of a dream and an icon of failure. Back among his old neighbors and household servants, surrounded by leaders of the Cappadocian Church, his thoughts seem to have been divided between his responsibilities to the community of his childhood and his memories of more dramatic responsibilities in the Empire's eastern capital.

For that final decade of his life, narrative sources are slim; Gregory's interests and activities are mainly known from his letters, the writing of which now became a central part of his theological and political activity. Doubtless soured, more than ever now, on the life of public leadership in the Church, even under the orthodox and generally supportive Theodosius, Gregory maintained contact with the major figures in the controversies of the day by the highly cultivated art of letter writing. Like retired politicians today, his thoughts seem to have turned toward establishing his legacy. In the tranquil, if Spartan circumstances of his ancestral villa, he apparently devoted most of his time and energy to being a man of letters: editing and rewriting his best sermons and speeches, corresponding with friends and people of influence in the Empire, and composing the bulk of the large collection of verse he would leave behind, including the three long narrative poems, in epic style, recounting his own autobiography.

Like Apollinarius of Laodicaea, like his Western contemporaries Prudentius and Ausonius and Paulinus of Nola, in many ways like Augustine, Gregory took seriously the task educated Christians in the Roman Empire were coming to see as one of their chief obligations: producing a new body of classical literature, equal to what the pagans had written in subtlety of language, metrical precision, and rhetorical color and power, but based on the Biblical narrative of salvation and redemption rather than on the mythic and historical memories of Greece and Rome. Partly, it seems, Gregory's hope was to help create a new set of models for Christian youth to analyze and imitate in their own literary training, models

---

that offered the formal perfection of classical models without their occasionally harmful content. Partly he did it for amusement, as a literary exercise, and even for consolation. Partly he wanted simply to prove that Christians could be Hellenists, too. So he writes, tellingly, in his poem *On his own Verses*, which probably comes from his final years of retirement:

> I do it not to win myself a name,
> As most folk, with less principle, might think …
> My first desire, working on other things,
> Was so to put constraints on my prolixity
> That I might write, but never write too much—
> Verse is an effort! Second, I thought of youth,
> And of the folk who find such joy in words:
> My verse could be for them a pleasant potion,
> Leading them towards the Good by mild persuasion …
> Thirdly, I must confess my thought was this—
> A petty thing, perhaps, but still I thought it:
> I cannot bear that strangers should possess
> The prize in letters, rather than ourselves …
> It is for you, O Sophists, that I write—
> Such is my lion-hearted gratitude!
> Fourth, I have found these poems a consolation
> When, weighed by illness, like an aging swan,
> I make the whistling of my wings a song:
> Not mournful, but a kind of parting hymn.[116]

As Gregory declined into old age, style and language, preaching and politics, the discipline of virtue and the pursuit of contemplation, all fused into a single preoccupation. The complexity of his life had itself become a work of art.

GREGORY THE HUMANIST

Although he seems to have been nicknamed "the Theologian" shortly after his death,[117] Gregory was remembered in later Byzantine tradition and in the Western Renaissance more as a literary figure than as a theologian in the modern academic sense. By the mid-fifth century, manuscripts of his orations seem already to have been freighted with marginal notes,[118] proof not only that his style of expression was considered difficult for ordinary Greek readers and students but that understanding his work was considered worth the effort. The first commentary on some of Gregory's Orations, by the so-called Pseudo-Nonnos (probably composed in the sixth century) explains classical references in his works, apparently having in mind young readers who may not be up to Gregory's level of classical learning. Glossaries of difficult words in his writings were assembled in medieval Byzantium;[119] full-scale commentaries, at least on the orations that were read in the monastic office, began to appear by the tenth century.[120] For Michael Psellos, the Byzantine connoisseur of Greek letters, Gregory was not simply the Theologian *par excellence* but Christian Hellenism's worthy counterpart to the orator Demosthenes:

> Since there are three categories of the rhetorical art,[121] Demosthenes has the highest reputation in the forensic genre, and in parliamentary oratory is cleverer than the rest; but when asked to give a panegyric, he is less good than in his other work and than other writers. But Gregory, when compared to him, not only excels Demosthenes's linguistic gifts in the panegyric form, but not even the Heavenly Trumpet,[122] as we call him, can hold his own against him in this sphere.[123]

Psellos goes on to compare Gregory's style with that of the other classical Athenian orators and prose writers—Aristides, Pericles, Lysias, Thucydides, Isocrates, Herodotus—seeing in his prose a fusion of all their best qualities and something unique as well:

> It is not as if what he draws together from many rhetoricians is then distributed, piece by piece, over the different aspects of his style. But as colors, when mixed, form a different shade altogether, and it is not simply what they are, but what is formed from them can at times be more beautiful than they are themselves, so the coloring of Gregory's speech blooms with a thousand colors, but is something else in comparison with them all, and is much more beautiful than they … I am not, then speaking of his style as a collection of unrelated elements, but as homogeneous in nature, just as the rose comes forth from the bowels of the earth in its natural color, yet also multiform, if one is capable of distinguishing in that color a mix of different shades, from which an artist might contrive something of this kind.[124]

Five centuries later, the Western humanist Desiderius Erasmus wrote to Parisian publisher Claude Chevallon, in a letter that was to serve as the preface for a new collection of Gregory's works in Latin translation: "In Gregory of Nazianzus, piety almost contends on an equal footing with eloquence. He loves meaningful wit, which is all the more difficult to translate into Latin, because it is mainly verbal."[125]

Gregory's prose style, in fact, is classically representative of the spoken and written artistic Greek characteristic of the "second Sophistic" period. This epithet, coined by third-century Athenian biographer and litterateur Flavius Philostratus (died A.D. 244–249), designates the dramatic revival of the art of rhetoric in the Greek world that began in the mid–first century of our era and lasted through a temporary decline from roughly 250 to 350, until the early fifth century. Cultivated especially in Athens and the old Greek cities of western Asia Minor, this new rhetoric of the Imperial period was, according to Philostratus, mainly focused on declamation: public performances by professional orators or "sophists" who often toured the Eastern Mediterranean, giving elaborate speeches addressed to historical figures or praising the Emperors and court officials of the day. Like modern concert musicians, these orators often supplemented their income from these performances by teaching, sometimes in imperially endowed chairs, and were occasionally also appointed to diplomatic posts or hired as imperial secretaries. Members of a highly competitive profession, the sophists of the early Christian era often tended to cultivate their own egos by inflating the egos of their living subjects; yet, their message was above all a celebration of traditional Greek ideals of virtue and heroism, transplanted now from the culture of small cities to that of a highly bureaucratic and centralized Empire.[126] The literary style esteemed in the second Sophistic era tended to be characterized by learning and self-conscious artifice and constantly attempted to wear its classical inspiration flamboyantly on its sleeve. Like the work of the "metaphysical poets" or Donne's sermons in Jacobean England, Second Sophistic writing was meant to be an exercise in wit, so much so that its meaning occasionally sank into obscurity beneath its highly wrought skin of cleverness.

The 44 "orations" that form the core of Gregory's literary legacy all represent the taste and technical achievements of Second Sophistic rhetoric.[127] Highly structured sentences built on a foundation of symmetrically arranged *cola* or phrases; sheer verbal abundance; clever plays on words and tricks of sound; abrupt changes of rhythm and reference; dramatic metaphors; and the constant presence of Scriptural and classical allusion, providing his entire train of thought with a parallel world of remembered significance, evoked in a kind of running semiotic counterpoint—all these features turn Gregory's lectures and sermons (at least in their present edited form) into exquisitely self-conscious works of art. Gregory's poetry, too, is heavily influenced by the style and taste of the rhetoricians of the late Empire, many of whom also wrote verse in laboriously classical forms. The eight solemn *poemata arcana* or "mystery-

poems," found in the beginning section of his poetic works as collected in
Migne's *Patrologia*, are clearly meant to imitate the Homeric hymns in
meter and dialect. They celebrate the central subjects of the Christian
"rule of faith"—Father, Son, Holy Spirit, the created world, providence,
the soul, the Bible—outlined by Origen in the preface to his *De Principiis*.[128]
Other poems use the conversational iambic trimeter of the dialogue passages
of Greek drama, still others the more personal elegiac distichs of Greek
epigrams or the more complex lyric meters of monodic song. The subjects
of Gregory's poems include not only theological themes but highly personal
prayers and meditations on the shortness of human life, moral and ascetical
treatises, satirical pieces, and brief personal perceptions of family members
and friends. The celebrated *Palatine Anthology*, a collection of classical and
Christian Greek poetry compiled in the mid–tenth century from earlier
collections, includes as the whole of Book VIII some 240 personal epigrams
and epitaphs by Gregory of Nazianzus: evidence that for Byzantine *literati*
of the early Middle Ages, Gregory's poetry represented Hellenistic taste
and poetic achievement at its best.[129] Yet, its content, its message, was
almost exclusively tied to the Christian Gospel and Christian life. As
Michele Pellegrino observed,

> Under fortunate circumstances, the soul of a poet who is also a
> saint finds itself confronted with the marvelous reality revealed
> by Christianity. What for others is profound doctrine and moral
> purity, he sees in the light of beauty; he stands before a world
> that he contemplates and loves … Saint Gregory Nazianzen, as
> we have seen, often succeeded in feeling the poetry that
> Christianity offered to him in his internal world and in the reality
> around him, especially in what was new in that reality with respect
> to the classical tradition.[130]

The esthetic element, both of Gregory's poetry and his prose, cannot be
separated from his theological vision or his pastoral aims. Throughout his
life, he seems simply to have been driven to communicate his Christian
sense of reality with all the resources that his education in Greek language,
philosophy, and literary style had put at his disposal.

Even Gregory's letters, of which some 249 have been preserved, belong
to the realm of self-consciously literary production, despite the mundane
or ceremonial character of many of them. Although the art of the letter in
both verse and prose had been cultivated for several centuries, the fourth
century witnessed a new interest in the private correspondence of celebrated
literary figures. The first set of Greek letters preserved as a body was that
of Gregory's older contemporary, the Emperor Julian; Libanius, the most

famous rhetor of the day, also left a collection of letters. Gregory, however, is the first Greek writer known to have edited and circulated his own correspondence. Probably during his years of retirement, he complied with the request of his great-nephew, Nicobulus the younger, who was himself studying rhetoric at the time, and sent him "as many of my letters as I have been able to gather together;" he included even some letters sent to him by Basil, as proof to the world of their friendship.[131] His purpose in collecting his letters, he says, is to make available to others "the instructive character of our writings, wherever that is possible, in both opinion and doctrine."[132]

In Letter 51, also to Nicoboulus, which may have served as a programmatic foreword to the collection, Gregory briefly outlines his view of good epistolographic style. A letter should, first of all, be characterized by a length appropriate to the subject: "One should neither write at length when there are not many things to talk about, nor skimp on one's writing when there are."[133] In another brief note to Nicoboulus, he explains the real nature of epistolary brevity:

> The laconic style does not mean, as you may think, to write just a few syllables, but rather to write little about much. So I would say, myself, that Homer is extremely brief in what he says, while Antimachus is prolix. Why? I am judging their length in terms of content, not of words.[134]

Second, Gregory explains to Nicoboulus in Letter 51, a good letter is characterized by both clarity and simplicity, so that the less educated reader can understand it, while the more educated will still find its content interesting.[135] Third, a good letter needs to have "grace," and to be judiciously—but sparingly—spiced with proverbs and witty sayings and with the rhetorical flavoring of artistic prose, without being overly mannered.

> One ought to use these tools to the degree that one uses purple wool in weaving: we do make use of stylistic figures, but only a few of them, and that with modesty! We abandon antitheses and parallel structures and symmetrical phrases to the professional rhetoricians; and if we do use them, we do it more in jest than in earnest.[136]

In prose with as personal an intended audience as a letter, good rhetoric consists in a cultivated informality, even a touch of irony, and must strive first of all to convey meaning directly and concisely.

Gregory's concern for literary accomplishment was by no means unique among Christian leaders and thinkers of the late fourth century, the period that led to what is sometimes called the "Theodosian renaissance" in the cultivation of the arts and literature. One of the formative influences on this revival was the challenge that had been raised by the Emperor Julian (361–363) briefly but menacingly against Christian involvement in the continuing cultural life of the Empire. The son of Constantine's half-brother Julius Constantius, Julian was orphaned as a child and had been brought up by tutors and servants, in bookish isolation, on various imperial estates in Asia Minor. He was carefully instructed in Christian teaching, baptized as a teenager, and even ordained a lector but, as he continued to immerse himself in classical studies, Julian became increasingly alienated from the faith of his family and Christian teachers and devoted himself more and more to the philosophical religion of Greek Neoplatonism. By the time he succeeded his cousin, Constantius II, as Eastern Emperor in November of 361, Julian had begun to participate publicly, as most Neoplatonist philosophers did, in traditional sacrificial rituals directed to pagan gods. An enthusiastic, highly cultivated intellectual with little interest in the sensual amusements available at court, Julian set about curing what he saw as the moral and spiritual decadence of his time by reforming both the administrative and financial structures of the Empire and by attempting to restore traditional religion in a new, systematically rationalized and institutionally unified form modeled, as he himself admitted, on the charitable structures and probing theology of the Christian Church.[137]

Besides allowing the official reopening of pagan temples and the resumption of sacrifice, which had been legally restricted by his predecessor, Julian also took steps to dismantle the public support and social recognition that Christians had increasingly received since the reign of Constantine, forty years earlier. State subsidies and tax exemptions awarded to the Churches were discontinued; heretical and schismatic Christian leaders were allowed to return from exile, under the guise of a general policy of religious tolerance. However, the measure that most aroused Christian fear and anger and continued to embitter Christian writers against Julian for decades afterward was his decree of June 17, 362[138] requiring every schoolteacher both to be approved by the local council and to have that approval officially sanctioned by the Emperor. The decree seems to have been recognized immediately by Christians and non-Christians alike as an attempt to exclude those whom Julian labeled "the Galileans" from the culturally central task of teaching the young. Julian explained, in a letter probably written to a Christian official shortly after the decree was issued, that his concern was to safeguard the moral content of classical education. He was not requiring Christian teachers to change their beliefs, but simply intended to make sure that no one taught young people to interpret and imitate a literary corpus embodying religious ideals in which the teacher did not personally believe: "For whoever thinks one thing and teaches something else to those before him, seems to me to be just as deficient in his quality as an educator as he is in being an honest person."[139] The real target of the measure, he says, is teachers of rhetoric and grammar who handed on the linguistic and symbolic core of classical culture.

Schools, after all, are not simply places where information and "skills for living" are passed on to eager young minds. In every society, they are also places where the values and ideals of human culture are expressed and communicated within the dominant perspective of those who teach in them and who direct their operation. School curricula are always value-centered and teaching always reflects and promotes a vision of society, even if the lines of that vision are not always consciously recognized or openly avowed. Julian understood this. By the fourth century, all literary education passed moral as well as esthetic judgments on ancient texts, made liberal use of allegory to interpret the classics and their myths in morally and intellectually edifying ways, and had a human ideal of excellence in view as its goal. Julian's concern was that such interpretation be kept within classical philosophical (by now mainly Neoplatonic) lines and not be given a Christian coloring or mingled with the teachings of the Christian Scriptures.

> If they think that those whose works they expound, and for whom they occupy, as it were, the position of prophets, were wise, then let them be first to imitate their piety towards the gods. But if they think that they [the ancient poets] were in error in regard to those whom they held in highest honor [i.e., the gods], let them make their way to the churches of the Galileans and expound Matthew and Luke, since they are the ones you trust when you lay down rules barring people from the temples. I want their ears and their tongues to be 'born again,' as you would say ...[140]

In any case, Julian had decided that professing Christians were not to be recognized publicly as experts on the language and intellectual heritage forming the cultural web of the Empire, as purveyors of the "words" that conveyed the heart of Hellenism.

For Gregory and for many educated Christians like him, Julian's new restriction cut deeply into their very identity, implying that their Christian faith and practice, officially tolerated and even promoted by the Empire for the last few decades, were now judged incompatible with the cultural mainstream. In a bitter two-part invective against the Emperor (Or. 4 and

5, *Against Julian*)—probably finished in the spring of 364, less than a year after Julian's unexpected death in battle on the Persian frontier[141]—Gregory accuses the late Emperor of confusing Greek literature with Greek religion: "therefore he has driven us away from literature like thieves from alien property, as if he could fence us off from any of the arts discovered by the Greeks!"[142] "Do you own Hellenism?" Gregory later asks the dead emperor in a brutally pointed apostrophe: "Do you own Attic style? Whose are the draught-board and numbers and the art of calculation,[143] measures and weights, tactics and the art of war? ... Do you own poetry?"[144] What right does even so learned an emperor as Julian have to claim the human λόγος— the power of reason, itself a participation in the Reason or Word of God, and all the verbal skill and beauty in which this created reason clothes and communicates itself—as something subject to imperial legislation? Gregory continues:

> Although there are many serious issues for which he might be justly hated, there is no other point on which he seems more to have acted lawlessly than this. Let anyone who loves literature and who devotes himself to this occupation—which I will not deny I do myself—join me in my anger! For I leave everything else for those who wish to pursue them: wealth, noble birth, a good reputation, power, all of which belong to the endless pursuits and illusory joys of this lower world; I cling to the things of the mind[145] alone, and I do not grumble at the labors on land and sea which won these things for me.
>
> Let me, then, and let anyone who is my friend, have power over words; this is what I have embraced first of all and continue to embrace, after the One who is first of all—I mean the divine realm and our hope that lies beyond visible things. So that if, as Pindar says, 'all that is ours weighs us down,' it is, in my view, necessary to speak words about these things, and especially right— more than anything else I can imagine—to render thanks in words, for words, to the Word!
>
> Where, then, did you get the idea, most lightweight and most undisciplined of mortals, to deprive Christians of words? This was not just a threat, but part of enacted legislation. Where did you get this—and what was your reason?[146]

The threat against Christians and their place in Hellenic culture that was implied in Julian's decree had only begun to be implemented in the withdrawal of patronage from Christian thinkers and institutions and in the support of overtly pagan ones when Julian met his death on June 26,

363.[147] However, for Gregory, as for his friend Basil and many of their contemporaries, the challenge raised by the apostate Emperor never entirely went away. What, indeed, was the right of Christians, who belonged by their faith to a higher world than the visible one, who followed a crucified and risen Lord, to call the tradition of Greek culture their own? How should Christian teachers approach the classics, to help their pupils grow both in their faith and in the world's wisdom? What modifications did Christians need to make in their use of Greek rhetorical and poetic forms, even of Greek technology and the visual arts, if they were to remain authentically Christian and still draw on the cultural riches of their society? What was Christian education at its best? It does not seem an exaggeration to see Gregory's own staggering mastery of literary technique—put always at the service of the Church's internal struggle to remain faithful to her own tradition—as a first, still unsurpassed effort to answer Julian's still disturbing challenge: to show his contemporaries and all later devotees of Greek literature how one could be both a Christian and a humanist.[148]

GREGORY THE PHILOSOPHER

Gregory of Nazianzus was hardly what a modern academic would think of as a "philosopher." Like most well-educated people of late antiquity, his schooling had been focused largely on the effective use of language: immersing himself in the long tradition of Greek literature to learn both its ethical and cultural ideals and its ability to persuade. At Alexandria and at Athens, he had had the opportunity to attend lectures by representatives of the great philosophical "schools" of antiquity and probably used it: a liberally educated person was expected to be familiar with the strategies of reasoning and the various conceptions of the world's fundamental reality that had been handed on, through almost a thousand years, in Hellenic culture. Yet as far as philosophical doctrine goes, Gregory was, in John McGuckin's words, "a pragmatic eclectic" like Origen and most other Christian thinkers before him:[149] able to use Aristotelian dialectics in argument, sometimes speaking of the relationship of God's transcendent reality to the created world in terms of the eternal intelligible forms in God's mind, aware of Stoic speculations on the inherent order of the world, and ready to admire even the Cynics for their radical freedom from material attachments, yet certainly not committed to the teaching of any of these schools as the dominant vehicle for his thought. His thoughts about God and the human person certainly echo many themes from late antique Greek philosophy, but he seldom engages in direct conversation with the classical philosophers.

In his philosophical eclecticism, Gregory was not unusual among educated fourth-century Greeks. Even though the teaching of philosophy in the later Empire consisted mainly in commenting on classical texts and drawing reverently on earlier traditions, most late antique philosophical writings combined ideas from a number of earlier streams. Plotinus, for instance, the first representative of what we moderns call *Neoplatonism*, drew on both the Platonic and the Aristotelian tradition in constructing his own original and highly influential intellectual system. Through the sixth century, later school commentators on the classical texts of Plato and Aristotle tended to read them through Neoplatonic lenses that belonged, strictly speaking, to neither tradition. The reason was not simply the normal process of the evolution and cross-fertilization of ideas but the fact that, from the beginning, Greek philosophy had had a fundamentally practical, even pastoral purpose: training young minds to seek the wisdom that would enable them to live well, to "care for the self," by using the powers of reason to reflect critically on their assumptions, analyze the structures of a good argument, and focus on the ethical and esthetic implications of our knowledge of what is real.[150] In the classical model, as Pierre Hadot has observed, the objects of philosophical discourse—crucially important to the entire analytical and persuasive enterprise of literary training—"cannot be considered realities which exist in and for themselves" but always form part of a "way of life" embodied first by the philosopher who developed them and then by his disciples.[151]

Gregory himself was aware of this interplay between the speculative and existential aspects of the rational study we call *philosophy*. In his first oration *Against Julian*, he makes the point clearly:

> All philosophy is divided into two aspects, contemplation and practice. The one is loftier, but hard to approach through the warrants of experience; the other is humbler, but more useful. In our view, each is seen as valuable because of the other. For we make contemplation our companion on the way to the next life, and practice our means of access to contemplation; after all, it is impossible to share in wisdom without behaving wisely.[152]

On the one hand, this sense of the practical implications of philosophic contemplation accounts for the high value Gregory places in his orations on speculating about the relation of the transcendent, ineffable Creator to the circumscribed world of time and space. In the five Theological Orations, for instance, he speaks several times about both the importance and the challenge of "philosophizing about God:" it is not something to be done by those untrained in virtue or by those with simply an academic interest in the divine nature;[153] it is to be done only when there is time to contemplate the subject at length and in an atmosphere of reverence;[154] and it must be done in consciousness of the limits imposed on what one can say both by tradition and by an awareness of the utter incommensurability distancing our minds from God.[155] Still, the very attempt to turn the finite mind towards God, as the source of all intelligibility and the force sustaining all intelligence, is central to the human vocation: to our conversion from being immersed in sensible things and to life-giving union with God. So, at the beginning of his panegyric on St. Athanasius, Gregory describes the work of "true philosophy":

> God is to intelligible things what the sun is to the things of sense. The one lightens the visible, the other the invisible world ... And just as that which bestows on the things which see and are seen the power of seeing and being seen is itself the most beautiful of visible things, so God—who creates, for those who think and for that which is thought of, the power of thinking and being thought of—is himself the highest of the objects of thought; in him every desire finds its goal, beyond him it can go no further. For not even the most philosophic, the most piercing, the most curious intellect has, or can ever have, a more exalted object. For this is the utmost of things desirable, and they who arrive at it find an entire rest from speculation. Whoever has been permitted to escape, by reason and contemplation, from matter and this fleshly cloud or veil (whichever it should be called), and to hold communion with God, and to be associated, as far as human nature can attain, with the purest light: blessed is he, both for his ascent from here and for his deification there. This is conferred by true philosophy, and by rising superior to the dualism of matter, through the unity which is perceived in the Trinity.[156]

The generally Platonic tone of this passage is echoed in a number of places in the Orations, where Gregory attempts to put into words the confrontation of the finite mind with God's infinite intelligibility. The most extended of these is a section of his oration *On the Theophany* (Or. 38), wherein Gregory begins his account of why the Church celebrates the human birth of Christ with a reflection on what can be said about the being of God.

> God always was and is and will be—or better, God always *is*. For "was" and "will be" are divisions of the time we experience, of a nature that flows away; but he is always, and gives himself this

name when he identifies himself to Moses on the mountain. For he contains the whole of being in himself, without beginning or end, like an endless, boundless ocean of reality; he extends beyond all our notions of time and nature, and is sketchily grasped by the mind alone, but only very dimly and in a limited way; he is known not directly but indirectly, as one image is derived from another to form a single representation of the truth: fleeing before it is grasped, escaping before it is fully known, shining on our guiding reason—provided we have been purified—as a swift, fleeting flash of lightning shines in our eyes. And he does this, it seems to me, so that, insofar as it can be comprehended, the Divine might draw us to itself …[157]

Gregory goes on to reflect, in a few dense sentences, on how the finite, temporally limited mind might conceive of God's eternity[158] and then on God's initiative to share the Good, which he is, by "pouring himself out" in creation—first in the creation of immaterial, intellectual beings, then in the formation of the world of sense and the human creature, who unites both visible and invisible in "a kind of second world, great in its littleness: another kind of angel, a worshipper of mixed origins, a spectator of the visible creation and an initiate into the intelligible …"[159] It is on this grand stage, depicted in broadly Platonic terms, that the drama of sin and redemption will be played.

In most of Gregory's works, however, "philosophy" and "philosophize" are used primarily to refer not so much to a body of speculative doctrine or a systematic analysis of ultimate reality as to the cultivated practice of self-mastery, the ability to live in peace even among life's most difficult circumstances, because one has learned to seek what is ultimately important—which the Christian realizes is union with God. So Gregory writes to his family friend, Philagrius, in a tone of sympathy for what seems to be a bout of illness, but cautions:

> You must find in your vulnerability a place to philosophize, and purify your mind now more than ever, and show yourself stronger than the things that hold you in check, and consider this illness a profitable training—namely, to look down on the body and bodily things, and on all that is fleeting and disturbing and passing away, and so become completely focused on what lies above, to live not for this present world but for the world to come, making this life here what Plato calls "a preparation for death," and loosing the soul, as far as possible, from what, in his words, we call either its body or its prison.[160]

To a woman named Thecla, Gregory writes in a similar vein:

> As far as the things that trouble all of you are concerned, what
> should I write? Only that I wish you to consider this an occasion
> for the utmost philosophical behavior, to steel yourselves against
> your sufferings, and so to struggle against those who are causing
> you grief. Anything else would be neither possible nor holy![161]

To his friend Basil, who in 372 was facing the prospect that both the civil
province of Cappadocia and his own ecclesiastical province would be divided
in two, Gregory recalls their common commitment to a life free from
political intrigue:

> I have no fear at all, then, that you will experience any
> unphilosophical emotions in your troubles, or anything unworthy
> of yourself and both of us. But I consider this moment, in fact, to
> be really the time when my Basil will show his true colors, and
> when the philosophy you have been putting together for yourself
> all this time will be fully revealed: when you will rise above these
> threats, as on the crest of a wave, and remain unshaken while
> others tremble.[162]

To Christian friends such as these, Gregory offers comfort in rational but
not explicitly Christian terms. He seems simply to have assumed that "our
philosophy"[163] included both a vision of the world and of human life based
on the Scripture and a disciplined pattern of life, purified by reason and
dedicated practice from the fears and obsessions that come from a disordered
love of creatures.

Gregory's heroes, correspondingly, are frequently described as
"philosophers," even if their actual occupation is something more mundane.
His sister Gorgonia, whose life was spent running a household, appears in
Gregory's funeral oration for her (Or. 8) as a model of all the principal
virtues elaborated in Aristotle's *Nicomachean Ethics*: she has "reached such
a stage of philosophy," in fact, "that she does not even pride herself in her
spiritual gifts."[164] Gregory's great, if short-lived, attraction to the flamboyant
Maximus of Alexandria, too, seems to have been based largely on Maximus's
claim to be living a genuinely philosophic life in the free-spirited style of
the Cynic school. Thus, Gregory's oration in praise of Maximus, introducing
him formally to the Nicene congregation of Constantinople as a supporter
in their cause of Christian orthodoxy, begins:

> I shall speak in praise of the philosopher, even though I am sick
> in body: for that's philosophy! And it is wholly right that I shall

praise him: for he is a philosopher, and I a devotee of wisdom, so that praise makes sense. As a result, I shall also be a philosopher in this respect, if in no other: by admiring the philosophic life.[165]

Light-heartedly addressing the long-haired, unconventional visitor as "one who lives our kind of philosophy in an alien garb,"[166] a "dog" (or "Cynic") "not in shameless behavior but in freedom of speech,"[167] Gregory paints him above all as a "witness to the truth,"[168] which, in his view, includes Trinitarian orthodoxy, a frugal, passion-free life, and a readiness to speak out freely for justice.[169] For Maximus, as for the heroes of the Biblical narrative, the vision of God that is the goal of the philosophic quest is found first in quiet and withdrawal but leads to the active charity that hopes to communicate that same vision to others. As Gregory explains,

> Piety does not consist in little things, nor philosophy in a downcast eye, but in firmness of soul and purity of understanding and a noble inclination towards the good, whatever the clothes we wear and whomever we associate with—whether we withdraw our mind from sensible things to be by ourselves, or find our own way publicly among the throng of those just like us, living as philosophers amidst those who do not ...[170]

After Maximus's real ambition—to become bishop of Constantinople himself—had become clear, Gregory again withdrew from the city, presumably to assess his own position and to reflect on his choices for the future. As we have mentioned, Oration 26, couched in terms of a mutual "accounting" between him and his flock and delivered shortly after his return, is largely a meditation on the life of the Christian philosopher, a role Gregory now claims for himself in terms that seem calculated to distance him from the spurious Christian "Cynic" he had lionized in Oration 25. After criticizing those "dogs who try by force to become shepherds" for the essentially destructive effect of their ambitions,[171] Gregory asks his congregation whether they have remained true to their Christian profession in orthodox faith and the works of love.[172] For his own part, he explains that his "experience of the desert" has given him a chance to reflect on the instability of human affairs.[173] Those who "make use of philosophic reasoning and have risen above the mediocrity of the crowd" endure like rocks battered by the sea, because they "bear everything without being shaken or disturbed."[174] Gregory goes on to paint a portrait of the true philosopher as a person of extraordinary stamina, genuine nobility, and unfailing generosity. Like Paul, he can "endure all things;"[175] like Christ, he forgives all insults and offenses.[176] So, the Christian philosopher, as Gregory describes him, is transformed by his practice of virtue into a supremely free being:

> There is nothing more impregnable, nothing more unconquerable than philosophy. Everything else collapses before the philosopher does! He is a wild ass in the desert, as Job says, unfettered and free …[177] Let me put it in a nutshell: two things stand beyond our control—God and an angel; and in third place comes the philosopher! He is an immaterial being in matter, uncircumscribed while in a body, a citizen of heaven on earth, impassible in the midst of vulnerability, beaten in all things except his thoughts, a conqueror of those who think they have subdued him—simply by letting himself be conquered.[178]

By his own confession, at least, this was the state of mind Gregory tried all his life to acquire by quiet and scholarly withdrawal in the midst of heavy responsibilities; it became the central preoccupation of his final years. In some of his works—his orations in memory of Gorgonia, for instance, or *On the Love of the Poor*—Gregory echoes the widespread ancient conviction that the body as we presently experience it usually is more of a hindrance to the life of philosophic balance and freedom than a means for obtaining it. Yet to see him simply as a world-denying ascetic or even as a practical dualist is to misread his idiom in a serious way. Gregory's philosophic style was not the organized eremitical pattern of the Egyptian desert monks or even that of Basil's sister, Macrina;[179] it was to be alone with his books and his writing-paper, in the simple security of his family estate in Arianzus, and to struggle there to maintain a virtuous and productive calm as a disciple of Christ in the face of illness, age, and isolation.[180]

The main thing that stood in tension with his achieving this philosophic state, Gregory readily admits, was his need for companionship. He writes to a certain Amazonius (probably an associate from Constantinople) after his return to Cappadocia:

> If one of our mutual friends (and I believe there are many of them!) asks you, 'Where is our Gregory now? What is he doing?' say confidently that he is philosophizing in peace, and that he thinks no more of those who have wronged him than of events whose existence is unknown. But if the same person asks you further, 'How does he endure being separated from friends?' don't say confidently that he is philosophizing— say, rather, that he is in a very bad way! Some people have other weaknesses; ours is friendship and friends …[181]

Like the classical philosophers before him, Gregory realized that philosophy was not simply theoretical speculation but commitment to virtue, detachment from cares and passionate fixations, and longing for union with God. It began in conversion of heart and led, if fully realized, to total transformation; but it could be fully realized only in the company of friends. To be a philosopher, one needed not only books and ideas but a community, even if that community was mainly bonded together by letter.[182] In this way, writing for Gregory was an essential part of his philosophical and his literary vocation.

GREGORY THE THEOLOGIAN

Since at least the mid-fifth century, as we have said, Gregory of Nazianzus, along with the writer of the Fourth Gospel, has been dubbed "the Theologian."[183] His first biographer, the early Byzantine writer known as Gregory the Presbyter, writes:

> In the loftiness of his teaching and in his discussion of God (θεολογία), his power was so great that, although many men known for wisdom had spoken of God (θεολογήσαντων) through the centuries, he alone, after John the Evangelist, was named "the Theologian" (ὁ θεόλογος), and this title became, in a way, his own distinctive characteristic.[184]

The reason for this title is clearly Gregory's urgent championing of a Trinitarian conception of God and his insistent care to articulate a theological terminology—indeed a theological grammar—for speaking of God in a way consistent with Scripture and the Church's tradition of faith. Like his friends Basil and Gregory of Nyssa, like his contemporary Didymus of Alexandria, and the slightly younger Augustine of Hippo, Gregory insisted that Christian orthodoxy requires a notion of the Divine Mystery as a unique and inseparable unity of three irreducible hypostases or "persons." In their polemical works against the Eunomian "Arians," who used the principles of a philosophy of language to resist predicating divine substance of Christ, and against those who opposed the application of the term *consubstantial* (ὁμοούσιον) to the Holy Spirit, these authors were the first in the Christian tradition to articulate in formal terms a comprehensive Trinitarian model of thought that would set the boundaries for mainstream Christian understanding of God, based on faith in Christ as Lord and on the continuing experience of his Spirit in the Church. Among them all, it was Gregory of Nazianzus who offered the clearest, most economical, and perhaps the most paradoxical parameters for articulating this Mystery and who most insistently emphasized the centrality of this Trinitarian confession for the whole of Christian life.

"Theology," along with its cognates, was a term with a long history in Greek religious thought. For Plato[185] and Aristotle,[186] "doing theology" was telling the ancient stories of the gods, as Hesiod and Homer had done, to give some account of the world. In a famous passage in *Metaphysics* 6, however, Aristotle also designates the "theological philosophy" as the "most honorable" form of speculative thought, because it concerns the causes of things insofar as they are both unchanging in themselves and "separate" from the objects of direct experience: it is what Aristotle calls here "the primary philosophy," the role of which is to study "Being insofar as it is" or ultimate reality.[187] Origen was the first Christian writer to use the word *theology* to refer not to pagan myths or to considerations of the divinity in general terms, but to the understanding of God implied by the Gospel. So he writes in his *Contra Celsum* that Jesus' words about his own relationship to the Father are the foundation of what Christians have to say about the divine Mystery: "He revealed to his true disciples the nature of God and told them about his characteristics. We find traces of these in the Scriptures and make them the starting-points of our theology."[188] In one passage of his *Commentary on John*, Origen—speaking about the content of Jewish prophecy—even suggests that the real heart of theology for the Christian is not simply Christ's teaching or the full Biblical witness to his coming, but Christ's place in the divine reality:

> Perhaps the testimonies of the prophets do not only proclaim that Christ is to come, nor do they teach us only this and nothing else; but one can learn much theology, and the relation of Father to Son and Son to Father, no less from the prophets, in what they promise concerning him, than from the Apostles, who narrate to us the greatness of the Son of God.[189]

Origen's disciple Eusebius of Caesaraea, writing almost a century later in his *Church History*, uses θεολογία to refer even more explicitly to the Christian way of speaking of God, as revealed by Jesus and contained in Scripture and the Church's tradition; he distinguishes such language from the narrative of what God has done in history through Jesus, the plan that he calls the "economy" (οἰκονομία):

> My narrative will begin, as I have said, from the narrative of God's plan (οἰκονομία) and the way of speaking of God (θεολογία) that are according to Christ—something understood to be higher and better than what is simply human.[190]

By the end of the fourth century, this distinction of "theology," as Christian language about God, from "economy," the Biblical narrative of creation and redemption—culminating in the story of the Incarnation of the Word—on which this understanding of God is based, would be a standard part of Christian terminology. Yet it is important to realize that the approach to theology of the Council of Nicaea, in the strict sense (with its confession that the Son and Word of God, through whom the mysterious and inconceivable God of Israel created all things, is "of the same substance" as that God) remained for most fourth-century Greek Christian thinkers dangerous and radical. It seemed to undermine the personal distinctness that enabled Jesus to be, himself, a divine savior present in the world: the one who reconciled a fallen creation with the God who sent him and whom he called "Father." And when some Christian writers, including Athanasius in the 350s, even began to apply to the Holy Spirit the title "consubstantial" given by Jesus to his Church—the Spirit who makes us divine by allowing us to participate in the life of God through Jesus—a large body of Christians in Egypt and Asia Minor resisted this terminological innovation, too; if the Spirit is sent by Father and Son, it seemed he must be produced by them in some fundamental way: created, brought into being as God's second intermediary in the work of salvation.

Although Gregory of Nazianzus has left us a number of passages that sum up the "economy" of the Incarnation in classical terms (notably Or. 38.13–16, and his two anti-Apollinarian letters to Cledonius [Epp. 101–102]), it was his careful, unrelenting attempt to emphasize and refine the *theologia* at the heart of Christian life and practice that won him his lasting nickname.[191] In his view, being a "theologian" was a daunting, totally preoccupying challenge. To speak accurately and appropriately of the Mystery of God, as Gregory frequently emphasizes, involves not simply learning and intellectual subtlety but a commitment to the entire pattern of Christian life that begins in conversion and is sealed in the sacraments of the Church. In Oration 20, for instance, *On Theology, and the Appointment of Bishops*, a brief treatise that seems to have been a preliminary sketch for the more elaborate "Theological Orations," Gregory begins by emphasizing the need for purification of heart and mind, for a life of "philosophy" in the Christian sense, if one's talk of God is to be more than idle chatter. Speaking of our human potential to reflect the self-communicating light of God, he writes:

> One can scarcely achieve this except ... by training oneself in the discipline of philosophy for a long time, and so breaking off the noble and luminous elements of the soul, little by little, from what is base and mingled with darkness ... But before one has

elevated this materiality as far as possible, and has sufficiently purified one's ears and one's intelligence, I do not think it is safe either to accept a position of spiritual leadership or to devote oneself to theology.[192]

Later in the same oration, Gregory invokes incidents from the Old Testament to suggest how dangerous it is to approach God with rash familiarity, reminding his readers that each of us needs to be healed inwardly, purified by God-given wisdom, before we may "safely" speak of what and who God is.[193]

Gregory goes on to describe the Christian's "safe" understanding of God as a "middle" position between the exaggerated stress on divine unity proposed by "Sabellian" modalism and the exaggerated, ontological distinction of Father from Son and Spirit suggested in the various anti-Nicene theologies of the mid-fourth century:

> Our argument should not lump the three together into one individual (*hypostasis*), for fear of polytheism, and so leave us with mere names, as we suppose Father, Son and Holy Spirit are the same, as if we were just as ready to define all of them as one as we are to think each of them is nothing—for they would escape from being what they are, if they were to change and be transformed into each other. Nor should our argument divide them into three substances: either substances foreign to each other and wholly dissimilar, as that doctrine so aptly called 'Arian madness' would have it, or substances without origin or order, which are, so to speak, gods in rivalry.[194]

Here and repeatedly throughout his orations, Gregory offers a more complex model than either of these "extremes" for thinking of the Father, the Son. and the Holy Spirit. He envisions seeing all three figures revealed in the long narrative of Scripture as divine and as communicating divine life to creatures; invoked in baptism as the single "name" in whom the believer finds renewed existence; and therefore *one* in their substance or being as God (as Aristotle's "Being insofar as it is"), yet permanently *three* in the order in which their being is possessed and shared. As a result, they are also abidingly distinct in their relationship to the believer, who shares divine life through all of them. Christian orthodoxy must therefore avoid the extremes of both confusion and separation in its thought of God:

> So, according to my argument, the unity of God would be preserved, and Son and Spirit would be referred back to one

original cause, but not compounded or blended with each other; their unity would be based on the single, identical movement and will of the divine being, if I may put it that way, and on identity of substance. But the three individuals (*hypostases*) would also be preserved, with no amalgamation or reduction or confusion conceived in our thought, so that the whole might not be destroyed by theories that honor the unity of God more than is appropriate. And their individual characteristics are these: the Father is conceived and said to be both without origin, and origin himself— origin, in that he is cause and spring and eternal light; but the Son is not at all without origin, yet himself is the origin of all things that are …[195]

After further reflection on how one ought and ought not to understand the eternal "begetting" of the Son if one is to avoid thinking of him as a creature (as less in the fullness of his reality than the one who begot him), Gregory concludes by reminding his hearers of the limits of human understanding with regard to all our language about God:

> If you are not indulging in idle curiosity about the Son's begetting (if one must call it that) or his hypostasis, or whatever other term one might invent that is more precise than these (for what we are thinking and talking about defeats my powers of speech!), then do not waste your efforts, either, on the procession of the Spirit … Do you hear mention of a begetting? Do not trouble yourself about how it occurs. Do you hear that the one who proceeds forth from the Father is the Spirit? Do not exercise your curiosity about the manner … If you trust me, then—and I am no rash theologian!—grasp what you can, and pray to grasp the rest. Love what already abides within you, and let the rest await you in the treasury above. Approach it by the way you live …[196]

However closely one tries to cling to the familiar language of Scripture and Church tradition, one must bear in mind that Trinitarian speech is language with rules of signification that have been permanently altered, bent beyond the shape and contexts of its normal use, to point to the ineffable.

Despite his cautions about the limits of language, Gregory is creative, even bold, in plotting out the semantic boundaries within which the Church's faith may rightly and safely be articulated. Along with Gregory of Nyssa,[197] he continually promotes a standardized terminology for speaking of what is one and what is three in the divine Mystery revealed by Christ to his Church in the power of the Spirit. God, as Israel knew, is radically one—a single reality, a single "substance" (οὐσία) or "nature" (φύσις), a single "what," a single, infinite "thing" that transcends all our powers of categorization but underlies all our understanding of what is real. Yet God is, at the heart of this eternal and unchanging reality, three "individuals" (ὑποστάσεις, hypostases), whose very individuality is defined simply by their relationship to each other: three "*personae*" (πρόσωπα) or agents, playing three "roles" like the *personae* in a Greek drama, even though the action they perform always constitutes one story, produces one unified effect.[198] All these terms clearly are to be used with an awareness of how different their referents are from what is signified by them when we speak of the created world. God is not a single "stuff" formed into three distinct portions, nor are Father, Son, and Holy Spirit three "people," three self-contained centers of consciousness and will, related to each other by shared knowledge and love as a kind of divine family. Yet, for lack of better conceptions, these terms at least allow us to speak of Father, Son, and Spirit as constituting the single Mystery of God's ultimate reality in their unified threeness—a threeness, as Augustine would argue, revealed in human history and sweeping the person of faith into its own internal process of giving and receiving, loving and sending and returning from multiplicity to union.

Much of our traditional understanding of this Trinitarian life of God comes from Gregory himself. One stratagem he occasionally uses is to speak of the relationship between God's unity as "substance" or reality and God's threeness as the eternally related "individuals" Father and Son and Spirit. This gives rise to a kind of timeless, unchanging rhythm—a dynamic, nonspatial "movement" in which there can be priority and productivity without isolation or alienation. So he writes in a famous passage of the *Third Theological Oration*:

> We honor a Single Source (*monarchia*) of all: not a Single Source defined by a single agent (*prosopon*, "person")—for it is possible that even what is single could come to be in conflict with itself and become multiple—but one that a shared dignity of nature and harmony of will produces, an identity of movement, and a convergence towards the One of what comes forth from it. All of this is impossible on the level of created nature. The result [i.e., in God] is that even if there is difference in number, there is no separation in substance. For this reason, the Monad, which is from the beginning, stirred into movement as a Dyad, comes to rest in the state of a Triad. In our language, this is the Father and the Son and the Holy Spirit: the one is the Begetter, the Producer

(but I mean this in a sense that implies no passion, no time, no body); and of the others, one is begotten, the other produced (or whatever way one might designate their origins, abstracting these terms completely from the world of sense) ... So let us remain within our boundaries, and use the language of "Unbegotten" and "Begotten" and "What proceeds from the Father," as God the Word himself puts it.[199]

In his *Second Irenical Discourse* (Or. 23), one of several pieces Gregory delivered during his ministry in Constantinople in the attempt to give new theological depth and subtlety to the Nicene cause, he sketches out in admittedly paradoxical terms the conceptual alternative to a theology that sees Son and Spirit as created intermediaries between the Father and the world:

> For my part, I propose a divine source beyond time, inseparable, indivisible; I reverence in equal measure the Source and those who are from the Source—the One, because he is their Source, the other Two, because in this way they are what they are and he is what he is, without any distance among them in time or nature or holiness. They are one in distinction and divided in unity, if I may utter such a paradox—not less to be honored because of their relationship to each other than each one is when understood and taken on his own: a perfect Triad of three perfect members, with the Monad stirred into motion by its own richness, the Dyad surpassed (for it is something beyond matter and form, from which bodies are composed), the Triad defined by its perfection. For being first, it goes beyond the composition proper to what is twofold, so that the divinity does not remain confined, nor is spilled outwards to infinity ...[200]

In his laudatory address to Maximus the Cynic (Or. 25), Gregory includes in his advice to the rising Christian philosopher a detailed exposition of right faith in God. After warning him against various false conceptions of the place of Father, Son, and Holy Spirit within the divine Mystery, Gregory urges:

> [Teach] that the Father is truly a father, much more truly so than is the case with us; for he is so in a unique way (in his own way, that is, and not as occurs with bodily beings), as unique Father (for he is not married) of a unique Son (for he is only-begotten), uniquely (for the Son was not before him); and he is wholly Father,

of one who is wholly Son (for with us this is unclear), and from the beginning (for he did not beget later on).

[Teach] that the Son is truly a son, for he is unique, of a unique Father, in a unique way and uniquely—for he is not a Father … [Teach] that the Holy Spirit is truly holy: for no other [spirit] is like him, nor holy in such a way. His sanctification does not come by way of addition, but is holiness in itself, becoming neither more nor less, neither having a beginning nor coming to an end. For common to Father and Son and Holy Spirit is both the fact of not coming to be, and divinity; common to Son and Holy Spirit is being from the Father. Particular to the Father is being unbegotten; to the Son is being begotten; to the Spirit is being sent forth (ἔκπεμψις).[201] And if you seek for the manner, what will you leave for them who are attested [by Scripture] as alone knowing each other and known by each other,[202] or even for those of us who will later be illumined in the life to come?[203]

Not content simply to define and use the language of "substance" and "hypostasis" that he and his fellow Cappadocians have promoted as a unified Christian terminology for expressing the divine Mystery, in a number of passages Gregory draws on all the grammatical and syntactical resources of the Greek language to paraphrase the conceptual model of the Triune God in as simple terms as the paradox will allow. So in his "Farewell Address," for instance, he weaves such a paraphrase into a summary of the essence of the orthodox faith (cc. 14–18):

The One without beginning, and the Beginning,[204] and the One who is with the Beginning,[205] are one God. Being without beginning is not the *nature* of the One without beginning, nor is being unbegotten; for nature is never a designation for what something is not, but for what something is. The affirmation of what is is not the denial of what is not. Nor is the Beginning kept separate from that which is without beginning, by the fact that it is a beginning: for being the beginning is not his nature, any more than being the One without beginning is the nature of the other. These characteristics 'surround' nature, but are not nature. And the One who is with the One without beginning and with the Beginning is not something else than what they are.

The name of the One without beginning is 'Father,' of the Beginning 'Son,' of the One with the Beginning 'Holy Spirit.' There is one nature for all three: God. The unity is the Father, from whom and towards whom everything else is referred, not so as to be mixed together in confusion, but so as to be contained, without time or will or power intervening to divide them. These three have caused us to exist in multiplicity, each of us being in conflict with ourselves and with everything else. But for those beings whose nature is simple, and whose existence is the same, the principal characteristic is unity.[206]

Gregory emphasizes here the single being shared by Father, Son, and Holy Spirit, a singleness not ruptured by their distinctiveness as related individuals, and he makes it clear that this single being—this simple nature, this unified existence—is so not in a generic sense, not as a universal class to which these three individuals belong, but as a relationship of origin and issuance, of independence and dependence, contained in the Father's gift of what he primordially is: "the unity *is* the Father."

Gregory's real contribution to the formation of the Church's classical Trinitarian understanding of God is, as we have said, his formation of a new, paradoxical, yet brilliantly consistent style of discourse: a "grammar" for using the language of substance and individual, universal and particular, in a way that allows real growth in the understanding of the Church's baptismal faith without upsetting the delicate internal balance of its paradoxes. Like most of Gregory's theology, it is also a rhetorical achievement, a way of using this carefully crafted network of Biblical and philosophical terms in a moving and persuasive way; to be the emblem of a common tradition of faith that enables a Christian community to worship and live as one; and to draw his hearers more deeply into a pattern of life that promises a share in the internal relationships of the God of the "economy," the God who saves us in Christ and in his Church.

However, it is clear, too, in Gregory's frequent attempts to summarize orthodox Christian theism and to stake out its boundaries, that all of this is not, in his view, simply an issue of pedantic dogmatic correctness. The dogma of the Trinity, after all, is not something Christians believe *about* God, not a theory or an explanation, so much as the briefest of Christian creeds: a summary of what Christians find revealed in the one long narrative of Israel's history, the life and death and resurrection of Jesus, and the Church's continuing life in the power of his Spirit as Christ's Body. And the implications of this creed are always "for us" and for the world. Because God is what God is, because the Son has become one of us and has poured forth on us his own Spirit, who "proceeds from the Father," we too can walk with him as brothers and sisters, children of the same Father, sharers in the same life. So Gregory begins the final section of his address to Maximus the Cynic with a word of encouragement addressed to one he still thinks of as a fellow athlete in the struggle for a right faith:

> Teach people to fear only one thing: to dissolve the faith in sophistries. There is nothing terrible about losing an argument, for not everyone can argue; the terrible thing is to be deprived of the reality of God—for he is the hope of us all … And when you are ready to make a good departure from this life, remember, I beg you, the Trinity, who dwells in tents—if it is right at all to say that God dwells in what is made by human hands—and remember this little harvest, growing from religious seeds that are by no means small, but still little and poor itself, and only partly gathered …[207]

The life and even the language of this "partly gathered" Church of orthodox believers, Gregory realizes, remains incomplete, limited by the poverty of its beginnings. However, the basis of the Church's hope, of its courage in the face of struggle, is "the Trinity who dwells in tents:" God not simply as God but as "God with us."

GREGORY THE PRIEST

Towards the end of his "Farewell Address" (Or. 42), Gregory comments ruefully about the faithful in Constantinople: "They are not seeking priests, but rhetors—not pure hands to offer sacrifice, but strong hands to hold the reins!"[208] The remark contains a hint of self-reproach, for Gregory goes on to admit that "this is the way we have trained them by being 'all things to all people,' and I do not know whether we have saved all or lost them!"[209] Eloquence, even in a renowned preacher, could be a means of pandering as well as an instrument for communicating the Gospel, especially in so verbally sensitive a society as ancient Byzantium.

Beneath the remark lies the hint of a tension that Gregory seems to have felt within himself for much of his adult life: the tension between his desire to be a literary figure, perhaps even the creator of a new, recognizably Hellenic (yet thoroughly Christian) body of literature, and his sense of responsibility to provide pastoral leadership for a local Church in the way his father and his friend Basil did. Born and educated for a position of power in fourth-century Christian society and surrounded since birth with an extensive network of ecclesiastical connections, Gregory constantly had to struggle with the competing claims of community needs and his own retiring temperament as he discerned the right form in which to put power and privilege to their best use.

Gregory's letters reveal him as someone deeply concerned to offer guidance and other kinds of help to relatives and friends, even to use his connections for the benefit of others. His most revealing reflections on priestly ministry, however, in all its dimensions, are found in Oration 2. This work is a long apologia, supposedly delivered at the Paschal festival of 362 to his home congregation in Nazianzus, for fleeing to rural solitude immediately after being ordained a presbyter there by his father, the previous Christmas.[210] This oration, which clearly influenced John Chrysostom's celebrated dialogue *On Priesthood*, written some twenty years later,[211] is the earliest extended work we have in Greek on the responsibilities and the spiritual and personal challenges of Church ministry.[212] Here and in a number of his other works, particularly his panegyrics in honor of bishops (including Athanasius, Basil, and his own father), one glimpses the complex set of categories in which Gregory understands the role of headship within the Christian community.

Although he rarely develops the parallel thematically, Gregory usually speaks of ministry in the Church, as Christians of both East and West had done since the start of the third century, in the vocabulary of cultic priesthood taken from the Old Testament: a role of sanctification and reconciliation that especially the Letter to the Hebrews recognizes as having reached its providential fulfillment in the sacrifice of Jesus' death and in his entry into the heavenly sanctuary.[213] In explaining his own panic and flight at the time of his presbyteral ordination, for instance, Gregory draws on Biblical examples of people who greatly fear to "draw near to God" or who are destroyed for doing so in a rash way; he writes:

> Since I knew this, and knew that no one is worthy of the great God, who is both sacrifice and priest, if one has not already "offered himself to God as a living sacrifice, holy," or "offered up pleasing spiritual worship,"[214] or sacrificed to God a "sacrifice of praise"[215] and a "contrite spirit"[216]—the only sacrifice that the one who gives us all things requires of us—how could I be bold enough to offer to him the exterior sacrifice that is the copy[217] of the great Mysteries? How could I put on the vestments and the title of priest, before perfecting my hands in holy works, before letting my eyes grow used to gazing on creation in a wholesome way, in wonder at the creator and not to the detriment of the creature, before my ears had been sufficiently opened to the education of the Lord ...?[218]

In his orations for the festivals of Christ's birth and epiphany, as well, Gregory deliberately presents himself as both "participant and leader of these Mysteries" of initiation,[219] as host at a great banquet of "spiritual delicacies."[220] Liturgical celebration, conceived in terms of both Jewish and Greek ritual practice, is clearly at the heart of his understanding of his role in the Church.

This underlying image of the presbyter and bishop as the one who sanctifies and purifies the people is, in Gregory's view, the explanation of the serious moral obligations incumbent on the clergy. So, in his poem *On Himself and the Bishops*, he writes in a sharply critical vein against those who see priesthood as an administrative office:

> You've been considering a bishop as you would an accountant, laying stress on mere rubbish, where I've been concerned with important issues. A priest should have one function and one only, the sanctification of souls by his life and teaching. He should raise them towards the heights by heavenly impulses. He should be serene, high-minded, reflecting like a mirror the godly and unspotted images that he has inside. For his flock he should send up holy offerings, until the day when he, too, shall perfect them into an offering. Other matters he should relinquish to those skilled in them.[221]

In fact, Gregory's understanding of priesthood, sacrifice, and liturgy tends to emphasize their spiritual significance, their effectiveness in purifying human hearts from sin. So in his poem, "Inexact Definitions," he characterizes the elements of cult in a figural way:

> The Temple is that sacred place that makes us holy;
> Our gift to God, all purifying sacrifice;
> The place for offering our gifts, the holy table
> Where God comes down; our priesthood purifies the mind,
> Brings us to God as reconciled, and God to us;
> The Mystery is what we seek in wordless awe.[222]

The priest of the Christian dispensation stands within a world of types that have come to their fulfillment in the one atoning sacrifice of Christ, "God with us," now mirrored in the celebration of the Eucharistic community.

However, Gregory's understanding of priestly ministry was clearly not simply that of a celebrant. It was headship in a broader sense: an office of leadership and direction conceived in the familiar image of a shepherd protecting and leading his sheep. So Gregory, in the same Oration, expresses his alarm at having received the leadership of souls (ψυχῶν ἡγεμονίαν), and authority (προστασίαν) over them, even though we have not yet properly learned to follow a shepherd ourselves, nor have been purified in our souls as much as is proper, in order then to be trusted to rule (ἐπιστατεῖν) over a flock …[223]

His "fear of rule," he later explains, is rooted in his awareness of the account to which God promises in the Bible to hold "those who lead my people and rule over them."[224] The task of the shepherd in the Church, in fact, is not simply that of guiding docile and willing subjects; often enough, it resembles more the role of an animal tamer dealing with a moody and resistant beast: "a composite animal with no parallel, characterized by many different temperaments and languages."[225] The "person who presides" over such a many-headed body clearly needs both extraordinary competence and extraordinary virtue and experience.[226]

The task of the shepherd in the Church, of course, is not simply to guard and direct his flock but to feed them, principally by "distributing the word," which is "the first of our tasks."[227] This consists, in Gregory's view, not only in simple catechesis but in elaborate and nuanced instruction, adapted to the capabilities and desires of each hearer:

In my opinion, it seems no small matter, nothing suited for the narrow of spirit, 'to give to each his measure of grain' from Scripture 'in due season,'[228] and to distribute the truth of our teachings with discernment, whether we are speculating about the world or worlds, about matter, about the soul, about the intellect and intellectual natures, good and evil, about the providence that holds all things together and guides their course— whatever seems true according to the whole of reason, and whatever lies beyond this human reason here below.[229]

To teach profitably about these subjects and—even more important— to communicate the Christian understanding of God as a Trinity of Persons[230] requires not only learning and moral purification but the discretion that enables the teacher to judge the talents, the prior knowledge, and the silent prejudices of each of his hearers, and to adapt his instruction accordingly.

For some need to be nourished with the milk of simple, elementary teaching—those who are like newborn infants in their state of mind, one might say, and cannot bear adult intellectual food. If one were to offer it to them beyond what they have strength to bear, perhaps they would be oppressed and weighed down by it, and their intelligence would not be sufficient to take in and assimilate what is offered, just as happens with our material body, and [their mind] would lose even its original power. But others need "the wisdom that is uttered among the perfect,"[231] a higher and more solid form of nourishment, because their perception has been sufficiently trained to distinguish truth from falsehood, and if they were to be offered milk to drink and vegetables to eat, the food of the weak, they would rightly take it ill, because we would not be providing them with strength in Christ ...[232]

Understandably, Gregory invokes Paul in crying out, "Who is sufficient for this task?"[233]

And the work of the leader and teacher is not, in Gregory's understanding, simply a matter of giving directions and offering doctrinal information. It is a subtle, highly complicated skill: "In reality," he writes, "this seems to me to be the art of arts and the science of sciences: to lead the human being, who is the most cunning and many-sided of animals."[234] What adds to its complexity is the fact that Christian ministry is always essentially a work of therapy or rehabilitation; the pastor is a "physician of souls" whose aim is to heal the mind and spirit of the would-be believer from the disorder and weakness that darken his or her knowledge of the things of God and dull his desire to pursue them. Like any other physician, the pastor needs both a wealth of diagnostic knowledge, so as to recognize the particular weaknesses of each member of his congregation, and an equally large repository of therapeutic technique, so as to provide an effective "cure." And like other physicians, he often faces ingratitude or hostility on the part of his patients because the medicine prescribed can be unpleasant.[235]

> These are the reasons why I consider our kind of medical skill much more laborious than the kind that is concerned with bodies, and more valuable for this reason. In the case of bodily medicine, which does not examine much of our deepest selves, most of the activity concerns what appears to the senses; but with us, all the treatment and practice concerns 'the hidden person of the heart,'[236] and the battle is against the one who wars on us and wrestles with us from within, who uses our very selves as arms against us, and—worst of all—who hands us over to the death of sin. Against these forces, in my opinion, we need a great and perfect faith, and even greater cooperation on the part of God, and also no small measure of skill in offering our own resistance.[237]

The goal is nothing less than transformation of the human in the image of the divine. Alluding to Plato's famous simile in the *Phaedrus*,[238] Gregory sums up the therapy practiced by the pastor by saying,

> [I]n this art, the purpose is to give the soul wings; to snatch from the world and give to God what is made in his image; to preserve what remains of the image, to lead along carefully what is at risk in it, to restore what has been deformed; to bring Christ to dwell in human hearts through the Spirit;[239] above all, to make divine, a sharer in heavenly blessedness, everyone who has committed himself to heaven.[240]

This kind of healing, Gregory goes on to argue, is not just a human answer to a limited human predicament; it reveals the overarching purpose of God's long history of involvement in his creation, the very "economy" or plan of salvation, in which our human ministry simply shares in finite ways:

> This is what the Law, our schoolmaster, intended for us; this is what the prophets—who come between Christ and the Law—intended; what Christ intended, the perfecter and goal of the spiritual Law; this is the goal of the 'emptied' Godhead,[241] the assumed flesh, the new mixture,[242] God and human, one from both and both through one ... For this reason the New was brought in to replace the Old, the suffering One called back to life through suffering; for this reason everything that is above us was given in exchange for everything that is ours, and the arrangement of love, directed towards the one who had fallen through lack of faith, came to be a new Mystery ... All this is a kind of training-plan (παιδαγωγία) of God concerning us, a healing of our weakness, which raises up the old Adam from the place where he had fallen, leading him to the tree of life, from which the tree of knowledge—tasted inappropriately, ahead if its time—had led us away.[243] Of this healing, we, who have a position of authority over others, are servants and collaborators ...[244]

Precisely because it forms an integral part of God's own plan of ministry to a fallen race, human ministry reveals its enormous importance as well as its terrifying challenge: "what is at stake for us is the salvation of the soul."[245] Ministry is a human representation of the love of God; the pastor acts as "best man" in the marriage of the heart with its divine Lover, the "matchmaker" between God and his earthly bride.[246]

Gregory's understanding of the exalted goal of ministry in the Church is interwoven, then, with a sense of its almost impossible difficulty, its superhuman scope. In the second half of Oration 2,[247] he draws on the whole array of Old Testament prophets who criticized the priestly class in Israel, along with the other "leaders and teachers of wickedness"[248] who exercised power over the people, and concludes by reminding his readers of Jesus' sharp rebukes of the Scribes and Pharisees. In contrast to these hereditary priests and religious power-seekers, Gregory holds up the Apostle Paul as his chief example of a tireless and selfless pastor: by his own admission living in continual strain and danger, reaching out to people of every kind in a constantly changing array of styles and tones, allowing himself to be more and more conformed to Christ, to preach Christ in his person and his deeds and in his words.[249] The portrait of ministry that emerges is clearly a prophetic, rather than a predominantly institutional or clerical one. Identifying his own concerns with those of the prophets and Paul, Gregory suggests that the minister must be consumed by the word he proclaims, become personally an embodiment of his own message, if his work of mediation is to be fully authentic.

Faced with such a challenge, Gregory readily admits his own inadequacy for Church ministry in Oration 2, his own need first to undergo the process of cleansing and healing that a priest is expected to provide for others:

> I am myself preoccupied with these considerations night and day. They consume my marrow and eat away my flesh; they do not allow me to live in courage, or to walk forward with eyes upraised. They depress my soul and contract my thoughts and put a leash on my tongue; they do not lead me to considerations of leadership, or of reproving and directing others—which calls for wide resources—but rather to thinking how I myself might 'flee the wrath to come,'[250] and in some small way scrape from myself the rust of wickedness. One must first be purified, and then purify others; first be made wise, and so make others wise; first become light, and then enlighten; first draw near to God and then lead others forward; first be made holy and then sanctify others, lead them by the hand, offer them understanding counsel …
>
> When will this happen, according to my calculations, my noble friends? Not even extreme old age would be too distant a date to set …[251]

Gregory goes on to confess his particular sense of inadequacy before the challenges of a divided, hotly polemical Christian society. The Empire and the Church—both clergy and people—are engaged, he suggests, in a kind of civil war, each side "claiming the faith as pretext" for promoting their own positions.[252] Gregory confesses not only to a lack of taste for conflict and to confusion about the right course to pursue,[253] but to personal moral weakness:

> I have not yet spoken about the war within—even within ourselves—that rages among the passions. We are engaged in war with them night and day, brought on by our "lowly body,"[254] sometimes in secret and sometimes openly, and by the turmoil that sweeps over us like a wave from above and below, whirling through our sensations and the other delights of this life, and by the "miry clay"[255] in which we are stuck, and the "law of sin that wars against the law of the Spirit"[256] and is attempting to destroy the royal image in us, as well as whatever foundation of divine self-communication has been laid in us … Before one has gained control of this, as far as he is able, and has sufficiently purified his way of thinking, and before one has far surpassed the others in growing near to God, I am certain that it is unsafe to receive the office of leading souls or of mediating between God and human beings—for that, one might say, is what a priest does.[257]

Gregory emphasizes that preparation for ministry also involves an external process of education and gradual advancement. In several places, he opposes the contemporary practice (exemplified in the appointment to episcopal rank of such lay bureaucrats as Ambrose in Milan and Nectarius, his own successor, in Constantinople) of ordaining bishops who had not yet been baptized, let alone ordained to lower ecclesiastical offices. One must first be "worthy of the Church" through baptism, he insists in Oration 2, and then become "worthy of the pulpit" by being given the office of lector or deacon, before one can be thought "worthy of presidency" as a bishop or as one of the presbyters who represent and assist him.[258] To be an adequate teacher, one must spend sufficient time as a pupil to become a wise person,[259] but

> [T]o attempt to educate others without having been sufficiently educated oneself—to "learn the art of ceramics by making a large vase," as the saying goes[260]—and to practice piety by developing it in the souls of others, seems to me, quite simply, to be the practice of foolish or rash people: foolish, if they do not even perceive their own lack of learning; rash, if they do recognize it, but still attempt the job.[261]

Like dancing and flute-playing, he insists, the life of virtue and the practice of faith that are essential prerequisites for a life of preaching the Christian Gospel must be learned and cultivated carefully. To carry out their ministry without being paralyzed by vainglory, even such great apostles as Peter and Paul not only displayed the ability to "control themselves in word and deed" but "received the charism of 'becoming all things to all, in order to gain all.'"[262] Gregory says in another discourse from his early years that it is only because he is aware of himself as a diligent hearer of God's Word, as one struggling to grow in the wisdom of the Scriptures, that he feels empowered to "welcome ... my friends and brothers and set before them the table of the Word and the abundant bowl of the Spirit."[263]

By cultural and economic position and by family connections, Gregory had every reason to assume some entitlement to a position of power in the Church of his time; as Andrew Louth observes, "in their role as bishops—and, more to the point in Gregory's case, in their view of the nature of the Episcopal office—Basil and Gregory were exercising a right to rule that was theirs by virtue of their birth and education."[264] But Gregory confesses, in addition, a deep sense of vocation to priestly office, a personal desire to be involved publicly in the things of God that he identifies with his mother's prenatal dedication of him to God's service:

> And yet I was called to this from my youth, if I may tell something most people do not know; I was "thrown" onto God "from the womb,"[265] and given to him as a gift by my mother's promise. Afterwards, I was confirmed in this at a time of danger;[266] my longing grew, my reason led in the same direction; I brought everything forward, and offered it all to the one who had received my lot and had saved me: my property, my reputation, my well-being, my very ability with words—from which I have derived only this benefit: to be able to see beyond it, to have had something that I rank second to Christ.[267]

As a result of this long-cherished awareness of being called to serve, and of his father's wishes, Gregory concludes Oration 2 by speaking of his decision to accept the priesthood in terms of personal obligation, specifically of obedience. Love for his townsmen, he says, for the members of the little congregation at Nazianzus, has ultimately persuaded him not to prolong his flight from pastoral responsibility; so has his sense of responsibility to care for his aging parents and to assist his father in his work.[268] However, even more important than these considerations, Gregory continues, the Biblical story of Jonah, the reluctant prophet, has brought home to him the central importance in any prophet's life of obedience to God as a duty outweighing even his own sense of inadequacy and his fear of judgment:

> To distinguish the issues more clearly, perhaps the law of obedience might even relieve my fear of taking leadership (προστασία), since God gives recompense for faith in his goodness, and makes the one who trusts in him and places all his hope in him fit to exercise leadership perfectly; but if the danger of infidelity becomes a reality, I do not know who can help us escape, or what argument can command our confidence.[269]

It is only in obedience to a call from God, revealed in Gregory's own deepest long-lived desires and mediated through the expectations of family and friends, that Gregory feels himself freed from his well-founded reluctance to exercise the priestly office.

Gregory's misgivings about priestly ministry and authority reveal a deep sense of conflict about his real vocation and identity. As we have just seen, he admitted to a lifelong desire to serve God whole-heartedly. His temperament and his literary education inclined him to do this as a reclusive man of letters, as an intellectual well connected with those who operated the levers of power in fourth-century Asia Minor, but not operating them directly himself. Leadership in the Church both fascinated and repelled him; constantly aware of the struggles between Nicenes and anti-Nicenes, supporters and opponents of imperial policy, Gregory hoped in his own time to participate as an opinionated bystander, a "philosopher" standing at a critical and ascetical distance from the fray. In Oration 2, however, he confessed to his audience that it was his commitment to the philosophic life that now had led him, paradoxically, to accept a share in his father's ministry. Having resolved to support his parents in their old age,

> I filled this task as far as I have been able, so as to neglect philosophy itself, which is more precious to me than any possession or title—or to speak more truly, having first resolved philosophically not simply to give the appearance of living the philosophic life, I could not bear that all my labor should be wasted simply by my sticking to a single plan, or that that blessing, which one of the saints of old is said even to have taken by theft, should be lost to me ...[270]

In the course of his ministry as presbyter and bishop, Gregory came to realize that "the government of souls and leadership" is itself a form of the philosophic life,[271] indeed, one more demanding than his previous "spiritual exercises" had prepared him to accept, and that, as Athanasius had discovered in his visits with the desert monks during his times of exile, "there is a form of priesthood that is philosophical, and a form of philosophy that needs to initiate others into the Mysteries."[272] Gregory's own lifelong struggle was to hold these two forms of "philosophy" together.

THESE TRANSLATIONS

In his preface to the Paris edition of Gregory of Nazianzus in Latin translation (1532), Desiderius Erasmus remarked, "The cleverness of his expression, as well as the loftiness of his subjects and his more-than-obscure allusions, has always prevented me, at least, from translating Gregory."[273] The caution of such a great Hellenist should serve, perhaps, to warn the rest of us against attempting such a foolhardy task! Yet Gregory's brilliance as a Christian writer and thinker, and the extraordinary power and detail with which he has revealed to us his complex personality, render him a figure of unique interest in the Patristic era. Until very recently, few of his poems or letters and only approximately half of his forty-four orations have been available in English, most of the orations in Victorian translations that often sound archaic and are occasionally inaccurate.[274] The publication in the *Fathers of the Church* series of Martha Vinson's fine new translations of most of the orations not included in the earlier collections has made at least this part of his work available at last to English readers, but most of his shorter poems and three-fifths of his letters remain inaccessible to those who cannot penetrate his difficult Greek. As in the other volumes of this series, it is my hope that this collection will be yet another step towards making Gregory a figure more familiar to the modern English reader.

The challenge, of course, is to make a selection from his works that will offer a representative sampling of his writings within the limited scope offered by a volume such as this. My choices have been guided by the following general goals:

A. To translate works for which (at least until the publication of Vinson's volume) modern translations have not been readily available. Important and powerful as the *Theological Orations* or the letters on Christology are, for instance, offering new versions of them here did not seem necessary.

B. To include Orations representative of Gregory's approach to a variety of subjects and situations, yet expressing theological and Biblical themes central to his thought, which reveal his distinctive power as a Christian rhetorician.

C. To include a selection of poems and letters, most of them not translated into English before, dealing with both literary and religious themes and showing his characteristic style and persona as a Christian humanist.

D. To offer a new translation of Gregory's will, which affords us a distinctive glimpse of his relationships and concerns as he faced the prospect of death.

My aim has been to provide translations of these works that will represent Gregory's thought as accurately as possible, but that will also convey, in contemporary English, a sense both of his classical, yet highly individual, voice as a poet and letter writer and of the ornate and powerful—if sometimes rather fervid—style of his oratory. Rhetoric and argument, form and content, are as inseparable today as they were in the fourth century. I hope that these translations succeed in some measure in rendering that connection clear.

2

ORATIONS

INTRODUCTION: GREGORY'S ORATIONS

It seems more accurate to describe Gregory of Nazianzus as an orator rather than as a preacher. His ministry to congregations in Cappadocia and Constantinople doubtless required him to give frequent homilies, interpreting Scriptural texts and developing the central meaning of liturgical celebrations. Even so, the 44 of his speeches that have come down to us have little in common with the Biblical homilies of Origen or with Augustine's *sermones ad populum*. Although they usually end with the doxology characteristic of a liturgical sermon, they are also self-conscious, highly finished works of late antique prose: theological lectures, commemorative addresses and panegyrics, polemical arguments, occasional pieces. All of them, as we now have them, are composed in the form of speeches made before a live audience; but their very complexity of style and thought suggests at least heavy reworking, and we have no way of knowing with certainty which, or which parts, were delivered orally in their present form.

Some of the orations are clearly intended to persuade their hearers or readers of Gregory's doctrinal or pastoral concerns, much as Demosthenes or Lysias strove to persuade their Athenian contemporaries on civic issues of the day; they are, in a sense, "political" speeches in the context of a Christian Empire and its official Church. Others are clearly "epideictic" in form: formal speeches meant to celebrate a person's life or actions—the story of a saint, a friend, a departed family member—as a way of urging the audience to follow an example of virtue. Only one oration (Or. 37) deals directly with a Biblical passage: Jesus' words on marriage and divorce (Matt 19.1–12); but even this work in its present form is more a treatise on marriage and celibacy than a straightforward attempt to expound a text in a liturgical setting.

Although relatively short in comparison with the discourses of other fourth-century Greek orators, such as Libanius or Themistius, Gregory's orations clearly are meant to respond to the tastes and expectations of a cultivated society, for whom a rich and florid style and verbal wit and learning were both persuasive and esthetically satisfying. Their distinguishing characteristic, however, is their consistently religious subject matter and evocation of a context of worship, their relentless focus on the main doctrinal themes of the Gospel and Nicene Christianity, and the constant allusions to the Christian Bible woven into their texts, much as a pagan orator might color his arguments, and establish his own credentials as bearer of a cultural tradition, with allusions to Homer, Plato, or the tragedians.

I have chosen to translate eight of Gregory's orations here as representative both of the variety of styles and literary forms of his rhetoric and of the theological and spiritual themes that often recur in his work.

1. ORATION 8: *FUNERAL ORATION FOR HIS SISTER GORGONIA*

Gregory left commemorative discourses on his younger brother Caesarius, his father Gregory, and his older sister Gorgonia, all of them blending intimate, affectionate remembrance and grief with the rhetorical formality of the classical panegyric. This oration in memory of Gorgonia is perhaps the most remarkable, as an example of Gregory's ability to hybridize classical form and Christian content. Wife of Alypius, a native of Iconium, and mother of at least three daughters, Gorgonia died in Iconium in 369 or 370, while Gregory was still a presbyter, little more than a year after the death of their younger brother, Caesarius.[1] Following the general outline of a funerary discourse as given by late antique handbooks on rhetoric, Gregory here holds before us the figure of a Christian woman, whose life (doubtless unknown to most people outside her family circle) has transformed the classical virtues praised in the pagan tradition into a new, Biblically anchored image of self-effacing Christian heroism. Apparently the head of a substantial household, Gorgonia has reshaped her life and the lives of those around her by the relentless pursuit of Christian "philosophy" and has begun to radiate from her own person the signs of moral and spiritual transformation promised to the faithful Christian, through identification with the crucified and risen Christ. The portrait Gregory offers us of his sister may strike us as high-flown in its language and challengingly austere in its details, by most modern standards: closer, perhaps, to the image of a desert ascetic than to that of a middle-class Christian wife and mother. The paradox is intended; Gorgonia lives "in the world," Gregory suggests, but her heart is set on the Kingdom of God. In the context of the new perspectives of the fourth-century Church and society, Gregory's eulogy of his sister is really a discourse on Christian holiness.

Oration 8: *Funeral Oration For His Sister Gorgonia*[2]

1.   In praising my sister, I shall be relating the wonderful deeds of my own family.[3] I shall not be telling lies about her, simply because she is my sister; I shall rather be telling things that give her credit, because they are true— and telling the truth not just because it is right to tell it, but because it is already well known. No place will be given here simply to what delights the ear, even if we should wish to do so; for the listener stands here, like a skilled umpire, between my speech and the truth, giving no praise to words that are undeserved, but demanding what is deserved—and that is only just. What I fear above all, then, is not that I should go beyond the bounds of truth, but just the opposite: that I should fall short of the truth in some way, and, by grossly misrepresenting her real worth, that I should lessen her reputation by this oration in her honor. For it is difficult to equal the virtues of this woman, either in action or in words. Let not, then, all sorts of good qualities that were not hers be the object of my praise—that would be unjust—nor let what did belong to her, if it was worthy of praise, be without honor; in the first case, something foreign would become her reward, and in the second, what properly belonged to her would turn out for her discredit. In either case, whether the former qualities are praised or the latter allowed to go unspoken, the order of justice would be damaged. So we shall take the truth as our norm and measure, and look to it alone, not regarding any other considerations that might sound attractive to the lowly crowd. We shall praise what is worthy of praise, and keep silence about what deserves silence.[4]

2.   Listen to the most absurd thing of all! If we do not think it decent to deprive our friends of something, to insult them or accuse them or in some other way, small or great, to do them an injustice, surely the worst thing of all would be to commit such a wrong against our nearest relatives. Yet when we deprive them of a memorial discourse—that duty owed to the virtuous above all others, the means by which we might raise up for them an everlasting memorial—we convince ourselves we are doing the right thing, and take more account of those unprincipled people who charge us with favoritism than we do of the respectable ones who demand that we acknowledge real merit. Nothing seems to prevent outsiders from praising what they do not know, what they have not witnessed themselves—even when silence would be much more justified. But family affection, and envy masked as popular opinion, does prevent us from praising those we know, especially once they have departed this life, when it is too late to give them pleasure; after all, they have left behind both those who praise and those who blame them, with all the rest.[5]

3.   Now that we have sufficiently justified our approach to these subjects, and have shown how necessary this oration is to us, come—let us move on

with our encomium![6] We will spurn all attempt to make our language elegant and graceful, since the one we are praising also went unadorned, and her very lack of ornament was her beauty; we will fulfill our duty of paying her memorial honors, as the most pressing of debts, and at the same time we will try to educate the public to imitate her virtue eagerly, since our most serious concern is to use each of our words and actions to form those entrusted to our care.

Let someone else speak in praise of the native land and race of the departed one. At least one will be at no loss for fine words in abundance, if one should want to adorn her with outward details, as one decks out a noble and beautiful form with gold and precious stones, adornments worked by human hand and art—adornments that make a homely face seem even worse by comparison, and that bring no added beauty to a fair one, beauty which of itself puts such things to shame. But I will begin by following the laws governing such topics at least to this extent, that I will recall our common parents—after all, it would not be a holy thing to pass over the parents and teachers of a person of such goodness! Then, as quickly as possible, I will turn my words towards her, and will not frustrate the longing of those who have come expecting to hear her praises.

4.   Who, then, does not know our latter-day Abraham, and the Sarah of our time? I mean Gregory and his spouse Nonna—for it is right not to pass over their names, since they encourage us to virtue.[7] He was made just by his faith,[8] and she shared the life of the just one; he has been "the father of many nations"[9] in hope, and she has labored to give them spiritual birth; he fled from servitude to his ancestral gods, and she was both daughter and mother of the free;[10] he left his family and household for the sake of the "land of promise,"[11] and she was the cause of his departure—for in this respect alone, I dare to say, she has even surpassed Sarah; he has "sojourned" well [as a Christian],[12] and she has eagerly joined in his sojourn; he has given himself to the Lord, while she has called and thought of her husband as her own lord, and in part has become holy for this reason; both received a promise, both received Isaac—insofar as his coming depended on them—and both offered him back as a gift.[13]

5.   He has been her "good shepherd," whom she has prayed for and guided on his way; from her he has received the model for being a good shepherd. His call it was to flee sincerely from idols and then to put idols to flight; hers never even to share a table[14] with idol-worshippers. Both are of one dignity, of one mind, of one soul, no less in a partnership of virtue and closeness to God than in a partnership of flesh. They compete with each other equally in length of life and silver of hair, in prudence and in brilliance—but they far surpass all the rest. They are held back little by the flesh, far advanced in the spirit, even before those elements have been

separated. The world is both not theirs and theirs—one world they ignore, the other they far prefer. They have disposed of their riches,[15] and have become rich through the industry of holiness, despising one sort of wealth and buying instead the riches of the world to come. Only a brief span of this present life is left for them, and what remains they have dedicated to piety; but abundant and everlasting is the life for which they have labored. And let me simply add one thing to what I have said about them: it is good and right that they belong to different sexes, he to be the ornament of men and she of women—and not simply ornaments, but also patterns of virtue!

6.   From them, Gorgonia received both her existence and her good name; from that source, too, she took the seeds of piety. From them, finally, she received the ability both to live well and to depart gracefully, with the best of hopes. These are all great gifts, surely, and are not shared by those many who plume themselves on their noble birth, and swell with pride in their pedigrees.[16]

But if one is to explain her at a higher and more philosophical level, Gorgonia's native land was "the Jerusalem above,"[17] the city not yet seen but known, the place of our common life, towards which we hasten—where Christ is citizen, and his fellow citizens the festal gathering and "assembly of the first born, whose names are written in heaven,"[18] where they celebrate their great founder by contemplating his glory, circling round him in a dance that will never come to an end. There nobility consists in preserving his image and keeping one's likeness to the archetype; there reason and virtue and pure desire, and the gift of knowing whence and who we are and where we are heading, all bring this image to full reality, as they continue to form, on God's own pattern, genuine initiates in the sublime mysteries.

7.   That is how I understand these things. And therefore I know and proclaim that her soul was the noblest "among all the children of the East."[19] I use as my rule and measure something better than what common opinion uses to judge nobility and its lack, marking these things not on the basis of blood, but of a certain manner of living, judging whom to praise and whom to blame not on the basis of clan, but as individuals. This discourse on her virtues is given among people who knew her—let each one come to its aid by contributing some new detail! It is not possible, after all, for one person to grasp them all, even if one has mastered the art of retaining and analyzing all that has been said about her.

8.   She was so outstanding in self-control,[20] so far above her contemporaries in embodying it—to say nothing of those women of old, whose self-control is so much the stuff of legend—that while most people distinguish two patterns of living, marriage and celibacy, and consider the latter higher and more divine, but also more laborious and dangerous,[21] and think the former less exalted but safer, she escaped the negative aspect

of both states, and succeeded in garnering from both all that is best. She was able to bring both together into a single life—the loftiness of the one, the safety of the other—and to become chaste without becoming proud;[22] she mingled the beauty of celibacy with marriage, and showed that neither of them binds us completely to God or to the world, or completely separates us from them, in such a way that the one should be utterly shunned because of what it is, or the other unreservedly praised. The mind, rather, must be the good supervisor of both marriage and virginity, and both must be arranged and molded into virtue by the craft of reason.[23] For when she was joined to flesh, she was not, by that same action, separated from spirit; nor, because she looked on her husband as her head,[24] did she disregard our chief head. Rather, after paying service for a little while to the world and to nature, as far as the law of flesh—or rather, as far as the one who gave flesh its laws—demanded, she then consecrated herself entirely to God.

The most beautiful and exalted part is that she also brought her husband to act in agreement with her, and so gained for herself a virtuous fellow servant, rather than a virtual tyrant. Not only this, but she turned the fruit of her body—I mean her children and grandchildren—into the fruit of the Spirit, consecrating her whole family and household, not just a single soul, to God, and giving marriage a good reputation, both through what was pleasing to God in marriage itself and through the good fruit that it produced. She presented herself, as long as she lived, as a model of every good virtue to her descendants; and when she was called from this life, she left behind a testament to her household that was itself a silent exhortation.

9.   Holy Solomon, in his introduction to wisdom—I mean the Book of Proverbs[25]—praises the female works of housekeeping and loving one's husband; he contrasts the woman who wanders about, dishonored and without self-control, entrapping the souls of honorable men by lascivious gestures and words,[26] with the one who spends her time virtuously indoors, doing a woman's tasks with a man's endurance, constantly setting her hands to the spindle, making cloaks of double thickness for her husband, buying a field at an opportune time, providing food abundantly for her household, welcoming friends with a plenteous table[27]—and all the other activities he praises in a modest and industrious woman. But if I were to begin to praise my sister for such activities, I would be praising the statue on the basis of its shadows or the lion on the basis of its claws, and be missing the greater, more perfect things.

Who was more worthy to appear in public? But who appeared less frequently, or made herself more inaccessible to male observation?[28] Who knew better than she the limits of both gravity and joy? Her serious behavior never seemed inhuman, nor her tenderness unrestrained—the one was always intelligent, the other gentle, and the definition of decorum for her became a mixture of friendliness and lofty distance. Listen, all you women who are too demonstrative and too easy-going, and who show no respect for the veil of modesty! Who was her equal in knowing how to temper the eye? Who was so much a scorner of vulgar laughter as to feel, as my sister did, that even the urge to smile was excessive? Who kept a better watch over the doors of her hearing? Who was so open to the word of God—or rather, who so made her mind the guide of her tongue—that she could always speak of the judgments of God? Who has imposed such order on her own lips?[29]

10. Shall I tell you another of her virtues? It concerns something that seemed of little worth to her, or to any woman who is truly modest and decorous in her ways, but that women in love with the world and its honors, not yet purified by the words of those who should teach us such things, consider of great importance. Gold, worked up to an excess of beauty by human art, never adorned her; blond braids—now strikingly obvious, now tucked discreetly away—did not surround her face, nor spirals of curls, the artifices of stage designers, which only dishonor an honorable head; neither the extravagance of flowing, diaphanous robes was hers, nor the charm and glitter of stones that color the air around them and light up the forms that bear them. She was not concerned with the arts and trickery of painters, nor with cheaply bought beauty; she had no dealings with the earthly creator, God's rival, who conceals God's creation with treacherous colors and spreads shame by the honors he bestows, setting forth the divine form as an idol of lewdness for hungry eyes, so that spurious beauty might steal away the natural image meant for God, and for the age to come. She knew, in fact, the many, varied forms of external ornament women wear, but considered none of them more precious than her own manner of living and the brilliance hidden away within her. The only rouge she valued was the blush of modesty; her only white powder was the pallor of self-denial. Highlights and eye-shadow, the fleeting prettiness of living portraits, she left to the women of the theatre and the public square, to those for whom a sense of shame is itself a source of shame and a reproach.

11. So much for that! As for her prudence and her piety,[30] no words could come close to them, nor could many parallel examples of them be found, besides those of her parents in the flesh and in the spirit. She looked towards them alone; and although she was in no respect behind them in virtue, she took second place—and quite gladly so—on this one point alone, that she drew her goodness from them, and knew and acknowledged openly that they were the root of the light within her. What was more acute than her intelligence? Not only the members of her family, nor even simply her own people, the sheep of the same fold, recognized her as their common counselor; all those who lived around her accepted her advice and exhortation

as absolute law. Whose words were more apposite than hers? What could be more thoughtful than her silences? But since I have recalled her silence, I must add the aspect of it that was most proper to her, most fitting for women, most useful for this present moment: who knew the things of God better [than she did], both from the divine Scriptures and from her own wisdom? Yet who spoke less about them, remaining within the proper limits of reverence?[31]

One thing must be said of her in justice, as a person who truly knew what piety is; one appetite she had that was both insatiable and virtuous: who else adorned so many of God's temples with votive monuments— churches elsewhere, but especially this one, which may never be adorned again after her time? More important, who ever offered herself in such a way to God as a living temple? Who has given such honor to priests, above all to the one who was her fellow combatant in the struggle for piety—her teacher, who sowed good seed and who produced a pair of children consecrated to God?[32]

12.   Who, more than she, put her own house at the disposal of those who live in God's way?[33] Who ever offered them a more handsome and generous welcome? More important still, who ever welcomed them with such modesty, with such efforts to walk in God's footsteps? And beyond this, who has shown a mind less adversely affected by suffering, yet a soul more compassionate towards the sick? Who has extended a more lavish hand towards the needy? I feel I might even dare to adorn her with what is said of Job: "Her door was open to everyone who came, and no stranger ever had to camp outside."[34] "She was an eye for the blind, a foot for the lame,"[35] a mother of orphans.[36] Why need I say more about her tender-heartedness towards widows than that she bore its fruit: she was never called a widow herself.[37] Her hearth was a common place of refuge, both for the poor and for her own relations; her possessions belonged to all the needy, in the same way that each possessed what was his own. "She shared, she gave to the poor;"[38] through the promise that can never be defeated, never deceive, she laid up ample stores in the vats of heaven, and she often welcomed Christ by welcoming so many beneficiaries in his name. Best of all, appearances did not count more than truth with her: she cultivated her piety in secret, for the eyes of him who sees in secret.[39] She snatched everything from the grasp of the "ruler of this world,"[40] transferred it all to a safe storehouse.[41] She left nothing behind on this earth except her body. For everything else, she exchanged the hope of heaven. One form of riches she left to her children: an example to imitate, and the desire to rival her in these things.

13.   And it was not the case that she showed such signs of generosity as these, incredible as they may seem, but indulged her body in luxury and the

pleasures of unrestrained consumption,[42] that raging and savage hound; she did not rely on her acts of benevolence, as most people do, and think she was purchasing a right to luxury by compassion for the poor—not healing evil by good, but remaining in vice as compensation for virtue. Nor did she overthrow her "earthen" self by fasting, and leave the remedy of sleeping on the ground to others; still less did she discover this support for her soul, but set less of a measure on her sleep than others might do; nor did she lay this law on herself, as if she were bodiless, but lie on the ground while others remained erect all night in vigil—a special feat of men dedicated to "philosophy." Nor did she merely show herself, in this way, as a person of courage—more courageous not only than women, but even than men of noble heart. In her thoughtful way of chanting the psalms, in her reading and explanation and timely recall of holy Scripture, in the bending of her hardened knees, which almost seemed glued to the ground, in the tears that cleansed away stain "with a contrite heart and a humble spirit,"[43] in her prayer lifted up on high, her unwavering and elevated mind—in all these things, what is there that any man or women could boast of that would surpass her?[44]

It may seem a great deal to say, but it is nonetheless true: she would strive for one virtue while being, in another, already the model for striving; as she found her way towards one, she surpassed the other. And if, in each of these respects, she achieved something for others to rival, she conquered everyone else in being able to bring all of them together in a single life. So she managed to make all these qualities her own, though others can scarcely achieve one with even moderate success; in fact, she brought each of them to such a peak of fullness that one alone, in place of all the rest, would have been enough!

14.   O unwashed body, and clothing that bloomed with virtue alone![45] O soul supporting a body, almost as if without nourishment, as if the body were without matter! O body rather, forced to be mortified, even before its separation from the soul, that the soul might find its freedom and not be entangled in the senses! O sleepless nights and psalmody and standing erect, as day trailed on into day! O David, singer of songs, which only to faithful souls never seem too long! O tender limbs, cast down on the earth and roughened against their nature! O springs of tears, "sown in sorrow" that they might be "reaped in joy!"[46] O cry in the night, piercing the clouds and reaching heaven itself! O fervor of spirit, braving the dogs of night in its eagerness to pray, defying frost and rain and thunder and hail and the ungodly hour! O woman's nature, defeating that of men in our common struggle for salvation, proving that female and male are differences of body, not of soul! O purity after the bath,[47] and soul made a bride of Christ in the chaste bridal chamber of the body! O bitter taste,[48] and Eve, mother of our race

and our sin, and deceptive serpent, and death—all overcome by her self-mastery! O emptying of Christ, and form of a servant, and suffering now honored by this woman's mortification!

15.   How shall I enumerate all her virtues, or fail to deprive of profit those who never knew her, if I omit the rest?[49] It seems best now, however, to add instead a few words about the rewards of her piety; for those of you who knew her in life have been longing to hear for some time, I think—and have been seeking in my discourse—not simply something about her present state and the joys she now shares in heaven (all far beyond our minds, and our human hearing and sight), but also something of the blessings which here on earth the one who justly repays us bestowed on her as a reward. This, too, after all, often works to build up faith in unbelievers, when one shows in little things a promise of greater ones, and in visible things a pledge of the invisible. I will recount some things known to everyone, but also others of which most are ignorant—since her asceticism[50] reached also to this, that she did not preen herself on the graces she received.

You know about the mad mules who ran away with her carriage, that unexpected swerve, the irresistible speed, the awful wreck—and also about the scandal that first resulted for unbelievers because the just are allowed to suffer thus, and then the swift correction of their lack of faith. Everything in her was crushed and broken: bones and limbs, internal and external parts; yet she allowed no physician near her except Him who allowed the accident to happen. For one thing, her modesty made her shy of the eyes and the touch of men—even in her suffering, she maintained her sense of propriety. For another, she sought the explanation [of her pains] from the one who permitted her to suffer these things, and she received her cure from no one else but him. As a result, some were less disturbed by her suffering than astonished by the miraculous return of her health; the tragedy seemed to have happened that she might be glorified in her sufferings. Suffering in a human way, she was healed superhumanly, and so left posterity a story that was great for revealing faith in the midst of pain and toughness in the face of adversity, but even greater as a revelation of God's kind concern for people such as her. For to the verse which so beautifully portrays the plight of the just man, "when he falls, he will not be shattered,"[51] a new clause has now been added: even if he is shattered, he will quickly be raised up and glorified.[52] Although she suffered in an extraordinary way, she also returned to herself with extraordinary speed, so that her misfortune was almost obliterated by her recovery of health, and the cure became more celebrated than the injury.

16.   O praiseworthy, wonderful accident! O suffering more exalted than invulnerability! O text of Scripture, "He will strike, he will bind the wounds and heal, and after three days he will raise up"[53]—words with a greater and more mystical significance, one which has indeed already come to fulfillment,

but which apply none the less to this woman's sufferings. All of this is obvious to everyone, even to those with few connections to her, since the miracle became known to all, the story was on everyone's lips and in everyone's ears, among all God's other wonderful deeds of power.

But do you command me to relate what most people, until now, do not know, O best and most perfect of shepherds, shepherd of this holy sheep?[54] Shall I speak of what still lies concealed because of the ascetical discipline[55] I have mentioned, and the unpretentious, unadorned manner of her piety? Do you approve of my also telling this other anecdote—since only we were entrusted with the mystery, witnesses to each other of the miracle—or should we still keep faith with her who is departed? It seems to me, at least, that just as there was once a time for silence, so now is the time for full disclosure: not only for the glory of God, but also as a comfort to those undergoing trials.

17. Her body was sick, and she was in serious condition. The disease was strange and unusual: sudden fever throughout the body, with a kind of seething and boiling of the blood; then a coagulation of the blood, with numbness and unbelievable pallor, and a paralysis of mind and limbs—and all of this not separated by long intervals, but at times quite continuously. The calamity seemed not to be of human proportions. The skill of physicians could make no difference, although they examined her symptoms very painstakingly, each by himself and in consultation with each other; her parents' many tears, which often seem so powerful, were also fruitless, as were the common prayers and intercessions which her whole community made for her, as if for their own salvation. Indeed, her good health was the health of all, just as her suffering from this bodily illness was a matter of common suffering.

18. What, then, did that great soul do, who deserved the greatest of rewards? How was her illness cured? Let me now tell you her great secret. Giving up on all other doctors, she took refuge in the universal Physician. Waking once in the dead of night, when her illness had receded a little, she threw herself with faith before the altar,[56] and calling out in a loud voice to him who is honored there, naming him by all his names and reminding him of all his powerful deeds of the past—for she was well schooled in "things old and new"[57] —she ended by indulging in a kind of reverent and benign shamelessness, imitating the woman who dried up her flow of blood by touching the fringe of Christ's cloak.[58] What did she do? First she leaned her head against the altar, crying out as before, and drenched the altar with her abundant tears, as once a woman had done to the feet of Christ,[59] threatening that she would not let go before she regained her health. Next, she anointed her whole body with a medicine she had devised herself: having privately stored away some of the sacraments of the precious body and blood

[of Christ], and she now mingled them with her tears! And O wonder! She immediately sensed that she was healed, and went away, lightened in body, soul, and mind, receiving as the reward of her hope the thing she had hoped for, and securing new strength for her body by the strength of her soul.

These words may amaze you, but they are no lie. Believe them, all of you, both sick and healthy, that the well may preserve their health and the sick regain it. And that the story is not just boasting is clear from facts that she kept in silence while she lived, but which I have now revealed. I would not have publicized them even now, I assure you, if I were not in some way afraid to conceal such a great miracle from believers and unbelievers, now and for the time to come.

19.   Such is the story of her life—we have omitted most of the details in order to keep some due proportion in our discourse, and not to seem greedy for her praise.[60] But I would probably be doing an injustice to her holy and celebrated death, if I did not recall some of its beautiful moments—especially since she so longed for it, and sought it so. I shall call them to mind, then, as briefly as I can.

She longed for her departure: indeed, she spoke her mind freely to the one who would call her to himself, and prized "being with Christ"[61] before all earthly blessings. No one so yearns[62] for the body —not even those who love it with irresistible excess—as much as she yearned to fling away these fetters and cross beyond the slime in which we pass our lives, to live purely in the presence of the Good and to receive a full share of the Beloved (who is, I must add, also her Lover), whose rays now illumine us in a small degree, but from whom we still live at a distance, as far as full knowledge is concerned. She was not disappointed of this desire, divine and lofty as it was; more remarkable still, she had a foretaste of its beauty, due both to her own sense of the future and to her frequent nightly vigils.[63] One dream, of the most blessed kind, was bestowed on her as a reward; one vision concerned her departure at its appointed time, and let her know the day of it, as if God himself were making sure that she would be ready, and would not be disturbed.

20.   In her own life, in fact, the blessings of purification and perfection[64] were then a recent thing —something that all of us must receive as a free gift, as the foundation of our second life. Or rather, all of life was for her purification and fulfillment: the gift of rebirth itself she had from the Spirit, but its security came from the way she had lived before. For her alone, I almost dare to say, the sacrament was a seal, but not an empowering grace. The one thing that she sought to add to all of this was her husband's perfection [in baptism] —and do you want me to describe her husband in a word? He was her husband; I do not think one need say any more!—so that she might be consecrated to God in her whole body,[65] and not depart

from life only half-perfected, or leave anything belonging to herself imperfect. She was also not disappointed in this request, by the one who accomplishes the will of those who fear Him, and brings their earnest longings to completion.

21.   When everything had taken place according to her plans, and none of her desires remained unfulfilled, and the appointed day was near, she made final preparations for death and for her departure from this world, and fulfilled the law that governs these things by taking to her bed for the last time. And having given the kind of instructions to her husband and children and friends that might befit one who loved husband and children and fellow human beings as she did, having reflected luminously about the things of heaven and so turned her last day into a festival,[66] she fell asleep: not full of years according to human reckoning—for she never asked that from God, knowing that human days are evil, and most of them full of dust and error—but indeed full of days according to God, to a degree that one who dies in rich old age, and counting many turns of years, might not so easily claim. So she found her end[67]—or, to put it better, she was taken up, or flew away; she was brought to a new dwelling place; she withdrew for a while, in advance of her own body.

22.   But think of what I have almost omitted from her story! Yet perhaps you would not have allowed me to do so—you who were her spiritual father, who carefully observed the wonder and made it known to us.[68] It is a great thing, both for her own credit and as a way of reminding us of her virtue and leading us to long for a death like hers. Yet a shiver runs over me and a tear starts in my eye, as I recall the marvel.

She was at the point of deliverance and was breathing her last; a chorus both of family and outsiders stood around her, chanting the funeral prayers. Her aged mother was bowed beside her, her soul torn apart by a kind of envious desire to experience such a departure. For all, affection was mingled with anguish: some longed to hear something, as an ember for the memory;[69] others wished to say something, but did not dare. Their tears were mute, the agony of their grief incurable, for it seemed irreverent to honor one departing in such a way with lamentations. The silence was deep—death seemed a rite of initiation! She lay, to all appearances, without breath or motion or sound; the silence of her body seemed due to a kind of paralysis, as if her organs of speech were already dead, because that which could set them in motion had slipped away. But her shepherd, who observed every aspect of her life with care, because all of them were wonderful, noticed that her lips were gently moving and put his ear near them; he drew courage to do so from his own manner of living, and from his sympathy with her. You tell us, now, the mystery of her peace—what it was, what was its meaning! No one will disbelieve it if you say it! It was a psalm that she was murmuring—psalmody was her language in death! Blessed be anyone who goes to his rest with words such as these: "In peace, all at once, I shall lie down and fall asleep."[70] That is what she, the most beautiful of women, prayed in your ear, and indeed, it came true: the psalm-verse both described what happened, and became a motto to accompany her departure. How well you have come to peace after all your sufferings, receiving the sleep due the beloved, as well as our common sleep of death! This was only fitting for you, who have lived and died with the words of piety on your lips![71]

23.   Your present joys, I know well, are far more precious than the joys of this visible life: the sound of festival, choruses of angels, the heavenly army, a vision of glory, and yet another, higher illumination, purer and more perfect than that of this world, the light of the Trinity, which no longer eludes a mind bound and diffused by the senses but is contemplated as a whole by the whole mind, grasping us now and letting its radiance illumine our souls with the full light of the godhead. Now you enjoy all the things which, while yet on earth, you possessed only in distant distillations, through the clarity of your instinct for them.

If you still take any account of the honors we pay you—if this, too, is part of the reward God gives holy souls: to be aware of such things: then receive our discourse, too, in place of, even in preference to, the many memorial gestures we have paid, to Caesarius before you[72] and now to you in your turn. For we have been spared by God to speak the funeral orations of our brother and sister! Whether or not anyone will honor us in a similar way, after both of you, I cannot say. In any case, let us only be honored with the honor that is in God, whether we still live here in exile, or have finally come to live in Christ Jesus our Lord, to whom be glory along with the Father and the Holy Spirit, for all ages. Amen.

2. ORATION 14: *ON THE LOVE OF THE POOR*

One of Gregory's most moving orations, *On the Love of the Poor* is an appeal to a Christian congregation to notice the destitute (especially the homeless victims of an outbreak of leprosy) in their own city and to open their homes to them in compassion; probably it was originally delivered in Caesaraea during the years 369–371. Like the two Biblical homilies of Gregory of Nyssa dealing with the same theme, it seems to form part of a campaign to win public support for the efforts of Basil of Caesaraea to organize relief for the poor and sick, a project that culminated in the opening of a new hostel for the homeless just outside Caesaraea during the early years of Basil's work there as bishop (370–379).[73] Gregory begins here with a discussion of human virtue, leading to the conclusion that it is human kindness, or "love of humanity" (φιλανθρωπία), that makes us most closely resemble God. After a reflection on the highly ambivalent situation in which our present condition of embodiment places us, Gregory moves on to speak of physical disease and human want, of the deceptiveness of material pleasures and possessions, and of the hidden ways of Providence in allotting different degrees of well-being to the human race. Drawing on a dazzling array of Biblical texts, he then makes an eloquent appeal to his listeners to use their own resources to express their love for their neighbors in misery, reminding them that love of one's neighbor is, for the Christian, the most direct way of loving Christ.

Oration 14: *On Love of the Poor*[74]

1.   Brothers and sisters, poor with me—for all of us are beggars and needy of divine grace, even if one of us may seem to have more than others when measured on a small scale—accept my words on love of the poor, not in a mean spirit but generously, that you may be rich in God's Kingdom; and pray that we may bestow these words on you richly, and nourish your souls with our discourse, breaking spiritual bread for the poor. Perhaps we may make nourishment rain from heaven, as Moses did in ancient times, lavishing on you the bread of angels; or perhaps we may feed many thousands in the desert with a few loaves, and leave them satisfied, as Jesus later did, who is the true bread and the source of true life.

Now it is no easy matter to find the supreme virtue and award it first place, as conquering the rest—just as in a flowery, fragrant meadow it is not easy to find the fairest and most fragrant flower, since each one draws our sense of smell towards itself, urging us to pluck it first of all. But as it seems best to me, at least, to divide the subject, let us consider these things as follows.

2.   "Faith, hope and love, these three,"[75] are all a good thing. And the example of faith is Abraham, who was justified by faith.[76] The example of hope is Enos, who was first to be moved by hope to call on the name of the Lord,[77] along with all those just ones who suffer because of their hope. And the example of love is the divine Apostle, who dared to speak out even against his own best interests for Israel's sake,[78] and also God himself, who is called love.[79] Hospitality is a good thing; among the just its example is Lot, who came from Sodom but did not imitate Sodom in his actions, while among sinners it is Rahab the harlot, who was not a harlot by choice and who was praised and spared because of her hospitality. Love of one's brothers and sisters is a good thing; its example is Jesus, who was ready not only to be called our brother, but even to suffer for our sakes. Love of humanity is a good thing; its example is the same Jesus, who did not only

create the human person for the sake of good works,[80] and unite his image to clay as a guide towards the highest things and a harbinger of heavenly life, but himself also became a human being for us. Patience is a good thing; again, he is its example, who did not only decline the help of legions of angels against those who had risen up against him to oppress him, nor only rebuke Peter when he drew his sword, but who restored the ear of him who had been struck.[81] Gentleness is a good thing; its examples are Moses and David, who embodied this virtue before all others, as well as their teacher, who "did not quarrel or cry out, or make his voice heard in the streets,"[82] nor struggle against those who led him away.

3. Jealous zeal is a good thing; an example is Phineas, who slew the Midianite with the sword along with the Israelite,[83] to remove shame from the children of Israel, and who made a name for himself by this decision. After him, there were others who said, "With zeal I have been jealous for the Lord,"[84] and "I am jealous for you with a divine jealousy,"[85] and "Jealous zeal for your house consumes me."[86] Mortification of the body is a good thing; let Paul persuade you, who continued to keep himself in training, and who was fearful for Israel because they relied on themselves and indulged the body; Jesus himself fasted, and in time of temptation conquered the tempter. Prayer and watching are a good thing; let God himself[87] persuade you, who stayed awake to pray the night before his passion. Chastity and virginity are a good thing; let Paul persuade you, who laid down rules for these things, and acted as impartial judge on questions of marriage and celibacy.[88] And Jesus himself was born of a virgin, that he might both honor childbirth and give first honor to virginity. Self-control is a good thing; let David persuade you, when he gained control of the well at Bethlehem and then did not drink, but only poured out the water on the ground, not being willing to slake his own thirst at the cost of others' blood.[89]

4. Solitude and silence are a good thing; my teachers in this are Elijah's Carmel, or John's desert, or Jesus' mountaintop, to which he often seems to have withdrawn, to be by himself in silence and peace. Frugality is a good thing; here my teacher is Elijah, who lodged with a widow, and John, who was cloaked in camel's hair, and Peter, who fed himself on a few pennyworth of lupines.[90] Humility is a good thing, and there are many examples of this on all sides; before all the rest is the Savior and Lord of all, who did not only humble himself as far as taking "the form of a slave,"[91] or simply expose his face to the shame of being spat upon, and let himself be "counted among sinners"[92]—he who purged the world of sin!—but who washed the feet of his disciples dressed as a slave. Poverty and contempt for money are a good thing; examples here are Zacchaeus and Christ himself: the former, by putting almost all his wealth at the disposal of others when Christ entered his house,[93] the latter by defining perfection in these terms when he spoke with the rich

man.[94] To put it still more concisely concerning all these virtues, contemplation is a good thing, and action is also a good thing: the first, when it raises us up and leads us to the Holy of Holies, guiding our mind upwards towards what is akin to it; the second, when it receives Christ as its guest and looks after him, revealing the spell of love by its works.

5.   Each of these virtues is one path to salvation, and leads, surely, towards one of the blessed, eternal dwellings; just as there are different chosen forms of life, so there are many "dwelling places" with God,[95] distributed and allotted to each person according to his merit. So let one person cultivate this virtue, the other that, another several, still another all of them—if that is possible! Let each one simply walk on the way, and reach out for what is ahead, and let him follow the footsteps of the one who leads the way so clearly, who makes it straight and guides us by the narrow path and gate to the broad plains of blessedness in the world to come. And if, following the command of Paul and of Christ himself, we must suppose that love is the first and greatest of the commandments, the crowning point of the law and the prophets, I must conclude that love of the poor, and compassion and sympathy for our own flesh and blood, is its most excellent form. For God is not so served by any of the virtues as he is by mercy, since nothing else is more proper than this to God, "before whom mercy and truth march as escorts,"[96] and to whom mercy is to be offered as a sacrifice in preference to justice;[97] nor will human kindness be repaid with anything else than the same kindness, by him who makes just recompense and weighs our mercy with his balance and scales.[98]

6.   We must open our hearts, then, to all the poor, to those suffering evil for any reason at all, according to the Scripture that commands us to "rejoice with those who rejoice and weep with those who weep."[99] Because we are human beings, we must offer the favor of our kindness first of all to other human beings, whether they need it because they are widows or orphans, or because they are exiles from their own country, or because of the cruelty of their masters or the harshness of their rulers or the inhumanity of their tax-collectors, or because of the bloody violence of robbers or the insatiable greed of thieves, or because of the legal confiscation of their property, or shipwreck—all are wretched alike, and so all look towards our hands, as we look towards God's, for the things we need. But of all these groups, those who suffer evil in a way that contradicts their dignity are even more wretched than those who are used to misfortune. Most especially, then, we must open our hearts to those infected by the "sacred disease" [i.e., leprosy], who are being consumed even in their flesh and bones and marrow, just as some have been threatened in Scripture.[100] They are being betrayed by this deceiving, wretched, faithless body!

How I am connected to this body, I do not know, nor do I understand how I can be an image of God, and still be mingled with this filthy clay; when it is in good condition, it wars against me, and when it is itself under attack, it causes me grief! I love it as my fellow servant, but struggle against it as an enemy; I flee it as something enslaved, just as I am, but I show it reverence as called, with me, to the same inheritance. I long that it be dissolved, and yet I have no other helper to use in striving for what is best, since I know what I was made for, and know that I must ascend towards God through my actions.

7.   So I treat it gently, as my fellow worker; and then I have no way of escaping its rebellion, no way to avoid falling, weighed down by those fetters that drag me or keep me held down to the earth. It is a cordial enemy, and a treacherous friend. What an alliance and an alienation! What I fear, I treat with honor; what I love, I fear. Before we come to war, I am reconciled to it, and before we have made peace, I am at odds with it again. What wisdom lies behind my constitution? What is this great mystery? Is it God's will that since we are part of him, drawn in an upward stream, we should always look towards him from the midst of a fight and struggle with the body, so that we might not be lifted up by our own dignity and think ourselves so high that we begin to look down on our creator? Is this weakness with which we are joined a kind of training for that dignity, making us aware that we are both the greatest and the most lowly of creatures, earthly and heavenly, temporal and immortal, heirs of both light and fire, or even of darkness, depending on which way we may lean? Such is the blend of our nature, and for this reason, it seems to me, whenever we are exalted in spirit because of the image [of God], we are humbled because of the earth. Let anyone so inclined speculate[101] about these things—we will speculate with him at a more appropriate time!

8.   Now, however, as I feel pain at the weaknesses of my own flesh and sense my own weakness in the sufferings of others, what reason urges me to say is this: brothers and sisters, we must care for what is part of our nature and shares in our slavery. For even if I lay charges against it, because of its passibility, still I stand by it as a friend, because of the one who bound me in it. And we must, each of us, care no less for our neighbors' bodies than our own, the bodies both of those who are healthy and of those who are consumed by this disease. "For we are all one in the Lord, whether rich or poor, whether slave or free,"[102] whether in good health of body or in bad; and there is one head of all, from whom all things proceed: Christ. And what the limbs are to each other, each of us is to everyone else, and all to all. So we must by no means overlook or neglect to care for those who experience our common weakness before we do, nor should we delight more in the

fact that our bodies are in good condition than we grieve that our brothers and sisters are in misery. Rather, we must consider this to be the single way towards the salvation both of our bodies and of our souls: human kindness shown towards them. Let us examine this point together.

9.   For most people, only one thing causes misery: something is lacking. Perhaps time, or hard work, or a friend, or a relative, or the passing of time has taken it away. But for the people I am speaking of,[103] misery is present even more abundantly, in that the resources to work and to help themselves in need have been taken away along with their flesh, and the fear of growing weaker is always greater to them than the hope of recovery. Indeed, they find little support in hope, which is the only drug that really helps the unfortunate. In addition to their poverty, illness is a second evil: the most abominable and depressing evil of all, suggesting to many the most obvious formula for a curse! And a third evil for them is the fact that no one will approach them, that most will not look at them, that all run away from them, find them disgusting, try to keep them at a distance. So that for them something still more burdensome than the disease is to perceive that they are hated because of their misfortune. I cannot bring myself to think about the suffering of these people without tears, and I am brought to confusion when I recall them; you should feel the same way yourselves, that you might put tears to flight with tears. I know, in fact, that those among you who love Christ and love the poor do feel this way; for you have received the gift of sharing God's mercy from God himself, and you give witness to your feelings yourselves.

10.   There stands before our eyes a terrible, pitiable sight, unbelievable to anyone who did not know it was true: human beings both dead and alive, mutilated in most parts of their body, scarcely recognizable either for who they are or where they come from; they are, rather, wretched remnants of once-human beings. As marks of identification, they call out the names of their fathers and mothers, brothers and sisters and homes: "I am the son of so-and-so, so-and-so is my mother, this is my name, you were once my dear companion!" They do this because they cannot be recognized by their former shape; they are truncated human beings, deprived of possessions, family, friends and their very bodies, distinctive in being able both to pity themselves and hate themselves at once. They are uncertain whether to lament for the parts of their bodies that no longer exist, or for those that remain—those which the disease has consumed, or those left for the disease to work on. The former have been consumed most wretchedly, the latter are still more wretchedly preserved; the former have disappeared before their bodies are buried, the latter have no one who will given them a burial. For even the kindest and most humane of neighbors is insensitive to them; in this instance alone, we forget that we are flesh, clothed in this lowly body,

and we are so far from caring for our fellow creatures that we think the safety of our own bodies lies in fleeing from them. One approaches a body that has been dead for some time, even if it has begun to reek; one carries about the stinking carcasses of brute animals, and puts up with being full of filth; yet we avoid these lepers with all our might (what inhumanity!), almost taking offense at breathing the same air they breathe.

11. Who could be more upright than a father? Who more sympathetic than a mother? But nature's operation is shut off even for them. The father looks at his own child, whom he begot and raised, whom alone he considered the light of his life, for whom he prayed often and long to God, and now both grieves over that child and drives him away—the first willingly, the second under compulsion. The mother recalls the pangs of childbirth and her heart is torn apart: she calls his name wretchedly, and when he stands before her she laments for her living child as if he were dead: "Unfortunate child of a miserable mother, bitter disease has come to share you with me! Wretched child, unrecognizable child, child whom I have raised only for the cliffs and mountaintops and desert places! You will dwell with wild beasts, and rock will be your roof; only the holiest of people will ever look on you!"[104] Then she will utter those pitiable words of Job, "Why were you formed in the womb of your mother? Why did you not come forth from her belly and immediately perish, so that death and birth might have been simultaneous? Why did you not depart prematurely, before tasting the evils of life? Why did these knees receive you? Why were you allowed to suck at these breasts, since you were going to live so wretchedly, a life more difficult than death?"[105] So she speaks, and lets loose floods of tears; the unfortunate woman wishes to embrace her child, but fears his flesh as if it were the enemy. From all the neighbors come loud shouts and gestures, driving him away—cries not directed against criminals, but against the wretched. There have been instances when people have allowed a murderer to live with them, have shared not only their roof but their table with an adulterer, have chosen a person guilty of sacrilege as their life's companion, have made solemn covenants with those who have wished them harm; but in this person's case suffering, rather than any injury, is handed down as a criminal charge. So crime has become more profitable than sickness, and we accept inhumanity as fit behavior for a free society, while we look down on compassion as something to be ashamed of.

12. They are driven away from the cities, driven away from their homes, from the market-place, from public assemblies, from the streets, from festivals and private celebrations, even—worst of all sufferings!—from our water; not even the springs flow for them, though they are common property for everyone else, nor are the rivers allowed to wash off any of their impurities. Most paradoxical of all, we drive them away as bearers of pollution, yet we

draw them back towards us again, as if they caused us no distress at all, by giving them neither housing, nor the necessary food, nor treatment for their lesions—by not cloaking their disease, as far as we can, with some form of covering.[106] For this reason they wander around night and day, destitute and naked and homeless, showing their disease publicly, talking of the old times, crying out to their Creator, crafting songs that constrain us to pity, asking for a bit of bread or some tiny scrap of food, or for some tattered rag to protect their modesty and offer some relief to their sores. The kindest person, for them, is not someone who supplies their needs, but someone who does not send them off with a sharp word. Most of them, too, are not ashamed to appear at festivals—just the opposite: they thrust their way into them, because of their want. I am speaking both of public festivals and of the sacred ones that we have instituted for the care of our souls, when we come together either because of some mystery of faith or to celebrate the martyrs who witnessed to the truth, so that by paying honor to their struggles we might also imitate their piety. These people feel shame at their condition, surely, before their fellow human beings, since they are human themselves; they would wish to be hidden by mountains or cliffs or forests, or finally by night and darkness. Yet they throw themselves into the midst of the crowd, nonetheless, a wretched rabble worthy of our tears. Perhaps this all has a reason: that they might remind us of our own weakness, and persuade us not to lean on any of the present things we see around us, as if it were stable. They throw themselves into our midst, some from a longing to hear the human voice, others to see a face, others in order to gather up some scanty provisions from those who are feasting—all of them making their laments public, in hope of tasting some form of gentleness in return.

13. Whose heart is not broken by the mournful cries of these people, sounding forth a kind of pitiable music? Whose ear can bear the sound? What eye can take in the sight? They lie alongside each other, drawn into a kind of sickly bond by their illness, each one contributing another instance of misfortune to the general misery. They add to each other's suffering, wretched in their weakness and still more wretched in the fact that it is shared. A mixed audience gathers around them, touched with compassion—but only for a moment. They toss around in the hot sun and dust, at the feet of their fellow men and women; at other times they will lie there, suffering in the bitter frost, in rainstorms and violent winds. The only reason they are not trampled under our feet is that we shrink from touching them. The wail of their begging offers a counterpoint to the sacred singing within the church, and a miserable dirge is produced, in contrast to the sounds of the Mysteries. Why must I depict all their misfortune to people celebrating a feast day?[107] Perhaps it is that I might stir up some lament in your own hearts, if I carefully play out every detail; perhaps suffering will triumph

over celebration! For I say all this, since I have not yet been able to convince you that sadness is sometimes more precious than joy, and gloom than celebration—a tear more praiseworthy than unseemly laughter.

14.   This is how they are suffering, and much more miserably than I have said: our brothers and sisters before God (even if you prefer not to think so) who share the same nature with us, who have been put together from the same clay from which we first came, who are strung together with nerves and bones in the same way we are, who have put on flesh and skin like all of us, as holy Job says when reflecting on his sufferings and expressing contempt for our outward form.[108] Or rather, if I must speak of greater things, they have been made in the image of God in the same way you and I have, and perhaps preserve that image better than we, even if their bodies are corrupted; they have put on the same Christ in the inner person,[109] and have been entrusted with the same pledge of the Spirit;[110] they share in the same laws as we do, the same Scriptural teachings, the same covenants and liturgical gatherings, the same sacraments, the same hopes. Christ died for them as he did for us, taking away the sin of the whole world;[111] they are heirs with us of the life to come,[112] even if they have missed out on a great deal of life here on earth; they have been buried together with Christ, and have risen with him;[113] if they suffer with him, it is so they may share in his glory.[114]

15.   And what about us, who have inherited the great new name, in being called after Christ—us who are "the holy people, the royal priesthood, the people set apart,"[115] specially chosen, "eager for good and saving works,"[116] disciples of the gentle and kindly Christ, who "bore our weaknesses"[117] and humbled himself so far as to share in the mixture of our nature, who "became poor for our sakes"[118] in this flesh and "this earthly tent,"[119] and suffered pain and weakness for us, so that we might be rich in divinity? What about us, who have received such a great example of tenderness and compassion? How shall we think about these people, and what shall we do? Shall we simply overlook them? Walk past them? Leave them for dead, as something loathsome, something more detestable than snakes and wild animals? Surely not, my brothers and sisters! This is not the way for us, nursed as we are by Christ, the Good Shepherd, who brings back the one gone astray, seeks out the lost,[120] strengthens the weak;[121] this is not the way of human nature, which lays compassion on us as a law, even as we learn reverence and humanity from our common weakness.

16.   Yet they live their wretched lives under the open sky, while we live in splendid houses, adorned brightly with stones of every color, glittering with gold and silver and mosaics[122] and colored paintings, deceptive allurements for the eyes! We live in some of these houses; we are in the process of building others—but for whom? Perhaps not for our heirs, but

for strangers and foreigners, or even for those who do not love us, but are hostile and envious enemies—the worst fate of all! These people shiver in thin and tattered rags—perhaps they are not so lucky as to have even that—while we corrupt ourselves with soft and flowing robes, woven of linen and silk light as air, and make with them an impression more of disorder than of dignity; our clothes are stored away for us in chests—a useless and unprofitable precaution!—as food for the moths and for time, which consumes all things. These people are not even supplied with the most basic nourishment (how can I be so refined, while they so repine?), but lie before our doors, faint and starving, not even possessing the bodily power to beg; they have lost voices to lament with, hands to stretch out in supplication, feet to approach those with possessions, noses to give resonance to their complaints; and—though they judge this heaviest of all burdens to be lightest—with their eyes they can only give thanks, because they cannot look on their own mutilation.[123]

17.   Such is their condition. Yet we, by contrast—glorious figures that we are—lie back in splendor on high, raised beds, with coverings so exquisite one scarcely dares handle them, and we are annoyed if we hear so much as the sound of their pleading. For us, the floor has to be scented with flowers, often even out of season, and the table must be sprinkled with perfumes of the most fragrant and expensive kind, to encourage our decadent tastes all the more. Serving boys stand nearby; some of them in an orderly row, with flowing hair and effeminate appearance, their locks fashionably cropped around their faces, groomed far better than they should be, for the sake of hungry eyes; others hold wine cups carefully with their fingertips, trying to be as proper and as safe as possible, while still others use woven fans to circulate the air above us, cooling our fleshy hulks with artificial breezes. Beyond all this, the table is laden with food, which all the elements—air, earth, water—abundantly put at our service; it is crowded with the masterpieces of chefs and pastry-makers. There is a competition among them all, as to who can most flatter our hungry and ungrateful belly, that heavy burden that is the root of all our ills, that insatiable and untrustworthy beast, soon to be eliminated along with the foods it eliminates. For those standing outside, it is a great thing to have enough water; but for us, the bowls of wine are kept full until we feel merry—or rather, until the more intemperate of us are well beyond merriment. We send one of the wines away, savor another for its "nose," wax philosophical about a third, and are disappointed if one of the well-known foreign names does not subdue our local wine as reigning emperor. For we simply must be—or be thought to be—people of refined tastes, furnished well beyond our needs; it is as if we were ashamed not to be thought wicked, not to be slaves of the belly and the regions below it!

18.   What do you make of all this, my friends, my brothers and sisters? Why do we suffer ourselves from this spiritual sickness—a sickness much more serious than that of the body? I am convinced, after all, that as much as the one is involuntary, the other comes from our choice; as much as the one ends with this life, the other goes with us when we are brought to the next; as much as the one is pitiable, the other is hateful, for anyone of sound mind. Why do we not help our own natural kin, while we have time? Why do we not take steps to protect them in the lowly state of their flesh, since we are flesh ourselves? Why do we feast in the face of our brothers' and sisters' misfortunes? Let it not be so with me—let me not be rich while they are destitute, nor be in good health if I do not tend their wounds, nor have enough food or covering, nor rest under a roof, if I do not offer bread to them, and give them something to wear and a shelter to stay in, as far as I am able! Surely we must either give all things away for Christ's sake, so that we may follow him truly, taking up our cross, so that we might take our flight unburdened towards the world above, well equipped and held back by nothing, so that we might gain Christ at the expense of all else,[124] exalted through humility and made rich by poverty; or else we must share our goods with Christ, so that our possession of them may at least be sanctified by our possessing them well, by our sharing them with those who have nothing. Even if I were to sow for myself alone, I would still, surely, be sowing what others would later eat. To use the words of Job again, "Instead of wheat, nettles would come forth, and instead of barley, brambles;"[125] a burning wind would come up, and a violent storm would carry off my efforts, so that I would have labored in vain. And even if I were to build storehouses to save what my money has earned, this very night I would be asked for my soul,[126] and must give account for what I have improperly acquired.

19.   Shall we not finally come to our senses? Shall we not cast off our insensitivity—not to say our stinginess? Shall we not take notice of human needs? Shall we not identify our own interests with the troubles of others? By nature, nothing human is lasting or in equilibrium, nothing is self-sustaining, nothing remains the same. There is a cycle in our affairs, often bringing new changes, of different kinds, in a single day or even in a single hour; and it makes more sense to trust in the inconstant breezes, or the wake of a ship sailing on the ocean, or the deceitful dreams of night that offer us joy for a while, or the forms that children make in the sand as they play on the beach, than it does to trust in human prosperity. The prudent ones, then, are those who do not rely on present circumstances, but make their treasure of what is yet to come, and who, because of the inconstancy and irregularity of human welfare, love that human kindness that never passes away. As a result, they will profit in one of three ways: either they will

never undergo misfortune themselves, since God so often forms bonds between his reverent followers and those who will later be kind to them, letting kindness call forth a similar response; or else they will feel free to ask for what they need from God, knowing that when they experience misfortune, it is not in return for wickedness, but for some providential reason; or else, finally, they will be able to ask for generosity from other prosperous people as something that is their due, since when things were prosperous for them they gave to those in need.

20. "Let not the wise person boast about his wisdom," we read, "nor the rich about her wealth, nor the mighty about his strength"[127]—even if they should have reached the very summit of these things: one of wisdom, the other of possessions, the third of power. And in the same line of thought, I will add this: let not the person of good reputation boast in his glory, nor the healthy person in her bodily well-being, nor the handsome person in his good looks, nor the youth in her tender years, nor let the person puffed up with pride, to put it in a word, boast in any of the things that are praised in this world. Rather, let the one who boasts boast only in this: that he knows and seeks God, and grieves along with those who suffer, and lays away a deposit that will serve him well in the age to come. For these temporal things are fluid and temporary, and like the pieces in the game of draughts will be thrown away or passed on, in other circumstances, to other people; nothing belongs so properly to its owner that it will not either cease to exist out of age, or be transferred to others out of envy. But our possessions before God stand firm; they remain and are never taken away, never collapse, nor do they deceive the hopes of those who trust in them. For this reason, it seems to me that none of the good things of this world is trustworthy or long-lasting for us who are mortal. Rather, it seems that this has been devised best of all by the creative Word, by the Wisdom which surpasses every mind: that we should be set here to play among visible objects which change and are changed, now in one direction and now in another, and which are borne up and cast down again, vanishing and eluding us before we can grasp them, so that when we consider the instability and variety in all these things, we might turn to pursue what still lies ahead. For what would we have done if our prosperity here were something that abides, seeing that even when it is unstable we are so attached to it, and the deceptive joy it brings with it so enslaves us that we cannot imagine anything better or more valuable than the things of this present world—and this even though we have heard and believe that we are made in the image of God, an image which exists in a higher world and draws us towards itself?

21. "Who is wise, and understands these things?"[128] Who will pass beyond the things that are passing away? Who will attach himself to the things that last? Who will come to recognize the things now present before

us as destined to leave us, and the things we hope for as all that stands firm? Who will make a distinction between what is and what only seems to be, and pursue the one while letting the other go? Who will distinguish mere pictures from truth? Or this tent below from the city that is above? Or a temporary residence from a permanent home? Or darkness from light? Or the slime of the abyss from holy ground? Or flesh from spirit? Or God from the ruler of this world? Or the shadow of death from eternal life? Who will purchase what is to come for the price of present realities? Or the wealth that cannot be destroyed with that which is always in flux? Or what is unseen with what is seen? Blessed is the one who can make such a distinction, wielding the sword of the Word to separate what is better from what is worse! As holy David says, he has built steps in his heart,[129] and fleeing this deep valley of tears as far as he can, he "seeks the things that are above;"[130] crucified to the world with Christ, he rises from the dead with Christ and ascends with Christ to inherit the life that never fades or deceives—where no serpent lies on the way, ready to strike, watching for his heel and guarding its own head.[131] To the rest of us, the same David cries out with good reason, like a loud-voiced herald shouting from a high public platform, and calls us slow of heart, lovers of lies,[132] so that we might not be excessively attached to visible things, or suppose that all our happiness in this world consists only in satiating ourselves with corruptible bread and wine. Perhaps, too, this is what blessed Micah was thinking when, struggling to resist the specious blessings that come from below, he said, "Draw near the eternal mountains; rise and move on, for this is not the place of your rest."[133] This phrase, after all, is almost the same as the very words which our Lord and Savior gave us as a command. What did he say? "Rise, let us go from here!"[134] He was not simply urging the disciples of that time to move on from that place, as one might think; rather, he was attempting to draw all his disciples, in every age, away from earth and the things that surround it, towards heaven and heavenly things.

22.   For this reason, let us now follow the Word. Let us seek our rest in the world to come, and cast away our surplus possessions in this world. Let us only hold on to what is good from all these things: let us come to possess our souls in acts of mercy, let us share what we have with the poor, in order that we may be rich in the things of the world to come. Give a portion of your goods to your soul, not simply to your flesh; give a portion to God, not simply to the world. Take something away from the belly and consecrate it to the spirit. Snatch something from the fire, store it far from the flame that eats away from below. Snatch it from the tyrant, and entrust it to the Lord. Give a share to the "seven"—that is, to this life—and also to the "eight"—to that which awaits us after this.[135] Give a little to him from whom you have received much; even give your all to the one who has given

all to you. You will never surpass the lavish generosity of God, even if you throw away all things, even if you add yourself to the possessions you give away. For this, too, is a way of receiving: to be given to God! However much you contribute, there is always more left over; and you are never giving away what is your own, since everything comes from God. And just as it is not possible to step over our own shadow, which moves along exactly as far as we do, and always reaches out the same distance before us—just as the height of a body cannot exceed the head, since the head is always above the body—so, too, it is impossible to outdo God in our giving. For we never give him anything apart from what belongs to him, nor beyond his munificence.

23.   Recognize the source of your being, your breath, your power of thought, and (greatest of all), your power to know God and to hope for the Kingdom of Heaven, for equality with the angels, for the vision of glory—which now you have only "in a mirror and in riddles,"[136] but which someday will be more perfect and pure—for the chance to become a child of God, a fellow-heir with Christ, even (I make bold to say) to become yourself divine. From where do all these gifts come—and from whom? Just to mention the small and obvious things: who gives you the ability to look on the beauty of heaven, the course of the sun, the cycle of the moon, the multitude of stars, and the harmony and order that rules in all these things as in a lyre, always remaining the same? To witness the passing of the hours, the changes of season, the turning of years, the equal measures of day and night; the products of the earth, the abundance of the atmosphere, the breadth of the sea as it constantly flows yet remains, the depths of the rivers, the blowing of the winds? Who gives you the rains, the skill to raise crops, food, crafts, houses, laws, civilized society, an easy way of life, family relationships? Whence is it that some animals are tame and are subject to you, while others are provided for your food? Who appointed you lord and king of all things on earth? I will not mention every detail—but who endowed you with all the gifts by which the human person stands out over all other creatures? Is it not he who now, before all else and rather than all else, demands from you kindness towards other human beings? Are we not, then, ashamed, if receiving so much from him, either in fact or in hope, we do not give back this one thing to God: kindness towards our fellow men and women? God has separated us from the wild beasts, and honored us alone, of all creatures on earth, with reason; shall we, then, make ourselves into beasts? Are we so corrupted by our luxurious life, or have we gone so mad, that—I find it hard to put it into words—we come to think we are better by nature than others, as if we were barley mixed with bran in a careless harvest? And just as there was once (or so the myths tell us) one race of giants and another of ordinary humans, shall we be lofty and super-human in contrast to them,

like the famous Nimrod, or the race of Enak, who once harassed Israel, or like those who made it necessary that the flood purge the earth? God is not ashamed to be called our Father, though he is our God and Lord; shall we, then, deny our own human family?

24.   Surely not, my friends—my brothers and sisters! Let us not be irresponsible stewards of the good things that have been given us, lest we hear St. Peter say, "Shame on you, who hold back what belongs to others! Imitate the even-handedness of God, and no one will be poor!"[137] Let us not labor to gather up treasure and protect it, while others labor in poverty, lest someone rebuke and threaten us in the words holy Amos once used: "Come, now, you who say, 'When will the month be over, so that we may begin selling again? And the Sabbath, that we may open up our money-boxes?'"[138]—and in the words that follow, in which those who have devised long and short weights for themselves are threatened with the wrath of God. In the same vein, blessed Micah[139] was perhaps attacking the same thirst for luxury when he insisted that surfeit breeds arrogance, while people behaved wantonly on their ivory couches, vainly anointing themselves with choice perfumes, feasting on tender calves from their stables and kids from their flocks, applauding in time with the music of pipes, and—worse still—thinking that there was something about all this that was stable and lasting. Yet perhaps he did not regard all this as so serious, compared with the fact that in their affluence they were not the least affected by the oppression of Joseph,[140] for he adds this to his charge of over-consumption. Let us not allow this to happen to us, nor carry our own fine tastes to such an excess that we, too, begin to make little of the kindness of God; he is angered by such behavior, even if he does not express his wrath against sinners immediately, or simultaneously with their crimes.

25.   Let us imitate God's highest and first law, which makes the rain fall on the just and sinners, and makes the sun rise equally on all.[141] He has spread out the unsettled land for everyone on earth, with springs and rivers and forests; he provides air for the winged species, and water for all whose life is spent there; he lavishes the basic supports of living ungrudgingly on all—not putting them under the power of force, or the limits of law, or the divisions of geographical boundaries—but sets them forth as the rich and common possessions of all, not in any way lessened for this reason. Beings of like rank in nature he honors with equal gifts, and so he shows how rich his own generosity is. But human beings, in contrast, bury their gold and silver and their soft, unneeded clothing in the ground, along with their shining jewels and other riches of this kind—all tokens of violence and discord and primeval oppression—and then they raise their eyes in incomprehension, shutting off the stream of mercy from their unfortunate fellow mortals. They do not even wish to use their surplus to help others in

need (what lack of feeling! what foolishness!), nor do they even consider this, as a final argument: that the things we call poverty and riches, freedom and slavery, and other, similar names, are themselves only later acquisitions of the human race, and are like a kind of common disease that attacks us along with sin, and is a symptom of it. "From the beginning," however, as the Lord says, "it was not so."[142] The one who created the human person in the beginning made him free and able to determine his own behavior, subject only to the law he had commanded, and rich in the luxury of Paradise. And God willed to bestow this freedom on the rest of the human race as well, through the single seed of our first ancestor. Freedom and riches consisted simply in observing the commandments, while true poverty and slavery came from their transgression.

26.　But ever since envy and quarreling have appeared among us, and the treacherous domination of the serpent, who constantly trips us up with lust for pleasure and sets the more aggressive of us against the weaker, the human family has been shattered into a variety of names, and greed has destroyed the noble beginnings of our nature, making an ally even of law, the surrogate of political power. Yet think, I beg you, of humanity's original equality, not of its later diversity; think not of the conqueror's law, but of the creator's! As far as you can, support nature, honor primeval liberty, show reverence for yourself and cover the shame of your race,[143] help to resist sickness, offer relief to human need. Let the one with good health or with riches come to the aid of the ailing and the needy; let the one who has never stumbled help the one who has fallen and is being trodden down. Let the one in good spirits comfort the dispirited, the one who flourishes in the best of circumstances support the one who is bowed over beneath the worst. Give some sign of thanks to God, because you are one of those who can do favors for others, rather than one of those who need favors done for them—because your eyes are not fixed on the hands of others, but others' eyes are on yours. Make someone else rich, not only with your surplus but with your piety, not only with your gold but with your virtue—or better still, only with this! Become more eminent than your neighbor by showing yourself more generous; become a god to the unfortunate, by imitating the mercy of God.

27.　For a human being has no more godlike ability than that of doing good; and even if God is benefactor on a grander scale, and humans on a lesser, still each does so, I think, to the full extent of his powers. He created us, and restored us again by setting us free; you must not overlook the one who has fallen. He has shown mercy to us in the greatest ways, above all by giving us the law and the prophets, and even before them the unwritten law of nature, the standard of judging all our deeds; he examines us, admonishes us, trains us, and finally he has given himself as ransom for the life of the world. He has lavished on us apostles, evangelists, teachers, shepherds, healers, wonderful signs, a way that leads to life, the destruction of death, a trophy of victory over the one who had conquered us, a covenant in shadow and a covenant in truth, gifts that let us share in the Holy Spirit, the Mystery of new salvation. As for you, if you are also capable of greater things, do not fail to do good for the needy with the gifts with which your soul is blessed—for God has made you rich in this way, too, if you only wish to be so. Give a share in these things, first and foremost, to the one who asks your help, even before he asks you; all day long, "have mercy and lend" him God's word,[144] and earnestly demand your loan back, with the growth of the one you have helped as your "interest"—for he always adds something to the word you have given by letting the seeds of piety grow a little more within himself.

But if you cannot do this, give the secondary, smaller gifts, as far as is in your power: come to his help, offer him nourishment, offer her a scrap of clothing, provide medicine, bind up his wounds, ask something about her condition, offer sage advice about endurance, give encouragement, be a support. Surely you will not pose any danger to yourself by doing this much! Surely you will not catch the condition, even if skittish people, deceived by foolish rumors, may think so—at least, they offer this excuse for what is either timidity or impiety on their part, and take refuge in cowardice as if it were some great sign of wisdom. Let the scientists, members of the medical profession, and those who live with these poor people and care for them, convince you that no one ever ran any danger by associating with people suffering in this way.[145] And even if the reality is frightening and moves us to take precautions, do not you, O servant of Christ—lover of God and of your fellow men and women—fall into a sordid state yourself! Have confidence in your faith; let your mercy conquer your cowardice, your fear of God overcome your squeamishness; let your piety take precedence over your thoughts for the welfare of your flesh. Do not overlook your brother, do not pass your sister by, do not turn them away as something polluting or unclean, as some alien thing, to be avoided and cursed. This is part of your body, even though it is bowed down by misfortune. The poor man is left to your mercy, as he is to God's.[146] Even if you are hurrying by, full of arrogance, perhaps I can shame you with these words! The opportunity for being generous is before you, even when our Adversary tries to turn your heart against receiving God's gifts.

29. Such things reason teaches, as well as the law; so do people of moderation, for whom good action is more precious than passivity, and mercy more worth pursuing than profit. But what would you say about those considered wise among us? I will not even speak of the pagans, who consider the gods as conspirators in the life of passion, and offer their first-

fruits to Apollo the Money-Maker.[147] Worse still, they believe that there are spirits, active among certain peoples, who encourage manslaughter; cruelty is for such people a part of piety, and they both enjoy performing human sacrifice themselves and think their gods enjoy it, too, for they are wicked priests and initiates of wicked deities. But there are also some among us—although it is enough to make one weep—who are so far from offering compassion and help to the oppressed that they even blame them bitterly, and trample them down. They develop vain and empty theories about them, and speaking really "from the earth," they shout their words into the wind, not addressing those understanding ears that are used to divine teachings. They dare to say, "The suffering of these people is God's work, just as prosperity is God's work in us. Who am I, then, to countermand the judgment of God? Shall I seem kinder than God is? Let them be sick, let them suffer, let them be unfortunate! Such is God's will!" These people only talk about loving God when they feel the need to guard their pennies, and to make silly speeches against the wretched. They make it crystal-clear from what they say that they do not believe their own prosperity comes from God. For who would think in such a way about the needy, if he recognized God as the source of his own possessions? It is part of the same attitude, after all, to consider what we have a gift from God and to use the things we have according to God's will.

30.   It is not clear whether or not the sufferings of the poor are from God, as long as this material realm is characterized by disorder, as if it were a flowing stream. Who can tell if one person is being punished for his vices, while another is being exalted as a gesture of praise? Could it not be just the opposite: the one is exalted because of wickedness, the other put to the test because of virtue? The one is being raised higher, in order to fall more grievously, allowing all his own viciousness to break out, that he might then be all the more justly punished. The other, contrary to our expectations, is oppressed, so that, being tried like gold in a furnace, he might allow to melt away even whatever little vice remains. No one, as we hear, is completely pure of every stain—no one, at any rate, who is born to share in this nature—even if he should appear quite respectable. I find a mystery of this kind expressed in holy Scripture, although I have no intention to enumerate all the sayings of the Spirit that lead me to this conclusion. But "who could measure the sand of the sea, or the drops of rain, or the depth of the abyss?"[148] Who could trace out in every detail the profundity of God's Wisdom, from which God made all things and by which he governs it in the way he wills and knows? It is enough for us, with the divine Apostle, simply to contemplate this inexplicable, inconceivable Wisdom and to exclaim in wonder: "O the depth of the riches and wisdom and knowledge of God! How unsearchable are his judgments, how untraceable his ways!"[149] "Who

has known the mind of the Lord?"[150] "Who has come to the end of his Wisdom?" as Job says.[151] "Who is wise, and understands these things?"[152]— and does not rather measure what is beyond measuring by the standard of the unattainable?

31.   Let someone else speak rashly and arrogantly about these things— or better still, let no one dare to do so. I, for one, am hesitant to explain all this life's trials as punishment for vice, or all human comfort as a reward for piety. There are times, rather, when the bad experiences of the wicked serve a useful purpose in checking wickedness, and when the positive experiences of the good open the way to virtue—but not always or in every case. Such universality only belongs to the time to come, when the one group will receive the rewards of virtue, the other the punishment of vice; "for these shall rise," Scripture says, "to the resurrection that is life, but those to the resurrection of judgment."[153] The events of this present life are of a different form and have a different moral purpose, although all lead in the same direction; surely what seems to be unfair to us has its fairness in the plan of God, just as in the physical world there are prominent and lowly features, large and small details, ridges and valleys, by which the beauty of the whole comes into visible existence in their relationship to each other. It is, after all, very much within the skill of the Craftsman if he should adapt the occasional disorder and unevenness of the material realm to achieve the purpose of his creation; and this will be grasped and acknowledged by all of us, when we contemplate the final, perfect beauty of what he has created. But he is never lacking in the skill of his art, as we are, nor is this world ruled by disorder, even when the principle by which it is ordered is not apparent to us.

32.   But if we must use some image to describe our situation, it might not be off the mark to speak of nauseous or dizzy people, who think that everything is revolving around them, when in fact it is they who are in a spin: that is what the people are like, of whom I speak. For they do not allow that God may be wiser than they are, if they become confused about some event in their lives. In fact, what they should do is either struggle to find the reason, trusting that the truth will be revealed to earnest labor, or consult seriously with those wiser and more spiritually gifted than themselves—since this, too, is one of the Spirit's gifts, and knowledge is not shared equally by all—or else pursue this knowledge by purifying their lives, and seek wisdom from Wisdom itself. But they, in their supreme ignorance, turn to easy answers, and falsely complain of the irrationality of the universe, when it is they who do not understand what reason is. They are wise through ignorance; or rather, through their exaggerated claims to wisdom, if I may call it that, they have come to be without both wisdom and understanding. So some of them put forward theories about fate and determinism—ideas which are themselves constructed in a purely accidental and unplanned way;

others speak of a certain irrational, indestructible domination by the stars, which weave our affairs as they will—or rather are also subject to determination in the way they weave it—and of the conjunctions and withdrawals of the planets and fixed stars, and the sovereign movement of the universe. Still others attribute whatever their imagination can contrive to the long-suffering human race, and divide among a variety of theories and titles all the aspects of Providence that they cannot fathom by their contemplative powers. And there are others, too, who detect great poverty on the part of Providence; although they think that the things beyond our senses are governed by it, they shrink from bringing it down to our level, who need it most—as if they feared that by saying God showers blessings on all of us, they should show their benefactor to be too generous, or suspected that God might grow tired by doing good for too many!

33.   But let us dismiss these people, as I have said, since Scripture has already well refuted them in the words, "Their foolish heart has been led into vanity; by saying that they are wise, they have been made foolish, and they have traded away the glory of the incorruptible God,"[154] slandering the Providence which works in all things by talking of myths and shadows. As for us, let us not produce such monsters as these, if reason matters at all to us, who claim to be reasonable people and servants of Reason himself;[155] nor let us be receptive towards those who think this way, even if they score some verbal points with fanciful phrases and doctrines, and delight in novelty. Let us, instead, believe that God is the maker and shaper of all that is—for how could the universe exist, unless someone had given it being and arranged it harmoniously? And let us include with our faith belief in God's Providence, containing and connecting this universe, since it is necessary that the one who is creator of all things should also have providential care for them. Otherwise, the universe would be borne along by its own internal forces, like a ship before a whirlwind, soon to be shattered and scattered by the unruliness of matter, and reduced to the disorder of the primal, pre-cosmic confusion. Let us rather accept that our own maker or shaper (whatever you prefer to call him) is fully in charge of our affairs, even if the course of our lives is influenced by opposing forces—forces which remain unknown, perhaps, precisely that we might wonder at the Reason above all things, because it is so difficult to recognize. For what is easily grasped seems utterly despicable; but what is above us is all the more wonderful, the more difficult it is to attain. Everything that lies beyond the reach of our appetite simply stimulates our longing.

34.   For this reason, let us not admire every form of health or reject all illness; let us not allow our hearts to become attached to the wealth that passes away, or be devoted to unstable things more than is good for us, and so allow some part of our soul to be consumed along with them. Let us not

struggle against poverty as if it were wholly to be detested and condemned, wholly on the side of things we should hate. Let us rather learn also to despise health without understanding, for its fruit is sin, and to honor the illness that is holy; let us admire those who are victorious through their suffering, recognizing that a Job may be hidden among the sick, far more worthy of our reverence than the healthy, even though he may be scratching his running sores and suffering night and day under the open sky, hard pressed by the plague, and by wife and friends. Just so we should learn to be dismissive of unjust riches, for whose sake Dives rightly suffers in the fire and begs a little drop of water for refreshment, and to praise a grateful and philosophic[156] poverty, in which Lazarus is saved and enjoys the riches of rest in Abraham's bosom.[157]

35.   For this reason, too, then, kindness towards our fellow human beings and compassion towards the needy seem to me necessary: that we might restrain those who have such an attitude towards them, and might not give in to their foolish arguments, making cruelty into a law turned against our very selves. Rather, let us respect the commandment—and the example—that is greater than all the rest. Which commandment? Just notice how constant and how noble it is! For the instruments of the Spirit have not simply spoken once or twice about the needy and then fallen silent; nor was it simply some of them and not others, or some more and others less, as if they were dealing with no great matter, with nothing of pressing importance. No—all of them laid this command on us, each with the greatest urgency, either as the first of our duties or as one of the first. Sometimes they exhort us, sometimes they threaten, sometimes they rebuke; and there are times, too, when they give recognition to those who have done it well—all as a way of making the command efficacious by keeping it constantly in our memory.

Scripture says, "Because of the wretchedness of the poor and the groaning of the deprived I shall arise, says the Lord."[158] Who does not fear the Lord when he rises? And further: "Rise up, Lord my God, let your hand be raised; do not forget the poor."[159] Let us pray that he may not rise this way, let us not hope to see his hand raised against the disobedient, much less in action against the hard-hearted! And: "He has not forgotten the cry of the poor;"[160] and: "The poor person will not always be forgotten;"[161] and: "His eyes gaze on the poor" (a stronger and more important action than simply raising his eyelids!) "and with eyelids raised he examines the race of mortals"[162] (which is, one might say, a lesser, secondary kind of supervision).[163]

36.   But perhaps someone may say, "All this concerns the poor and needy who are treated unjustly." I do not disagree—but this, too, should spur you towards active kindness! For if so much is said about them when they are unjustly treated, clearly when these same people are well-treated God will look upon it all the more favorably. If "the one who dishonors

poor people arouses their creator to anger,"[164] then the one who treats the creature kindly honors the creator. And again, when you hear, "Poor and rich oppose each other, but the Lord made them both,"[165] do not suppose that he made the one poor and the other rich, so that you may rise up against the poor person all the more readily. For it is not clear that this distinction is from God; the text simply says that both are likewise creatures of God, even if their external circumstances are unequal. Let this shame you into being more compassionate and loving towards your brothers and sisters, so that when you are puffed up by texts like the one we have mentioned, you may be deflated again by this thought, and grow more moderate than you were. What other texts do we have? "The one who has mercy on a poor person lends to God."[166] Who would not take on such a debtor, who will repay our loan in due time with interest? And again, "Through acts of mercy and fidelity sins are purged away."[167]

37.   Let us be purged, then, by showing mercy! Let us cleanse the filth and stains of our souls by this beneficial herb; and let us make ourselves white—some "white as wool,"[168] others "white as snow,"[169] in proportion to the mercy we show. And I will tell you something to put fear in your hearts: even if there is no lesion or scar, no inflamed wound, no leprosy of the soul, no sign of infection[170] or white spot, which the Law makes clean in a small way but which needs the healing touch of Christ, still you must reverence the one who was wounded and made weak for our sakes. And you will reverence him, if you show yourself kind and generous towards one of Christ's members. But if perhaps the robber who terrorizes our souls has wounded you, as you were "going down from Jerusalem to Jericho"[171] or some other place, falling upon you unarmed and unprepared, so that you rightly cry out, "My wounds stink and are putrefying, as a result of my foolishness"[172]—if you are in such a state that you do not even seek a cure or know the way of your healing—then alas! this is truly to be wounded, and to sink into the depth of wretchedness! But if you have not completely despaired of yourself, if you are not in an incurable state, then go up to the healer, speak to him imploringly, heal wounds by wounds, regain likeness by likeness—or rather, be healed of major things by minor things![173] Say to your soul, "I am your salvation,"[174] and "Your faith has saved you,"[175] and "See, you have become well again,"[176] and all the phrases that express his kindness, just as long as he can see you showing kindness to those who are suffering.

38.   "Blessed are the merciful," Scripture says, "for they shall obtain mercy."[177] Mercy does not come last amid the Beatitudes! And "blessed is the one who is understanding towards the poor and needy;"[178] and "that person is kind, who has pity and lends;"[179] and "all day long the just one is merciful and lends."[180] Let us lay hold of the beatitude for ourselves, let us

be called understanding, let us become kind. Let not even night interrupt your acts of mercy; "Do not say, 'Get up and go home, and tomorrow I will give you something.'"[181] Do not let anything come between your inclination and your good deed; only one thing brooks no delay: kindness to others. "Break your bread with the poor person, and bring homeless beggars into your house"[182]—indeed, do it eagerly! "Let the one who is merciful do so gladly," Scripture says,[183] and your goodness will be doubled by your readiness of heart. For what is done with a sorrowful spirit or under compulsion is done without grace, and bestows no beauty on the doer. Celebrate, then, and do not lament when you do good![184] "If you do away with the fetter and with selectiveness"[185]—with your stinginess, in other words, and with your close scrutiny [of the poor], or perhaps with your hesitancy and your grumbling words[186]—what will happen? Something grand and wonderful! How great and how fine the reward of this generosity will be! "Your light will break forth like the dawn, and your healing will rise up quickly."[187] And who does not yearn for light and for healing?

39.   I revere greatly Christ's ointment-box, which invites us to care for the poor,[188] and the agreement of Paul and Peter, who divided up the preaching of the Gospel but made the poor their common concern,[189] and the way of perfection of the young man, which was defined by the law of giving what one has to the poor.[190] Do you think that kindness to others is not a necessity for you, but a matter of choice? That it is not a law, but simply an exhortation? I used to wish this very much myself, and supposed it to be true. But that "left hand" has instilled fear in me, and the "goats," and the rebukes that will come from him who raises them to stand before him:[191] condemned to be in this class, not because they have committed theft or sacrilege or adultery, or have done anything else forbidden by the Law, but because they have not cared for Christ through the needy!

40.   If you believe me at all, then, servants and brothers and sisters and fellow heirs of Christ, let us take care of Christ while there is still time; let us minister to Christ's needs, let us give Christ nourishment, let us clothe Christ, let us gather Christ in, let us show Christ honor—not just at our tables, as some do, nor just with ointment, like Mary, nor just with a tomb, like Joseph of Arimathea, nor just with the things needed for burial, like that half-hearted lover of Christ, Nicodemus, nor just with gold and frankincense and myrrh, like the Magi who came to him before all the rest. But since the Lord of all things "desires mercy and not sacrifice,"[192] and since "a compassionate heart is worth more than tens of thousands of fat rams,"[193] let us give this gift to him through the needy, who today are cast down on the ground, so that when we all are released from this place, they may receive us into the eternal tabernacle,[194] in Christ himself, who is our Lord, to whom be glory for all the ages. Amen.

3. ORATION 20: *ON THEOLOGY, AND THE APPOINTMENT OF BISHOPS*

The oration *On Theology, and the Appointment of Bishops* seems to date from the early days of Gregory's work in Constantinople; most modern scholars place it sometime in the spring of 380, and John McGuckin suggests it may be a reworking of his "first lecture" in the capital, given as early as September or October 379.[195]

In its present form, this brief piece incorporates a number of sections that also appear in other orations (Or. 2, 27, 28, 29, and 39)[196] and seems to be intended as a sketch or a summary of material he will develop at greater length elsewhere, particularly in the five "Theological Orations."[197] Its content is mainly a dense statement of Gregory's synthetic view of the orthodox doctrine of the one God, as a Trinity of persons. Here as elsewhere, he emphasizes that the ability to approach this central understanding of faith in the right spirit depends, first of all, on the moral and intellectual purification of the believer. As the title suggests, too, he insists here that such purification, and the contemplation of God for which it is a preparation, are together the necessary prerequisite for "accepting a position of spiritual leadership, or devoting oneself to theology." Gregory seems to be offering here his own confession of Nicene faith, in its classical Cappadocian form, as a proof of his readiness for episcopal office and as a doctrinal challenge to his opponents. Although a composite piece, this carefully constructed oration gives us a clear, concise synopsis of Gregory's understanding of θεολογία: right discourse about God, within the community of worship.

Oration 20: *On Theology, and the Appointment of Bishops*[198]

1.   When I see the endless talkativeness that haunts us today, the instant sages and designated theologians, for whom simply willing to be wise is enough to make them so, I long for the philosophy that comes from above; I yearn for that "final lodging," to use Jeremiah's phrase,[199] and I want only to be off by myself. For nothing seems so important to me as for a person to shut off his senses, to take his place outside the flesh and the world—not to fasten on human realities unless it is completely necessary, and so, in conversation with himself and with God, to live above the level of the visible, and always to bear the images of divine things within himself in their pure state, free from the stamp of what is inferior and changeable. In this way, one is—and one is always becoming—a spotless mirror of God and divine things, assimilating light to light, and adding clarity to indistinct beginnings,[200] until we come to the source of the light that radiates in this

world and lay hold of our blessed end, where mirrors are dissolved in true reality. One can scarcely achieve this, except either by training oneself in the discipline of philosophy[201] for a long time, and so detaching the noble and luminous elements of the soul, little by little, from what is base and mingled with darkness, or else by obtaining God's mercy—or by a combination of the two; so, making it one's concern, as far as possible, to turn one's gaze upwards, one might gain mastery over the materiality that drags one downwards. But before one has elevated this materiality as far as possible, and has sufficiently purified one's ears and one's intelligence, I do not think it is safe either to accept a position of spiritual leadership or to devote oneself to theology.[202]

2.   Let me tell you how I was led to this fear, so that you may not suppose that I am an undue coward, but may rather praise my prudence. I hear the story of Moses, when God began to communicate with him: several people were invited to come near the mountain, including Aaron with his two priestly sons; all the rest were commanded to worship from afar, but Moses alone was told to approach, while the people were not allowed to go up the mountain with him.[203] Just a little before this, flashes of lightning and claps of thunder, trumpet-calls and the sight of the whole mountain covered with smoke, awful threats and other terrifying signs of this kind, held them below. It was a great thing for them simply to hear the voice of God—and this was allowed them only when they had very thoroughly purified themselves. But Moses went up, walked into the cloud, met God and received the law[204]—for most people, the law of the letter, and for those who can rise above the crowd, that of the Spirit.

3.   I am aware, too, of the stories of Eli the priest, and—a little afterwards—of a certain Oza.[205] The first was held accountable even for the transgressions of his sons, which they had dared to commit against the rules of sacrifice—and this, even though he did not approve their impiety, but had reproved them for it again and again.[206] The second was punished when he simply dared to touch the ark as it was being pulled about by the ox: he saved the ark, but himself perished, as God acted to preserve the sacred mystery associated with the ark.[207] I know, further, that it was not safe for the people in general even to touch the walls of the Temple, and therefore they needed yet another set of outer walls, and that the sacrifices themselves were not to be consumed by those not allowed to do so, or at a time and place that were not fitting; much less was it allowed for just anyone to dare approach the Holy of Holies and look at the curtain or the altar of sacrifice or the ark, let alone to touch them.

4.   Knowing this, then, myself, and knowing that no one is worthy of the great God, who is both victim and high priest, unless one has first offered oneself to God as a living sacrifice,[208] or rather has become a holy,

living temple of the living God, how should I be hasty to engage myself to speak concerning God, or approve anyone who might engage himself to use such words in a rash way? To desire such a thing is not praiseworthy, and to attempt it strikes fear in the heart!

Therefore the first requirement is to purify oneself,[209] then to associate oneself with the One who is pure. Otherwise, we run the danger of sharing the experience of Manoah, and of saying with him, as we come before an apparition of God, "We are lost, O woman—we have seen God!"[210] or of asking Jesus, as Peter did, to withdraw from our boat, since we are not worthy of such presence as his,[211] or—like the centurion—of begging for a cure without receiving the healer into our house.[212] Let each one of us, as long as we are "centurions," who rule over many in wickedness and still serve Caesar, the world-ruler of those creatures who creep along on the ground,[213] say also, "I am not worthy that you should come under my roof." And when I gaze on Jesus, even though I may be small in spiritual stature, as Zacchaeus was, and hanging on a sycamore tree—putting to death my earthly members, and treating this lowly body as a foolish thing[214]—still I shall receive Jesus, and hear him say, "Today salvation has come to this house."[215] And I shall lay hold of salvation, and practice philosophy in a more perfect way, dispensing well what I have gathered ill—either my goods or my teaching.

5.   Since we have now purified the theologian in our discourse, come— let us also briefly discuss the subject of God, trusting boldly in the Father and the Son and the Holy Spirit, with whom our discourse will now be concerned. I pray to have Solomon's state of mind: not to think or say anything about God that is simply my own. For when he says, "I am the most foolish of all people, and human prudence is not in me,"[216] it is not, surely, in recognition of his own lack of understanding that he speaks this way. For how could one say this who asked from God before all else—and who received—wisdom and contemplative vision and a wideness of heart, richer and more abundant than the sand?[217] If one is as wise as this, and has obtained such a gift, how can he name himself the most foolish person of all? Surely it is because he has no natural wisdom of his own, but is enlivened by the more perfect wisdom that comes from God. After all, when Paul said, "I live, now no longer I, but Christ lives in me,"[218] he was surely not referring to himself as dead, but as alive with a life superior to that of most human beings, since he shared in the true life that knows not the limit of death. So we adore the Father and the Son and the Holy Spirit, dividing their individualities[219] but uniting their godhead; and we neither blend the three into one thing, lest we be sick with Sabellius's disease, nor do we divide them into three alien and unrelated things, lest we share Arius's madness.[220] Why should we act like those who try to straighten a plant bent

over completely in one direction by forcibly training it the opposite way, correcting one deviation by another? Rather, we should straighten it midway between the two, and so take our position within the bounds of reverence.

6.   When I speak of such a middle position, I mean the truth; we do well to make it the sole object of our vision, rejecting both a cheap approach to unity and an even sillier version of distinction. Our argument, as a result, should not lump the three together into one hypostasis, for fear of polytheism, and so leave us with mere names, as we suppose Father, Son and Holy Spirit are the same individual. That would suggest we were just as ready to define all of them as one as we were to think each of them is nothing: for they would escape from being what they are, if they were to change and be transformed into each other. Nor should our argument divide them into three substances:[221] either substances foreign to each other and wholly dissimilar, as that doctrine so aptly called "Arian madness" would have it, or substances without origin or order, which would be, so to speak, gods in rivalry. By the first of these moves, we find ourselves locked into Judaism's narrow way of speaking, in that we define divinity simply by the notion of being unbegotten;[222] by the second, we fall into the opposite but equal evil, supposing there are three ultimate principles and three gods, which is still more foolish than what we mentioned before. The right thing is that we should neither be such partisans of the Father that we end up canceling his Fatherhood (for whose Father would he be, if the Son's nature is alienated from him, and made into something else, through this talk of creation?), nor such partisans of Christ that we no longer even preserve his Sonship (for whose Son would he be, if he does not look towards the Father as his cause?). Nor should we minimize the Father's rank as ultimate cause, insofar as he is Father and begetter (for he would be the cause of minor and unworthy beings, if he were not cause of the divinity that we recognize in the Son and the Spirit). If, then, we must necessarily hold on to the one God while confessing the three hypostases, surely we must speak of three Persons,[223] each one with its own distinctive properties.

7.   So, according to my argument, the unity of God would be preserved, and Son and Spirit would be referred back to one original cause, but not compounded or blended with each other; their unity would be based on the single, self-identical movement and will of the divine being, if I may put it that way, and on identity of substance. But the three hypostases would also be preserved, with no amalgamation or reduction or confusion conceived in our thought, so that the whole might not be destroyed by theories that honor the unity of God more than is appropriate. And their individual characteristics are these: the Father is conceived and said to be both without origin, and origin himself—origin, in that he is cause and spring and eternal light; but the Son is not at all without origin, yet himself is the origin of all

things. When I speak of "origin," do not insert there a notion of time, nor put some third thing in between the begetter and the begotten, nor divide the divine nature by mistakenly including something else with those two, who are equally eternal and fully joined. For if time is older than the Son, surely the Father would be its cause first of all; and how then would [the Son] be the maker of all times, if he is subject to time? How would he be the Ruler of all things, if he is bound and ruled by time himself? The Father, then, is without origin, for his being does not come from some other source, nor even from a source within himself. But the Son is not without origin, if one understands as his origin the Father—for the Father, as cause of the Son, is his origin also; but if you conceive of origin here on the basis of time, then he, too, is without origin—for the Master of time does not have time as his source.

8. Now if you think that the Son is subject to time because bodies are subject to time, then you will have fenced in the Bodiless One by a body; and if you insist that the Son must have come into being from what was not, because those who are begotten in our world once did not exist and then came to be, you will be comparing incomparable realities: God and the human, the body and what is without body. In that case, God will experience suffering and be destroyed, because that is what happens to our bodies. You seem to think, in fact, that God is begotten in this way, because that is the way our bodies are begotten; but I think that he is not begotten in this way, because our bodies are begotten thus! If the being of two things is not alike, then their begetting will also not be alike; but if this is not so, then God will be subject to material circumstances in every other respect, suffering and experiencing pain and hunger and thirst and all the other things that the body, or body and soul together, undergo. But your mind cannot accept that—for our conversation is about God! Do not, then, take his being begotten in any sense but a divine one.

9. "But," you say,[224] "if he is begotten, how has he been begotten?" Answer me this, dialectician—for now you have no way out! If he is created, how is he created? You ask me, "How has he been begotten? Is there any possibility[225] involved in his begetting?" There is possibility involved in creating, too! Is it not possibility to imagine and to plan, and to break down into a myriad of details what has been thought of all as one? "Is time involved in his begetting?" Created things, too, come to be in time. "Is there place in it?" There is place in creating, too. "Is there an element of misfortune in begetting?" Misfortune is involved in creation, too. These are the things I hear behind your philosophical arguments; for often the hand does not put its final signature on what the mind has subscribed to internally.

"But all things have come to be," you say,[226] "by his word and his will. 'For he spoke and they came into being; he gave the command and they were created.'"[227] When you say that all things were created by the word of God, you are not making use of our human notion of creating; for none of us makes things happen simply by a word. Nothing would be beyond us, after all, and nothing would require less effort than this, if simply our saying the word were the way to complete an action. But if God creates what is created simply by a word, creating for him is not like our human activity. Either show us some human being creating something by a word, or accept the fact that God does not create as a human being does. Design a city any way you choose, and let the city arise before you! Will that a son be born to you, and let the son stand there! Make the decision that something else be done, and let your willing lead to reality! But if none of these things follows upon your willing it, whereas with God willing is acting, then a human being creates in one way, and God, the creator of all things, in another. How, then, will he create not in a human fashion, yet be forced to beget in a human fashion? In your case, first you did not exist, then you came into being, and next you gave being to another. For this reason, you bring what has no being into being—or, if I may touch on something more profound, perhaps even you yourself do not bring into being from non-being, since Scripture says Levi was already in the loins of father, before he actually came to live himself.[228] But let no one use this text as a weapon against us! For I am not saying that the Son has come into being from the Father in this way, that he first was in the Father, and after that made his way towards being—he was not, after all, first incomplete and then complete, as is the law of our own process of generation.

10.   All of this is what our abusers argue; all of this belongs to those who rashly attack everything we say. We do not think this way—this is not our opinion. But together with the Father's ingenerate being—he always was, for mind never slips away into non-being—the Son, too, was, in a generate way. As a result, the begottenness of the Only-begotten runs parallel with the being of the Father; he has his existence from him and not after him, except in respect of the concept of source—source, that is, in the sense of cause.

I am constantly repeating the same argument, since I fear for the crude and material style of your thought. But if you are not indulging in idle curiosity about the Son's begetting (if one must call it that) or his hypostasis, or whatever other term one might invent that is more precise than these (for what we are thinking and talking about defeats my powers of speech!), then do not waste your efforts, either, on the procession of the Spirit. For me it is enough to hear that there is a Son, and that he is from the Father, and that the one is Father and the other is Son. I do not trouble myself beyond this, lest I become just like those voices that go completely hoarse from shouting too loudly, or the eye that strains towards the rays of the sun. For the more fully, the more exactly one wishes to see, so much more one's sense-organs are damaged, and one is, in the end, deprived of the ability to see at all: the object of sight itself increasingly overcomes our ability to see, if we want to see everything, and not just what it is safe to see.

11.   Do you hear mention of a begetting? Do not trouble yourself about how it occurs. Do you hear that the one who proceeds forth from the Father is the Spirit? Do not exercise your curiosity about the manner. Or if you pry curiously into the begetting of the Son and the procession of the Spirit, I will pry curiously into your own mixture of soul and body! How is it that you are both earth and the image of God? What is the source of movement in you, and what is moved? How can the same thing both cause motion and be set in motion? How can sensation both remain inside yourself and absorb what is outside you? How can the mind remain within you and beget a concept within some other mind? How is thought handed on by speech?

I have not yet mentioned puzzles on a grander scale: what is the rotation of the heavens?[229] How do you explain the motion of the stars, their order and measure and conjunction and disjunction? What are the boundaries of the sea? Whence come the blasts of the winds, the changes of the seasons, the deluges of rain? If you do not understand any of these things, my fellow human—and perhaps you will understand them someday, when perfection is within your grasp: "for I will look on the heavens," Scripture says, "the works of your fingers,"[230] which suggests that what we now see is not the truth but only images of the truth—if you, who discuss these things, do not know who you really are, if you do not fully grasp these things, of which your own sense faculties are witnesses, how do you suppose you can know with accuracy what and how great God is? This is really a lot of foolishness!

12.   If you trust me, then—and I am no rash theologian!—grasp what you can, and pray to grasp the rest. Love what already abides within you, and let the rest await you in the treasury above. Approach it by the way you live: what is pure can only be acquired through purification. Do you want to become a theologian someday, to be worthy of the divinity?[231] Keep the commandments, make your way forward through observing the precepts: for the practical life is the launching-pad for contemplation.[232] Start with the body, but find joy in working for your soul. Now what human being is there who can be raised up high enough to meet the measure of Paul?[233] Yet he, too, says that he sees "through a mirror, dimly," and that the time is yet to come when he will "see face to face."[234]

Are you more philosophical than others in your speech? In any case, you speak on a lower level than God. Are you, perhaps, more clever than others? Still you fall short of the truth, to the degree that your being stands second to the being of God. We have the promise that we will someday "know just as we are known."[235] If it is impossible to have perfect knowledge of all things here in this life, what remains for me? What is there to hope for?

Perhaps you will say: the Kingdom of Heaven. Yet I consider this to be nothing else than to share in what is purest and most perfect; and the most perfect of all things that exist is the knowledge of God. Let us, then, hold on to what we have and acquire what we can, as long as we live on earth; and let us store our treasure there in heaven, so that we may possess this reward of our labor: the full illumination of the holy Trinity—what it is, its qualities and its greatness, if I may put it this way —shining in Christ himself, our Lord, to whom be glory and power for the ages of ages. Amen.

4. ORATION 26: *ABOUT HIMSELF, ON HIS RETURN FROM THE COUNTRY*

About Himself, on his Return from the Country seems to come originally from the autumn of 380, after the imposture of Gregory's former protégé Maximus had been uncovered. Gregory had briefly left Constantinople— perhaps simply to rest and compose his thoughts, perhaps also to escape the critical questions of a shocked and confused congregation, as news of Maximus's own episcopal ambitions became known—but now he has returned. Oration 26 is Gregory's version of his and his Church's mutual "accounting" to each other after the recent crisis, in which he subtly deflects accusations of incompetence and maladministration. In some manuscripts, the title is simply, "About Himself." One gives a more elaborate and descriptive heading: "About Himself, the People, and the Shepherds (i.e., bishops), when he Returned from the Country after his Struggle against Maximus." In the Latin translation by Rufinus and in an early Armenian translation, it is as we give it here. Gregory's real emphasis, in fact, is on the nature of the true "philosophy" practiced by the faithful Christian, in implied contrast to Maximus's elaborate philosophical and theological poses. In the process, the oration becomes a gentle but winning apologia for Gregory's own behavior in Constantinople: as a philosopher, he lives detached from all needs for office, recognition, and material support, ready at any time to return to his simple, scholarly life in Cappadocia. In affirming his own vulnerability, as well as his internal freedom, Gregory seems, paradoxically, to be trying to make himself appear viable to the people once again as their spiritual leader.

Oration 26: *About Himself, on His Return from the Country* [236]

1.   I have missed you, my children, and you have missed me just as much! If I must add some proof to what I say, let me use the saying of Scripture: "I

swear it by my pride in you, which I have in Christ Jesus our Lord."[237] For the Holy Spirit has assured me of this on oath—the Spirit, by whom we have been moved to come to you, that we might prepare for the Lord "a people of his own possession."[238]

See how great my confidence is: I testify to my own feelings, and make every effort to express yours! And this should not raise eyebrows—when people share the same Spirit, they share the same sensibilities; and if they feel the same things, they also believe the same things. If one has never felt something oneself, one would find it hard to believe it of another; but if one has felt it, one is more ready to acknowledge similarities, to be the invisible witness of unseen feelings, to act as mirror to a form outside oneself. This is why I could not bear to abandon you any longer, even though I find life here a heavy burden, quite hard to endure. The burden is not just what cities impose: crowds, noise, public places; theatres, opulence, arrogance; criminals and victims, winners and losers, the bereaved and those for whom they mourn; people weeping and rejoicing, marrying and burying, being blessed and being cursed; the temptation to sin, a world in simmering agitation, fortunes that constantly shift like the winds or the Euripus.[239] It is also this more exalted and precious burden you see here—I mean the burden that clings to this pulpit and the holy table. We claim authority over them, we are counted among those who draw near to God, but I fear that we may not draw near in the right way—that, like straw before a fire, we may not be able to endure the flame.

2.   In any case, I have come back to you. I fled under pressure, but have returned—not under pressure, but in fact very willingly. My feet moved themselves, as the saying goes; the Spirit led me to do it, like a stream of water that must be forced to go uphill but that rushes downhill eagerly. Truly a single day is like a whole human life for those who are weighed down with longing! The case of Jacob does not seem to me to be any different: he worked for Laban the Syrian fourteen years for the sake of Laban's two young daughters, and never felt burdened; for Scripture says that all those days were to him as a single day, because of his love for them[240]—perhaps because the object of his longing was within sight. So what is available for us as our own is slow to stir our desire, as one of those before us has remarked.[241] For my part, when I was here I hardly noticed my affection for the place, but when I was far away I came to know longing as a sweet tyrant! But this is nothing new.

For if the cowherd so grieves over the calf that has wandered from the flock, and the shepherd laments that one sheep of ten is missing, and a bird mourns for the nest that it has left for a little while—so much so that the herders take up their pipes and climb up on some lookout point, and fill their reeds with the sounds of sadness, to summon the wandering beasts back, as if they were endowed with reason; and if they respond, the herders rejoice more than over all the rest together, who have caused them no concern;[242] while the bird makes its call and goes to its nest, and perches over its chirping nestlings and covers them with her wings—how important must a flock of rational creatures be to an upright shepherd, especially if he has run some danger for them in the past (since that, too, adds power to the potion of love)!

3.   How I have feared that fierce wolves, watching for us to disappear in the dark night, would tear the flock apart with thieving and violent words[243]—for they watch for our unguarded moments, since they cannot defeat us openly! I have feared that thieves and robbers, climbing into the pasture, would either carry the flock away shamelessly or steal them by trickery, to sacrifice and kill and destroy them[244]—"snatching booty and devouring lives," as one of the prophets put it.[245] I have feared, too, that someone who recently, even yesterday, was one of us, might find the side door unlocked and then enter, as if he belonged, only to plot against us as a stranger might do.[246] Many and varied, after all, are the stratagems of the one who sets such plots in motion, and there is no architect of any of these varied schemes to match the Enemy, the expert on all wickedness.

I have feared, too, in the past, those dogs who try by force to become shepherds:[247] this is a strange phenomenon, since they have contributed nothing to the shepherd's work except shearing the fleeces they had so dishonorably cultivated. They would not remain as dogs, but never became real shepherds; all they did was tear apart and scatter and destroy the efforts of others! After all, to destroy is always easier than to preserve. "It is by labor that a man is born," as Job says,[248] or that a ship is built and a house is raised; but to kill or to sink or to set on fire is free to anyone who wishes. Let those who now set the dogs upon the flock not give themselves airs, then, since they cannot claim to have added a single sheep to the flock, or saved even one from danger. They were practicing mischief, after all, not learning to do good.[249] And if they scatter the flock, this is but a small squall, this is just a minor plague, this is merely one wild beast, attacking us by surprise!

Let them stop, then—those who boast of their own shame; let them give up their wickedness if they can, let them "bow down and prostrate themselves, and weep before the Lord who made them;"[250] and if they are not completely incurable, let them mingle in with the flock.

4.   This is what I have to say—I, the cowardly and over-cautious shepherd, accused of being slack because I have tried to be safe! I am not one of those shepherds who gulp down the milk and wrap themselves in the wool, who slaughter the sheep, oppress them with hardship and sell them off, saying, "Praise the Lord—we're rich!" They are shepherds for themselves,

not for the sheep, if you will remember the saying of one of the prophets, by which he tried to evict the wicked shepherds.[251] I belong, rather, to those who can say with Paul, "Who is weak, and I am not weak? Who is made to fall, and I am not indignant"—or concerned?[252] "For I do not seek what is yours, but you."[253] "I have been burned up," too, "by the heat of the day, and stiffened by the cold of the night,"[254] to use the words of that patriarchal shepherd, who cared for those spotted sheep that were striving to conceive their young, there by the feeding troughs![255]

This is why I stand before you, then, just as I am and just as you are. And since I am here, let us give each other an accounting of what we have accomplished since last we were together. For it is good policy for you to demand a reckoning from us, not simply for our words and deeds, but even for each brief and insignificant moment of the day itself; and you must report to me what you have been doing, while I lay out before you the philosophy I have been practicing, while I lived with myself, alone in silence.

5. What vision of the highest things have you preserved, from all that you learned from me? What new contribution do you have to make from your own resources, either concerning how we speak of God,[256] or any of the other doctrines which I so often explained to you at such length? I seek, after all, not simply the principal, but the interest —not simply the talent, but what it has produced, lest one of you hide what has been entrusted to you, or bury it, and then deceive the one who gave it to you, on the grounds that he is harsh and wants what belongs to others![257] And how have you carried out those practices I recommended to you? Have you borne fruit without your "left hand knowing it,"[258] or in such a way that "your light may shine before men and women"?[259] Have you lived so that "the tree may be known from its fruit,"[260] and the teacher recognized through his disciples, so that someone observing our affairs—and there are many who do, some out of good will and others out of malice—might say, "God is truly among you, not simply proclaimed in the right way, but also worshipped as he should be"?[261]

For just as it is impossible for our practice to be worthy apart from faith—whereas most people also cultivate the good for glory's sake, and so hold true to nature—so, too, "faith, apart from works, is dead."[262] "Let no one deceive you with empty words"[263]—none of those who are ready to excuse everything if only you will speak impiously on doctrine; they are ready to repay base action with a base reward! Prove your faith, then, from your works; prove the fertility of your land—if we have not sowed in vain, if there is some harvest in you—by producing strong wheat worth storing in barns, so that we may cultivate you all the more eagerly.[264] Who will bear fruit a hundredfold, who sixtyfold, who even as much as thirtyfold?[265] Or who, conversely, is progressing from thirty to sixty (for we have this order, too, in the Gospels[266]) and ends at a hundred, so that he might grow to be great like Isaac,[267] advancing "from strength to strength,"[268] singing the "songs of ascent" and achieving those ascents "in his own heart"?[269]

6. I seek the profit that has accrued in your account. The gain, after all, is yours, not mine —or if it is also ours, then only because it is yours, the benefit returning from you to us like rays of reflected light. If you have fed the poor man, if you have sheltered the stranger, if you have "washed the feet of the saints;"[270] if you have found your luxury in an empty belly (please excuse my language!) and feasted on the commandments—for there is no luxury superior to this hunger, or more enduring for those who seek delight; if you have given refreshment to those who serve at the altar of sacrifice, who are appropriately poor (excuse me for saying this, too!), so that they might attend to the sacrifice with fewer distractions, sharing in what is yours and offering you in return what is theirs: how shameful it would have been, if we had requested such things as these and you had not offered them! I did not suggest all this to you, so that I might stand to benefit from it.[271] For it would be better for me to die than to have my boast made empty,[272] and to let the Gospel lose its reward for me by reaping a reward in this life. Preaching the Gospel, after all, is a matter of necessity for me,[273] and my ambition is to have it go unrewarded! But I suggested all this[274] that you might learn to do good for Christ by doing good for one of his little ones.[275] The reason is that just as he became everything that I am except sin,[276] for my sake, so he accepts the least of my needs and refers them to himself[277] —whether you share your roof or your clothing, whether you visit one in prison or go to see someone who is sick; or most insignificant of all, whether you refresh a parched tongue even with a drink of cold water, as the rich man suffering in the fire begged from poor Lazarus: for he enjoyed luxury in this life, and ignored Lazarus's poverty and sores, and received in return the fate of begging from Lazarus in the next life, and receiving nothing.[278]

7. This, then, is what I hold you responsible for. And I know you will not stand ashamed, either when held to accounts by us now or on the last day, when all our affairs will be reckoned up together—just as it is written, "And I am coming, to hold a reckoning of all your thoughts and actions,"[279] and "Behold the man, and his works and his recompense with him."[280]

But now we will show you our own accounts—what we accomplished in the desert. Elijah, too, loved to live the philosophic life on Carmel, and John in the desert; and Jesus himself, for the most part, performed his deeds among the crowds, but confined his prayers to solitude and desert places. What principle was he teaching us? Our need, I think, to be quiet for a while, so as to converse with God without disturbance, and to lift up the mind for a little, above changeable things. For he himself had no need to draw apart—there was no place to which he could withdraw, in fact, since as God he filled all things; but it was that we might learn that there is a time for activity and a time to be occupied with higher things.

What happened, then, in my experience of the desert? As a good merchant,[281] making profit everywhere, I want to deliver some freight to you that I acquired there.

8.   I was walking alone, just as the sun was setting. My path led out on a promontory—for it is a kind of habit of mine to relax from labor in this way; the bowstring cannot bear the tension if it is always stretched tight, but needs to be released from the notches for a short while if it is going to be stretched again, and not become unserviceable to the bowman, or useless in time of need! I was walking, in any case, and as my feet moved along my gaze was fixed upon the sea. It was not a pleasant sight, even though there are other times when it is very pleasant—times when it glows with a serene purple, and breaks sweetly and gently on the headlands. But what happened on this day? I prefer to quote the words of Scripture: "The sea started up and was rough, because a great wind was blowing."[282] And as happens in such weather, some of the waves were raised up far out and crested for a moment, then broke and dispersed themselves quietly along the headlands, but others crashed against nearby rocks and were beaten into a frothy foam and sprayed high into the air. Then pebbles and seaweed and trumpet shells and tiny oysters were churned up and scattered about; some of them were drawn back again, as the wave receded, but the rocks themselves were unshaken, immovable—no less than if nothing had disturbed them, despite all the battering they received from the waves.

9.   I know that I drew some profit from this for the philosophic life; and being, as I am, the kind of person who relates everything to myself, especially when I find myself staggered by some aspect of my situation (which then was the case), I took in what I saw as not at all irrelevant. The scene became a lesson for me! For surely, I said to myself, is not the sea our life and all our human affairs—since so much about them is salty and unstable? And are not the winds the trials and unforeseen events that fall upon us? David, that marvelous seer, seems to me to have recognized this when he said, "Save me, Lord, for the waters have risen up to take my soul,"[283] and "Save me from the depths of the waves!"[284] "I have come into the depths of the sea, and the storm engulfs me!"[285]

When people undergo trials, some always seem to me to be swept away like things without weight, breathless and offering no resistance to what threatens them; for they do not seem to have within themselves the firmness and weight of measured thinking, which is capable of holding out against the things that assault them. Others seem like rock, worthy of that Rock on whom we stand, and whom we worship:[286] these are they who make use of philosophic reasoning, and have risen above the mediocrity of the crowd, who bear everything without being shaken or disturbed, and either laugh at those who would shake them or look on them with pity—the first because of their philosophical mind, the second because of their charity. But as far as dishonor goes, when it is absent they are disposed to overlook it, or rather not to think it so dreadful, but when it faces them they are overcome by it. And what kind of dishonor? Passing things, that seem to them enduring! They act like philosophers apart from the decisive moment, but in time of need they are shown not to be philosophers at all—just like the person who thinks himself the best of athletes, but never goes down into the stadium, or thinks himself a tried and true steersman, and makes much of his skill in fair weather, but when the winds blow, hands over the rudder to someone else!

10.   Once I had formulated these thoughts for myself, I also came upon another image, which fits my present circumstances perfectly. Perhaps you will consider me a garrulous old man, if I explain this to you, as well. But I must explain it, since I know that Scripture, too, often uses images such as this to spell things out more clearly.

There is a legendary plant which sprouts when it is cut, and fights back against a steel blade.[287] If one may speak about paradoxical realities in paradoxes: it lives from death, it flourishes on pruning, it grows when it is made to diminish. That is the story, in any case—a free expression of the creative imagination. But it seems to me that a philosopher is clearly something of this kind. He finds his good reputation in the midst of suffering; he makes painful things into the stuff of virtue, and takes pride in adversity. He is not elated when "the arms of justice"[288] work well for him, nor crushed when they work badly; but he always remains the same, although his situation does not, and is even found to have grown in value, like gold purified in a furnace.

Let us look at it this way.[289] Is he of noble birth? He will reveal that his upright behavior is in a kind of tension with his blood, so that he is thought of highly for two distinct reasons: the genealogy people calculate, and the person they see. Is he unprepossessing in form, and in the underlying clay (if clay can really be all that different from clay)?[290] He will produce, as a substitute, nobility of intellect, and of that faculty by which one forms oneself into a better or worse person; but he will write off all other forms of nobility—whether by genes or by decree—as worthless and spurious.

There are, after all, three kinds of noble ancestry. One originates from above; by it, all of us are equally well-born, since we have all come to exist according to the image of God. The second originates from the flesh, and I am not sure if it really is something noble; this kind is produced by corruption.[291] And the third is recognized on the basis of vice or virtue: we share in it to a greater or lesser extent, I think, to the degree that we preserve the image or help to destroy it. That person who is truly wise, truly a philosopher, will love this third kind of nobility. But the fourth kind of noble ancestry, based on patents and decrees,[292] I will only consider worth noticing when I am also willing to call painted complexion beauty, or to bend my knee before a monkey who has been dubbed a lion!

11.   Is he young? He will mature as a man by resisting his passions, and will benefit from his youth in this: that he is not undergoing the things most young people do, but shows an elder's wisdom in a body still at the crest of its powers. He will enjoy his victory more than those crowned at Olympia; for he will win it in the common theatre of the world, and his victory will be beyond price. Is he tending towards old age? Still, he does not grow old in the soul, too—he welcomes the end of life as the time appointed for a necessary liberation, and crosses over graciously to that life to come, where no one is immature or aged, but everyone shares the age of spiritual perfection! Is he enjoying the prime of life? One beauty will sparkle in the other—that of the soul in that of the body. Has he already passed the flower of age, and kept it well preserved? Is he focused on himself, unaware of how he looks to others? Is he ugly in appearance? Still, he is lovely in his hidden self, like a rose in bud: a flower not yet in bloom, the most fragrant of blossoms in its odorless sheath! "In his beauty, he is fairest among the children of men;"[293] yet he gives no opportunity to be observed externally, but turns the onlooker's gaze to "the inner person."[294]

Is he in good health? He will use his health for the best purposes: he will give advice, strike a blow for goodness, speak words of freedom, keep watch through the night, sleep on the ground, fast, empty out his possessions, look contemplatively on both earthly and heavenly things, prepare for death with utter seriousness. Is his health poor? He will struggle, and if he gets the worst of it he will win the prize of no longer having to struggle. Is he wealthy? Philosophy will mean disposing of his riches, sharing his possessions with the one in need, as if he were a steward of what belonged to another, so that the poor person benefits by receiving a share, and he himself is united to God, having nothing of his own except his cross and his body. Is he poor? He will be rich in God, and will laugh at those with possessions, who are always acquiring more, and always poor in their need for something else—always drinking that they might still be thirsty!

12.   Is he hungry? He will be fed as the birds are, whose livelihood comes without sowing or ploughing.[295] He will live along with Elijah, staying with the widow of Zarephath; "The flask of oil will not run out, the vessel of flour will not be emptied," but the one will continue to flow and the other will abound richly, so that the hospitable widow may be honored, and may nourish the one who gives her nourishment.[296] Is he thirsty? Springs and rivers shall be his drink—a drink that is never intoxicating, never

rationed. If all sources give out due to drought, he will probably be "drinking from the brook."[297] Is he cold? So was Paul[298]—but for what a great purpose! And there is such a thing as a garment of rock: let Job persuade you, when he says, "Because they had no shelter, they wrapped themselves in rock."[299]

And consider with me still greater perfection. Is he insulted? He will conquer, by not insulting in return. Is he persecuted? He will endure it. Is he cursed? He will offer consolation. Is he slandered? He will pray for his slanderers. Is he struck on the right side? He will offer the other as well,[300] and if he had a third side he would also bring that forward, in order to give the one striking him a better lesson in patience—teaching by deed what he is not able to teach in word. Is he abused? So was Christ; he will be honored by sharing in his suffering. And if he hears, "Samaritan!"—if he is accused of having a demon—he will accept all of this along with God.[301] Even if he suffers a great deal, much will still be lacking: vinegar, gall, a crown of thorns, a reed sceptre, a scarlet cloak, a cross, nails, thieves as companions on the cross, passers-by who mock. For God has to win the prize in bearing yet more dishonor!

13.   There is nothing more impregnable, nothing more unconquerable than philosophy. Everything else collapses before the philosopher does! He is a wild ass[302] in the desert, as Job says, unfettered and free; "he scorns the tumult of the city, he does not hear the abuse of the tax-collector."[303] He is a unicorn,[304] an independent animal. "Will he be willing to serve you?" Will you tie him to a manger? Will he be led under a yoke?[305] When he is shut out of all earthly things, "he will be fitted out with wings like an eagle's, and will turn again towards the home of the one he serves"[306]—he will fly up to God. Let me put it in a nutshell: two things stand beyond our control— God and an angel; and in third place comes the philosopher! He is an immaterial being in matter, uncircumscribed while in a body, a citizen of heaven on earth, impassible in the midst of vulnerability, beaten in all things except his thoughts, a conqueror of those who think they have subdued him—simply by letting himself be conquered.[307]

Now that our discourse has sketched a portrait of the philosopher, come— as I said when I began—let us examine our own behavior by his standard. "For I, too, think that I have the Spirit of God,"[308] even if on some of these points I am vulnerable, an easy target. So if those who hate me and attack me find that I am below the standard, their actions—if not their intentions— may be forgiven; but if they find me stronger and better than my enemies, they should either give up their wickedness or think up a new way to wrong me, since this present approach has been discredited. But let them not risk being accused of foolishness as well as malice, because they plot evil to no purpose, and do not know how to accomplish the wickedness they are so eager to do.

14.   For what real pain can they cause, even though they are ready to try everything? Let us consider just how many ways one human being can be maligned by another. Will they call me uneducated?[309] I know only one kind of wisdom, to fear God—for "the fear of the Lord is the beginning of wisdom,"[310] and "hear it all, the end of the argument: fear God!"[311] This is what Solomon says, the wisest of men. Let them prove, then, that I do not fear God, and they will have conquered me; but as for other forms of wisdom, some of them I have avoided, others I hope and pray to acquire, putting my trust in the Spirit.

Will they accuse me of being poor—which is my wealth? If only I could take off even these rags, to run naked across the thorns of life! If only, too, I could put off this heavy garment quickly, so that I might put on a lighter one![312] Will they stigmatize me as a fugitive from my native country? How little regard they have of us, these arrogant xenophobes! Do I have a native land, my friends? Everywhere is my country, and nowhere! And are you not a stranger and a sojourner, too? I will not praise the place where you live, if you have such a place, for fear that you might abandon your true homeland, where it behooves us to reserve our citizenship.[313] Surely you will not blame us for our age and our ill health? Is not this the whole story of material nature? Let me reveal to you one of my secrets: there is also a food which the mind consumes,[314] and there I have some little fare I can boast of! But you, my plump and over-nourished friend: you are a pleasant spectacle! If only you sported a few gray hairs and a pale complexion, so that you might be credible yourself as a person of understanding—as a philosopher!

15.   What, then? Will they depose me from the episcopal throne? But was there ever a throne I was happy to occupy, in the past or now? Do I call them blessed who ascend it? And you—do you make ambitious people attractive, by approaching the throne as unworthily as you have?[315] Did not these recent events reveal my state of mind to all of you? Or was this simply coyness [on my part], a test to see if you would miss me? Artists might be able to project all their own thoughts onto others, either in suspecting their motives or in putting their thoughts into words.[316] What did this desolation mean? What were the curses we pronounced publicly against ourselves? What did our tears mean, and the fact that we seemed so wretched to you, even detestable, because of our resistance?[317]

Will they deprive me of my position of leadership? Who in his right mind ever admired such a position? Rather, it seems to me, the first sign of intelligence would now be to flee from it, since everything is in commotion, our whole life shaken, because of it; since the ends of the earth are gripped by suspicion because of it, in a kind of silent and unnamed war; since we run the risk, because of it, of being just another human being, even though our origin is from God, and of losing the great new name that is ours.[318] It would have been a good thing if there had never been an office of leadership, or regional primacy, or the prerogatives of rule, so that we all might be recognized for virtue alone! But now this business of right and left, of middle and high and lowly rank, of walking first and walking behind,[319] has put all our life in shambles, to no purpose; it has thrust many people down into the pit, and led them off to the side of the goats[320]—not just subordinates, but even shepherds, unaware of the fact that they are "the teachers of Israel."[321]

16.   Will they bar us from the altars? But I know of another altar, of which those we see now are simply types, an altar untouched by chisel or hand, on which no iron, no tool of clever craftsmen, has been heard, an altar wholly produced by the mind, to which we must ascend by contemplation. Before this altar I shall stand; on this altar I shall sacrifice acceptable offerings, "sacrifices and offerings and holocausts,"[322] as much superior to the offerings made in this present life as truth is superior to shadow. The great David seems to have been philosophizing about this sacrifice when he said, "I shall go in to the altar of God, who gives joy to my spiritual youth."[323] No one can pull me away from this altar, even if they wish to!

Will they drive me out of the city? Not, surely, from that City which is above! Let those who hate us accomplish this, and they will truly have made war on us! But as long as they cannot do it, they are pelting us with raindrops, beating us with the breezes, playing a game with dreams—that is how I regard their "war"!

Will they seize our possessions? Which ones? If they are my own, let them clip me of wings I never put on to fly![324] But if it is the Church's goods—this is the cause, over which the whole war is being fought, the reason the thief coveted the strongbox and (most terrible of all!) betrayed God for thirty pieces of silver.[325] So much was the betrayer worth—not the one who was betrayed!

17.   Will they lock us out of our house? Will they cut back our livelihood? Will they alienate our friends? Of course, you can see we have imposed ourselves on the generosity of many! Yet when we did take advantage of their offers of support—for I will not seem ungrateful—we did so sparingly rather than eagerly. Here is the charge: a certain pious, God-loving household gave us refuge, and became for us like the Shunammite's house for Elisha[326]—a household related to us in body and in spirit, respectable in every way. There this people took root, stealthily carrying on a religious practice still subject to persecution, not without fear or without danger. May the Lord repay this house its due, on the day of retribution!

And if we have pursued material support, let those who hate us feast at our expense—I can invoke no greater curse on myself than that! As for friends: some, I fully realize, have not abandoned me, even when they have suffered evil—for to be subject to the same injustice causes the same pain; but if we receive the disdain of others, we have already been trained to bear it. For among my friends and family, some "openly draw near and stand facing me,"[327] but the others, in their great kindness, "stand far off;"[328] and "in this night all have been made to stumble."[329] I might almost say that Peter has denied me, and that he may not even be weeping bitterly to heal his sin![330]

18.   It may seem that I am the only one with daring, the only one bursting with confidence; that only I am hopeful in the face of fearful threats, that only I remain steadfast when shown public deference but scorned in private, known in both East and West as a focus of controversy. What nonsense! "If an army encamp against me, my heart shall not fear; if war should break out against me, even then do I hope."[331] I am so far from thinking that any of the present circumstances are dreadful that I forget what is happening to me, and simply grieve for those who do me harm.

You who once were members of Christ—members precious to me, even if you are now corrupted—members of this flock which you have nearly betrayed, even before it was fully gathered: how is it that you are both scattered and scatterers, like oxen released from their harness?[332] How is it that you have raised up an altar in opposition to an altar? How is it that you have suddenly found yourself in a place of desolation?[333] How is it that by this schism you have brought about your own death, and have made us suffer such pain? How is it that you are exploiting the simplicity of the shepherds to scatter the flock?[334] For I do not blame them for their inexperience—I blame you for your malice! "Who shall come to your assistance, O Israel, in your state of corruption?"[335] What medicine shall I find to heal your wounds? What shall I use as a bandage? How shall I join together what is broken? With what tears, with what words, with what prayers shall I treat the fracture? Perhaps this is the way:

19.   Holy and adored Trinity, perfect in yourself, rightly seen and honored by us as one, yours is the work, yours its accomplishment![336] May you restore them to us again, who have been separated just far enough to be trained, in division, to seek for harmony; in return for our sufferings in this life, may you give us the serene blessings of heaven! The first and greatest of those blessings is to be more perfectly and purely enlightened, by your grace, to see how the same Mystery can be understood as one, yet discovered to be three; how the Unbegotten and the Begotten and the One who Proceeds are one nature, three particularities,[337] 'One God, who is above all and through all and in all,"[338] neither exalted nor changed nor lessened nor divided:[339] now partly grasped and partly sought for, but someday, perhaps, to be fully grasped by those who have sought you well here on earth, by their way of living and their contemplation.[340] To you be all glory, honor and power for the ages! Amen.

5. ORATION 38: *ON THE THEOPHANY*

Along with Orations 39 and 40, *On the Theophany* forms a trilogy celebrating the birth and manifestation of the incarnate Word—what Western Christians commemorate in the feasts of Christmas, the Epiphany, and (more recently) the Baptism of the Lord. The three orations are remarkable examples of Christian theological and liturgical rhetoric and were probably delivered at the end of 380 and the beginning of 381, in the Basilica of the Holy Apostles in Constantinople, where Gregory, under imperial patronage, was now permitted to preside and preach as bishop. Some manuscripts give the title of Oration 38 as "For the birthday of the Lord" or "For the birthday of Christ;" the more usual title, "For the Theophany" (which simply means "manifestation of God") probably reflects the earlier name of this feast and is the name still used in many Orthodox Churches for the celebration of Christ's birth. Most modern scholars assume Or. 38 was given at the main liturgy celebrating the birth of Jesus on December 25, originally a Western feast, imported into the Greek Church around this time; Or. 39 and 40 would have been given a few weeks later at the celebration of the full manifestation of God's presence in the world in the baptism of Jesus on January 6, the traditional Eastern date for celebrating the Theophany.[341] John McGuckin prefers to assume that all three were given during a single two- or three-day festival concluding on January 6.[342]

Oration 38 begins with a reflection on the character of this and any Christian feast, in contrast to the pagan tradition of religious celebration. Gregory then turns to the theological content of the Christmas-Epiphany cycle, offering a terse but grandly conceived reflection on the mysterious being of God and on the narrative of creation, fall, and redemption: the long history of God's care for the human race, which culminates in the incarnation of the Word in human flesh and in the saving events of the human career of Jesus. Dense in its theological diction yet continually poetic in its proclamation of the Gospel of redemption, this oration is an astonishingly broad and fresh exposition, in Christian terms, of the Mystery of God's redeeming presence in time. It has deservedly become one of the most frequently quoted classics of Greek Patristic theology.

Oration 38: *On the Theophany* [343]

1.   Christ is born—give praise! Christ comes from heaven—rise up to meet him! Christ is on the earth—be lifted up! "Sing to the Lord, all the earth!"[344] Or, to speak of two places together, "Let the heavens rejoice and the earth be glad,"[345] because of the heavenly one who now lives on earth! Christ is in the flesh—rejoice with trembling and joy: with trembling, because of sin;

with joy, because of hope! Christ is born of a Virgin—women, preserve your virginity, that you may become mothers of Christ! Who does not worship the one who "is from the beginning"?[346] Who does not glorify the one who is "the end"?[347]

2. Once again darkness is put to flight, once again light comes into being, once again Egypt is punished by darkness, once again Israel is illumined by the pillar [of fire].[348] Let "the people who sit in the darkness" of ignorance see "the great light" of divine knowledge.[349] "Old things have passed away; behold, all things have become new."[350] The letter gives way, the Spirit gains ground,[351] the shadows disappear, the truth takes their place. Melchisedech finds his fulfillment: the one without mother comes into being without father—motherless first, fatherless next! The laws of nature are shattered; the world above is fully realized. Christ is in command—let us not resist him! "All nations, clap your hands,"[352] for "a child has been born for us, and a son given to us, whose rule is upon his shoulder"—for he is lifted up, along with his cross—"and his name is 'Angel of great counsel'"[353]—the counsel of the Father. Let John cry out, "Prepare the way of the Lord!"[354] I shall cry out the meaning of this day: the fleshless one is made flesh, the Word becomes material, the invisible is seen, the intangible is touched, the timeless has a beginning, the Son of God becomes Son of Man—"Jesus Christ, yesterday and today, the same also for all ages!"[355] Let the Jews take offense, let the Greeks scoff,[356] let the heretics wear out their tongues with chatter![357] They will believe one day, when they see him ascending into heaven—or if not then, at least when he comes from heaven again, enthroned as judge!

3. But more of this later. Today is the feast of God's Appearing,[358] or of the Nativity: both names are used, both titles given to the one reality. For God has appeared to human beings by being born: he is unique always, existing always from the One who always is, above all cause and language—for there was no word prior to the Word;[359] but he became the other [i.e., born] later for our sake, so that the one who gave being might also give well-being—or rather, so that when we had fallen away from well-being through wickedness, he might lead us back to himself again by becoming flesh. The name of the feast, then, is "Theophany" because he has appeared, but "Nativity" because he has been born.

4. This is our feast, this is what we celebrate today: God's coming to the human race, so that we might make our way to him, or return to him (to put it more precisely), so that we might put off the old humanity and put on the new,[360] and that as we have died in Adam so we might live in Christ,[361] being born with Christ and crucified with him and buried with him and raised with him.[362] For I must experience the lovely reversal: as pain came out of happiness, so happiness must return from pain. "Where sin has abounded, grace has

abounded all the more,"[363] and if the taste of fruit brought judgment upon us, how much more have Christ's sufferings brought us righteousness? Let us celebrate, then: not like a public festival, but in a divine way; not like the world, but above the world; not celebrating what is ours, but what belongs to the One who is ours—to our Lord; not celebrating weakness, but healing; not celebrating this creation, but our re-creation.

5. And how will this happen? Let us not garland our porticoes, or form dance troupes, or adorn the alleys; let us not feast the eye, or charm the ear with music, or pamper our nostrils, or titillate our taste-buds, or delight our touch—all means of access to wickedness, entry-ways to sin; let us not make ourselves effete by soft and flowing clothes, whose greatest beauty is their uselessness, nor by glittering gems or the glow of gold, nor with the deceiving colors of cosmetics, which give the lie to natural beauty and are devised to deface God's image, nor by "drunkenness and revels," which, I am certain, are linked to "debauchery and licentiousness"[364]—for bad teachers dispense bad knowledge, or better: bad seeds lead to bad crops! Let us not build high, leafy canopies as a shelter for the luxury of the belly![365] Let us not revere the bouquet of wine, nor chefs' sleight-of-hand, nor the costliness of perfume! Let not earth and sea bestow on us their treasures of dung—for that is my term of honor for luxury! Let us not make efforts to outdo each other in moral weakness. For moral weakness is what I call all excess, all consumption that goes beyond need—especially when others, formed of the same clay, are hungry and in need![366]

6. But let us leave all this to the Greeks, to Greek feasts[367] and celebrations: for they call beings "gods" who delight in the aroma of cooking meat, and consequently pay honor to Divinity with the belly; they come to be wicked themselves by being the sculptors and priests and initiates of wicked demons. As for us, who worship the Word, if we must live luxuriously, let us luxuriate in the word,[368] and in the law and the narratives of God—all of them, but especially the story behind this present feast—that our luxury may be appropriate, and not alien to the one who has called us together.

Would you like me, as your host today, to set words about these things before you, my honored guests, as abundantly and ambitiously as I can?[369] If I do, you will come to know how a stranger can nourish local natives, how a rustic can feed city folk, one ignorant of luxury those who are used to it, one poor and homeless those who glitter with abundance! That is where I shall begin; purify, I beg you, your mind and hearing and thinking, all of you who will enjoy luxuries such as these! For our discourse is about God, and therefore divine, and its purpose is that you may go on from here to share in true luxuries that will never come to an end. It will be at once both as full as possible and as concise as possible, so that it may not disappoint you by lacking substance, nor be distasteful through sheer excess.

7.   God always was and is and will be—or better, God always *is*.[370] For "was" and "will be" are divisions of the time we experience, of a nature that flows away; but he is always, and gives himself this name when he identifies himself to Moses on the Mountain.[371] For he contains the whole of being in himself, without beginning or end, like an endless, boundless ocean of reality; he extends beyond all our notions of time and nature, and is sketchily grasped by the mind alone, but only very dimly and in a limited way; he is known not directly but indirectly,[372] as one image is derived from another to form a single representation of the truth: fleeing before it is grasped, escaping before it is fully known, shining on our guiding reason[373]—provided we have been purified—as a swift, fleeting flash of lightning shines in our eyes. And he does this, it seems to me, so that, insofar as it can be comprehended, the Divine might draw us to itself—for what is completely beyond our grasp is also beyond hope, beyond attainment—but that insofar as it is incomprehensible, it might stir up our wonder, and through wonder might be yearned for all the more, and through our yearning might purify us, and in purifying us might make us like God; and when we have become this, that he might then associate with us intimately as friends—my words here are rash and daring!—uniting himself with us, making himself known to us, as God to gods, perhaps to the same extent that he already knows those who are known by him.[374]

The Divine, then, is boundless and difficult to contemplate; the only thing completely comprehensible about it is its boundlessness—even though some think that the fact of its simple nature makes it either completely incomprehensible or perfectly comprehensible! Let us, then, investigate what it means to be of a simple nature. Simplicity, after all, is not itself its nature, just as being composite is not the whole nature of composite beings.

8.   The boundless can be considered in two ways: with regard to beginning and with regard to end; for what is beyond these, and not contained within them, is boundless. So when the mind turns its gaze to the abyss above us, and finds no place to stand and settle down in its imaginings about God, it calls that boundless, inescapable realm "without beginning;" but when it turns its gaze below, to what comes after, it calls it "immortal" and "indestructible;" and when it brings the whole image together, it calls it "eternal." For eternity is neither time nor a part of time—it cannot be measured, after all—but what time is for us, measured by the movement of the sun, eternity is for eternal things: spread out coextensively with their being, like a kind of temporal movement and interval.[375]

So much for our present philosophical reflections on God. For this is not the time for such things, since our present task is to speak not about God in himself but about what God has done for us![376] And when I say the word "God," I mean Father and Son and Holy Spirit: we do not speak of

the divinity as being spread out beyond them, lest we introduce a whole
crowd of gods, nor as held within limits short of them, lest we be accused of
being stingy with divinity—speaking like Jews by emphasizing the divine
monarchy, or speaking like Greeks by emphasizing the divine abundance!
The weakness of both positions is the same, even if it is found in opposite
extremes. So the Holy of Holies, concealed by the seraphim and proclaimed
"holy" in their triple cry,[377] converges in a single Lordship and a single
Godhead—all this has been set out philosophically by one of our predecessors
in a beautiful and lofty way.[378]

9. And since it was not enough for Goodness to be set in motion simply
by contemplating itself, but the Good needed to be poured out, to undertake
a journey, that there might be more beings to receive its benefits—for this,
after all, is the height of Goodness!—it first thought of the angelic, heavenly
powers; and that thought was an action, brought to fulfillment in the Word
and made perfect in the Spirit. So a second set of splendors came into being,
ministers to the primordial splendor; we must understand them either as
intelligent spirits, or as some kind of immaterial, bodiless fire, or as of some
other nature, as close as possible to the beings we have mentioned.[379] I am
tempted to say that they are immovable towards what is evil, and only possess
movement towards the good, since they surround God and are the first
glimmerings to shine forth from God; for beings in this world belong to a
second phase of that shining.[380] But what persuades me to suspect and to
say that they are not immovable, but only difficult to move, is the one who
was called "Morning Star" because of his brilliance,[381] but became and is
called "Darkness" because of his proud rebellion—as well as those powers
who turned away under his influence, crafters of evil in their flight from the
good, patrons of evil in us.

10. In this way, then, and for these reasons, the intelligible world came
into being before God—at least, as I reflect on these things, weighing such
great matters by my tiny reason. And when the first creatures were, in his
judgment, in a good state, he conceived of a second world, material and
visible; this is the structure compounded of heaven and earth and all that
lies between them—praiseworthy, surely, for the natural excellence of each
of its parts, but still more praiseworthy for the proportion and harmony of
all of them together, each part standing in good relation to every other, and
all of them to the whole, in order to bring a single, ordered universe to
completion. In doing this, he not only revealed his own nature to himself,
but showed he is capable of bringing into existence something wholly other.
For intellectual natures, graspable by the mind alone, are clearly related to
the godhead; but whatever is subject to sense is utterly alien, and things
that are completely without soul or movement lie still further removed.

"How does all this concern us?" some impatient person may ask, over-eager, perhaps, to get on with the celebration. "Spur your horse around the turn! Tell us something deep about the festival, about the reason why we are seated before you today!" I will do this, certainly, even if I have begun on a somewhat more lofty plane; my desire and the shape of my discourse forced me to do so!

11.   Mind, then, and sensation, thus distinct from each other, had remained within their own boundaries and bore in themselves the greatness of the Word who had fashioned them, silently praising the majesty of his work and heralding it everywhere.[382] There was not yet a mingling of both realms, nor any mixture of these opposites—that mark of a still greater wisdom and generosity concerning created natures—nor was the full richness of his goodness yet evident. But when the creative Word willed to reveal this, and to form a single living being from both spheres—from both invisible, I mean, and visible nature—he crafted the human being. From matter, which already existed, he took the body, putting within it the breath that comes from himself, which Scripture understands to mean the intellectual soul, which is God's image. So he set upon the earth a kind of second world, great in its littleness: another kind of angel, a worshipper of mixed origins, a spectator of the visible creation and an initiate into the intelligible, king of the things on earth yet ruled from above, earthly and heavenly, subject to time yet deathless, visible and knowable, standing halfway between greatness and lowliness. He is at the same time spirit and flesh: spirit because of grace, flesh because of pride—the one, that he might always remain in being and glorify his benefactor; the other, that he might suffer, and in his suffering come to his senses, and be corrected from his ambitions of grandeur. He is a living being: cared for in this world, transferred to another, and, as the final stage of the mystery, made divine by his inclination towards God.[383] For that, I believe, is where the modest splendor of truth, in this life, is leading us: to see and experience the brilliance of God, a glory befitting the one who has bound us together, will dissolve us, and will again bind us together in a still more lofty way.

12.   This creature God placed in Paradise—whatever this Paradise was!—and honored him with self-determination, so that the Good might belong to him by choice, no less than it belonged to the one who provided the seeds.[384] He was the cultivator of immortal plants—divine thoughts, perhaps, both of a simpler and a more perfect kind; he was naked in his own simplicity, his life free from artifice, and needed no covering or defense. This is the way the original man was meant to be. And God gave him a law, as matter for his self-determination. Now the law was a command concerning which plants he was allowed to partake of, and which one he was not to touch. This latter was the tree of knowledge; it was not originally planted

with evil intent, nor prohibited out of ill-will—let not God's enemies exercise their tongues on this point, or imitate the serpent!—but was a good thing, if partaken at the right time. For the plant was contemplation, by my interpretation—something which may only safely be attempted by those who have reached perfection in an orderly way. So it was not beneficial for those still in a state of immaturity, greedy in appetite, just as mature food does not profit those who are still infants, still in need of milk. And when, by the envy of the Devil and by his bullying of the Woman—something she suffered because she was weaker, and something she passed on because she was more persuasive; alas for my weakness! for my ancestor's weakness is my own—he forgot the command that had been given him, and was overcome by that bitter food. Then he was banished, all at once, because of his wickedness, from the tree of life and the Paradise and God; he was dressed in tunics of skin—coarse, mortal and rebellious flesh, perhaps. So this was the first thing he came to know: his own shame; and he hid himself from God. But even here he drew a profit of a kind: death, and an interruption to sin; so wickedness did not become immortal, and the penalty became a sign of love for humanity.[385] That, I believe, is the way God punishes!

13.   Humanity was disciplined in many ways, in former ages, in return for many sins, which the root of wickedness caused to spring up in many different situations and times: disciplined by exhortation, by law, by prophets, by blessings, by threats; by calamities, by floods, by conflagrations; by wars, by victories, by defeats; by signs from heaven, signs from mid-air, from the earth, from the sea; by unexpected moves from men, cities, tribes—the aim of all which was to drive out wickedness. In the end, stronger medicine was needed, for maladies which had grown more severe: internecine murders, adulteries, perjuries, homosexual lust, and first and last of all evils, idolatry, which transfers worship from the creator to creatures. Since all these things required a greater help, they received one that was greater! This was the Word of God himself, who is before the ages, invisible, beyond comprehension, bodiless; cause from cause, light from light, the spring of life and immortality, the impress of the original beauty, the unquestionable seal, the unchangeable image, the Father's definition and Word. He came to his own proper image and bore flesh for the sake of flesh, and mingled with a rational soul for my soul's sake, wholly cleansing like by like.[386] In every respect save that of sin, he became human: conceived from the Virgin, who had first been purified in soul and flesh by the Spirit (for it was right both that childbirth be honored, and that virginity be honored still more highly); coming forth as God, along with what he had taken on; one from two opposites, flesh and Spirit—the one of which shared divinity, the other of which was divinized. O new mixture! O unexpected blending![387] He who is

has come to be, the uncreated one is created, the limitless one is contained, through the mediation of a rational soul standing between divinity and the coarseness of flesh.[388] He who is rich is a beggar[389]—for he goes begging in my flesh, that I might become rich with his godhead! He who is full has emptied himself[390]—for he emptied himself of his own glory for a while, that I might have a share of his fullness.[391] How rich is his goodness? What is this Mystery all around me? I had a share in the image, and I did not preserve it; he took on a share in my flesh, so that he might both save the image and make the flesh immortal. He establishes a second communication,[392] far more amazing than the first: just as then he gave us a share in what was better, so now he takes on a share of what is worse. This is more godlike than the first gift—this, to those who have any sense, is loftier still!

14.   What do the opportunists have to say to us about this—those malicious calculators of the divinity, talking down what should be held in honor, in the dark about the light, ignorant when it comes to wisdom, people for whom "Christ died for nothing,"[393] creatures without gratitude, shaped by the Evil One? Do you charge against God his own benefaction? Is he any the less, because he humbled himself for your sake? Because, as the Good Shepherd, he came after the wandering sheep, laid down his life for the flock, on the mountains and the hills, on which you offered sacrifice,[394] and found the one who had wandered; and when he found him, took him on those shoulders on which he also bore the wood; and lifting him up, he raised him to life on high; and raising him there, counted him along with those who had never gone astray?[395] Because he lit a lamp—his own flesh— and "swept the house," cleansing the world of sin, and searched for the coin, that royal image caked with the mud of passions, and called together all the powers friendly to him when he found the coin, and let them share his joy, because they had also been privy to his plan of restoration?[396] Because the light which floods all things followed on the lamp that went before him,[397] and the Word followed the voice,[398] and the Bridegroom his attendant,[399] who "prepared for the Lord a people of his own"[400] and cleansed them by water to be ready for the Spirit?[401] Are these the things you charge against God? And do you suppose he is inferior, simply because he girded himself with a towel and washed the feet of the disciples, and showed that the best road to exaltation is humiliation?[402] Because he humbled himself through a soul bowed down to the earth, that he might also raise with himself what had been bent under the weight of sin? Why, then, do you not also accuse him of this: that he ate with tax collectors, in the houses of tax collectors, and made tax collectors his disciples, that he himself might profit in the process? What profit? The salvation of sinners! Unless someone will also criticize a physician for bowing over illness and putting up with bad

odors, that he might give health to the sick; or criticize someone for leaning, out of kindness, over a pit, in order to rescue the beast who has fallen into it, as the Law commands![403]

15.   He was sent, but as a human being—for he was twofold, since he grew tired and hungry and thirsty, and was distressed, and shed tears, by the law of the body.[404] And if he also did these things as God, what can that mean? Think of the good pleasure of the Father as a mission, and that [the Son] refers all that is his back to him, both because he reveres him as his timeless source and in order not to seem to be God's competitor. For it is said in Scripture both that he "was handed over"[405] and that he "handed himself over,"[406] and that he "was raised by the Father"[407] and "was taken up,"[408] but also that he himself "rose"[409] and "ascended" once again[410]—the former a proof of [the Father's] good pleasure, the latter of [his own] power. But you speak of the things that suggest he is less, while you pass over the things that exalt him; you take account of the fact that he suffered, but neglect to add that he did it willingly. The Word now undergoes the same treatment: by some he is honored as God, and blended in; by others he is dishonored as flesh, and broken off![411] With whom is he more angry? Or better, whom is he likely to forgive? Those who join him [to Father and Spirit] in a perverse way, or those who divide him? After all, the first group ought by right to divide him, as well, and the second group to join him—the first in number, the second in divinity.[412] Do you take offence at the flesh? The Jews do as well. Will you also write him off as "a Samaritan"?[413]—and I will leave what follows unsaid![414] Do you refuse to believe in his divinity? Not even the demons did that! You, who are more faithless than the demons, more lacking in judgment than the Jews! The latter considered the title "Son" an expression of equal honor,[415] while the former recognized the God who expelled them[416]— for they came to believe on the basis of what they suffered. But you will neither accept his equality with God nor confess the divinity. It would be better for you to be circumcised and possessed by a demon (if I may say something that is a bit ridiculous) than to be uncircumcised and in good health, but still wicked and godless!

16.   A little later, then, you will also see Jesus cleansed in the Jordan with the same bath that cleanses me[417]—or rather, making the water holy by his cleansing, for the one who "takes away the sin of the world"[418] had no need of purification; and [you will see] the heavens rent open, and Jesus witnessed to by his kindred Spirit; [you will see him] tempted, and conquering his tempter, and served by angels; [you will see him] "healing every disease and every weakness,"[419] and giving life to the dead—as he must also do to you, who are dead in your heretical opinions[420]—and driving out demons, some by himself and others through his disciples; [you will see

him] feeding thousands with a few loaves, and walking on the sea, and betrayed and crucified—and crucifying, with himself, my sin: offered as a lamb, offering as a priest, buried as a human being and raised as God, and then ascending and coming again with the glory that is his. How many festivals there are, for each of the mysteries of Christ! Yet there is one conclusion to all of them: my perfection, my re-shaping, my return to the first Adam.

17.   Right now, however, accept his conception, and leap with joy—if not in the womb, like John,[421] then at least as David did when the ark came to rest.[422] Revere the census, by which you were enrolled as a citizen of heaven; be in awe of that birth, by which you were released from the bonds of your birth; honor little Bethlehem, which has pointed you on the way to Paradise; venerate the manger, at which you, an animal without reason, were nourished by the Word.[423] Like an ox, recognize your owner—so Isaiah exhorts you[424]—and like an ass, know the manger of the Lord himself: whether you are one of the clean beasts, subject to the Law, who chew on the cud of the word and are fit for sacrifice, or whether you are still unclean and unsuited to be food or victim, from the Gentile race. Run with the star;[425] bring gifts, with the Magi, of gold and frankincense and myrrh— gifts for your king, for your God, for the one who became a corpse for your sake! Give glory with the shepherds, sing praise with the angels, dance with the company of archangels! Let there be a common festival for the powers of heaven and earth! For I believe that they, too, are rejoicing and holding festival along with us today, if it is true that they are friends of both humanity and God, like those David portrays as "ascending on high"[426] with Christ after his passion, going out to meet him and urging each other to "lift high the gates."

18.   You should hate just one thing about the birth of Christ: Herod's murder of children. Or rather, reverence even this as a sacrifice of Christ's own contemporaries, offered in place of the new Victim. If he flees into Egypt, accompany him eagerly on his flight; it is a fine thing to flee with Christ when he is persecuted! Walk uncomplainingly through all the ages and miracles of Christ, as Christ's disciple.[427] Be purified, be circumcised, remove the veil with which you were born! Then teach in the Temple, drive out those who make a business of God! Be stoned, if this is what you must suffer—you will give the slip to those who cast stones at you, I am sure, and will escape through the midst of them as God did; for the Word cannot be touched by stones![428] If you are brought before Herod, remain, for the most part, silent; he will respect your silence more than the long speeches of all the others. If you are scourged, then seek out the other sufferings, too: taste the gall, because of that earlier taste;[429] drink the vinegar, seek out the spitting, accept the blows, the slaps on your face; be crowned with thorns—the harsh

side of a godly life; put on the scarlet cloak, receive the reed, be reverenced by those who make a game of truth! And in the end, be crucified with him, die with him, be buried eagerly with him, so that you may also rise with him and be glorified with him and reign with him, seeing God, so far as that is attainable, and being seen by him: the one who is worshipped and glorified in a Trinity, who we pray might be revealed to us even now, as far as that is attainable in the bonds of flesh, in Christ Jesus our Lord, to whom be glory and power for the ages of ages. Amen.

6. ORATION 39: *ON THE HOLY LIGHTS*

The oration *On the Holy Lights* is the second in the Christmas-Epiphany trilogy we mentioned above[430] and seems originally to have been delivered in the Church of the Holy Apostles at one of the liturgies of the feast of Epiphany, probably during the night-vigil preceding January 6, 381. In some manuscripts, it is given the simple title, "On the Lights;" in others, it receives a fuller description, such as "On the Holy Lights; this, too, is a dogmatic discourse, and was given in Constantinople." The celebration seems to have been focused on the baptism of Jesus as the revelation of the divine light in the world and the full manifestation of God in history, as Father, Son and Holy Spirit. The title of the oration comes from this connection with baptism, to which Gregory refers frequently by the common Greek title, "enlightenment" (φωτισμός); the liturgy of the feast also may have included the use of lamps to brighten the interior of the basilica during the winter night. Gregory presents the "grace of the day" as God's sharing of his own light with men and women to purify them from the darkness of sin, and contrasts this Christian Mystery, shared through the Church's baptism, with pagan mysteries of initiation.

Here and in Oration 40, which we have not translated here, Gregory uses the feast as an occasion for developing a theology of Christian baptism and renewal, for insisting on the lasting opportunity for repentance and conversion in the Church, and for urgently appealing to unbaptized members of the congregation not to defer their own "enlightenment" to the end of life but to begin preparation immediately for the sacraments of initiation that would be completed at Easter. Like the oration that precedes it, Oration 39 is a stunningly dense and complex meditation on the meaning of Christ's person and work for the Christian faithful, and on the continuing reality of redemption and the reconciliation of sinners, as realized in the Church's sacraments.

Oration 39: *On the Holy Lights* [431]

1.   Once again my Jesus, and once again a Mystery! It is not a deceptive, disorderly mystery, not pagan error and drunkenness: for that is what I call their solemn feasts, as I think any right-thinking person would do! It is a lofty and divine Mystery, the harbinger of the glory that is on high. For the holy Day of Lights, to which we have come and which we are judged worthy to celebrate today, begins with the baptism of my Christ, "the true light, which enlightens every man and woman coming into the world,"[432] and it sets in motion my own purification and comes to the aid of that light which we received from him as a gift from above, in the beginning, and which we darkened and confused by sin.

2.   Hear then, the voice of God, echoing strongly in me, a participant in and leader of these Mysteries, and perhaps also in you: "I am the light of the world."[433] Therefore, "come towards him and be filled with light, and let your faces not be put to shame,"[434] signed as they are with the true light. It is the moment of rebirth: let us be born from above![435] It is the time of new creation: let us take up the first Adam once again; let us not remain what we are, but let us become what we were! "The light shines in the darkness,"[436] in the darkness of this life and of this poor flesh, and is pursued but not captured by the darkness: by the hostile power, I mean, which sprang shamelessly upon the visible Adam, but was defeated when it encountered God.[437] His purpose was that we might put off our garments of darkness and draw near the light, and then become perfect light, begotten of perfect light. Do you see the grace of this day? Do you see the power of this Mystery? Have you not been raised up from the earth? Have you not been placed clearly on high, lifted by our voice and our instruction? You will be placed there more clearly still, if the Word gives a favorable direction to the word I speak!

3.   Surely this is not a kind of legal, shadowy purification, offering us the benefit of simply temporal washing, sprinkling those who participate in it with the ashes of a heifer?[438] Surely it is not the kind of Mystery the Greeks practice? All such rites of initiation, all such mysteries, are falsifications, in my view: the dark invention of demons, the creation of minds controlled by an evil spirit, a practice supported by time and controlled by myth.[439] What they adore as true, they conceal in mythic narrative; yet if they are true, these things must not be called simply stories, but should be proved to be free from shameful content, while if they are false, they should not be admired. The difficulty is that the pagans hold radically opposed views on the same subjects, like children playing in the marketplace or men who are really possessed by evil spirits—not like people in conversation

with men of reason, worshippers of the Word—even if they do express contempt for this contrived and shabby credibility [claimed for the myths].

4. Our Mystery is not a story of the affairs and frauds of Zeus, who once ruled the Cretans as tyrant—even if the Greeks also disapprove; nor is it the song and beat and movements of armed dancers, meant to drown out the god's cries and so help him escape the notice of his hostile father—for it is strange how one who had been swallowed like a stone should whimper like a child![440]

Nor is it like the ritual mutilations, the flute-playing and dancing of the Corybantes, and all the other things people do in the frenzied rites of Rhea, as they initiate themselves and one another into the cult of the mother of the gods—in ways that befit the mother of gods such as these![441] It has no connection with the story of a kidnapped maiden, and Demeter deceived, nor does it introduce any Celes or Triptolemos, or snakes—as Demeter shows herself both active and passive.[442] For I blush to bring this initiation, performed in darkness, to the light of day, or to call something so disgraceful a Mystery. Eleusis knows the story, as do those who have viewed these things wrapped in—and truly worthy of—silence! Nor does it include an androgynous god and a chorus of drunks, an army formed by loose morals, the mindlessness of those Thebans who honor him, and the thunderbolt of Semele, which is worshipped as well.[443] Nor is it the licentious sexual mysteries of Aphrodite, who was born and is honored, they tell us, in a shameful way.[444] Nor is it a matter of phallic and ithyphallic dancers, disgusting both in appearance and in fact. Nor is it the killing of strangers, as practiced by the Taurians,[445] or the altars in Sparta sprinkled with the blood of teenage boys, lacerated by whips in order—so perversely!—to make them men: and all of this to honor a god who is a virgin![446] The same worshippers, apparently, were attempting to honor her gentleness and worship her brashness!

5. And where will you place the butchering of Pelops to serve a meal to hungry gods—a nasty and inhuman sort of hospitality?[447] Where are the dark and frightening phantoms of Hecate, or the childish shows and oracles of Trophonius, or the silly ramblings from the oak of Dodona, or the trickeries of the Delphic tripod, or the prophetic drink of Castalia?[448] The one thing these oracles never prophesied was their own future silence![449] Nor is it the sacrificial prophecy of the Magi, drawn from their cutting of the victim, or Chaldaean calculations of stars and birthdays, which bring our movements into harmony with those of the heavens, although they cannot know what they themselves are or will become![450] Nor is it the orgies of Thrace, where religion is supposed to have originated,[451] nor the rites and mysteries of Orpheus, whose wisdom the Greeks so venerated that they ascribe to him the origin of the lyre, which draws all things into harmony

by its notes.[452] Nor is it the just punishment of Mithras, directed against those who allow themselves to be initiated into such things;[453] nor is it the wounding of Osiris, another misfortune honored among the Egyptians;[454] nor is it the trials of Isis and the goats venerated by the Mendesians[455] or the manger of Apis, that calf who feasts on the foolishness of the people of Memphis,[456] nor any of the honors by which they insult the Nile, which gives them fruitfulness (as their own hymns admit), raises the wheat high, and lets them measure the depth of their prosperity by the cubit.[457]

6.   I will not even mention honors paid to snakes and wild animals—the general competition in disgrace, in which each initiation and festival has its own character, but all share in diabolical inspiration. So that if it were indeed necessary for them to commit sacrilege and "fall short of the glory of God,"[458] being led to fall down before idols and the works of human craftsmanship, things formed by hand, those in their right mind would not wish anything else for them but to go on worshipping and honoring these things, "so that they might receive the recompense due to their error,"[459] as Paul puts it, precisely in the objects of their religion. They do not so much pay honor to these objects of worship themselves, as receive dishonor from them. They are disgusting because of their error, still more disgusting in the vileness of what they worship and revere; as a result, they are even more lacking in perception than the idols they worship,[460] surpassing what they adore in mindlessness to the same degree as their gods surpass them in worthlessness!

7.   Let the children of Greece, then, play these games with the demons, from whom their foolishness comes! It is the demons who wrested God's honor away for themselves,[461] dividing Greek society up, in various ways, into shameful opinions and fantasies. Even after they drove us away from the tree of life, through our sharing in the tree of knowledge at the wrong time and in the wrong way, they have attacked us in our present weakness, taking captive the mind that should rule us, and opening the door to our passions. Being themselves a naturally jealous and hateful race[462]—or rather, becoming such through their own wickedness—they could not bear that lower creatures should share in higher blessings, since they themselves had fallen to earth from above, nor could they endure such a transformation of glory and of their original natures. These are the grounds for their persecution of the human creature, these the reasons why the image of God has been brought into contempt; and because we did not see fit to keep the command, we were handed over to a pattern of deviation that continues on its own. As we wandered further from God, we were led into dishonor by the very things we venerated. For the strange part is not just that we who were made for good works, in order to glorify and praise our maker and (as far as possible) imitate God, should become the base of

operations for every kind of passion, which perversely feed on us and eat up the very person we inwardly are; it is also that we have set up gods as advocates for these passions, so that sin might not just go unpunished, but might be thought divine, since it takes its refuge in precisely this kind of excuse: the gods it worships.

8.   Since, then, we have been given the gift of escaping from superstitious error, of living in the company of truth and serving the true and living God,[463] of ascending above creation, moving beyond the limits of all that stands subject to time and the primordial motion, let us consider what concerns God and divine things, and let us speculate[464] about them. And let us begin our speculation where it is best to begin: that is where Solomon commands us to begin, when he says, "As a beginning of wisdom, acquire wisdom for yourself!"[465] To what is he referring, in speaking of "the beginning of wisdom"? Fear![466]

For one ought not to begin with contemplation and then finish in fear—after all, a free-wheeling kind of contemplation might push you over the cliff! Rather, being instructed in fear, cleansed and (one might even say) lightened by it, one should then be lifted on high. Where there is fear, there is observation of the commandments; where the commandments are observed, there is a cleansing of the flesh, that cloud that blocks the soul's vision and keeps it from seeing clearly the rays of divine illumination; but where there is cleansing, there is also illumination, and illumination is the fulfillment of desire for those eager to share in the greatest things—or in the greatest Thing, or in That which is beyond the great![467]

9.   For this reason, one must first purify oneself,[468] then associate oneself with what is pure, if we are not to undergo what Israel experienced, when it was unable to bear the glory shining on Moses' face, and so demanded a veil;[469] or what Manoah experienced, when he said, after seeing a vision of God, "We are lost, woman—we have seen God!"[470] Nor should we, like Peter, ask Jesus to leave our boat, because we are unworthy of his presence.[471] And when I mention Peter, whom am I talking about? The one who walked on the waves![472] Nor should we, like Paul, let our vision be blinded, before we are purified from our acts of persecution by contact with the one we persecuted, or rather, by a brief, shining glimpse of the great light.[473] Nor should we, like the centurion, seek healing but not receive the healer into our house, through praiseworthy timidity.[474] As long as one is yet unpurified and still a centurion—in charge, that is, of many who live in vice, and serving in the army of Caesar, the world-ruler of those who creep along on this earth—any of us may well say: "I am not worthy that you should come under my roof."[475] But when he glimpses Jesus, even though he is small in spiritual stature, as Zacchaeus was, and when he climbs up the sycamore, "putting to death his earthy members"[476] and ascending beyond "the body

of our lowliness,"[477] then let him receive the Word as guest and hear, "Today salvation has come to this house;"[478] and let him accept salvation and bear more perfect fruit, scattering abroad to share, for a good purpose, what he has wrongly acquired as a tax-collector.

10.   For it is the same Word, fearful because of his nature to the unworthy, accessible because of his kindness to those converted in the way we have described, who have driven the unclean, material spirit from their souls and have "swept and adorned"[479] their souls by deep knowledge,[480] not leaving them idle or inactive lest they be captured again, with greater planning, by the seven spirits of evil, whose number matches that of the virtues[481]—for whatever is harder to conquer is all the more worth a struggle! These converted souls work to acquire virtue, after putting evil to flight, and bring Christ to dwell within them, either whole and entire or as much as they can, so that the power of evil might not encounter emptiness and fill it again with itself, "and the last state become worse than the first"[482] because of the greater intensity of the attack, and the greater ease of defending it against recapture. But when we "guard our soul with all vigilance"[483] and "build upward paths in the heart,"[484] "breaking up our fallow ground anew"[485] and "sowing the seeds of righteousness,"[486] as Solomon and David and Jeremiah advise us to do, and so enkindle within ourselves the light of knowledge—at that point, let us begin to utter God's wisdom, which is hidden in Mystery, and let us shine forth this light on others. Until then, however, let us first purify ourselves, and be initiated into the Word, so that we may do as much good to ourselves as possible, forming ourselves in God's image and receiving the Word when he comes—not only receiving him, in fact, but holding on to him and revealing him to others.

11.   Since we have cleansed this theatre of ours[487] by the Word, come, let us speculate[488] now about the feast, and let us celebrate it along with those souls who love festivals, and love God. And because the heart of any feast is godly recollection, let us remember God! For I believe that the ringing echo of those feasting there, in "the dwelling-place of all who rejoice,"[489] is nothing other than this: God, praised and glorified by the people found worthy to live in his city. And if this present discourse contains anything of what I have said before,[490] no one should be surprised. I shall not only say the same words, but shall speak of the same things, trembling in tongue and in mind when I utter words about God, and praying that you, too, may experience this same laudable and blessed feeling. And when I speak of God, let yourselves be surrounded with a flash of that light which is both one and three: three in properties, or indeed in hypostases, if one wants to call them that, or indeed in "persons"—for we will not become involved in a battle over names, as long as the syllables point towards the same notion— and one with regard to the concept of substance, or indeed divinity.[491] It is

divided without division, if I may put it that way, and is joined together in the midst of distinction. The divinity is one in three, and the three are one—those three in whom the divinity exists, or to put it more accurately, who are the divinity. Let us leave out the approaches of excess or of deficit, not turning unity into confusion or distinction into complete separation. Let Sabellius's aggregation and Arius's alienation be equally far from us— diametrically opposed evils, equal in their impiety. For why should we either make God coalesce into an unholy mass, or cut him into unequal pieces?

12. "For us there is one God, the Father, from whom are all things, and one Lord Jesus Christ, through whom are all things,"[492] and one Holy Spirit, in whom are all things.[493] The phrases "from whom" and "through whom" and "in whom" do not divide natures—for then there could be no change of prepositions or of the order of the words[494]—but rather express the peculiar characteristics of one unconfused nature. This is clear from the fact that they are, in another context, applied to only one, if one reads with full attention that other passage in the same Apostle: "From him and through him and to him are all things; to him be glory for the ages. Amen."[495] The Father is Father and without beginning, for he is from no one. The Son is Son and not without beginning, for he is from the Father. If you understand "beginning" in the sense of time, however, he too is without beginning; for he is the maker of all time, not subject to time. The Holy Spirit is truly Spirit, coming forth from the Father, but not in the manner of a son or by generation, but by procession (if one must create new terminology for the sake of clarity). The Father does not cease from his unbegottenness because he has begotten, nor the Son from his begottenness because he is from the Unbegotten—how could that be?—nor does the Spirit change into either a Father or a Son, because he has proceeded and because he is God, even if that is not acceptable to atheists,[496] for his characteristic property is unalterable.[497] How, after all, could it remain a property if it altered and changed? And those who suggest that "unbegottenness" and "begetting" designate natures of those who are called "God" in an equivocal sense— perhaps they will argue that Adam and Seth are different in nature from each other, for the one is not from flesh, but was a formation of God, while the other was from Adam and Eve! There is one God, then, in three, and the three are one, as we have said.

13. Since these things—or rather this reality—is so, it was necessary that adoration not be confined to creatures in the upper world, but that there should be some worshippers down here as well, so that all things might be filled with the glory of God,[498] since all belongs to God; therefore, the human person was created, and given the honor of being made by the hand of God, in his image.[499] And when humans were wretchedly separated from God their maker, by the envy of the devil and the bitter taste of sin, it

was not God's way to ignore them. What happened? And what is the great Mystery that involves us? Natures are made anew; God becomes human; the one who "rides on the heaven of heavens in the sunrise"[500] of his own proper glory and splendor, is glorified in the sunset of our ordinariness and lowliness, and the Son of God allows himself to become and to be called Son of Man: not changing what he was—for he is changeless—but taking on what he was not—for he loves the human race—so that the incomprehensible one might be comprehended, associating with us through the medium of flesh as through a veil, since it was not proper to a nature subject to growth and decay to bear his deity in its pure form.[501]

For this reason, what could not be mixed has been mixed: not simply God and change, not simply mind and flesh, not simply the timeless one and time, not simply the uncircumscribed and measured limit, but also birth and virginity, dishonor with the one who is higher than all honor, impassible being with suffering, immortal substance with decay. For since that clever salesman for evil[502] thought he was invincible, deceiving us with the hope of being gods,[503] he is himself deceived by the screen of flesh, and thinking he was attacking Adam, he encountered God. In this way the new Adam succeeded in saving the old Adam, and put an end to the condemnation of the flesh; death, in that flesh, was put to death.[504]

14.   We have already celebrated suitably on the feast of his birth—I, the leader of the festivities, and you, and all creatures in this world and the world above.[505] We ran with the star, we paid homage with the Magi, we were surrounded by light with the shepherds, we sang his glory with the angels.[506] With Symeon we have taken him in our arms, with Anna the wise old woman, we have given voice to our thanks. And thanks to him, who has "come to his own"[507] in foreign guise, for giving glory to the stranger![508] Now, however, there is a different action of Christ, a different Mystery. I cannot restrain my joy; I have become inspired! Like John, I proclaim good news—if not as forerunner, yet at least as one from the desert![509]

Christ is full of light: let us shine with him![510] Christ is baptized: let us go down with him, that we may rise up with him! Jesus is baptized—is that all? Or must we carefully observe the other details? Who is he? By whom is he baptized? And when? He is the pure one, baptized by John, as he begins his signs. What should we learn? How shall we be formed by this? We must be taught to be purified first, to be lowly in our thinking, to proclaim the Gospel in the fullness of our spiritual and bodily maturity.[511] The first of these messages is addressed to those who rush headlong to baptism and have not prepared themselves well beforehand, or assured the security of their redemption through good moral habits. For if the gift of God means the forgiveness of all that is past—and that is a gift!—then the gift now demands care from us all the more, lest we "return to the same vomit."[512]

The second message[513] is for those who rebel against the stewards of the Mystery, if they attain some eminence in rank. The third message[514] is for those who trust rashly in their youth, and think that any moment in life is the right one to become a teacher, and to take a position of responsibility in the community. Jesus is cleansed—and do you look down on this cleansing? He is cleansed by John—and do you struggle against the authority of your herald? He was thirty years old—and are you teaching your elders, even before your beard is grown? Do you think you can teach them, without perhaps gaining the respect that comes from maturity or manners? In reply, of course, the example of Daniel, or some young judge or another, is on your lips. Everyone who misbehaves always has a ready excuse! But the exceptional situation is not the Church's law, just as "one swallow does not make a spring,"[515] or one diagram a geometer, or one voyage a sailor!

15.   In any case, John baptizes; Jesus goes up to him—perhaps in order to sanctify the baptizer, but clearly in order to bury the whole of the old Adam in the water.[516] But first of all, and for both their sakes, he goes up to sanctify the Jordan: as he was both spirit and flesh, he makes us perfect by the Spirit and water. The Baptist does not receive him, and Jesus puts up resistance: "I need to be baptized by you,"[517] the lamp says to the sun,[518] the voice[519] to the Word, the friend to the Bridegroom,[520] the one "above all those born of woman"[521] to the First-born of all creation,[522] the one who leaped in the womb to the one adored in the womb, the forerunner who will go before him [in death] to the one who has appeared and will appear [in glory]. "I need to be baptized by you"—and add, "for your sake"! For he knew he was to be baptized in a martyr's death—or, as Peter knew, that he would not only be purified in the feet. "And do you come to me?"[523] This, too, is prophetic. For he knew that after Herod, Pilate would begin to rage, and that Christ would follow the way that John had first walked.

And what does Jesus say? "Let it be so for now."[524] For this is the plan of salvation. He knew, after all, that after a while he would himself baptize the Baptist. And what is the "winnowing-fan"?[525] Purification. What is the "fire"?[526] The consumption of chaff, the boiling heat of the Spirit. What is the "axe"?[527] The surgical removal of the soul that is incurable, its being cast on the dungheap. What is the "sword"?[528] The cutting edge of the Word, which divides worse from better and separates the faithful and the unfaithful person, and stirs up son and daughter and bride against father and mother and mother-in-law[529]—in other words, what is new and fresh against what is old and shadowy. And what is the "thong of the sandal," which you, the one baptizing Jesus, do not loosen[530]—you who lived without food in the desert, the new Elijah, the one who is "more than a prophet"[531] because you knew the one prophesied; you who link the Old Testament with the New? What does this "thong" mean? Perhaps it is the explanation of his dwelling among us in the flesh, of which even the tip is hard to unravel—not just for those still bound in the flesh, still infants in Christ, but even for those full of the Spirit, as John was!

16.   But now Jesus comes up out of the water.[532] He brings the world up with him, and sees the heavens split open,[533] which Adam caused to be closed for himself and those who came after him, just as paradise was closed by a flaming sword.[534] And the Spirit bears witness to his divinity (for he comes to support the one like him); so does the voice from heaven (for the one to whom it bears witness comes from there); and the Spirit descends like a dove (for he pays honor to his body—since this, too, is God by divinization—by being seen himself in bodily form). It is true, too, that a dove has long been accustomed to proclaim the good news of the end of a flood.[535] If you judge divinity by measures and weights, and for this reason think that the Spirit is something small because he appears as a dove—you who think small thoughts about the greatest things—you are on the verge of disparaging the Kingdom of heaven, since it has been likened to a mustard-seed, and of exalting the Enemy above the greatness of Jesus, because he is called "great mountain"[536] and Leviathan[537] and "king of those in the waters,"[538] while Christ is called a "lamb"[539] and a "pearl"[540] and a "raindrop"[541] and names such as this.

17.   Since our feast celebrates a baptism, and since we must suffer some small adversities for him who took on our form[542] and was baptized and crucified, come—let us speculate a bit on the difference between baptisms, that we may go from here in a purified state. Moses baptized, but in water;[543] and before that, in the cloud and in the sea.[544] This was by way of figure, as Paul also realized.[545] The Sea was a type of the water; the cloud, of the Spirit, the manna, of the bread of life; the drink, of the drink given by God.[546] John baptized, but not in the Jewish fashion, for it was not only in water, but aimed at conversion; but it was not completely spiritual, for he does not add the phrase, "in the Spirit."[547] Jesus also baptizes, but in the Spirit; the Spirit is baptism's perfect completion! And how can he [i.e., the Spirit] not be God—if I might add a little speculation on the side—if you become God by his gift?[548] And I know of a fourth kind of baptism: that conferred by witness and blood, by which Christ himself was baptized; it is all the more venerable than the other kinds, since it is not soiled by further stains. And I know of a fifth kind, too: the baptism of tears. This is more laborious, since the one baptized "washes his bed and his mattress each night with his tears;"[549] even "the wounds of his sin smell offensive to him;"[550] he goes forward in grief and "with a sad face;"[551] he imitates the conversion of Manasseh,[552] and the self-abasement of the Ninevites, which moved God to mercy;[553] he speaks with the words of the tax-collector in the temple, and is found righteous before the boasting Pharisee;[554] he bows to the ground

like the Canaanite woman, and seeks crumbs of compassion, the food of a famished dog.[555]

18.   I confess to being a human being, a changeable animal with a nature always in flux; I accept this gift eagerly, and adore the one who has given it, and I share it with others; I pronounce mercy [on others] before receiving it myself. I know that I, too, am "beset by weakness,"[556] and that I will receive "in the measure with which I measure."[557] And what do you say? Why are you laying down the law, O modern Pharisee, pure in title but not in behavior, blustering to us the propaganda of Novatus,[558] with the same weakness of argument? Will you not accept conversion? Do you leave no place for lamentation? Will you not shed a tear for tears? May you never come upon such a judge yourself! Do you not reverence the compassion of Jesus, who "took up our weaknesses and bore our ills,"[559] who "came not to the righteous but to sinners" for their conversion,[560] who "wished mercy rather than sacrifice,"[561] who pardons sins "seventy times seven times"?[562] How blessed your haughtiness is, if it is pure and not just puffery, as you lay down laws for your fellow humans, and destroy correction by refusing to recognize it! One evil is like the other: leniency that applies no restraints, and condemnation without any concessions. The first lets go of the rein altogether, the second holds it much too tightly. Show me your purity of life, and I will accept your harsh attitude. But as it is, I fear that while bursting with wounds yourself, you charge others with being incurable. Will you refuse to accept David in his spirit of conversion, although conversion preserved in him the gift of prophecy?[563] Or the great Peter, who suffered human pangs concerning the suffering of the Savior? Jesus received him, and by his threefold questioning and Peter's threefold confession healed his threefold denial.[564]

Will you not accept someone made perfect by the shedding of blood? That, too, is part of your foolishness! Will you not accept the Corinthian who has transgressed the law?[565] Paul confirmed the force of love, when he said that he had mended his ways; and the reason he gave was "that such a person might not be overwhelmed by excessive grief,"[566] weighed down by measureless blame. Will you not permit young widows to marry, because their age lets them easily be abused? Paul was bold enough to do this,[567] though you, it seems, are his teacher—as if you had gone on beyond him to the fourth heaven, and found another Paradise, and heard yet more unspeakable mysteries,[568] and embraced yet a wider circle by the power of the Gospel!

19.   But, the Novatianist says, this is not possible after baptism. What is the proof of this? Either show me, or do not condemn! If the case is in doubt, let compassion win the day! But Novatus would not receive such people, he says—those who had lapsed in persecution. What does that mean?

If they had not repented, he was right; I also do not receive those who will not bow their heads—or at least not in a worthy way—and who make no redress for evil by correction; and when I do receive them, I allot them the appropriate place.[569] But if it is a question of those consumed by tears, I shall not imitate Novatus! Why should the inhumanity of Novatus be a law for me? He did not curb his greed, that second form of idolatry, yet condemned sexual immorality as if he himself was without flesh or body. What do you say? Do we persuade you with these arguments? Come, stand with us who are human beings. "Let us magnify the Lord together!"[570] Let none of you dare to say, even if he has enormous confidence in himself, "Do not touch me, for I am pure,"[571] and who else is there like me? Share with us, too, something of your splendor! Or do we not persuade you? Then we will weep for you, too.

If they wish, these people may follow our way and the way of Christ; but if not, let them pursue their own path. Perhaps in the next world they will be baptized with fire, that final baptism, greater and more severe, which will consume matter like straw, and annihilate the insubstantiality of all that is evil.[572]

20.   But for ourselves, let us honor Christ's baptism today and keep an honorable feast—not indulging our belly, but rejoicing spiritually. How shall we feast ourselves? "Be washed, make yourselves pure."[573] If you are purple in sin, yet still less than the color of blood, "you shall be white as snow;"[574] and if you are scarlet, complete "men of blood,"[575] even you shall reach the whiteness of wool.[576] Be completely purified, and you shall be pure, since God rejoices in nothing so much as in the correction and salvation of a human being, on whose behalf is all our speech, and all this Mystery. It is so that "you may become as lights in this world,"[577] a living force for other men and women, so that as perfect lights you may stand with the great light, and in his presence be initiated into the Mystery of light,[578] illuminated yet more purely and clearly by the Trinity, of which you have now received, in modest measure, this one ray of the one divinity, in Christ Jesus our Lord, to whom be glory for the ages of ages. Amen.

7. ORATION 42: *THE FAREWELL ADDRESS*

The Farewell Address, Oration 42, is presented in Gregory's corpus as his valedictory in Constantinople, addressed to his fellow bishops assembled for the Council of 381, to his faithful congregation, to court officials, and even to those representatives of other parties in the imperial capital who had opposed his leadership. Some manuscripts add to the title "Farewell Discourse" (συντακτήριος—a term for the rhetorical genre of the valedictory) the information that "it was delivered in the Martyrium of Saint Anastasia in Constantinople"—apparently confusing the name of the oratory in which Gregory's Nicene community had gathered with the later shrine of St. Anastasia Pharmakolytria.[579] Still more manuscripts specify that it was "spoken in the presence of the 150 bishops" (i.e., at a session of the Council of Constantinople in June 381). It seems unlikely, however, that the piece was directly addressed in its present form to all these groups at once, and Jean Bernardi has argued persuasively that Gregory at least reworked it heavily in his Cappadocian retreat sometime after his retirement in July 381.[580] It is one of Gregory's most eloquent and moving reflections on his own career and his sense of vocation: a defense against charges of ineptitude in his pastoral ministry in Constantinople—with occasional echoes of Plato's *Apology of Socrates*—as well as a reflection on the responsibility of bishops in a time of turbulent theological debate, a triumphant announcement of the rehabilitation of the Nicene community in the Eastern capital, and a summary (in Chapters 14–17) of the Trinitarian understanding of the faith that Gregory constantly presents as the central burden of his preaching. Towards the end of the work, Gregory's critique of the contentiousness and cultural airs of the citizens of Constantinople becomes increasingly ironic as he continues to contrast them with his own simple, "philosophic" lifestyle. Yet, his final farewells to the liturgical and architectural surroundings in which he has served the Church there, and to those faithful who have continually supported him, have, for all their bitterness, a touching ring of sincere regret for the brevity and mixed success of his ministry.

Oration 42: *Farewell Address* [581]

1. What do you make of our plight, dear shepherds and colleagues—you whose "feet are beautiful," as you "proclaim peace" and the "good news" with which you have come?[582] Your feet are beautiful also in our eyes, since you have come just in time for us: not to rescue a wandering sheep, but to care for a shepherd[583] who is, like you, a wanderer far from home. What do you make of our exile, and what fruit do you think has come of it—or better, what is the fruit of the Spirit within us, by whom we are always stirred, and remain stirred even now? For we do not desire to possess anything as our own, and perhaps we have nothing to claim.[584] Do you already understand our situation for yourselves? Have you made up your minds? Are you friendly auditors of our accounts? Or must we, like those whose performance as a general or a civil leader, or a manager of funds, is subject to investigation, ourselves provide a public accounting to you of our time in office? We are not ashamed to be put on trial, after all, since we, for our part, will pass judgment as well—all of us in the same spirit of charity!

It is an old custom. Paul, too, shared his Gospel with the Apostles,[585] not in a spirit of competition, as he makes clear in what he writes about himself— for the Spirit keeps far away from competitiveness—but so that what was correct might be confirmed, and what was defective might be corrected, if indeed anything of that kind could be discovered in what he was saying and doing. For "the spirits of prophets are subject to prophets,"[586] according to the good ordering of the Spirit, who manages and distributes all things for the best. And if Paul gave his account privately and only before a few, but I do so publicly and before all, do not let that surprise you. For I crave, even more than he did, to be free from accusations that in some way I seem to have failed in my duty, "lest somehow I should be running or had run in vain."[587] And there is no other possible way to defend myself than by giving a full accounting to you all.

2.   What, then, is our defense?[588] If it is false, refute it; but if it is true, you yourselves must bear witness—you for whose sake, and in whose presence, I speak! For you are my defense, my witnesses, and "the crown of my boasting,"[589] if I, too, may dare to speak in the Apostle's hot-headed style. This flock you see[590]—once it was small and incomplete, as far as visible criteria go; it was not a flock, but some little trace or disorganized leftover of a flock, without bishop and without boundaries, having no safe pasture, no fence to surround it; it was "wandering on the mountains, in dens and caves of the earth,"[591] torn apart and scattered in all directions, sheltered and pastured as well as each sheep could manage for himself, each happily snatching his own safety, however possible; like a flock that "the lions have put to flight,"[592] or the storm has broken up, or darkness has scattered; a flock that the prophets mourn over, comparing it to the sufferings of Israel when she was handed over to the Gentiles, and that we have mourned over, too, just as we have lived in a way worthy of lamentation.[593] For in fact we, too, have been expelled, cast off, scattered onto every mountain and hill, as happens when there is no shepherd;[594] a bad storm has come upon the Church, savage beasts have attacked it; even now, in broad daylight, they do not leave us alone, but they are shameless enough to show their power more openly than one might expect at such a time;[595] a menacing darkness dominates and covers the scene, much more severe than the ninth plague of Egypt—a "palpable darkness"[596] in which, I might almost say, we cannot even see each other!

3.   Let me say something that will arouse your compassion still more, speaking as one who has placed his confidence in a father who has betrayed him. "Abraham did not know us, and Israel did not recognize us, but you are our father,"[597] and we look to you. "Aside from you we have not known anyone; it is your name we call on."[598] Therefore "I will make my case; in fact, I will declare to you my accusations," as Jeremiah says.[599] "We have

become as in the beginning, when you did not rule over us,"[600] and you have forgotten your holy covenant,[601] and have shut up your mercies from us. So we have become a reproach to your beloved one[602]—we who worship the Trinity, who seek our complete refuge in the completeness of the Godhead, and who do not dare drag anything that is above us down to our own level, nor to react so strongly against the tongues of atheists and the enemies of God that we make Lordly power into a fellow-servant![603] We have indeed been handed over to the most wicked and sinful people among all the inhabitants of the earth; and why else, but because of our sins, especially for not walking worthily in the way of your commandments, but following in the path of our wicked thoughts?

The first, Nebuchadnezzar,[604] oppressed us: he followed Christ, then raged against Christ, and hated Christ for the simple reason that he had been saved through him! He chose godless sacrifices instead of the holy Bible. He "devoured me, cut me in pieces, covered me with insubstantial darkness,"[605] to speak my lament without departing from Scripture. "If the Lord had not come to my aid,"[606] and justly turned him over to the hands of sinners, removing him deep into Persia—such are the judgments of God!—and if blood had not been justly shed because of unholy bloodshed,[607] in this one case when justice would not endure to be patient any longer, then "soon my soul would have made its home in the underworld."[608]

The second oppressor was no more kindly than the first; indeed, he was more oppressive, in that he bore the name of Christ.[609] He was a false Christ, both a menace and a reproach to Christians. To act with him was to deny God; yet to suffer under him lacked glory, because it seemed to be no injury, nor was the glorious name of martyrdom attached to such suffering. Even in this the truth was stolen from us: suffering for being Christians, we were punished on charges of irreligion!

Alas! We have grown rich in miseries; "fire has consumed the loveliness" of the world.[610] "What the caterpillar has left the grasshopper has eaten, and what the grasshopper has left the rust has consumed, then the locust,"[611] and I know not what comes next—one evil growing onto another! How could one dramatize all the tragic events of our time, or what one might call the taxes now levied upon us—our trial by fire? But, in fact, "we have gone through fire and water"[612] and have come to a place of rest, by the benevolence of God our savior.

4.   But what my train of thought has been urging me to say from the beginning is this: there was a time when this field was tiny and poor—not a field worthy of God, who cultivates the whole world and continues to plant it with the good seeds of piety and holy teachings; not even worthy of a poor farmer of limited and moderate means, as it seems; really not a field at all, not worth storehouses or a threshing floor, perhaps, nor even a sickle,

not worth piles or even handfuls of grain—at best only small, unripe handfuls, such as grow on the housetops, which do not fill the hand of the reaper or invite the blessing of those who pass by.[613] This was how our field was, this was the size of our harvest: great and well-grown and rich to the one who sees in secret,[614] worthy to belong to such a farmer—a harvest with which the inner valleys of souls abound when well farmed by the Word!—yet not recognizable to most people, not gathered in single place, but coming together piece by piece, each like a single stalk in the harvest or a small grape at the vintage, when the whole cluster is no longer there. I think I should also say this, since the time seems right to say it: I found Israel like a watched-for fruit in the desert, like the first or second ripe grape on an unripe vine,[615] a blessing preserved by the Lord, a sacred first-fruit; but still small and scarce, not filling the mouth of one looking for food; "like a signal on a hill, a mast on a mountain-top,"[616] or any other lonely thing not visible to many. Such was the state of our poverty at first, the cause of our dejection.

5.   But from the moment that God spoke—God "who makes poor and makes rich,"[617] "who brings death and gives life,"[618] who makes all things and reshapes them simply by his will, who brings forth day from night,[619] spring from winter, calm from a storm, rain from drought (and all this often through the prayers of one man, long persecuted[620]), who lifts the meek up to the heights and humbles sinners to the ground; from the moment God said to himself, "Behold, I have seen the affliction of Israel"[621] "let them not continue to labor in mud and brick-making," and in saying this, visited them; from the time he then visited and saved his people, and led them out, "with a mighty hand and an outstretched arm,"[622] "by the hand of Moses and Aaron,"[623] his chosen ones—what happened? What wonders were worked? Those that books and living memories report to us! For apart from the miracles that occurred along the way, and this "mighty buzz"[624] that has followed, let me put it most concisely: Joseph went into Egypt as a single person, and six hundred thousand came out of Egypt shortly afterwards. What is more wonderful, or a greater proof of God's generosity, than when he wills to open a way in human affairs where there was no way before? And the land of promise was given as an inheritance through one man who had been hated; the one who was sold sets whole nations free and is established as a great nation himself; one tiny offshoot becomes a luxuriant vine, so large as to spread across rivers and stretch out to the sea, expanding from border to border, to shadow the mountains with the height of its glory, and grow above the cedars[625]—and all of this is the work of God, however one understands these mountains and those cedars!

6.   Such was this flock before; and such is it now: flourishing and spreading. If it is not yet in perfect condition, at least it is making its way

towards perfection step by step, and I prophesy it will continue on that way. This is what the Holy Spirit has foretold to me—if I have any prophetic powers, even when I look to what lies before us. At the same time, I can take confidence both from the past and from a reasonable sense of the future, as one for whom reasoning is second nature. It is much more astonishing, after all, that such a Church should have come into being from what it once was, than that it should go on from its present state to the height of splendor. For the complete process of resurrection, I am convinced, is on the way to a necessary fulfillment, starting from the moment when it began to be restored by the one who gives life to the dead, bone to bone and joint to joint, as the spirit of life and rebirth was bestowed on dry bones.[626]

So "let not those who embitter us be exalted within themselves,"[627] nor let them—like those who try to hold on to a shadow or "the dream of those who are waking,"[628] or the breezes as they blow, or "the tracks of a ship in the water"[629]—think that they have something in their grasp. "Let the pine tree groan, for the cedar has fallen!"[630] Let them be instructed by the misfortunes of others, and learn that "the poor man shall not be forgotten forever,"[631] nor will God restrain himself from "changing course, and cutting off the heads of the mighty," as Habakkuk says[632]—that God who has been cut up and wickedly divided into the source and the one derived from the source, so that even Godhead should be supremely insulted by being brought down to earth, and creation burdened by being given like honors with Godhead![633]

7. I seem to hear, too, the voice of the one who gathers together a scattered people, and who welcomes the oppressed: "'Expand your allotments, spread out again to the right and the left, drive in stakes, do not be stingy with tent-cloth.'[634] I have handed you over, and I will come to your help. 'In a narrow spirit' I struck you, and 'in everlasting mercy' I will give you glory.[635] Great is the measure of my love for humanity—greater than the measure of my chastisement. My earlier actions were due to your wickedness, but these are due to your worship of the Trinity.[636] Those were due to impurity, but these are for the sake of my glory; 'I will glorify those who glorify me,'[637] and 'provoke to jealousy those who so provoke me.'[638] Behold, this is sealed in my presence,[639] and this law of retribution cannot be broken.

"But you build walls around me, and marble slabs and mosaic floors,[640] long colonnades and porticoes; you glitter and shine with gold, spending it like water and gathering it up like sand, forgetting that faith camping in the open is worth more than the richest impiety, and that three people gathered in the name of the Lord[641] are worth more to God than tens of thousands who deny the divinity. Do you value the Canaanites more than Abraham, all by himself? Or the Sodomites more than Lot on his own? Or the

Midianites more than Moses—though all of these were aliens and strangers?[642] What of the three hundred with Gideon, who manfully lapped up the water, while thousands were rejected?[643] What of Abraham's household slaves, a few more than these in number, who pursued and defeated many kings and their armies of thousands of men, few though they were?[644] And how do you understand this passage: 'If the number of the children of Israel should become as the sand of the sea, only a remnant will be saved'?[645] Or this: 'I have left for myself seven thousand men, who have not bent their knees to Baal.'[646] No, this is not the solution—God does not delight in numbers!

8. "You count your tens of thousands, but God counts those who will be saved; you the immeasurable grains of sand, but I the vessels of election.[647] Nothing is so magnificent in God's sight as a purified reason and a soul made perfect by the doctrines of truth. One cannot offer anything to God that is worthy of the one who created all things, from whom are all things and to whom are all things[648]—surely not the work of a single hand or a single person's wealth, but not even if one should wish to honor him by bringing together all human wealth and all human handiwork. '"Do I not fill heaven and earth?," says the Lord.'[649] 'What house will you build for me? What shall be the place of my rest?'[650]

"And since you necessarily fall short of my dignity, I demand of you a second thing: religious reverence, a kind of wealth I share and value along with you, in which the utterly poor man may perhaps surpass the lavishly rich, if he is great of heart. To seek this kind of honor is a matter of good will, not of good fortune. I will indeed receive gifts of this kind from your hands, as you well know. 'Do not continue to trample my courts;'[651] 'the feet of the meek will walk there:'[652] those who have recognized me and my only Son and the Holy Spirit in a sound and upright way. How long will you 'be in possession of my holy mountain?'[653] How long will the ark be held by foreigners?[654] Now, for a little while longer, feast on the goods of others and enjoy yourselves at will; for in the same way that you have chosen to reject me, I, too, will reject you, says the Lord almighty!"[655]

9. I thought I heard God saying this, sensed him doing this, and even crying out, in addition, to this people—a people now grown from small to great, from scattered to well-knit, from a pitiable even to an enviable state: "'Enter through my gates'[656] and spread out! Must you always languish, dwelling in tents, and must your oppressors always rejoice at your expense?" To the angels in charge of us (for I am convinced that different angels stand guard over different Churches, as John teaches me through the Apocalypse), he says, "Make a path for my people, and clear the stones from their way,"[657] so that there might be no stumbling-block[658] or obstacle for the people on God's entrance-way—now leading to a home made by hands, but a little

later to the Jerusalem above,[659] and to the holy of holies there, which I know will mean an end to the present suffering and straining of those on the right way." And you are among them, called to be holy:"[660] "a people of his own possession,"[661] "a royal priesthood,"[662] the Lord's choice portion, a whole river flowing from a single drop,[663] a heavenly lamp[664] lit from one spark, a tree growing from a mustard seed which offers rest to the birds. [665]

10.   These people are our gift to you, dear shepherds![666] We lead them forward; with them as gift, we greet our friends, our guests, our fellow exiles. After searching for the best of our possessions, we have nothing more beautiful to offer you than these people, nothing more splendid— that you may realize that we, too, are strangers, who nevertheless want for nothing, "poor, yet enriching many."[667] If this seems a small, unremarkable thing, I would like to be persuaded of what is greater and more worthy of note! For if it is no great thing to establish and strengthen, by wholesome arguments, a city that is the focal point of the world,[668] the citadel of earth and sea, the meeting-point of the regions of East and West, the city where extreme positions in the faith come together from every direction, and from which they spread forth as from a common marketplace— especially since it hums with so many languages, seemingly from everywhere—then it would be hard to think of anything else great or worthy of concern! But if this sight before you is something worthy of praise and honor—and grant me here the opportunity, also, to pride myself on what has happened—then we ourselves have made some contribution to all that you see.

11.   Life up your eyes and look,[669] everyone who wants to verify my words. See the crown of glory that has been woven, in place of "the hirelings of Ephraim, the crown of contempt."[670] See the council of presbyters, made honorable by grey hair and understanding; the good order of deacons, not far from the Spirit himself; the decorum of lectors; the eagerness of the people to learn—men and women equally, all equally admirable for their virtue. See this among the men, both learned and uneducated, all of them wise in divine things; see it among rulers and ruled, all of whom here are rightly governed; see it among soldiers, among nobles, among intellectuals and those striving to be so. All are soldiers of God—gentle in other respects, but warlike on behalf of the Spirit; all honor the high assembly,[671] to which access is given not by the pedestrian letter but by the life-giving Spirit;[672] all are truly people of reason,[673] and devotees of him who is the Reason of God. Among the women, see how those under the yoke of marriage are bound to God rather than to the flesh, how those not under its yoke and free are wholly consecrated to God. Among the young and among the old, see how the one group walks on the best path towards maturity, while the other makes every effort to remain immortal, renewed by the best of hopes.

12. As far as this crown[674] is concerned ("what I say, I do not say according to the Lord,"[675] yet still I say it), I am one of those who has contributed to its weaving. Part of this is the effect of my words—not words that we have tossed off recklessly, but words spoken with love, not meretricious words (as a certain verbal and moral prostitute has suggested,[676] slandering us), but very sober ones. Part of this is the offspring and fruit of my spirit, in the way only the Spirit can give birth to those who are leaving the body behind.[677] I am sure that my well-wishers among you—perhaps even all of you—will also be my witnesses, since we have cultivated the harvest in all of you. Our reward is simply the confession of faith;[678] we do not seek anything else, nor have we ever sought it. Virtue, after all, has no reward, so that it may remain virtue, its eyes on the good alone.

13. Will you permit me to add something that may sound a little rash? Do you notice that the tongues that opposed us are silent, and that those who make war on the Godhead are quiet in our presence? This, too, is the work of the Spirit; and this, too, is the result of our cultivation. We do not teach in an uncivilized way, we do not pelt our enemies with insults, which is what most people do, fighting not against arguments but against those who propose them; at times, too, they cover over the weakness of their reasoning with invective, like the cuttlefish who, they say, belches forth ink before itself to give its predators the slip, or to hunt without being seen. But we try to show that fighting the war on Christ's behalf consists in fighting as Christ did—the meek one, the peacemaker,[679] who sustains our weaknesses. We do not pursue peace to the detriment of truthful argument, making concessions to gain a reputation of fairness—we do not, in other words, pursue the good by doing evil; but we pursue peace through fighting by the rules, within both our own boundaries and the norms of the Spirit. Here, in any case, is my thinking on these things; I offer this as a rule for all who care for souls and take responsibility for the Word: don't be irritating by your harshness, or encourage arrogance by your submissiveness, but be reasonable[680] concerning the Word, not exceeding good measure in either direction.

14. And since you so wish it, perhaps I should set forth an explanation of the faith itself, as we understand its essence.[681] I shall find my holiness in continually remembering it, and my people here will benefit by rejoicing in teachings such as these, even under the lead of another; and you, too, will come to know whether or not we have been engaged in vain rivalry, competing with some and making advances on others in our exposition of the truth. As with subterranean rivers, some are completely hidden in the depths of the earth, others make a boiling noise in their narrow passages, and promise our ears they will break forth but have yet to do so, while still others have surged up to the surface. So it is with those who speculate[682]

about God (not to speak of complete agnostics). Some cherish a thoroughly secret and hidden piety within themselves. Others are close to giving birth to faith, inasmuch as they avoid impiety, but do not give piety frank expression; they take refuge in this approach either by employing diplomatic words to "manage" their language,[683] or through sheer cowardice. They are sound in their own understanding, they insist, but they do not communicate this healthy doctrine to the people—as if they had been entrusted with the responsibility of leading themselves but no one else. Still others share the treasure publicly, not cramping the birth of true religion, or considering it salvation if they alone are saved and the good never bubbles over to benefit others. May I be counted in this last group, as well as those who with me "dare the good dare" to confess our religion.[684]

15.   There is one concise, public expression of our teaching, a kind of inscription available for all to read: this people! They are authentic worshippers of the Trinity, so much so that any one of them would sooner be separated from this present life than separate one of the three from the Godhead. They think as one, praise as one, are ruled by one doctrine in their relationships to each other, to us, and to the Trinity.

To recount the details briefly: the One without beginning and the Beginning and the One who is with the Beginning are one God. Being without beginning is not the nature of the One without beginning, nor is being unbegotten;[685] for nature is never a designation for what something is not, but for what something is. The affirmation of what is is not the denial of what is not. Nor is the Beginning kept separate from that which is without beginning by the fact that it is a Beginning: for being the Beginning is not his nature, any more than being the One without beginning is the nature of the other. These characteristics "surround" nature, but are not nature. And the One who is with the One without beginning and with the Beginning is not something else than what they are. The name of the One without beginning is "Father," of the Beginning "Son," of the One with the Beginning "Holy Spirit." There is one nature for all three: God. The unity [among them] is the Father, from whom and towards whom everything else is referred, not so as to be mixed together in confusion, but so as to be contained, without time or will or power intervening to divide them. These three have caused us to exist in multiplicity, each of us being in constant tension with ourselves and with everything else. But for them, whose nature is simple and whose existence is the same, the principal characteristic is unity.

16.   Let us abandon the twists and turns and parries of argument that are born of our competitive urge; let us neither indulge a Sabellian love of the One over against the Three, and so destroy all distinction by a false conjunction, nor take an Arian delight in the Three over against the One,

and subvert unity by malicious separation. For we do not seek to exchange evil for evil; we wish only not to miss the good. These theories are the games the Evil One plays, maliciously swaying our opinions to and fro. But we walk the middle, royal road,[686] where the experts tell us the pursuit of virtue is to be found; we believe in Father and Son and Holy Spirit, beings of the same substance and the same glory, in whom baptism reaches its perfection by word and deed (as anyone who is initiated knows[687]), since it is a denial of atheism and a confession of divinity. So we are put into right order, as we come to know what is one in substance and indivisible adoration, and what is three in hypostases or persons—whichever you prefer. Let not those who bicker about these things disgrace themselves, as if true religion lay for us in names rather than in realities. For what are you saying, you who introduce the language of three "hypostases"? Surely you do not understand three essences by such words?[688] I know you cry out loudly against those who suppose such an understanding, for you teach a doctrine of one and the same essence shared by the Three. And what about the "persons"?[689] Surely you are not putting together some composite thing, a unit of three characters,[690] something completely anthropomorphic? Surely not, you cry, nor does the word "person," whatever it means, represent God in this way. What, then, do the "hypostases" or "persons" mean for you? (For I will continue to engage you in dialogue!) "Their being three signifies that they are distinguished not in natures, but in characteristics." Excellent! How could one agree with you more, or say the same thing, without sharing this conviction, even if one were to differ in terminology? Do you see what kind of umpire I am for you—moving away from the letter and towards the sense, just as one does with the Old Testament and the New!

17.   But return with me once more to the same point. Let us speak and think of the Unbegotten and the Begotten and the One who Proceeds, if you will agree to let me coin some words. We no longer fear that the incorporeal will be understood in a corporeal way, as those who speak abusively of the divinity see fit to do. Let us speak of a creature as being "of God"—for that is a great thing when said of us, after all!—but never as being God.[691] Only then will I accept that a creature is God, when I too may literally become God! This is the point: if something is God, it is not a creature, for the creature is classed with us, who are not gods. But if it is a creature, it is not God, for it began in time. And of what had a beginning there was, when it was not![692] And if its non-being is older than its being, that thing does not have being in the proper sense. But if something does not have being in the proper sense, how is it God?[693] So then, no one of the Three is a creature, nor—still worse—did any of them come into being for my sake: lest it be not merely a creature, but less valuable than we are. For if I exist for God's glory, but this one has come into being for my sake—as the

blacksmith's tongs exist for the sake of the wagon, and the saw for the sake of the door—then I am superior, by being the cause. And to the degree that God is higher than creatures, so much is what has come to be for my sake less worthy than I am, who exist for God's sake.

18.　With this in view, let there be no entry into the Church of God for Moabites and Ammonites[694]—for dialectical, mischievous arguments, which, busying themselves illegitimately with the begetting of God and his ineffable origin, rashly attack the divinity, suggesting that what lies beyond reason must either be accessible to them alone or be non-existent, because they have not been able to comprehend it.[695] We, for our part, follow Holy Scripture; by breaking up the stumbling-blocks that lie in it to trip up the blind, we shall hold on to salvation, and shall dare anything rather than speak out rashly against God. We will leave discussion of the proof-texts to others, since many people have already written about them on many occasions—as have we ourselves, in no trivial effort.[696] At the same time, it would seem to me, at least, a real shame to use this moment to gather together the creedal formulae of those who have professed our faith from of old. For the best order is not first to teach and then to learn—especially when we are dealing with the things of God and subjects similarly great, but not even on other, smaller, less worthy issues. So, too, to solve or rearrange the problems of interpretation in Scripture is not the proper work of the present time, but calls for greater, more perfect concentration than is possible in the thrust of this discussion now at hand.[697] Still this, to put it in a nutshell, is what our own line of argument has been; and I have laid it out here, not in order to do battle against my opponents—for we have already done battle many times, if only with moderate success—but to show you the characteristic shape of my teaching, and to suggest that I am your fellow-combatant, having taken my stand against the same enemies and on behalf of the same causes.

19.　This, gentlemen,[698] is my apologia for my presence here. If it seems worthy of praise, thanks be to God, and to you who have invited me here; if it falls short of what you had hoped for, I am grateful even so—for I am sure it is not completely reprehensible, and I do not lack confidence in the judgment you will express. Did we profit at this people's expense? Were we promoting our own interests—which I see as the motive of so many? Did we cause any sorrow to the Church? Perhaps to others, who believed we had already chosen the solitary life and whom we have opposed outspokenly here—but not at all to you, as far as I am aware. "I have not taken your ox," the great Samuel said to Israel, when he disagreed with them on the matter of a king, "nor have I taken any propitiatory offering for your souls, as the Lord is witness among you."[699] Speaking more broadly, I have not taken anything at all (lest I be forced to enumerate every detail), but I have observed the duties of my priesthood purely and without compromise. And if I have loved power, or a high throne, or walking the courts of kings, may I never possess any other kind of splendor, and may I throw away all I have gained!

20.   What, then, am I saying? I am not an unpaid worker in the virtue industry—I have not reached that high a level of virtue myself![700] Grant me the reward of my labors! And what is that? Not what some, who easily jump to all conclusions, might suppose; but what I, at least, can safely seek. Give me rest from my great labors, show respect for this grey hair of mine, honor the fact that I am a stranger; put someone else in my place, who is ready to be persecuted for your sake, who will have clean hands, who is not without some understanding for language, who will be up to pleasing you in every respect—and to bearing ecclesiastical responsibility with you, since this is the foremost need of the present moment. As for me—see the condition of this body of mine, consumed by time and illness and labor. What use do you have for a timid old man, lacking in courage, dying day by day, as the saying goes, in every way—not only physically but mentally, so much so that I can barely speak these words to you? Do not refuse to believe what your teacher tells you, since you have never disbelieved me before! I have worn myself out under accusations of being too easy-going. I have worn myself out struggling against arguments and ill-will—those of my enemies, and also those of my own supporters. Some strike at you frontally and hit the mark less often; for it is easy enough to guard against open opposition. Others watch your back, and cause more trouble, for the unexpected wound is more likely to be mortal. If I were a steersman, even a very skillful one, and the sea were raging strongly around us and our ship, and the passengers on board were quarreling with each other—each one bickering with the others about something, all clashing against each other and against the waves—how long would I be able to lean against the rudder, fighting the waves and the passengers at the same time, so as to bring the ship to safety through a double storm? If it is difficult, in any event, to achieve the safety of those who struggle on your side, how can one avoid going under when they struggle against you?

21.   Do I need to keep on talking? How, I ask you, shall I wage this holy war? How shall I unify and bring to agreement these bishops, who have taken contrasting positions and use their shepherds' authority against each other, and a people who have been fragmented into opposing factions with them—like adjacent parts of a neighborhood broken by the cracks of earthquakes, or nurses and family-members visited by a plague, each easily catching the sickness from the other? And this is not all. The divisions have affected the whole world as a consequence of these conflicts; East and West are now divided into opposing factions, so that these risk becoming not only names of directions, but of ideologies.[701] How far shall we go with

"mine" and "yours," "old" and "new," "intellectual" and "spiritual," "noble" and "commoner," "well-supported" and "unsupported" in popular backing? I am ashamed of my years, if I should be labeled with the name of others when I am saved by Christ!

22.   I cannot stand your horse-races, your theatre, and this expensive, overpowering craze for rivalry! We hitch ourselves together and unhitch again, we whinny competitively, we almost seem to beat the air with our hooves as the horses do; we throw dust up to the sky like madmen, and fulfill our own need to be winners in the person of others.[702] We have become bad umpires in the conflict of ambitions, ignorant judges of human affairs. Today we all share a throne and a theological position, if those who have supported us will allow it; tomorrow our thrones and our opinions are in opposition, if the wind blows in the other direction. Along with hatred and friendship, too, go labels; worst of all, we do not scruple to regale the same audience with opposite positions, nor do we hold fast to the same principles when ambition drives us in different directions. These are like changes of tide, shifting currents in the straits!

Just as when lads are playing in the square, it would be extremely undignified, not appropriate to us, to leave our ordinary occupation and join in the game with them—for children's play is not becoming to the mature—so not even if I knew that one position, as others lead or are led this way and that, were better than the rest, would I agree to be part of the team, rather than remaining obscure and free, just as I am.[703] Besides all the issues, this is simply my temperament: on most subjects, I do not agree with the crowd, nor can I endure walking the same path as they do. That may be rash or ignorant, but it is nevertheless the way I habitually feel. The things that others enjoy annoy me, and I delight in what is annoying to others. So that I would not be astonished if I were to be locked up as a trouble-maker, or considered an idiot by the crowd; one of the Greek philosophers of the past is said to have suffered in this way, his temperance accused of being madness because he laughed at everything, and saw the things most people strive for as ludicrous.[704] Or perhaps I will be thought to be "full of new wine,"[705] like the disciples of Christ later on, because they spoke in tongues, and no one realized that this was the power of the Spirit, rather than an abandonment of their senses.

23.   Consider, after all, the charges that are made also against us. "For all the time that you have been in charge of this Church," they say, "with its changing moments of opportunity and changing imperial policies on such an important matter, what change has all this meant for us?[706] How many insults have been offered to us in the past? What dreadful things have we not suffered? Were there not insults? Threats? Exile? Thefts and confiscations of funds? The burning alive of presbyters at sea?[707] Churches

profaned by the blood of the saints, and being used as assembly halls[708] rather than Churches? The public murder of venerable bishops—patriarchs,[709] I should more properly say? Has not every place come to be off limits for the devout—and for them alone? Have we not experienced any dreadful deed one might mention?"

And what have we done in return to the perpetrators of these things, when the power to act changed for the better, and it was incumbent on us to punish the arrogant? I pass over the rest; but to speak of our own experience—lest I try to speak of yours—were we not persecuted? Were we not driven from our Churches, our residences—worst of all, from our very hermitages? Did we not endure a raging crowd, arrogant officials, emperors insulted along with their decrees?[710] And what then? We came to power, and the persecutors fled. In my view, it was sufficient retribution against the criminals to have the power of retaliation.[711] But others did not think this way; they are most meticulous and just when it comes to retribution, and for that reason they demand what the moment allows. "What official," they ask, "has been fined? What crowd has been forced back to sobriety? Which inflammatory rabble-rousers? What fear have we inflicted, for our own benefit and with an eye to the future?"

24.   Perhaps, too, someone will reproach us—indeed, they have already reproached us—with charges such as this: the pretensions of our table, the dignity of our dress, our public appearances, our haughty way of encountering others. I was unaware that we were competing with consuls and prefects and distinguished generals, we who do not have enough space to throw down what we own! Or that we must curb the appetite of our belly—we who feast on the fare of beggars—and that we restrict our use to what is necessary, rather than what is excessive, and pour out the rest on the altars![712] Or that we are drawn by fine horses and lifted high on litters, and parade around in splendor, and are whistled at all over town, so that everyone draws back from us like wild beasts and separate themselves, and that we are conspicuous from afar when we are making our way![713] If crimes such as these occurred, I missed them—forgive me this injury! Appoint someone else who will please the crowd; give me the desert, and rusticity, and God, whom alone I will please by my simplicity of life! It will be dreadful if we are deprived of speeches and conferences and liturgical festivals, and these bursts of applause which lift us up on wings—deprived of servants and friends and honors, and the beauty and grandeur of the city, and the brilliance that shines on us from all directions, giving light to those who look for such things but never turn their gaze within! But it will not be so dreadful as if I should be swallowed up in turbulence, and soiled by the disturbances and agitations among us, and by all the changes of position needed to follow the crowd. They are not seeking priests, but rhetors;[714] not pure hands to offer

sacrifice, but strong hands to hold the reins.[715] And I will say something on their behalf: this is the way we have trained them, by being "all things to all people;"[716] and I do not know whether we have saved all or lost them!

25.   What do you say? Do I persuade you with these arguments? Have I won? Or do I need stronger words to convince you? In the name of that very Trinity which I and you represent, in the name of our common hope and of the stability of this people, grant me this favor. Send me away with prayers; declare the results of the contest; give me my discharge papers as the Emperors do for their soldiers—if you are willing, with a handshake as testimony, so that I may have my honorary bonus! But if not, do as you will—I will raise no objections about it, but wait until God surveys the state of my affairs. Whom shall we install in my place? The Lord will provide himself with a shepherd to rule his flock, just as he "provided a lamb for the burnt offering."[717] This is the one thing I ask: let it be a person who is envied rather than pitied, not someone who gives in to everyone on every subject, but someone who knows how, on occasion, to strike a blow for what is right![718] The one attitude may be the most welcome here on earth, but the other is the most profitable in the life to come. As for you, think about what you will say to send me on my way, and I shall offer you my departing words.[719]

26.   Farewell to you, Anastasia,[720] my synonym for religion! For you were the one who challenged me to speak a word that was still held in contempt; you are the place of our common victory, the new Shiloh, where we first set down the tabernacle after carrying it on our wanderings for forty years in the desert.

And you, great and celebrated temple, our new inheritance: you now receive your greatness from the Word! Formerly you were the place of the Jebusites, but now we have made you Jerusalem![721]

And you, Churches immediately following her in beauty: one by one, you divide up the parts of the city, but join them together like sinews, teaching us how to be neighbors! Given our weakness, it was not we, who now retire, who filled you, but grace working with us.[722]

Farewell, Holy Apostles,[723] my beautiful home away from home: all of you were my teachers of the Truth! And if I have not often celebrated festivals in your midst, perhaps it is because I bear about in my body, for my own good, that Satan your own Paul bore,[724] because of whom I now must leave you.

Farewell, my episcopal throne, that lofty place bringing envy and danger to high priests! Farewell, college of priests[725] honored for reverence and for age, and all the rest who gather around God's holy table of liturgy, near to the God who draws near to us.

Farewell, choirs of Nazirites,[726] harmonious singing of the psalms, night-long vigils, holy virgins, modest women, institutions for widows and orphans, eyes of the poor turned towards God and towards us! Farewell, houses that welcome strangers along with Christ, sheltering even my own weakness![727]

Farewell, lovers of my language: the bustle, the crowds, scribes seen and unseen,[728] this barrier straining under the pressure of those crowding close around the word!

Farewell, kings and palace, and all who gather to wait on the Emperor and his domestic needs: whether or not you are faithful to the king, I do not know, but I do know that most of you are not faithful to God![729] Clap your hands, shout aloud, lift your orator[730] to the skies! The wicked, garrulous tongue you loved has fallen silent. It is not silent altogether—for it will continue to do battle with hand and ink—but for the moment it is silent!

27.   Farewell, great and Christ-loving city! (For I will still witness to the truth, even if my "zeal is not enlightened!"[731] Separation has made me a little kinder!) Draw closer to the truth; change your weapons, late as it is; fear God more than you have been accustomed to do! A change of position has nothing shameful about it, but holding on to evil leads to perdition!

Farewell, East and West, for whose sake and because of whose scheming we are all at war![732] The one who intends to make peace between you will bear witness to how few are willing to imitate me in retiring! Those who withdraw from their episcopal chairs, after all, will not lose God, but will have a throne on high, much loftier and safer than these!

Above all of them, before all of them, I want to cry: farewell, angels, guardians of this Church, of my presence and my departure—if it is true that all our lives are in God's hand! Farewell, my Trinity, my preoccupation and my pride! May you be preserved by these who stand before me, and may you preserve them, my people—for this is my people, even if your providence takes me elsewhere! May I always receive news that you are exalted and magnified, in word and in action!

Children, for my sake "guard what has been entrusted to you;"[733] remember my stoning![734] The grace of our Lord Jesus Christ be with you all! Amen.

8. ORATION 44: *FOR "NEW SUNDAY"*

Although little known to modern Western readers, the brief and beautiful oration *For "New Sunday"* was often quoted by later Patristic writers, and passages from it have been incorporated into the text of vespers for the consecration of a Church in the Greek Orthodox liturgy. According to Archbishop Nicetas of Heraclea (c.1050–after 1117), the chief medieval commentator on Gregory's works, "New Sunday" was the common title in Gregory's day for the Sunday after Easter. Apparently it was also a spring festival in Caesaraea, celebrating the dedication of the shrine of a local martyr, the semi-mythical shepherd St. Mamas, whose actual death was commemorated on September 2. This local feast was the setting for Gregory's oration; some manuscripts even give the fuller, explanatory title, "On 'New Sunday,' and on Spring, and the Martyr Mamas—for on 'New Sunday' his Memory is Celebrated in Caesaraea."

An allusion in the last paragraph to those who may "begrudge" Gregory the opportunity of preaching at this festival is, Nicetas suggests (PG 127.1434A), a playful remark addressed to Basil, to whose Church the martyr "belonged" and who also has left us a sermon in his honor.[735] This would place the date of the sermon sometime before Basil's death on January 1, 379, probably during the time of Gregory's shadowy ministry in Cappadocia as nonresident bishop of Sasima, in the mid-370s, and at the latest before his "flight" to Seleucia in 375. The great French Patristic scholar, Louis Le Nain de Tillemont (1637–1698), suggested that the sermon was, in fact, written after Gregory's return from Constantinople in mid-381, on the rather flimsy grounds that any allusion to Basil's "begrudging" him the opportunity to preach would be unseemly in a friend. Tillemont's suggestion has led to the general assumption that this is Gregory's latest sermon, datable perhaps to 383, when New Sunday fell on April 16, but there is no substantial evidence for this later dating.

In this oration, written for the annual "renewal" (ἐγκαίνια) or commemoration of the dedication of the shrine, Gregory skillfully weaves together the themes of God's renewal of humanity through the death and resurrection of Jesus, the renewal of nature with the coming of spring, and the spiritual renewal of the local faithful made possible by the martyr's feast. Echoes of the Easter liturgy are unmistakable (Chaps. 4–5), but Gregory moves beyond them to sketch out a concise portrait of how the life of a Christian, renewed by the risen Christ, might appear (Chaps. 6–8). The work is a fine example of Gregory's astonishing ability to turn a particular liturgical celebration into an occasion for reflecting profoundly on the broad themes of creation and salvation, and for enchanting his hearers with eloquence and learning.

Oration 44: *For "New Sunday"* [736]

1.   It is an old custom, and a worthy practice, to honor festivals of renewal[737]—or rather, by means of renewal festivals to honor newness, and to do so not once but often, as each revolution of the year brings the same day forward again. We do this, that fine things may not fade away through

time, or grow dim and slip into the abyss of forgetfulness. "The islands are renewed for God," we read in Isaiah[738]—whatever we are to suppose these islands to be! For myself, I think it refers to the Churches, which have now been formed from Gentile peoples, emerging from the bitter sea of unbelief and taking a firm hold, made stable in God.[739] A "bronze wall" is said to be renewed in another Prophet;[740] I think this refers to a solid soul, shining like gold and well constructed for a life of piety. We are commanded to "sing to the Lord a new song:"[741] whether we are those who had been dragged off by sin to a Babylon of perverse associations, and are now brought back, saved, to Jerusalem (and while we could not sing divine music there, in a foreign land, we have begun here a "new song" and a new way of life); or whether we have remained in the virtuous life and are making progress— having already realized some aspects of it, and still realizing others, by the grace of the Holy and renewing Spirit

2.   The tent of witness was dedicated,[742] and very richly—God revealed the design, Bezalel realized it, and Moses set it up.[743] David's kingly power was inaugurated,[744] and not just once, but first of all when he was anointed[745] and later when he was acclaimed.[746] The feast of renovation was celebrated in Jerusalem, "and it was winter"[747]—the winter of infidelity—and Jesus was there, both God and temple: God for eternity, a temple only recently, to be destroyed in one day and raised up again in three,[748] and remaining for all the ages, that I might be saved, renewed[749] from the ancient fall, and become a new creation, formed afresh by a love for humanity such as this. Holy David begged that a clean heart be created in him, and an upright spirit be renewed in his inmost parts:[750] not that he did not have them (for who could have them, if the great David did not?), but that he considered what is always being increased as something new. And why need I speak of more occasions of renewal, since it is easy to declare what the present festival means, and what we celebrate today? Our feast is one of renovation, my brothers and sisters—of renovation! Let us proclaim it over and over in joy. And what is being renewed? Let those who know be our teachers, and those who do not know be renewed in their ability to listen!

3.   There is one light, God: inaccessible, knowing no succession or beginning, never ceasing, never measured, always shining—triply shining![751]—yet few, I think, or less than few, are capable of reflecting on how great it is. And there are secondary lights, shining forth from that first Light: the powers that surround it, the spirits that serve it. But this light around us not only began recently, but is interrupted by night, and itself interrupts night in equal measure; it is entrusted to our sight, it is poured out in the air, it takes the very thing it gives—for it provides sight with the power of seeing, and is the first thing that our eyes see; by bathing visible objects, it gives us access to them.[752] For since God has willed that this

universe, composed of both visible and invisible beings, be put together as the great and marvelous herald of his greatness,[753] he himself is the light for eternal creatures, and there is no other (for why would those who possess the greatest of lights need a second one?); but for lower creatures—those all around us—he caused the power of this light to shine forth, first of all. For it was fitting that the Great Light begin the work of creation with light, by which he destroyed the darkness, along with the disorder and confusion that had prevailed until then.[754]

4.   He did not display this light at the beginning, in my opinion, through some instrument like the sun. It was disembodied, unconnected with a sun; only later was the sun given the work of shedding light on the whole world. For while, in the case of other creatures, he brought matter into being first and created form later, limiting each thing by order and shape and size, in this case—to work a still greater wonder—he caused the form to exist before the matter (for light is the form of the sun), and after this added the matter, creating the sun as the shining eye of day.[755] So one thing is numbered first in the list of days, another second and third and so on, until we reach the seventh day, which brings work to an end. The events of creation are divided up by these days, ordered in accord with God's ineffable reasons, and not attributed all at once to the omnipotent Word, to whom merely thinking or speaking is a work completed.

And if the human creature is mentioned last of all, and honored by reference to the hand and the image of God,[756] this should not surprise us. For the palace had to exist before the king, so that the king might be led in surrounded by all his attendants.[757] If we had remained, then, what we were, and had kept the command, we would have become what we were not, having access to the tree of life as well as the tree of knowledge. And what would we have become? We would have been made immortal, and have drawn near to God. But since, by the envy of the Evil One, death came into the world and took man captive by deceit,[758] God has come to suffer in the way we suffer, by becoming human, and has endured the poverty of being constituted as flesh,[759] "so that we might become rich by his poverty."[760] From this came death, burial and resurrection; and from them, new creation, and festival after festival. So here I am feasting again, celebrating the renewal of my own salvation!

5.   "What is the point?" someone may ask. "Was not the First Sunday[761] the feast of our renewal—the day after that holy night made bright by our candles? Why are you proclaiming it today? Are you simply a lover of festivals, inventing a multiplicity of splendid occasions?" Last Sunday was the day of salvation, but today is salvation's anniversary.[762] Last Sunday revealed the boundary between the grave and the resurrection, but today reveals, in all its clarity, our second beginning. So just as the first creation has its beginning

on a Sunday (and that is clear: for the seventh day after it is the Sabbath, which brings cessation from work), so the new creation must begin again with the same day: the first of the days that come after it, the eighth of those that come before, more exalted than what has been exalted before, more wonderful than previous wonders. For it refers to the state of things that lies beyond us, which holy Solomon seems to hint at when he commands that we "give a portion to seven"—that is, to this life—"or even to eight"[763]— that is, to the life to come—on the basis of our good works in this life and of the restoration of all things in the next. The great David, too, seems to be addressing his Psalms "on the eighth"[764] to this same hope, just as he labels another Psalm, which we use on this day of dedication and renewal, "a song for the dedication of the Temple."[765] That is what we are: we have been found worthy to be, to be called, and someday to become, "the temple of God."[766]

6.   Now you have the explanation of this day of renewal. So be renewed! "Put off the old man, and walk in the newness of life."[767] Put restraints on everything that is a source of death, train all your members, develop a hatred for all the evil fruit of the tree, or vomit it up again; let us only remember the old ways, that we might flee from them.[768] That fruit that brought me death was "lovely to look at and good to eat;"[769] let us flee from beautiful colors, and look only to ourselves! Do not allow a lust for beauty to overcome you. Do not become a captive of your eyes—not even, if possible, of a fleeting glance; think of Eve, of the lure of that delicious fruit, of the costly remedy. For how can the desire of another save a person, whose own desires have destroyed him?[770] Let not your throat become your garden of delights, where everything offered to you is simply swallowed up—precious before you consume it, but only dishonored afterwards. Does your sense of smell make you soft? Flee from fragrant things! Are you weakened by the sense of touch? Put away things that are smooth and soft! Has your hearing led you astray? Close the door on deceptive and elaborate words; open your mouth for the word of God, that you may breathe the Spirit—do not inhale death! If any of these forbidden things allure you, remember who you are, and how far you have fallen. If you turn aside from reason even a little way, return to yourself before you fall away completely and are swept towards death! Let your old person become new! Celebrate the renewal of your soul!

7.   Let your anger be directed only against the serpent, through whom you first fell. Let your yearning be only for God, not for any other thing, which can only betray and deceive you. Give your reason first place, before all else; do not allow your better faculty to be dragged down by what is worse. Do not hate—and gratuitously, at that—your brother or sister for whom Christ died; Christ, who is God and Lord, became your brother, too. Do not harbor grudges against the upright person—you who were the

object of a grudge, and were persuaded that God was grudging towards you, and so were made to fall.[771] Do not despise tears—you who have suffered things worthy of many tears, and who then received mercy. Do not send a poor person away—you who have been enriched by divinity; and if you cannot be generous, at least do not grow rich at the expense of the poor, for even that is a great deal to ask from people of insatiable appetite. Do not show disrespect towards the stranger—you for whom Christ became a stranger when we were all strangers and aliens to him, lest you be estranged from Paradise as in the beginning. Share your roof and your walls and your food with the person in need, since you have these things in abundance, far beyond your own need. Do not love wealth, unless it is a way of helping the poor. Forgive, for you have been forgiven; have mercy, because you have received mercy; earn kindness with kindness, while there is still time. Let your whole life, the whole way that you walk each day, be renewed!

8.   You who share the yoke of marriage, give something to God as well: for you have been made his partners. You who are virgins, give everything to God: for you have been left free. Do not become thieves of the pleasure that enslaves you, running away from your liberty by living with men who are not your husbands, but are your partners nonetheless.[772] I cannot endure the lingering disease of these hints of sensual pleasure—I loathe even airy forms of intercourse!

Men of power, fear the one who is more powerful than you; you who sit high on your thrones, fear the one who sits higher still! Do not wonder at anything that does not endure, nor overlook what does. Do not hang closely on anything that dissolves when it is grasped too tightly. Do not strive for the things that will not make you envied, but simply hated. Do not be lifted high, lest you fall even further; do not give thought to how you might appear superior to the wicked, but grieve that you have been bested by the good. Do not laugh at the downfall of your neighbor. Make your way forward as safely as you can possibly do, but give a hand, too, to the one who lies on the ground. When you are dejected, do not cast away all hope for prosperity, nor forget your times of dejection when you are faring well. Each year has its four seasons, each moment of time its many changes of fortune. Let care keep your pleasure in check,[773] and let hope for better things curb your grief.

This is the way a human person is renewed, this is how the Day of Renewal should be honored: with this kind of finery, with a banquet such as this! Scripture says, "Do not appear before me empty-handed,"[774] but if you have something good, bring it with you. Today, then, appear as a new person—a different person in your way of living, utterly changed! "The old things have passed away; behold, everything is new!"[775] Bring this as your offering to the festival: be changed for the better, and do not consider the change such a great thing, but cry out with David, "This change is worked by the right hand of the Most High,"[776] from whom comes every successful accomplishment of men and women. Scripture does not wish you to remain always as you are, but to be constantly in motion, beneficially in motion, even "a new creation"[777]—if you are a sinner, turning towards the good, and if you are upright, holding to your course.

9.   Yesterday you put your trust in temporal things; learn today to trust in God.[778] "How long will you go limping on both legs?"[779] How long will you simply go on with household business as usual?[780] You should also be eager, at some point, to build a new house! Yesterday you considered it important to *seem* like somebody; today, choose rather to *be* somebody. How long will you be concerned mainly with dreams? Realities, rather, should be your concern. Yesterday you were an actor; today, show yourself to be a contemplative.[781] Yesterday you were quarrelsome, rash; today be polite and gentle. Yesterday you were a reveler; today be a person of temperance. Today you drink wine; tomorrow drink water. Today you live wantonly, reclining on ivory couches and anointing yourself with the best perfumes; tomorrow, lie on the ground and keep watch through the night. Rather than a buffoon, be a thoughtful person; rather than a dandy, be a person of simple attire; rather than proud and pretentious, be frugal in your appearance; rather than living under a golden roof, live in a tiny hut, bowing low rather than holding your head high. If you think this way and act this way, you will possess "a new heaven and a new earth,"[782] and even grasp why they are as they are.

10.   Let us turn, then, and also celebrate together in a way that befits this present moment. For everything is conspiring together, rejoicing together, for the beauty of this feast. Look at all that meets your eyes! The queen of seasons leads the way in the procession for the queen of days, showering from her own treasure every exquisite and delightful gift. Now heaven shines more brightly, the sun stands higher and glows more golden; now the moon's orb is more radiant, the chorus of the stars gleams more clearly. Now the sea's waves make their peace with the shores, the clouds with the sun, the winds with the air, the earth with the plants, the plants with our eyes. Now the springs gush forth with a new sparkle; now the rivers flow more abundantly, released from the bonds of winter's ice. Now the meadow is fragrant, the shoots burst forth, the grass is ready for mowing, and the lambs skip through the rich green fields. Now the ship is launched from its harbor at the boatswain's commands—most of them in pious language!—and spreads its wings of sail.[783] And the dolphin dances around it, blowing as if in joy and leaping out of the water, accompanying the crew in high spirits.[784] Now the farmer plants his plough in the earth, looking up to heaven and calling on the one who gives fruit to the earth; he puts his

ploughing-ox under the yoke and cuts a sweet furrow, rejoicing inwardly in his hopes. Now the shepherd and cowherd, too, begin to fit pipes together and play their pastoral song, as they spend the spring among the shrubs and rocks. Now the nurseryman tends his plants, while the fowler builds his traps of reed and looks hard at the branches, wholly preoccupied with the feathers of a bird. And the fisherman gazes into the depths, cleans his net again, and takes his seat on the rocks.

11. Now the industrious bee lifts up its wing and leaves the hive; revealing her own wisdom, she flies to the meadows and takes her spoil from the flowers. One bee labors at making the combs, weaving together hexagonal chambers in an interlocking pattern, alternating straight lines and angles in a work aimed both at beauty and safety. Another bee stores the honey in these chambers, producing for its host sweet fruit without cultivation. If only we, too, as Christ's beehive, would take up this model of wisdom and industry! Now, too, the bird builds her nest: one flies up, another enters, a third flies about, and they fill the grove with song, charming the human hearer with their chattering.

All things sing God's praise, and give him glory with wordless voices. For God receives my thanks for all these things: so each of their songs becomes our hymn, for I make their hymnody my own! Now every race of living thing is laughing, and we make festival with all our senses. Now the noble, high-spirited horse grows tired of the stable, and breaking free of its fetters, it thunders across the field and prances into the rivers.

12. What else can I mention? Now martyrs go out into the open air and lead the procession; they summon Christ's faithful people to their gleaming reliquaries, and make public proclamation of their victories.[785] And one of these is my crowned hero—and he is mine, even if not part of my Church; so to those who understand me I say, let all grudging subside![786]—Mamas the illustrious, shepherd and martyr. Formerly he milked the deer, who pressed ahead of each other to nourish the holy man with unaccustomed milk;[787] now he shepherds the people of our metropolitan city,[788] renewing the spring today for the many thousands who press in on him from all around, ornamenting spring by the beauties of virtue, making it a time worthy of shepherds and victory orations.[789] To put it more briefly still; now is the world's spring, the spiritual spring, spring for our souls, spring for our bodies, spring visible, spring invisible. May we share in the spring which is above us, by being changed for the better here on earth; and may we be sent on, renewed, towards our new life in Christ Jesus our Lord, to whom be all glory, honor and power, with the Holy Spirit, to the glory of God the Father. Amen.

3

POEMS

INTRODUCTION: THE POEMS

From the vast number of Gregory's poems—rambling autobiographical narratives in Homeric style, theological meditations, prayers and hymns, celebrations of friends, didactic and moral discourses, and deeply personal cries of loneliness and despair—we can offer only a few brief samples. Following the principle of not duplicating what is already available in modern translation, I have included here mainly short pieces of a religious character and his revealing monologue, "On his own Verses."[1] Without any pretence at a poetic diction equal in quality to Gregory's own, I have translated these pieces in an English meter and style intended to convey something of the character of the original: sometimes solemn, sometimes conversational and informal. I have sometimes attempted to match the English meter to the Greek but at other times have chosen a somewhat simpler English meter, which seems better suited to capture the style of his poems in a new tongue.

Gregory's poem "On his own Verses" (*Carm.* 2.1.39), quoted in the introduction,[2] offers a kind of apologia for what seems to have been one of the main occupations of the bishop's retirement: writing classical Greek verse, both as an entertainment and educational resource for his contemporaries and as a way of finding consolation in his own linguistic gifts. His anacreontic "Hymn to God" (*Carm.* 1.1.30) and the brief "Hymn of Thanksgiving," in dactylic hexameters (*Carm.* 1.1.33), celebrate the Mystery of the Trinity as source of life and blessing, without particular reference to Gregory's own career. The "Evening Hymn" (*Carm.* 1.1.32) that I have also included is sometimes listed among Gregory's *dubia*, partly because it appears in only a few of the manuscript collections of his poems and partly because its meter is unusual.[3] Doubts about its authenticity do not seem to me strong enough, however, to exclude this lovely piece from the present collection. Gregory's "Prayer before Reading Scripture" (*Carm.* 1.1.35) and his little "Prayer before a Journey" (*Carm.* 1.1.37) suggest more particular moments in the bishop's life; with his "Prayer before a Journey to Constantinople" (*Carm.* 2.1.3), in the iambic trimeter used for dialog in classical tragedies, we are standing on the borderline between autobiographical reflection and the universal language of faith. The other poems I have included here—Gregory's "Prayer to Christ" (*Carm.* 2.1.74), his little cycle of "Three Prayers for a Day" (*Carm.* 2.1.24–26), and the dark dactylic lament entitled "Supplication" (*Carm.* 2.1.27)—all seem to reflect Gregory's mood of isolation and growing infirmity during the last years of his life, and show us most dramatically the deeply personal side of his poetic activity. They are cries of the heart, expressions both of self-pity and of unshakable faith, quarrels with the God whom Gregory never ceases to trust, even as he questions his own experience of Providence.

On His Own Verses[4]

Look at the crowd of writers living now,
All blithely gushing forth their streams of prose:
Spending much serious time upon their toil,
Yet, in the end, producing only words;
Issuing solemn essays like decrees,
Cluttered with insubstantial, silly things—
Like ocean's sand, or Egypt's plague of flies!
I'd love to give them all this one advice:
Get rid of every other text, but cling
To God's inspired books with all your might,
Like sailors seeking harbor in a storm!
If Scripture gives us safety-grips like this,
Your wisdom, Spirit, will bear richer fruit
Than all its misuse by your enemies
As ground for ill-intentioned, foolish talk.
When will *you* write, my friend, for simple minds,
Works unambiguously clear and straight?
But since this is, it seems, beyond our reach,
As parties split our world, and each one lays
A word-foundation for his deviant path,
Forging screeds to promote his own ideas,
I steer my writing down this other road—
One that I cherish, whether good or ill:
I spend my ink and energy on verse.
I do it not to win myself a name,
As most folk, with less principle, might think:
Glory, we say, is empty! And to please,

I'd have to write a different kind of verse,
Running in other tracks than mine now does.
Most people use the norms of their own work
To measure that of others—even God's![5]
May his word never leave me so alone!
"What is he thinking of?" you ask yourself.
My first desire, working on other things,
Was so to put constraints on my prolixity
That I might write, but never write too much—
Verse is an effort! Second, I thought of youth,
And of the folk who find such joy in words:
My verse could be for them a pleasant potion,
Leading them towards the Good by mild persuasion,
Sweetening by art the bitter taste of law.
Verse helps us to relax the tightened string,
If we but will, even if it be no more
Than lyric songs, musical interludes.
I write them simply, then, for your delight,
Lest other pleasures steal you from true Beauty.
Thirdly, I must confess my thought was this—
A petty thing, perhaps, but still I thought it:
I cannot bear that strangers should possess
The prize in letters, rather than ourselves—
Letters colored by art, I mean, although
For us real beauty lies in contemplation.
It is for you, O Sophists,[6] that I write—
Such is my lion-hearted gratitude!
Fourth, I have found these poems a consolation
When, weighed by illness, like an aging swan,
I make the whistling of my wings a song:
Not mournful, but a kind of parting hymn.
Beyond this, Sophists, let me share one thought:[7]
If you are bested, credit's mainly due
The words themselves—come, words, receive the trophy!
Nothing's too long, nothing beyond due measure,
Yet nothing, I think, without some useful point.
The words themselves will teach you, if you let them!
Some of them are my own, others are borrowed;
Some praise the good, others rebuke the wicked;
Some teach, some give opinions, some are hints
That bind the memory in the letter's cord.
If this seems trivial, *you* write something better!

You blame my verse? Of course! You have no ear—
Scribbler of doggerel, abortionist of words!
What blind man recognizes one who sees,
What snail can match a champion at his pace?
And yet I know you covet what you blame:
The very versifying you belittle
You strive, though clumsily, to craft yourself!
When you retort, "Honesty's my defender;
A simple, halting style's what I prefer,"
You Sophists just are spinning crafty words!
Is this not obvious lying, double-talk?
One minute a monkey, next a roaring lion,
The love of glory's easily entrapped!
Remember, there are many poems in Scripture,
As Hebrew sages tell us, and a rhythm
Supported by the plucking of a lyre:
The ancients sang instruction in their verse,
Making delight the vehicle of beauty,
Forming the heart for virtue by a song.
Saul is a prime example, whose troubled spirit
The music of a harp alone set free.
What harm, then, if we try to lead the young
To share in God by means of holy pleasure?
They cannot bear a sudden transformation,
So let us find a gentler form of contact.
Then, when the good is finally firm in place,
We can withdraw aesthetics, like the struts
Supporting some new vault, and see the Good
Standing alone. What profits more than this?
Do you not add some sweetness to your food,
My narrow and constricted, solemn friend?
Why do you slander my poetic gifts,
Weighing your neighbor's work by your own scale?
Mysia's far from Phrygia,[8] and the flight
Of crows a lowlier course than that of eagles!

A Hymn To God [9]

God, our ever-living monarch,
Give us voice to sing your glory:
You, immortal Lord and Sovereign,
To whom every hymn is chanted!

Through you all the choirs of angels,
All the ages, have their being;
Through you shines the sun in splendor,
Through you moonlight wanes and waxes
And the stars reveal their glory;
Through you man, your noblest creature,
Finds the grace to know your godhead
And to live endowed with reason.
For the whole is your creation
And you place each part in order,
Guiding all things by your knowledge.
As you spoke, they were created!
Now the Word you speak to form us
Is your Son, who shares your substance,
With his Father's glory equal—
He who fits all things together
So that you may rule and guide them.
And the bond that all embraces
Is your godly Holy Spirit,
Who protects all things by foresight.
So I name you living Triad:
Single, archetypal power,
Without source, unchanging always,
All-unspeakable in nature,
Mind of all-eluding wisdom,
Power of heaven, all-unconquered,
Without cause, and free from limit,
Source of light, still undetected,
Yet surveying all in brilliance,
Before whom no thing lies hidden,
From this earth to deepest heaven!
Father, look in mercy on me;
Let me always bow in wonder
At your majesty and glory.
Cast away my sins and failings;
Let my conscience stand unchallenged,
Free from every stain of malice.
Let me glorify your godhead,
Raising holy hands to heaven;
Let me sing to Christ in blessing,
And on bended knee beseech him
To receive me as his servant

When he comes again in glory.
Father, look in mercy on me;
Let me find your grace and pardon.
So to you be thanks and glory
For the ageless age unending!

A Hymn of Thanksgiving[10]

Thanks be to you, King of all things, maker of all;
Heaven is filled with your glory, filled is the earth
With your wisdom. Your Son, your Word has created all things;
Your Holy Spirit endows all creatures with life.
Show grace to the world, O Triad; have mercy on us,
O Son of God in the Spirit, of Man in the flesh.
You met and endured our mortal fate on the cross,
Yet passed, as God, on the third day through Hades' gates,
And rising, you broke the fetters of death itself,
Giving this mortal race a nature beyond us:
Life for endless days, to praise you as deathless forever.

Evening Hymn[11]

We bless you now, at twilight,
My Christ, God's Word, God's brightness
From light that knows no dawning,
And steward of the Spirit—
Your threefold radiance woven
Into one strand of glory!
You have abolished darkness,
Forming, on light's foundation,
A world that light embraces,
Shaping unstable matter
Into a stable order—
This beauty that delights us.
Our human mind you lighten
With reason and with wisdom,
Forming in us an image
Of heaven's transcendent brilliance,
That we, in light, may see light
And be ourselves its beacon.
The sky you have illumined
With lamps of varied brightness,

Commanding night and daylight
Gladly to yield their station,
And honor by example
The laws of kin and friendship.
By one, you ease the labors
Of flesh, with all its burdens;
You wake us by the other
To do the works that please you,
That we might flee the darkness
And come at last to daylight—
That day no night can conquer.
Send gentle sleep upon me,
Hovering on my eyelids;
Let not my tongue grow sluggish,
My praise for long be deadened—
Let not this earthen vessel
Long cease to echo angels.
Let sleep now be the forum
For holy thoughts, I pray you,
That night may not uncover
The hidden filth of daylight,
Nor dreams proclaim in vision
The shameful tales of darkness.
Let mind, now free from body,
Address you, God, in freedom:
Father and Son and Spirit,
Holy and undivided,
To whom be praise and honor
From age to age unending.
Amen.

Prayer Before Reading Scripture[12]

Father of Christ, all-seeing, hear our prayers;
Look kindly on your servant's solemn song.
He turns his footsteps down a godly path,
Who knows, while living, the ingenerate God,
And Christ, the king who bans all mortal ills.
Once, out of pity for our hard-pressed race,
Freely conforming to the Father's will,
He changed his form, taking our mortal frame
Though he was God immortal, freeing us all

From Tartarus's bondage by his blood.
Come now, refresh this soul of yours with words—
Pure, godly sayings from this sacred book;
Gaze here upon the servants of your Truth
Proclaiming life in voices echoing heaven!

Prayer Before a Journey [13]

Without you, not a footstep can we place,
Lord Christ, for mortals source of every good;
You are yourself our straight path through the world.
Trusting in you, I walk this present way—
Lead me unharmed, bless me with every gift
My spirit longs for, bring me to that poor home
Where night and day I'll seek your face in freedom.

Prayer Before a Journey to Constantinople [14]

In you our spirit finds its still point, Word of God.
When we're at home, you stabilize our leisure time;
Yours is the firm ground where we sit, and rise, and stand.
Yours, too, the way, and at the prompting of your will
Our journey prospers. Send me now an angel guide
To travel at my right hand, and to be my friend—
One who will lead me on, [15] a shaft of fire and cloud
To split the sea, stop rushing rivers with a word,
One who will sate me with the food of heaven and earth.
And let the cross my hands portray now hold in check
My Enemy's boldness; [16] let the burning heat of day
Not touch me, nor the night engulf me with its fears.
Let the steep path, now looming rough before my sight,
Be gentle, smooth and easy for your servant's steps,
Just as you sheltered me so often with your hand,
Saved me from mortal danger on both land and sea,
And wracking illness, and the threats of circumstance.
Let us now find success, the fullness of our hopes,
A happy outcome for our striving, and at journey's end
A safe return to friends and loved ones: home again,
Joyful that they rejoice to see us, free from care.
We bow in worship, Lord; grant that our final road
Be blest and happy, leading to a land of peace.

A Prayer to Christ[17]

Where's the injustice? I was born human—well and good!
But why am I so battered by life's tidal waves?
I'll speak my mind—harshly perhaps, yet still I'll speak:
Were I not yours, my Christ, this life would be a crime!
We're born, we age, we reach the measure of our days;
I sleep, I rest, I wake again, I go my way
With health and sickness, joys and struggles as my fare,
Sharing the seasons of the sun, the fruits of earth,
And death, and then corruption—just like any beast,
Whose life, though lowly, still is innocent of sin!
What more do I have? Nothing more, except for God!
Were I not yours, my Christ, this life would be a crime!

THREE PRAYERS FOR A DAY[18]

A Morning Prayer

At dawn, I raise my hand in oath to God:
I shall not do or praise the deeds of darkness.
Rather, this day shall be my sacrifice;
I shall remain unshaken, rule my passions.
My age would shame me, if I were to sin,
As would this altar over which I stand.
Thus my desire, my Christ: you bring it home!

An Evening Lament

O Truth, O Word, this morning I deceived you,
Marking this day as yours by consecration!
Night finds me now not fully in the light,
Although I prayed and hoped that might be so;
My feet have strayed and stumbled here and there.
The dark has come, begrudging me salvation.
Be light for me, O Christ—shine here once more!

A Prayer to Christ the Next Morning

Yesterday, Christ, turned out a total loss!
Rage came upon me, all at once, and took me.
Let me live *this* day as a day of light.

Gregory, look—be mindful, think of God!
You swore you would; remember your salvation!

Supplication[19]

Christ, light of mortals, pillar of glowing flame
For Gregory's soul, wandering this bitter waste:
Curb Pharaoh, hold his taskmasters in check,
Rescue my feet from Egypt's shifting mud,
Chasten my enemies with unsightly plagues—
Give me a level way! And if my foe
Should close on me in rage, come, split apart
The Red Sea, let me cross it like a road
To destiny and dry land, as you promised.
Stop the vast rivers, turn aside the spears
Of fierce invaders; if I ever reach
Your holy land, I'll sing your praise forever.
Lord Christ, why have you snared me in this flesh—
This chilly life, this muddy pit of squalor—
If I am, as they say, your heritage,
Truly divine? My limbs have lost their strength,
My knees won't hold me. Time has done me in,
And raging illness, and consuming care,
And friends whose thoughts are those of enemies.
My sins won't let me be, but track me down,
In weakness, just as dogs track down a hare
Or circle a fawn, craving to eat their fill.
Have mercy, bring this misery to an end,
Or else decide I've struggled long enough
And take me, set some measure on my pain;
If not, then let the sweet cloud of forgetting
Enfold my mind and shroud me in its veil.

4

LETTERS

INTRODUCTION: THE LETTERS

Like his poems, Gregory's letters are so numerous that we can offer only a small sample of them here. Like the poems, too, his letters are often short, occasional pieces: building relationships of client and patron, dealing with practical concerns, staying in touch with relatives and friends. In a number of them, however, Gregory reveals himself in a more homiletic role as a spiritual advisor, urging his addressee to live, along with him, the kind of philosophic life to which their common Hellenic culture and their common Christian faith invites them.

In Letter 11, probably addressed to Gregory of Nyssa, he criticizes Basil's younger brother (who does not seem ever to have been an intimate friend) for having been intimidated, by the anti-Christian or anti-Nicene sentiment of the 360s, into giving up his earlier desire to serve the Church in official ministry, and urges him to return to it. Gregory, trained as a rhetor, had been ordained a lector but has apparently ceased to be active and has instead begun teaching young people literature. Letter 20 is addressed to his own brother Caesarius shortly after the earthquake that ravaged western Anatolia in the autumn of 368, offering reflections on our experience of natural evils; Letter 30, written to the family friend Philagrius a year later, expresses Gregory's grief at Caesarius's untimely death. Letter 31, also to Philagrius, is a communication from one man of letters to another, urging his invalid friend to bear his chronic illness as a philosopher and offering to lend him a copy of the works of Demosthenes.

Two of the letters I include here—Letters 48 and 58—are addressed to Basil of Caesaraea, probably during the mid-370s, and offer us glimpses of the often tense relations that linked the two boyhood friends. In Letter 48, Gregory replies testily to Basil's complaint that he has not fully supported the metropolitan's campaign to resist the new imperial decision to divide Cappadocia into two provinces; Gregory here expresses his disdain for politics of every stripe. In Letter 58, Gregory tells Basil, with what may be a pretense at cheerful naïveté, of his efforts at a recent *soirée* to defend Basil's reputation in Cappadocia against the charge of excessively "managing" the truth, by refusing to declare his belief in the divinity of the Holy Spirit more forthrightly. Basil would later address a scathing reply to Gregory's report, accusing him of betraying their party by not denying the charge outright!

Lettter 51, to his great-nephew Nicobulus, a student of rhetoric, is a terse but fascinating treatise on the art of writing letters, probably composed after Gregory's retirement to Cappadocia; it is one of the few treatments of letter writing that we have from classical antiquity. Letter 76, to Gregory of Nyssa, is a message of consolation written after Basil's death on January 1, 379; Letter 80, to his friend Philagrius, expresses briefly, in less formal terms, Gregory's own grief at the loss of his domineering but heroic friend. Letter 90 to Anysius is a wry expression of Gregory's sense of injustice at being forced to retire from the see of Constantinople. Letter 178, finally, to Eudoxius—a Cappadocian rhetorician and the son of Gregory's friend by the same name—is a moving reflection on the philosophic life as lived by a Trinitarian Christian, and a satiric representation of careerism. Here he urges young Eudoxius to find in his own poor health an invitation to live simply, unencumbered by worldly ambitions and free to pursue the life of contemplation.

As will be obvious, Gregory uses the classical epistolary form in all these short pieces to engage in the same work of inspiration and persuasion that occupies him in his orations; here, however, the audience is a single individual, the style direct and usually informal, the message personal. Letters, as he explains to Nicoboulus in Letter 51, have their own rhetorical needs, and Gregory meets them expertly.

Letter 11: *To Gregory (of Nyssa)* [1]

I have one upright characteristic in my nature (for I will boast, even in my own name, of one thing in comparison with the rest): I am equally disgusted with my friends and with myself when we make a bad choice. So, since all of us who live by God's laws and submit to the same Gospel are friends and family to one another, why should you not hear us saying openly what everyone murmurs under his breath? They do not praise your disreputable thirst for reputation, if I may speak myself in your style,[2] or your slight shift of direction for the worse, or "that worst of demons, the love of honor," as Euripides puts it.[3]

What is wrong with you, my good sage,[4] what do you regret about your life, that you have thrown away those holy, thirst-quenching books, which you once proclaimed to the people—don't blush when you hear this!—and hung them over the fireplace like a rudder or a spade in wintertime?[5] Why have turned your hand to salty, undrinkable literature, and wish to be called "rhetor" rather than "Christian?" We prefer the second of these names to the first, thanks be to God! Now don't you suffer this sickness any longer, my good friend. Sober up, late as it may be, and return to your senses; explain yourself to the faithful, explain yourself to God, and to his altars and his mysteries, from which you have distanced yourself!

Don't speak to me clever, artificial phrases such as these: "What, then? Was I not still a Christian when I practiced the rhetorical art? Was I not a believer when I associated with the young?" Perhaps you may even call God to be your witness! But the answer, my good man, is: "Not at all!" Or if we even grant part of what you say, "Not at all as much as you should!" Why shock others through what you now are doing, when they are naturally more inclined to evil than to good? Why give them the opportunity to think and say the worst about you? Perhaps it is a lie—but what need is there to prompt it? One does not live simply for oneself, after all, but also for one's neighbor;[6] it is not enough to persuade oneself, if one does not also persuade others. If, for instance, you were a boxer in public arenas, giving and taking punches in the jaw, or if you twisted and turned in lascivious dances, would you say that you were still a solid citizen at heart? That kind of thinking does not belong to a sensible person; to accept it for yourself shows a lack of seriousness.

"If, then, you change your ways, then I shall rejoice," one of the Pythagorean philosophers once said, lamenting the fall of a comrade, "but if you do not"—this is what he wrote—"you are dead, as far as I am concerned!"[7] For myself, I will not go so far as to say about you, as the tragedy puts it, "A friend has become an enemy, dear though he still is."[8] I will be grieved, rather—that is the moderate way to put it—if you can neither recognize on your own what you ought to do (which belongs to the first class of praiseworthy people), nor follow the good advice of another (which belongs to the second).[9]

Here endeth the exhortation! You must excuse me: I feel pain through friendship; I am incensed as much on your account as on that of the whole priestly order—and I will add, as on that of all Christians. And if I must also pray with you or for you, then may God, who gives life to the dead, help you in your weakness!

Letter 20: *To Caesarius*[10]

Even fearful events are not useless for the wise; I would say they are highly beneficial and healthy! For although we certainly pray that they not happen, we learn something when they do. "The afflicted soul is near to God," says Peter in a truly wonderful passage,[11] and everyone who escapes danger is all the more attached to the one who has saved him from it. Let us not be troubled, then, by the fact that we sometimes experience evil, but let us give thanks that we have escaped it. Let us not show ourselves to God in one way in the moment of danger, and in another after dangers are over; but whether we are at home or away, living as private citizens or carrying out public duties (for I must speak this way, and not give up doing so[12]), let us make up our minds to follow the one who has saved us, taking little account of little, earthbound events. And we should give those who come after us a story to tell, something great for our own glory but also great for the profit of their souls. For this event can be a very useful instruction for many, teaching them that danger is better than safety and misfortune preferable to success, for the simple reason that before our terrors we belonged to the world, but after them we belong to God.

Perhaps we will seem heavy-handed in writing often to you about these same subjects, and you may think our words not exhortation but rhetorical show. For that reason, enough of this! Know that we are eager, and hoping very much, to visit you, so that we can rejoice with you over your safety and have the chance for more satisfactory conversation on these things. In any case, we hope to receive you here very soon, and celebrate our thanks to God together.

Letter 30: *To Philagrius* [13]

I have lost Caesarius. I will tell you something, even though such strong emotions are not philosophical: I love all that belonged to Caesarius, and whatever I see that reminds me of Caesarius I embrace and kiss, and seem, in a way, to see him, to be with him, to converse with him. I felt something like that even now, as I read your letter. As soon as I saw the address of your letter—something so welcome to me, with that welcome name, Philagrius—all our bygone joys[14] came over me in a rush: the cities, the things we did, our table, our poverty, what Homer calls "the delights of being the same age,"[15] our games, our serious interests, our literary labors, our common teachers, the loftiness of our hopes—all one might mention of past good things, which give me particular joy even now, as I remember them. Let me experience these comforts still more: put your pen in motion, indulge me by writing! This, at any rate, is no small favor to us, even if an envious fate has taken away the greatest thing, being together, and has shaped our affairs so sadly.

Letter 31: *To Philagrius* [16]

The things that are painful for you are truly painful for us, too. For we make common property of all that belongs to friends, whether good or otherwise—this, surely, is the definition of friendship. Still, if we must philosophize a little about these things and discuss with you what seems right (and surely we must, as the law of friendship demands!), then I do not wish—I do not suppose it is a good thing—that you, Philagrius, a person unusually well schooled in the things of God, should experience the same feelings as ordinary people, or succumb to the weakness that affects your body, or that you should lament over your suffering as something incurable. You must find in your vulnerability a place to philosophize, and purify your mind now more than ever, and show yourself stronger than the things that hold you in check, and consider this illness a profitable training—namely, to look down on the body and bodily things, and on all that is fleeting and disturbing and passing away, and so to become completely focused on what lies above, to live not for this present world but for the world to come, making this life here what Plato calls "a preparation for death,"[17] and loosing the soul, as far as possible, from what, in his words, we call either its body or its prison.[18] If you are a philosopher about these things, my good friend, and live in this frame of mind, you yourself will draw the greatest profit; and you will put our mind at ease about you, and will teach ordinary people to become philosophers about their sufferings. In addition, you will make no small gain—if this should matter to you at all—in being admired by everyone.

About the books you requested: I found one of them—the volume of Demosthenes—and have sent it to you gladly; the other I have lost. I don't have the book you want, the *Iliad*. But believe me, I only feel that I can enjoy those things—I only feel it is good to have those things—that you can share in yourself, and that you can use as if they were your own.

Letter 48: *To Basil* [19]

Will you never cease to attack us as ignorant, clumsy and unloving, as not even worthy to live, just because we have dared to understand our own situation? For we have not committed any other injustice, as you yourself would agree; nor are we aware of being involved in any other wrong, large or small, against you—we would never confess to that! The only thing we know is that we have been deceived; we realized it very late, but still we realized it! We accuse the episcopal throne, which all at once has raised you above us. We are tired of being blamed for your actions, and of having to apologize to those who clearly know both our former and our present way of life. And being in this situation, we have to undergo the most ridiculous, most wretched fate of all: being treated unjustly at the same time as being accused—for that is what is now happening to us!

Other people accuse us of one thing or another,[20] as each one prefers, each in his own way and in the measure of his anger against us. The kindest charge [against you] is disdain and contempt: that you have cast us aside when we were no longer useful, like the most common, worthless of tools, or like the supports under vaulting, which are taken away and disregarded after everything is solidly in place. But let us leave our accusers alone, to say whatever they will say—no one can restrain the tongue's autonomy! What you can do for me is strike down[21] those blessed, empty hopes you devised, according to those who abuse us, of manipulating us by Church office, because of our vain eagerness for such things.

For my part, I will explain my own position as it is; please do not be angry with me! For I will say what I uttered at the moment of high emotion,[22] when I was not so boiling with anger or offended at what had happened that I had lost my powers of reasoning, or was unaware of what I was saying. "I will not take up arms," I said, "or learn the tactics of battle; I didn't learn them before, when the time seemed more appropriate for them, with everyone armed and in an aggressive frenzy." (You know how powerless the sick can be![23]) "I will not fight the Arian Anthimus, even though he is an outdated warrior, since I am unarmed and unwarlike, more suited for wounds than war. Fight against him yourself, if that is what you choose to do—need often makes the weak into warriors! Or else look for comrades-in-arms, when he steals your mules, barricades the passes, and, like Amalek, keeps Israel at bay![24] But instead of all this, in any case, give us peace. What point is there, after all, in fighting over nursing lambs and poultry[25]—other people's livestock, in fact—as if we were fighting for souls and for the Church's laws? Why deprive the metropolitan city of jurisdiction over splendid Sasima, or lay bare and open your own hidden plans, which you ought to conceal?"

As for you, be bold, take control, steer everything towards your own way of thinking, as rivers take hold of spring torrents; do not honor friendship or intimacy over what is right and what is pious, do not be concerned about what kind of person you are as a result of acting this way, but belong to one alone: the Spirit![26]

For our part, we draw one profit from your friendship: not to trust in friends, and not to consider anything more valuable than God.

Letter 51: *To Nicoboulus* [27]

Among those who write letters (since that is what you ask about), some write more than is reasonable, some much less; both miss the right measure, just as some archers shoot their arrows short of the mark, others overshoot it. Missing the target comes down to the same thing, even if it happens for opposite reasons. The due measure in letters is what is appropriate:[28] one should neither write at length when there are not many things to talk about, nor skimp on one's writing when there are. What, then? Must we either "measure our verbal skill with the Persian cord,"[29] or else do it with a child's cubit[30] and draw with so few details as not to draw at all, but imitate noonday shadows—lines that stare us in the face, but whose full length is submerged, glimpsed rather than appearing, known by some of their beginnings and endings, so that (not to put too fine a point on it) we are only dealing with approximations of approximations?[31] The right thing is to avoid both kinds of distortion, and so strike the right measure.

That, then, is what I think about brevity. As far as clarity is concerned, the main point to notice is that one must avoid sounding like a speech, and lean rather in the direction of the conversational. To put it succinctly, the best and most beautifully constructed letter is the one that sounds convincing to both the simple and the educated reader: to the one, because it sounds like what everyone says; to the other, because it rises above the general level and is therefore worthy of note. It is just as inappropriate for a riddle to be obvious as it is for a letter to need interpretation.

The third characteristic of letters is grace. We assure this quality if we write neither in a style that is completely dry and graceless, lacking in adornment, "without order or border," as they say[32]—totally free of adages and proverbs and sayings, as well as of jokes and riddles, all of which contribute to a "sweetened" style—yet also if we do not seem to use these features to excess. The one extreme is clumsy, the other is self-indulgent. One ought to use these tools to the same degree one uses purple wool in weaving:[33] we do make use of stylistic figures, but only a few of them, and that with modesty! We abandon antitheses and parallel structures and symmetrical phrases to the professional rhetoricians;[34] and if we do use them, we do it more in jest than in earnest.

The conclusion of my treatise is something I once heard a literary connoisseur say about the eagle: when the birds were disputing about who should rule, and each one came forward congratulating himself for a different reason, the most beautiful thing about the eagle was that he did not consider himself a beauty. One should especially aim at this in letters, too: to be unadorned, and as near as possible to what is natural.

This is all we have to say to you about letters, in a letter of our own. Perhaps this is not our charge, since we have greater things to concern ourselves with. You will work this out by practice, since you are eager to learn; and those who have cultivated taste in these things will be your teachers.

Letter 58: *To Basil*[35]

I have considered you, from the beginning, my life's guide, my teacher of doctrine, and every other kind of good influence—and I consider you so now. If anyone sings your praises, he either does it with me or in my tracks. That is how much I defer to your piety, and how completely I am on your side! And no wonder: the more people live together, the more they know each other first-hand, and when that first-hand experience is abundant, the testimony one bears is all the more complete. If there is any benefit for me in living, it is your friendship and companionship. That is the way I feel about these things, and may I always feel this way! So what I now write, I write unwillingly—yet nevertheless I write it. Please do not be angry with me—I shall be very angry with myself, if I cannot make you believe that I say and write this to you out of good will.

Many people have accused us of not being firm in matters of faith—people who sincerely share our concerns. Some accuse us openly of sacrilegious opinions, others of cowardice: of sacrilege, those who think we are no longer in a healthy state of mind; of cowardice, those who charge us with concealing our real thoughts. But what need is there of rehearsing the opinions of others? Instead, I shall tell you what recently happened.

There was a party, and among the guests present were not a few distinguished people who are our friends; one of them belongs to those who bear both the name and the garb of piety.[36] We had not yet begun drinking, and the conversation turned to you and me, as often happens—we are preferred to any other chance topic! But while everyone admired your way of governing, and spoke, in addition, of our having shared a philosophic life—spoke of our friendship and of Athens, and of our agreement and like-mindedness on every subject—the so-called philosopher became indignant. "What is all this, my friends?" he said, crying out in an insolent way. "You are such liars and flatterers! Let these gentlemen be praised for their other qualities, if you like, and I will make no objection; but I will not grant the most important quality. Basil is wrongly praised for orthodoxy—and Gregory wrongly, as well! The one betrays the faith by the public discourses he holds, the other is an accomplice in the betrayal by not objecting!" "Why do you say this," I asked, "you foolish fellow—you modern Dathan and Abiram,[37] with your rebellious nonsense! Where do you come from, that you should be our teacher? How can you make yourself judge of questions such as this?" "I have come just now," he said, "from the gathering in honor of the martyr Eupsychius,[38] and there I heard the great Basil speaking excellent and perfect things about the divinity of the Father and the Son, as no one else could easily do, but gliding past the Spirit"—and he added some comparison to rivers that run over rocks but hollow out sand.

Then he said, turning to me, "And why on earth do *you*, my friend, speak so openly of the Spirit as God"—and he recalled one of my comments, when at a gathering of many people I was speaking of the Mystery of God and then applied to the Spirit that famous line, "How long shall we hide the light under a bushel?"—"while *he* plays down the fact in murky expressions, and only lays out doctrine in a sketchy way. He will not speak the truth frankly, but bathes our ears in language more political than pious, concealing the ambiguity in the power of his words."

"Since I live in obscurity," I said, "and am unknown to most people, and since both what I do say and the fact that I say anything at all is hardly noticed, I can be a philosopher[39] without risk. But his pronouncements are more important, since he is better known both on his own account and on account of his Church. Everything he says is public, and a great war is going on about him; the heretics[40] are eager to criticize a simple word, let alone Basil himself, so that he might be expelled from the Church—he who remains virtually the only spark of truth, the force of life, while everyone around him is tainted with heresy—and that this evil might take root in the city,[41] and then, using this Church as a kind of base of operations, overrun the whole world. The better path, then, for us is that the truth be managed prudently,[42] that we yield a bit to our times as one would to a cloud, rather than let the truth be destroyed by the bright clarity of our proclamation. For us, after all, there is no harm in recognizing the Spirit as God through other expressions that lead in that direction—for truth is found less in sounds than in the understanding; but for the Church, there will be a great loss if truth is put to flight through the defeat of a single man!"

The others present did not accept this idea of "prudent management," which seemed to them a vapid way of playing with words; instead, they joined in criticizing us angrily for "managing" cowardice rather than doctrine. It would be much better, they said, for us to protect our own interests through the truth, than to damage them, and so fail to win over the other party, through this so-called "management."

It would take a long time—and perhaps it is unnecessary— to rehearse now in detail all that I said, all that I heard, how I responded angrily to our opponents, almost without moderation and beyond my usual style. At the end of the conversation, I sent them away with arguments like those I have mentioned. But you must give me instructions, my divine and consecrated friend: how far should we come forward in speaking of the Spirit as God? What expressions should we use? To what extent should we "manage" our speech? We need to have a firm front against those who criticize us! For if I were to fail to learn this now—I who of all people know you and your thoughts the best, and who have often both given and received full assurance of this—I would be the most ignorant and the most wretched person of all.

Letter 76: *To Gregory of Nyssa*[43]

So this, too, has been destined to be part of this wretched life of mine: to hear of Basil's death[44] and that holy soul's departure, by which he has left us to dwell in the presence of the Lord, after making all his life a preparation for this moment. As for me, along with other losses—because I am still in a poor and very dangerous state of bodily health—I am even deprived of my desire to embrace the holy dust, to be with you, who will react to the event in a reasonable way, like a philosopher, and to give consolation to our mutual friends. To see the Church left alone, shorn of such glory and shaken free of such a crown, is, for anyone with sense, neither a sight to be endured nor a report one wants to hear.

Although there are many friends, many words available for your consolation, you seem to me not likely to be consoled by any of them, so much as by yourself and by Basil's memory; the two of you have been for all the rest a model of philosophy, and a kind of spiritual measuring-stick for ordered behavior in prosperity and for patient endurance in adversity, since philosophy knows how to do both: to take prosperity moderately, and to take adversity gracefully.

These are our thoughts for your Excellency. But how can any time or language console me, after writing this, unless I can share in your own presence and company—which the blessed one[45] has left us in place of all other legacies, so that we might see in you his features, as in a lovely and shining mirror, and might believe that he still is ours?

Letter 80: *To Philagrius*[46]

You ask how things are going with us. Very badly! I no longer have Basil, I no longer have Caesarius—neither my spiritual brother nor my bodily one! With David I cry, "My father and my mother have abandoned me" (Ps 26.10). My bodily state is wretched, old age shows on my head, cares weave together, practical concerns press on me, my friends are faithless, the Church is without a shepherd. Goodness has vanished, evil is out in the open; we are sailing in the dark, and there is no light anywhere. Christ is asleep! Why must we suffer? There is one end to my miseries: death! But even what lies beyond it is terrifying to me, if present circumstances are any indication!

Letter 90: *To Anysius*[47]

You ask how our affairs are going. We will answer with a story. The Athenians, they say, sent an embassy to the Lacedaemonians, when they were ruled by a tyrant. The point of the delegation was to ask that some act of generosity might be made towards them from the people of Sparta. And when the they returned from their mission, someone immediately asked them, "How did the Lacadaemonians treat you?" "As slaves, with great courtesy," they said, "but as free men, very arrogantly!" This, in fact, is what I have to write myself. We are being treated more humanely than those whom everyone writes off, but more roughly than those who might matter to God. Illness still troubles us—or rather, troubles us severely; our friends do not cease from doing us harm, injuring us any way they can. Pray, then, that the Divinity will be gracious to us, and that one of two things might be given us: that we will escape these dangers completely, or that we will endure them. The latter, at any rate, would probably mean some lessening of misfortune.

Letter 178: *To Eudoxius*[48]

There was an ancient custom in Athens, which had, I would say, excellent results. When young men came into their adolescence, they were introduced to the arts, and introduced in the following way. The tools of each of the arts were put on public display, and the youths were led up to them; whichever one each lad seemed to be drawn to and delight in, it was that tool's art he was taught. The assumption was that what accords with our nature generally leads to success, but what contradicts nature ends in failure. What is this story meant to prove? I am saying that you, too, who have an aptitude for philosophy, ought not to neglect it, or be pushed rather towards some other occupation that doesn't fit you, rather than embracing the art towards which you are inclined—not simply because it is the best of arts, but also because it comes more naturally to you. "Do not try to force a river's flow," the proverb tells us, and the poem insists that "the one who has learned horsemanship not try to be a singer"![49] Otherwise what might happen? You might fail at both horsemanship and at singing!

But what is this aptitude [for philosophy]? As I look at you, this is what strikes me. First, your manner, your calm and unpretentious temperament, so little suited to the changing fortunes of life that surround us. Second, the nobility of your soul, lofty and easily moved to reflection. Third, your poor health, your bodily weakness—for this, too, seems to Plato to be no small preparation for philosophy.[50] In addition, you are also at an age at which the passions have already begun to decline; you seem to me not to be oppressed by poverty, so much as to pride yourself on it; and you know how to be modest, unlike most rhetoricians! Your voice is not brutal, you have not lost your ethical principles, you are not a rabble-rouser—you have none of those qualities, to put it in a nutshell, with which Aristophanes forms Agoracritus into the classic demagogue![51] Although you style yourself a rhetor, you belong in that category, in the end, in every way except character. Don't let yourself, then, throw away all the progress you have made in philosophy; don't settle for second place in a second-rate occupation, rather than holding first place in the most important things. And even if we give the things of this life precedence, don't accept being the best of the cormorants when you can be an eagle!

How long will we be puffed up by insignificant, earth-bound things, and play games among boys with imaginary characters,[52] and be elated by applause? Let us leave this behind, let us become men, let us throw dreams away, let us run past the shadows, let us yield the delightful things of life—which are, more precisely, painful things—to others. Let others become the playthings of envy and time and fate—that name we give to the inconsistency and instability of human affairs; let others be shaken by them and be their pawns! Far from us be thrones, power, wealth, distinctions, promotions and falls, or that cheap and detestable thing, reputation, which leads rather to the disgrace of the one who lets himself be elated, instead of laughing at the farce and theatricality of this great stage! Let us, instead, embrace the life of the mind,[53] and choose to have God before all things, the one all-sufficient Good available to us; so we shall share in a good reputation here on earth, if we are still petty enough to seek it, and we shall surely have it in the next world, since the reward of virtue is to "become God" and to be lit up by the brilliance of that purest light, which we contemplate in the Triple Unity, of which even now we share some modest rays. Go towards this goal, make progress, give wings to your reason, lay hold of eternal life, never stand still in your hopes, until you reach the summit[54] of desire and blessedness. You will welcome our advice to some degree now, I know—but more abundantly in a little while, when you see yourself surrounded by the things we promise you, and find them no empty blessedness, no mere inventions of the mind, but the truth of all things.

5

GREGORY'S WILL

INTRODUCTION: GREGORY'S WILL

Gregory is, as far as I know, the only Church Father, Eastern or Western, whose written will has come down to us; according to one prominent Roman social historian, his is in fact the oldest extant complete will made under Roman law.[1] In this brief document, drawn up with all the formality of Roman testamentary law and signed in the presence of six other Cappadocian bishops and the presbyter Cledonius, Gregory makes a few bequests to friends and faithful staff members, but leaves the bulk of his possessions to the Church at Nazianzus for the benefit of the poor of the town. In doing so, he makes it clear he is carrying out his parents' wishes for the future use of their estate, even while he explicitly cuts out two nieces whom he deems unworthy of any inheritance at all. We have no idea how large his estate was, but it was at least large enough to justify his drawing up a formal document and setting up a kind of trust fund with the bulk of it for the poor of his father's Church. A number of the particular monetary bequests Gregory authorizes in the will represented considerable sums in his time. As a mirror of his concerns and of the combination of practical attention to detail and freedom from worldly ambition that apparently dominated his mind during the last decade of his life, it is a moving and revealing document.

The main problem facing us in interpreting Gregory's will, curiously, arises from its opening sentence. No critical edition of the document has been made, but the text reprinted in the Greek *Patrologia* begins by dating it to "the consulate of the most illustrious Flavius Eucherius and Flavius Evagrius, on the day before the kalends of January." "Flavius Evagrius" is clearly a scribal mistake for "Flavius Syagrius," who was consul along with Flavius Eucherius for the year 381; "Evagrius" is easily understandable as a misreading of "Syagrius" when both are written in Greek uncials. This means, however, that the date given for the making of the will is the last day of that same year: December 31, 381. Because Gregory refers to himself twice in

184

the will as "bishop of the Catholic church in Constantinople," modern scholars since at least Louis Le Nain de Tillemont in the seventeenth century have suggested that "the kalends of January" should also be emended to read "the kalends of June." This would render the date of the will May 31, 381, when Gregory was still acting as bishop in the capital and when a number of Greek bishops, including most (but not all) of the witnesses of the will, would have already gathered for the coming Council.[2] Raymond Van Dam has even offered a number of speculations about why Gregory may have wanted to draw up a will at that particular time: an assurance of the honesty of his financial accounting, a proof of his modest possessions, a sign of his readiness to renounce the episcopal throne at Constantinople in the face of mounting opposition.[3]

One problem, however, with changing the date given in the Greek text from "the day before the kalends of January" to "the day before the kalends of June" is that it is much more difficult to justify such an emendation of the Greek text on palaeographical grounds than it is to emend the consul's name. A further difficulty is that one of the six bishops who signed the will as witnesses—Theodulus of Apameia—does not appear on the lists of bishops who attended the Council of 381, and there is no reason to think he was in Constantinople at that time; among the signatories of the Council's canons, the Church of Apameia was represented by a presbyter.[4] Also, the presence of the presbyter Cledonius in the list of witnesses suggests that the will was made in Cappadocia, at a date after Gregory's return to his home district: Cledonius, a presbyter of Iconium, where Gregory's cousin Amphilochius was bishop, apparently was invited to Nazianzus shortly after Gregory's return to the region in the fall of 381 to act as administrator of the Church there until a successor to Gregory's father could be appointed, but we have no reason to suppose he attended the Council in any capacity.[5] In the absence of a critical text, then, it seems wiser to let the date stand as it appears in the *Patrologia* and to assume that Gregory made his will on the last day of 381, in the company of neighboring clerics who may well have come together for the Christmas or New Year's festival. That Gregory's mind should have turned to the end of life and his desires to the care of the poor in his native town, after the crisis of the early summer and his return home to face the diminishments of age and illness, seems to me to make more sense than that he would make such a will as this at the start of the Council the previous May.

What remains puzzling, of course, and surely significant, is that even though his name appears in the lists of bishops attending the Council six months earlier simply as "Gregory of Nazianzus," while his successor Nectarius already heads those lists as bishop of Constantinople, here in his will Gregory continues to refer to himself by the solemn title of "bishop of the Catholic Church in Constantinople:" a title that had never canonically been conferred on him and that the Council had rejected, in large part, because of his illegal move there from the little see of Sasima. Presumably it is either claimed here as a courtesy title—something retained because once possessed, like a retired senator or retired generals today—or else it signals that in Gregory's own mind, at least, the succession in the capital had not yet been ratified to his satisfaction. In any case, the use of his title here—if indeed the dating of the will is correct—has the slightly pathetic ring of fading dignity. As he settled back into the obscurity of rural Cappadocia, Gregory seems to have brooded over the sudden end to his pastoral career and to have been deeply concerned to put his economic legacy, as well as his literary and theological one, in good order. His thoughts have turned again, clearly, to his father's church at Nazianzus; his daily life is centered again on Karbala, his writing, and his books, but he remains, in his own mind, the priest burdened with great dignity and great responsibility—bishop of Constantinople, capital of the world!

Saint Gregory the Theologian:

An Exact Copy of the Original Document,
on Which are Preserved Both His Signature
and Those of the Witnesses Who Also Signed It.[6]

In the consulate of the most illustrious Flavius Eucherius and Flavius Syagrius, on the day before the kalends of January.[7]

I, Gregory, bishop of the Catholic Church in Constantinople, alive and in my right mind, with sound judgment and healthy reasoning, have drawn up this my testament, which I order and wish to be valid and in force before every court and governmental authority. For I have already made my intention clear, and have consecrated all my possessions to the Catholic Church which is in Nazianzus,[8] for the service of the poor who are under the care of the aforesaid Church. Therefore, I have also appointed three agents to care for the poor: Marcellus, deacon and monk; Gregory the deacon, who was born a slave[9] in my household; and Eustathius the monk, who himself likewise was born a slave in my household. So now, preserving that same mind with regard to the holy church which is in Nazianzus, I hold to the same course of action. If, then, it should be my lot to experience the end of life, let the aforementioned Gregory, deacon and monk, a member of my household whom I set free long ago, be heir of all the property that is mine, moveable and immoveable, wherever it may be, and let everyone else be disinherited.[10] But let him be my heir in such a way that he distribute all my property, moveable and immoveable, for the benefit of the holy Catholic Church which is in Nazianzus, holding back nothing at all besides that which I should leave to some individuals in this my testament by way of legacy or *fideicommissum*.[11] Rather, as I have already said, let him preserve everything precisely for the benefit of the Church, having the fear of God before his eyes, and knowing that I have commanded that all my property should go to the service of the poor of that same Church, and that I have named him heir for this purpose, that by his agency everything should be preserved, without remainder, for the Church.

As for the members of my household, whom I have set free, either by my own decision or by command of my blessed parents, I wish that all of them should abide in their freedom now, too, and that the funds[12] I have invested in them should all remain firm and undisturbed. Further, I wish that my heir, Gregory the deacon, along with the monk Eustathius, both of whom once belonged to my household, should possess the property in Arianzus which came to us from the possessions of Rheginus.[13] And I wish that the breeding mares and sheep, which I already ordered given to them while I was there, and whose possession and ownership I handed over to them, should remain securely theirs by right of ownership. Further, I specially direct that Gregory, the deacon and my heir, who has served me faithfully, should receive the sum of fifty gold pieces[14] as his own legal property.

To the venerable virgin Russiane, my relative, I have already commanded that a specified sum be given each year, in order that she might live decently;[15] I wish and command that all of this be paid to her each year without delay, according to the pattern I have established. Concerning her place of residence, I formerly made no arrangements, since I did not know where it would be most pleasing to her to pass her days. Now, however, I also wish the following: that in whatever place she should choose for herself, a house should be furnished that is fitting for her, a respectable woman, for a decent existence as a virgin. She shall possess this house undisturbed, in fact, for her use and profit, until the end of her life, and after that, it shall revert to the Church. And I wish that she should also be given two serving girls whom she shall choose, with the understanding that the girls will remain with her until the end of her lifetime. And if it should be agreeable to them, it will be her right to bestow freedom on them, but if not, they too shall continue to work for the same Church.

I have already freed my servant Theophilus, who has remained with me. I wish, then, that five gold pieces should now also be given to him as a legacy. And I wish that his brother, Eupraxius, should be freed,[16] and that five gold coins be given to him by way of legacy. Further, I wish that Theodosius, my notary,[17] should be freed, and that five gold coins should be given to him, too, by way of legacy. I wish that my sweet daughter Alypiane[18] might pardon me—for I take little notice of the other two,

Eugenia and Nonna, whose way of life is reprehensible[19]—if I am not in a position to leave anything to her, since I have already promised everything to the poor, or rather since I am following the promise of my blessed parents; to disregard their intent would be, in my view, neither holy nor trustworthy. However, whatever is left from the property of my blessed brother Caesarius—silk or linen or woolen garments, or ponies[20]—I wish to be given to her children; and I wish that neither she nor her sisters should contest any of these dispositions, either against my heir or against the Church.

Let it be known that my in-law Meletius[21] is in unlawful possession of the property in Apenzinsus,[22] which used to be part of Euphemius's[23] property. On this subject I have already written to Euphemius many times, accusing him of cowardice if he does not reclaim what is his. Now I call on all—rulers and subjects—to recognize that Euphemius is being treated unjustly; it is necessary to restore this property to Euphemius.

I wish that the purchase of the estate of Canotaloi[24] from my venerable son, bishop Amphilochius,[25] be revoked; for it is noted in our accounts, and everyone is aware, that the contract has been voided and I have received the payment back, and have already given back possession and ownership of the property.

To Evagrius the deacon,[26] who has labored much with me and shared in my thinking, and has shown his kindness in many ways, I confess my gratitude before God and men. God will repay him with greater kindnesses; but that we might not neglect even little signs of friendship, I wish that he should receive a shirt, a colored tunic, two cloaks, and thirty gold pieces. Likewise, I wish that our other deacon, our sweet brother Theodulus, be given a shirt, two colored tunics from those on my family estate, and twenty gold pieces from the account of my family estate. To Elaphius, my notary, who is so competent and who has made life more peaceful for us the entire time he has been in service, I wish that one shirt be given, two colored tunics, three cloaks, a simple robe,[27] and twenty gold pieces from my family estate.

I wish that this my testament be valid and in force before every court and every governing power. But if it should lack validity as a testament, I wish that the same document be valid as an expression of my wishes or indeed as a codicil.[28] Whoever attempts to overturn it will give account in the day of judgement, and will have his retribution.

In the name of the Father, and of the Son, and of the Holy Spirit.[29]

I, Gregory, bishop of the Catholic Church in Constantinople, having read the testament and being satisfied with all that is written here, sign it in my own hand, and order and wish that it be in force.

I, Amphilochius,[30] bishop of the Catholic Church in Iconium, being present at the making of the most reverend bishop Gregory's will and at his request, sign in my own hand.

I, Optimus, bishop of the Catholic Church of Antioch,[31] was present when the most reverend bishop Gregory make his will as written above, and at his request sign in my own hand.

I, Theodosius, bishop of the Catholic Church of Hyde,[32] being present at the making of the most reverend bishop Gregory's will and at his request, sign in my own hand.

I, Theodulus, bishop of the holy Catholic Church of Apameia,[33] being present, etc.

I, Hilarius, bishop of theCatholic Church in Isauria,[34] being present, etc.

I, Themistius, bishop of the Catholic Church in Adrianople,[35] being present, etc.

I, Cledonius, presbyter of the Catholic church of Iconium, being present, etc.

I, John, lector and notary of the most holy Church of Nazianzus, having made a copy of this sacred testament of the holy and illustrious Gregory the Theologian, which is kept in this holy Church where I work, certify it publicly.[36]

NOTES

1 INTRODUCTION

1 Michael Psellos, *Opusculum Theologicum* 19 (ed. Paul Gautier, *Michaelis Pselli Theologica* 1 [Leipzig: Teubner, 1989] 75.91–93).

2 See Peter Walter, "Erasmus von Rotterdam and Gregor von Nazianz," in Nabil el-Khoury, Henri Crouzel and Rudolf Reinhardt, *Lebendige Überlieferung. Prozesse der Annäherung und Auslegung* (Beirut: Rückert/Ostfildern: Schwaben, 1992) 365–383.

3 "New," presumably, in being a second Gregory Nazianzen!

4 See Jacques Noret, "Grégoire de Nazianze, l'auteur le plus cité, après la Bible, dans la littérature ecclésiastique byzantine," in Justin Mossay (ed.), *II. Symposium Nazianzenum. Louvain-la-Neuve, 25-28 août 1981* (Studien zur Geschichte und Kultur des Altertums, NF 2; Paderborn: Schöningh, 1983) 259–266, with evidence to substantiate the claim.

5 The date of his birth is normally put around the year 330. In his poem *On his own Life* line 239, however, he says that he returned home from his studies in Athens when he was "almost in my thirtieth year," an event that is usually dated in 356; given that date, he may have been born a few years before 330. Karbala is today the lovely village of Güzelyurt, where a Byzantine church of uncertain date is said to incorporate a building originally built by Gregory for his townspeople. For the details and interpretation of Gregory's life, I am especially indebted to the thoughtful and engaging book of John A. McGuckin, *St. Gregory of Nazianzus. An Intellectual Biography* (Crestwood, NY: St. Vladimir's, 2001)—the most complete modern treatment of Gregory's life. Other valuable modern biographies of Gregory are: Paul Gallay, *La Vie de Saint Grégoire de Nazianze* (Lyon/Paris: Vitte, 1943); Jean Bernardi, *Saint Grégoire de Nazianze. Le Théologien et son temps (330–390)* (Paris: Cerf, 1995); and Nicanor Gómez-Villegas, *Gregorio de Nazianzo en Constantinopla. Ortodoxia, heterodoxia y regimen teodosiano en una capital cristiana* (Madrid: Consejo Superior de Investigaciones Científicas, 2000).

6 See McGuckin 3 for further references.

7 See Gregory, Ep. 63; Libanius, Ep. 634, 671. Gregory refers to his cousin, the younger Amphilochius, who became bishop of Iconium and was a distinguished theologian in his own right, as "a friend on your father's side" of Themistius: Gregory, Ep. 24.

8 Gallay 22.

9   Nonna's brother Amphilochius is said to have come from "Diocaesaraea" (see *Anthologia Palatina* 8.134, 135), which most scholars identify as another name for Nazianzus: see Gallay 12–16.

10   See McGuckin 9–10.

11   *On his own Affairs* 424–467; *On his own Life* 69-94.

12   See Gregory's will, translated below, in which only one of them—Alypiane— is considered deserving of a bequest.

13   His cousin, the younger Amphilochius, became bishop of Iconium in 373 shortly after the younger Gregory had been ordained bishop of Sasima. Iconium (present-day Konya) is one of the cities visited by Paul on his first missionary journey: see Acts 13.51–14.7; 14.21–23; II Tim 3.11.

14   See Gregory's funeral oration for Caesarius, Or. 7.9.

15   See Gregory, Or. 7.11–13 and Ep. 7 (to Caesarius). In his funeral oration for Caesarius, Gregory tells the story of Julian's attempt before a crowd of other court officials to persuade Caesarius to abandon Christianity; when Caesarius diplomatically refused, Julian kept him on as palace physician anyway because he admired his learning.

16   See Ep. 20 below.

17   *On his own Affairs* 202–203 (trans. Denis M. Meehan: Fathers of the Church 75; Washington: Catholic University of America Press, 1987; 31–32 [altered]). For a description of Gregory's desperate grief at his brother's death and of the added burden of acting as executor of his will, see *ibid*. 165–229; Ep. 30, to Philagrius (translated below).

18   A classic study of education in the Greek and Roman world remains that of Henri-Irénée Marrou, *A History of Education in Antiquity* (trans. George Lamb; New York: Sheed and Ward, 1956). On the particular importance of rhetoric in the formation and preservation of classical culture, see George Kennedy, *The Art of Persuasion in Greece* (Princeton: Princeton University Press, 1963) and *Greek Rhetoric under the Christian Emperors* (Princeton: Princeton University Press, 1983); Peter Brown, *Power and Persuasion in Late Antiquity: Towards a Christian Empire* (Madison, WI: University of Wisconsin Press, 1992).

19   McGuckin 36–37.

20   Until c.400, when it was divided into three parts, present-day Israel, Palestine, and parts of Lebanon and Jordan constituted a single province, euphemistically called "Palaestina Salutaris."

21   Or. 7.6.

22   Epitaph 4 (PG 38.12–13).

23   McGuckin 45.

24   See McGuckin 47 and references there.

25   For a description of Caesarius's scientific studies there, which occupied him as long as Gregory's humanistic studies kept him in Athens, see Or. 7.7.

26   *On his own Life* 122–123.

27   *Ibid*. 129–204; cf. *On his own Affairs* 307–322.

28   *On his own Life* 162–169 (tr. Meehan 81–82).

29   *Ibid*. 182–199 (tr. Meehan 82 [altered]).

30   For the opinion that Gregory must have sought baptism soon after arriving in Athens, see McGuckin 55, 63–75. There is little evidence in the biographical sources to provide certainty about when he was baptized, however, and modern biographers come to a variety of conclusions; see, for instance, Gallay 67 and further references there. See also below p. 8 and n. 42.

31 See Gregory, Or. 43.15–24. Gregory describes here the acerbity of some of these debates (17) and suggests that Basil was more combative in them than he was himself. According to Gregory, Basil was one of the star students of Athens in their day: *On his own Life* 225; Or. 43. 22–23.

32 For perceptive, if speculative, reflections on this friendship, see McGuckin 76–80.

33 As Gallay puts it, "Au point de vue de l'enseignement, Athènes gardait un prestige incontesté; par ses écoles, elle était encore 'la demeure de l'éloquence' (PG 36.513A5). Pour appartenir à l'élite des gens cultivés, il fallait presque nécessairement avoir passé par Athènes" (37–38).

34 For a description of the academic resources of Athens in the mid–fourth century and a description of the typical course of studies for young men like Gregory and Basil, see Gallay 37–55. See also Gregory's own description, Or. 43.23.

35 See McGuckin 56–62.

36 Or. 43.20 (trans. Charles Gordon Browne and James Edward Swallow: *Nicene and Post-Nicene Fathers* Second series, 7 [repr. Grand Rapids: Eerdmans, 1983] 402). Cf. *On his own Life* 231–237.

37 Or. 43.24.

38 *On his own Life* 239.

39 Or. 7.8.

40 *Ibid.*

41 See, for instance, *On his own Affairs* 452–465.

42 PG 35.257B. If Gregory did in fact delay his baptism until he was ready to commit himself unconditionally to the single-minded pursuit of discipleship and Christian asceticism, he would not be unlike a number of his late-fourth-century contemporaries—Ambrose and Augustine in the West, for instance, or his own sister Gorgonia and Nectarius, his successor as bishop of Constantinople—for whom baptism seems to have come as the "seal" to an already well-formed sense of vocation to Christian life and service to the Church.

43 In his poem *On his own Life* 280–312, Gregory describes this inner conflict and insists that he freely chose a "middle way between the life without ties and the life of mixing, one which would combine the serenity of the former with the practical use of the latter" (trans. Meehan 86).

44 Ep. 3, to a certain Evagrius, father of Gregory's pupil by the same name.

45 Epp. 1, 2, 4, 5, 6.

46 See below, *Introduction*, section III.

47 Ep. 1, to Basil.

48 See the modern edition of this collection by Marguerite Harl, *Sources chrétiennes* 302. Mme. Harl is skeptical about the traditional ascription of the collection to Gregory and Basil; see also McGuckin 102–104, who defends it as at least plausible.

49 In Ep 115, to Bishop Theodore of Tyana, probably written at Easter 383, Gregory says he is sending his friend a copy of such a collection: "And that you may also have a memento from us, and similarly from holy Basil, we have sent you a volume of the *Philokalia* [= anthology] of Origen, with excerpts of passages useful to those who study texts." This has been understood as a claim that Basil and Gregory themselves compiled the collection, but it may simply mean that the volume was one they had used in their earlier study together.

50 *On his own Life* 337–345 (trans. Meehan 86–87). Allusions to the movements of the Emperor Julian in Or. 2, in which Gregory explains his "flight" after ordination, date the Oration to the spring of 362. In Or. 1, given during the Easter celebrations and immediately before Or. 2, Gregory says, "A Mystery anointed me; I withdrew a little while at a Mystery, as much as was necessary to examine myself; now I come back with a Mystery" (Or. 1.2; trans. Browne and Swallow 203 [altered]). This is usually taken to mean that he was ordained at the solemn celebration of the birth of Christ, that he left immediately afterward during the celebration of the Baptism of Christ, and that he returned in time for the Pascha. Uncertain, however, is whether the birth of Christ at this stage was celebrated on December 25 in Cappadocia, as it was in the West, or whether the birth, manifestation, and baptism of the Lord were celebrated on successive days around January 6: see below, p. 22 and n. 106; also Gallay 72, n. 3; McGuckin 101–102.

51 *On his own Life* 350–356. Gregory loved to joke about remoteness and the cloudy, wet climate of Basil's estate at Annesi in Pontus: see Epp 5-6.

52 Or. 2. This long oration provides the main model and source for John Chrysostom's celebrated treatise *On Priesthood*, which probably dates from 381 to 386, while John was a deacon in Antioch. For both authors, of course, "priesthood" refers primarily to the ministry of bishops as heads of local communities of worship but was a title also shared by presbyters, who were seen as associates of subordinate rank. See below, *Introduction*, section V.

53 See above, p. 8 and n. 42.

54 Orations 4 and 5. For Julian's challenge to Christian intellectuals, see below pp. 31–32.

55 Or. 7, from the end of 368 or the beginning of 369.

56 Or. 8, the date of which is uncertain; Gregory's parents are referred to in it, however, as still alive, but Caesarius is already dead. McGuckin dates Gorgonia's death as "369 or 370 at the latest" (166).

57 Or. 14. For the dating and circumstances of this oration and its relation to the second of two orations by Gregory of Nyssa on the same subject (from which Gregory of Nazianzus seems to make a number of explicit borrowings), see my article, "Building the New City: The Cappadocian Fathers and the Rhetoric of Philanthropy," *Journal of Early Christian Studies* 7 (1999), 431–461. See also McGuckin 145–155, who dates Or. 14 to 366–367. On Gregory's treatment of the Christian duty of philanthropy, see Bernard Coulie, *Les richesses dans l'oeuvre de saint Grégoire de Nazianze : étude littéraire et historique* (Louvain-la-Neuve: Institut Orientaliste, 1985); on the treatment of poverty by the three Cappadocian Fathers, see Susan R. Holman, *The Hungry are Dying: Beggars and Bishops in Roman Cappadocia* (New York: Oxford University Press, 2001).

58 See Gregory's explanation in his Panegyric on Basil, Or. 43.58: "When our country had been divided into two provinces, with two capital cities, and a great part of the former was being added to the new one, this again roused their [= Valens's supporters] factious spirit. The one [= Anthimus] thought it right that the ecclesiastical boundaries should be determined by the civil ones, and therefore claimed those newly added as belonging to him, and severed from their former metropolitan. The other [= Basil] clung to the ancient custom, and the division which had come down from our fathers. More painful results either actually followed, or were struggling in the womb

of the future. Synods were wrongfully gathered by the new metropolitan, and revenues seized upon. Some of the presbyters of the churches refused obedience, others were won over. In consequence, the affairs of the churches fell into a sad state of dissension and division." (trans. Browne and Swallow 414 [altered]). Gregory goes on to underline the economic motives for Anthimus's ambitions, although he acknowledges that Anthimus professed pastoral concern; in his poem *On his own Life* 460–463, he acknowledges frankly that the motive of both metropolitans was a desire for financial and administrative control.

59 On Amphilochius's place in the theological world of the Cappadocian Fathers, a fundamental study is still Karl Holl, *Amphilochius von Ikonium in seinem Verhältnis zu den grossen Kappadoziern* (Tübingen: Mohr, 1904; repr. Darmstadt: Wissenschaftliche Buchgesellschaft, 1969).

60 McGuckin 190–191.

61 *On his own Life* 440–450 (trans. Meehan 89–90). For other poignant references to Gregory's resentment at being "forced" to be ordained bishop of Sasima, see Orations 9–12; Epp. 48–50. Even in his panegyric on Basil (Or. 43.59), delivered to Basil's admirers some ten years later, despite the overall tone of fulsome praise, Gregory cannot refrain from venting his wounded feelings over the affair: "I am afraid that I myself was treated as an appendage to this scheme [of increasing his episcopal support in Cappadocia]. By no other term can I readily describe the position. Greatly as I admire his whole conduct, to an extent indeed beyond the powers of expression, of this single particular I find it impossible to approve, for I will acknowledge my feelings in regard to it, though these are, from other sources, not unknown to most of you. I mean the change and faithlessness of his treatment of myself, a cause of pain which even time has not obliterated. For this is the source of all the inconsistency and tangle of my life; it has robbed me of the practice, or a least the reputation, of philosophy..." (trans. Browne and Swallow 414 [altered]). Gregory could no longer claim a lofty distance from Church politics; yet, his actual opportunity for leadership in Sasima was ludicrously small. For further discussions of the entire affair, see Stanislas Giet, *Sasimes, une méprise de S. Basile* (Paris: Lecoffre, 1941); Gallay 104–116; Bernardi 138–142. See also Basil, Epp. 71, 74–76, 98.

62 So *On his own Life* 530–532 (referring to his decision to return to Nazianzus and assist his father, shortly after his episcopal ordination): "I had not touched at all the church allotted to me, even to the extent of offering a single sacrifice there, or leading the congregation in prayer, or ordaining a single cleric." (trans. Meehan 92).

63 Ep. 49. Gregory claims for himself here the Aristotelian virtue of magnanimity (μεγαλοψυχία see *Nicomachean Ethics* 4.2: 1122a19–1123a32), by which a person realistically measures his or her own worth and acts accordingly, expecting to be acknowledged by others in an appropriate way. Here, by an ironic twist, real magnanimity is said to consist not in taking a leadership role but in refusing to take one.

64 *On his own Life* 490–491 (trans. Meehan 91).

65 *Ibid.* 494–557 (trans. Meehan 91–93).

66 *Ibid.* 533–536. See also Or. 12, in which Gregory expresses his assent to his father's pressing invitation.

67 See Gregory's funeral oration for his father, Or. 18. Basil himself was present at the funeral of the elder Gregory, who had been bishop of his small Cappadocian community for 45 years. For the death of Nonna, see *Carmina* 2.1.90 (PG 37.1445–1446):

> Caesarius died first, to common grief;
> Gorgonia next; our father; then our mother.
> O Gregory's grieving hand, O bitter script!
> I'll write my own memorial last of all!

On the death of Gregory's parents, see also Gallay 124–126; McGuckin 223–225.

68 See *On his own Life* 539–547. Gregory explains the bishops' refusal: "Some wanted me to go on ruling because of their regard for me; others were perhaps on the high and mighty side!" (trans. Meehan 92).

69 This sermon is usually dated to the years of Gregory's retirement in Karbala, after the Council of Constantinople (so Gallay 224–225; Bernardi, *La Prédication des Pères Cappadociens* [Montpellier: Presses universitaires de France, 1968] 251–253; McGuckin 386–387), conjecturally even to 383. According to Nicetas of Heraclea, the medieval commentator, however, Gregory delivered it in the presence of his friend Basil, presumably before his own "retreat" to Seleucia. See below (Or. 44, introduction).

70 See Bernardi, *Saint Grégoire* 150–151; McGuckin 229–233.

71 *On his own Life* 550–551 (trans. Meehan 92).

72 An important discussion of the real intent of Apollinarius's Christology is Rowan Greer, "The Man from Heaven: Paul's Last Adam and Apollinaris's Christ," in William S. Babcock (ed.), *Paul and the Legacies of Paul* (Dallas: Southern Methodist University Press, 1990) 165–182. See also G.L. Prestige, *Basil the Great and Apollinarius of Laodicaea* (London: SPCK, 1956), and my article, "'Heavenly Man' and 'Eternal Christ': Apollinarius and Gregory of Nyssa on the Personal Identity of the Savior," *Journal of Early Christian Studies* 10 (2002), 469–488.

73 A famous phrase of Origen, included by Gregory in his Ep. 101 to Cledonius, against the Apollinarian Christology.

74 So McGuckin 236, relying on a vague remark of Gregory's in his panegyric on Basil that his work in Constantinople in the years 379–381 had been taken on according to the will of God and the "judgment" of his late friend: Or. 43.2.

75 *On his own Life* 592–599 (trans. Meehan 93–94).

76 McGuckin 236–238.

77 The location of Theodosia's house, and the domestic church Gregory called the *Anastasia* is still uncertain. The fifth-century church historians Socrates (*Church History* 5.7) and Sozomen (*Church History* 7.5) tell us that the oratory there was enlarged into a magnificent basilica by "later emperors," perhaps by Theodosius himself shortly after Gregory's resignation. Later sources attest its location as in the "portico of Domninus," in the "quarter of Maurianus." Historians continue to differ on just where this was. In the nineteenth century, Alexander G. Paspates (*Byzantinai Meletai. Topografikai kai Historikai* [Constantinople: Koromela, 1877] 364–374), arguing from Byzantine narrative material and the remains of ancient buildings nearby, suggested that the Anastasia stood on the site now occupied by the sixteenth-century

Sokollu Mehmet Pasha mosque, south of the Mese—the ancient Roman main street (today the Divan Yolu)—toward the Sea of Marmara, on a steeply descending site in what is now the Sultanahmet quarter, roughly halfway between the Hippodrome and Justinian's church of Sts. Sergius and Bacchus. Raymond Janin later rejected Paspates's theory, arguing that the Portico of Domninus lay on higher ground on the opposite side of the Mese running downhill toward the Golden Horn, between Çemberlitaş and Beyazit Square, near the site of one of the present entrances to the Great Bazaar (*La Géographie ecclésiastique de l'Empire Byzantin* 1.3 [Paris: CNRS, 1953] 28–29; for a discussion of the historical sources, see also Janin, "Études de topographie Byzantine," *Echos d'Orient* 36 [1937] 137–149). See also McGuckin 242–243, who cites "a recent archaeological report" confirming Paspates's hypothesis. In any case, Gregory's "Anastasia" seems to have been only a short walk from the imperial palace and the center of the city's life; in fact, when the present church of Hagia Sophia was dedicated in 537, after being rebuilt under Justinian I, the liturgical procession began at the Anastasia.

78   This dating of Gregory's move to Constantinople, rather than the more commonly accepted earlier one of spring, 379, has been suggested by McGuckin (236–240) and rests on the plausible assumption that he was persuaded to take on this new responsibility by the urging of the bishops at the synod of Antioch in the autumn of that year. The rest of his career in Constantinople suggests strong ties with the theological agenda of Melitius of Antioch and mounting tension with Antioch's rival see, Alexandria, which, as it had done for most of the fourth century, turned westward to the see of Rome for its support. For a lively description of Constantinople as a city and of the situation of the various Christian communities in it at the time of Gregory's arrival, see Bernardi, *Saint Grégoire de Nazianze* 155–185; also Gómez Villegas 79–103, 119–158.

79   See Or. 42.27 below and the further references given there.

80   For details of the dating of Gregory's pastoral activities and orations from this period, see Gallay 136–211, with a schematic summary on 252–253; McGuckin 243–369.

81   This strange piece, focused mainly on legends connected with another early martyr, Cyprian of Antioch, and showing little understanding of the activities or writings of the third-century bishop of Carthage, seems to have been given to meet the congregation's demand for some kind of public oratorical declamation by the newly arrived bishop.

82   For the practice of summary professions of faith by newly appointed bishops as a requirement for the maintenance of communion among the Churches which recognized one another as representing the apostolic faith, see the description of Ludwig Hertling, *Communio. Church and Papacy in Early Christianity* (trans. Jared Wicks; Chicago, IL: Loyola University Press, 1972), esp. 28–36, 41–42. Hertling presents his evidence from an anachronistically narrow Roman Catholic perspective, but his general description of what was involved in the concept of ecclesial communion remains classic. See also the fuller treatments of Jean-Marie-Roger Tillard, *Église d'Églises. L'ecclésiologie de communion* (Paris: Cerf, 1987); and *Flesh of the Church, Flesh of Christ: At the Source of the Ecclesiology of Communion* (trans. Madeleine Beaumont; Collegeville, MN: Liturgical Press, 2001).

83 For details of the story of Maximus and his relations with Gregory, see Jan Sajdak, "Nazianzenica I," *Eos* 15 (1909) 18–48; Jean Bernardi, *Prédication* 168–181; *Saint Grégoire* 191–194; Justin Mossay, "Note sur Héron-Maxime, écrivain ecclésiastique," *Analecta Bollandiana* 100 (1982) 229–236; McGuckin 311–325; Gómez-Villegas 103–112.

84 Sozomen, *Church History* 7.9.

85 *On his own Life* 750–772. The Cynics were notorious among the ancient philosophical sects for being Antiquity's hippies: challenging polite conventions of decorum while they engaged the young in largely destructive critical arguments about personal freedom and ethics.

86 *Ibid.* 773–775.

87 *Ibid.* 976–977.

88 *Ibid.* 784–786; 807–814 (trans. Meehan 99–100).

89 *Ibid.* 832–865.

90 *Ibid.* 834–844.

91 Hero (Greek: Ἥρων) was a first-century Greek mathematician of Alexandria and a minor local deity in Bithynia in Asia Minor; it was also the name of two early Alexandrian martyrs, one of them a disciple of Origen (see Eusebius, *Church History* 6.4.3; 6.41.19). It may have been a name connected with Maximus's family or may simply be a nickname used by Gregory for reasons now lost to us.

92 *Ibid.* 845–864.

93 *Ibid.* 891. Alexandrian sailors seemed to have a reputation for supporting nefarious theological causes in the fourth century. Both Arius and Athanasius had courted their support as they attempted to put political pressure on the Emperor and the local population.

94 *Ibid.* 885–939.

95 McGuckin 324.

96 *On his own Life* 941–946 (Meehan 103).

97 Socrates, *Church History* 5.7; see McGuckin 325.

98 *On his own Life* 1312–1324.

99 *Ibid.* 1325–1342 (trans. Meehan 114).

100 *Ibid.* 1371-1390.

101 *Ibid.* 1411–1418, 1424–1427, 1431–1436 (trans. Meehan 116).

102 *Ibid.* 1466–1473 (trans. Meehan 117).

103 *Ibid.* 1475–1484.

104 *Ibid.* 1500–1506.

105 McGuckin 329.

106 The dating of this important trio of sermons is somewhat unclear. Gallay, following earlier consensus, places Or. 38 at December 25, 379, on the assumption that the Western practice of celebrating the birth of Jesus on that day had already been imported to the Greek Church and was observed as a separate festival from that of his "epiphany" to the nations on January 6 (Gallay 153–159; for this position on the dates of the two festivals, see also B. Botte, *Les origines de la Noël et de l'Epiphanie* [Louvain: Mont-César, 1932]; J. Mossay, *Les fêtes de Noël et d'Epiphanie d'après les sources littéraires cappadociennes du IVe siècle* [Louvain: Mont-César, 1965]; Thomas J. Talley, *The Origins of the Liturgical Year* [Collegeville, MN: Liturgical Press, 1991] 134–141). For the most recent and complete discussion of the celebration, see Susan K. Roll, *Toward the Origins of Christmas* (Kampen: Kok Pharos,

1995) 189–193. The evidence normally supplied for dating the introduction of the Western Christmas, however, in Constantinople—and by implication in Cappadocia—is chiefly Gregory's Oration 38, so the usual argument for dating the oration on December 25 is, in fact, circular. Gallay's choice of 379–380 for the trilogy, rather than 380–381, is determined to a great extent by the earlier date he assigns to the start of Gregory's pastoral career in Constantinople. The three "theophany" sermons are so closely interwoven thematically and rhetorically that it seems to make more sense to identify them with a continuous, major liturgical feast and to assume that Or. 38 was given on January 5, the day before the main feast; Or. 39 was given during a night vigil (hence the emphasis on lights); and Or. 40 was given on January 6 itself, when baptisms were probably performed at the liturgy. See McGuckin 336–337; also Bernardi, *Prédication* 199–216 (dating Or. 38 to December 25, 380 and Or. 39 and 40 to the vigil and morning liturgies, respectively, of January 6, 381), and Claudio Moreschini, introduction to *Sources chrétiennes* 358 (Paris: Cerf, 1990) 16–22, who lays out the various hypotheses but follows Bernardi.

107   See McGuckin 348.
108   *Ibid.*
109   The most comprehensive treatment of the Council of 381 is that of Adolf Martin Ritter, *Das Konzil von Konstantinopel und sein Symbol. Studien zur Geschichte und Theologie des zweiten ökumenischen Konzils* (Göttingen: Vandenhoeck und Rupprecht, 1965). See also Ignacio Ortiz de Urbina, *Nicée et Constantinople* (Paris: L'Orante, 1963); J.N.D. Kelly, *Early Christian Creeds* (3rd edn; New York: McKay, 1972) 296–367. The formula we know as the creed of Constantinople was regarded, at least from the time of Chalcedon (451), as simply an expanded version of the Nicene creed but seems originally to have been a baptismal profession used in Syria and Palestine in the mid-fifth century, and is quoted by Epiphanius of Salamis near the end of his *Ancoratus*, as early as 374 (*Ancoratus* 118.9–12 [ed. Karl Holl: *Griechische christliche Schriftsteller* 25 (Leipzig: Hinrichs, 1915) 146–147]); the creed may have been considered as a possible formulation of faith by the bishops at Constantinople in 381, although it is not certain that the Council actually adopted it. For a discussion of various plausible explanations of the origin of the creed and its relationship to the Council, see Kelly 298–331. For a discussion of the Council's approach to speaking of the person of the Holy Spirit, see Anthony Meredith, "The Pneumatology of the Cappadocian Fathers and the Creed of Constantinople," *Irish Theological Quarterly* 48 (1981) 196–211.
110   *On his own Life* 1532–1559 (trans. Meehan 119–120).
111   Sozomen, *Church History* 7.7 (trans. Edward Walford, rev. Chester D. Hartranft; Nicene and Post-Nicene Fathers II/2 [repr. Grand Rapids: Eerdmans, 1983] 380.
112   The Greek text of the canons of the Council, which provides a list of the bishops who signed them, includes Gregory among the bishops from Cappadocia—as bishop not of Sasima but of Nazianzus! By the end of the Council, it seems clear that Gregory had given up all claim to the see of Constantinople and that Nectarius had been recognized as the new bishop. See C. H. Turner, "Canons Attributed to the Council of Constantinople, a.d. 381, Together with the Names of the Bishops, from Two Patmos MSs

POB α′ POΓα′," *Journal of Theological Studies* 15 (1914) 169. In fact, no bishop was officially elected to the see of Nazianzus until at least the mid-380s. Gregory never accepted the post canonically but appointed a presbyter of Iconium, Cledonius, as caretaker, probably in the fall of 381, until a bishop should be appointed. For a Syriac version of the canons and bishops' list of Constantinople, see Oskar Braun, "Syrische Texte über die erste allgemeine Synode von Konstantinopel," in Carl Bezold (ed.), *Orientalistische Studien für Theodor Nöldeke* 1 (1906) 463–478.

113 Sozomen, *Church History* 7.7 (see note 111). The statement that another was appointed in Gregory's stead is inaccurate (see note 112).

114 See his arguments in the introduction to *Sources chrétiennes* 384 (Paris: Cerf, 1992) 7–17.

115 For a discussion of the dating of Gregory's will, see the introduction to our translation of it below, pp. 170–172.

116 *Carmina* 2.1.25–57 (PG 37.1331–1333). For the entire text, see below.

117 Excerpts from Gregory's works are designated in this way in the florilegia included in the *Acta* of the Council of Chalcedon (451). See below, n. 182.

118 See Joannes Sajdak, *Historia Critica Scholiastarum et Commentatorum Gregorii Nazianzeni* (Cracow: Academia Litterarum, 1904); Friedhelm Lefherz, *Studien zu Gregor von Nazianz. Mythologie, Überlieferung, Scholiasten* (Diss. Bonn, 1958) 113. For a full discussion of all the known scholia and commentaries on Gregory's work through the eighteenth century, see Lefherz 109–195.

119 See, for example, the glossary in the thirteenth-century manuscript Oxford Baroccianus 50, published by J. Cramer, *Anecdota Graeca e codicibus manuscriptis Bibliothecarum Oxoniensium* 2 (Oxford, 1835) 475–487.

120 Lefherz 135–137.

121 Psellos is referring here to Aristotle's distinction of the three *genera* of artistically persuasive speech, or rhetoric: forensic speech, aimed at convincing jurors in a trial; political speech, aimed at moving an assembly to vote in a particular way; and "epideictic" or "show" speech, aimed at moving its hearers to share certain feelings and values, especially to avoid vice and pursue virtue. This third genre of oratory became dominant in the time of the Empire, when the democratic processes of the ancient city had gone into decline. Peter Brown has pointed out, however, its crucial political and social relevance as a vehicle of communicating classical ideals of behavior: see *Power and Persuasion in Late Antiquity: Towards a Christian Empire* (Madison, WI: University of Wisconsin Press, 1992); see also Malcolm Heath, *Menander: a Rhetor in Context* (Oxford: Oxford University Press, 2004). Psellos refers to epideictic oratory here as "panegyric" because one of its main forms was the speech in praise of some historical or contemporary figure.

122 I.e., John Chrysostom.

123 Michael Psellos, "The Characteristics of Gregory the Theologian, the Great Basil, Chrysostom, and Gregory of Nyssa" (PG 122.901 C8 – 904 A6).

124 *Ibid.* 904 D3–905 A4. In a similar vein, Psellos insists in his "Improvised Speech to Pothos the Cubicularius," after comparing Gregory to the major figures in classical Greek prose, that "he has mingled, in a more precise way, the outstanding features of each of them in his own written works, so that he does not give the appearance of collecting all these features to compete with them, but rather of being, on his own, the archetypal form of graceful

speech." (ed. A. Mayer, "Psellos' Rede über den rhetorischen Charakter des Gregorios von Nazianz," *Byzantinische Zeitschrift* 20 [1911] 48.20–23).

125 PG 35.309. The letter to Chevallon served as preface to the 1532 Paris translation of Gregory's works, edited by Erasmus and Johannes Straub. The Latin translations in the volume include several by Rufinus of Aquileia, dating from the late fourth and early fifth centuries, and others by the German humanists Petrus Mosellanus (1493–1524) and Willibald Pirckheimer (1470–1530).

126 See Brown, *Power and Persuasion* (above, n. 121). For the Christian adaptation of late antique rhetoric to the Church's own purposes in a Christianized Empire, see George A. Kennedy, *Greek Rhetoric under Christian Emperors* (Princeton: Princeton University Press, 1983); *Classical Rhetoric and its Christian and Secular Tradition from Ancient to Modern Times* (Chapel Hill, NC: University of North Carolina Press, 1999); Averil M. Cameron, *Christianity and the Rhetoric of Empire: the Development of Christian Discourse* (Berkeley, CA: University of California Press, 1991). For a discussion of the role of literary accomplishment in defining a person's Hellenic identity in this period, see Tim Whitmarsh, " 'Greece is the World': Exile and Identity in the Second Sophistic," in Simon Goldhill (ed.), *Being Greek under Rome: Cultural Identity, the Second Sophistic, and the Development of Empire* (Cambridge: Cambridge Univeristy Press, 2001) 269–305. More recently, Malcolm Heath has argued that Philostratus's portrait of the activities and concerns of late antique orators is one-sided and that judicial and deliberative oratory still had important public functions: *Menander: A Rhetor in Context* (above, n. 121). For a full and engaging account of the quieter, more scholarly role of the "grammarian," or literary critic, in ancient society as the arbiter of linguistic correctness and elegance, see Robert A. Kaster, *Guardians of Language: the Grammarian and Society in Late Antiquity* (Berkeley: University of California Press, 1988).

127 The most detailed study of the technical and stylistic aspects of Gregory's prose style is still Marcel Guignet, *Saint Grégoire de Nazianze et la rhétorique* (Paris: Picard, 1911). Čelica Milovanović has recently argued, through a detailed analysis of several of Gregory's orations, that classical models of forensic oratory have influenced him as much as the epideictic style, despite their largely declamatory or literary character: see "Sailing to *Sophistopolis*: Gregory of Nazianzus and Greek Declamation," *Journal of Early Christian Studies* 13 (2005) 187–232. For a sensitive study of the uniquely personal, even "confessional," character of Gregory's oratory, see Hans-Georg Beck, "Rede als Kunstwerk und Bekenntnis: Gregor von Nazianz," *Bayerische Akademie der Wissenschaften, Philosophisch-historische Klasse* Sitzungsberichte 1977.4 (Munich, 1977).

128 For a modern edition of these important poems, with English translation, see Claudio Moreschini and Donald F. Sykes, *Gregory of Nazianzus: Poemata Arcana* (Oxford: Oxford University Press, 1997).

129 For an analysis of the growth of this anthological tradition, see especially Alan Cameron, *The Greek Anthology from Meleager to Planudes* (Oxford: Oxford University Press, 1993). For the addition of Book VIII and the inclusion of doublets of some of these poems by Gregory elsewhere in the manuscript, see *ibid.* 99–108, 145–146, 325–327.

130 Michele Pellegrino, *La Poesia di S. Gregorio Nazianzeno* (Milan: Vita e Pensiero, 1932) 93.

131 Ep. 52.2; Ep. 53. We do not know how many letters were included in the collection Gregory sent to Nicoboulus, but it seems likely that it forms at least the core of the collection that has come down to us. For a brief discussion of the origin of the collection, see Paul Gallay, *Saint Grégoire de Nazianze. Lettres* 1 (Paris: Les Belles Lettres, 1964) xxi–xxiii.

132 Ep. 52.3.

133 Ep. 51.2. For a study of Gregory's epistolary style, see Paul Gallay, *Langue et style de Saint Grégoire de Nazianze dans sa correspondance* (Paris: Monnier, 1933); see also George T. Dennis, "Gregory of Nazianzus and the Byzantine Letter," in Thomas P. Halton and Joseph P. Williman (eds), *Diakonia. Studies in Honor of Robert T. Meyer* (Washington, DC: Catholic University of America Press, 1986) 3–14.

134 Ep. 54. This is the entire letter—a concise statement about concision! Antimachus, a poet who had a reputation for long-windedness and flourished around the end of the fifth century B.C., survives today only in fragments.

135 Ep. 51.4.

136 *Ibid.* 6.

137 For a description of Julian's intended religious reforms, and references to passages in his letters that express them, see especially Robert Browning, *The Emperor Julian* (Berkeley, CA: University of California Press, 1976) 167–168, 177–182. At his request, the Neoplatonist philosopher Salutius Secundus, whom Julian had promoted to the office of praetorian prefect of the Eastern Empire, composed a brief catechetical handbook on Platonized pagan religion, called *On the Gods and the World*; Julian himself wrote several treatises promoting a philosophical interpretation of traditional Roman cults and attacking the agnosticism of the Cynic school.

138 *Codex Theodosianus* 13.3.5.

139 Julian, Ep. 36 (422 B).

140 *Ibid.* (423 CD).

141 For a discussion of the date of these two orations, see the introduction by Jean Bernardi to *Sources chrétiennes* 309 (Paris: Cerf, 1983) 19–35. See also McGuckin 119–126.

142 Or. 4.5.

143 Literally: "counting on your fingers."

144 Or. 4.107–108.

145 Greek: λόγος, which could also mean "literature" or simply "the word".

146 Or. 4.100–101.

147 For the mysterious events surrounding his death, see Browning 183–186.

148 For a thoughtful synthetic view on these tensions in Gregory's work, see Brooks Otis, "The Throne and the Mountain: An Essay on St. Gregory Nazianzus," *The Classical Journal* 56 (1961) 146–165. Otis characterizes them (147–148) as the interplay of "three great issues": the "issue of the world," or the conflict between Christian institutions and the politics of the Empire; the "intellectual-theological issue," which grew from the attempt to interpret Christian Scriptural teaching with the explicit help of the Greek philosophical tradition; and the "issue of Christian Culture," which included both Christian use of Hellenic culture and Christian action in a world that was often crassly irreligious.

149 McGuckin 57. The best general survey of Gregory's use of the Greek philosophical tradition, although unfortunately difficult to find in libraries,

is Henri Pinault, *Le Platonisme de Saint Grégoire de Nazianze. Essai sur les relations du Christianisme et de l'Hellénisme dans son oeuvre théologique* (La Roche-sur-Yon: Romain, 1925). For Gregory's admiration of the asceticism of the Cynic school, whom he doubtless knew through the doxographical handbooks and biographical collections of late antiquity and through the self-consciously "Cynic" style of his Alexandrian rival Maximus, see J. R. Asmus, "Gregorius von Nazianz und sein Verhältnis zum Kynismus. Eine patristisch-philosophische Studie," *Theologische Studien und Kritiken* 67 (1894) 314–339. For the understanding and uses of the term φιλοσοφία in the Greek philosophical and early Christian tradition, see Anne-Marie Malingrey, *"Philosophia." Étude d'un groupe de mots dans la literature grecque, des Présocratiques au IVe siècle après J.-C.* (Paris: Klincksieck, 1961); for the Cappadocians, see 206–261.

150 Perhaps the most useful and persuasive recent exposition of the aims and character of philosophy in ancient Hellenic culture is Pierre Hadot, *What is Ancient Philosophy?* (trans. Michael Chase; Cambridge, MA: Harvard University Press, 2002). See also the more wide-ranging essays collected in Hadot's earlier volume, *Philosophy as a Way of Life* (ed. Arnold Davidson, trans. Michael Chase; Oxford: Blackwell, 1995).

151 *What is Ancient Philosophy?* 5–6.

152 Or. 4.113. For a thoughtful discussion of the interplay of "practical" and "theoretical" emphases in Gregory's writings, see Thomas Špidlík, S.J., *Grégoire de Nazianze. Introduction à l'étude de sa doctrine spirituelle* (Orientalia Christiana Analecta 189; Rome: Pontificium Institutum Studiorum Orientalium, 1971), esp. 49–155.

153 Or. 27.3.

154 *Ibid*. 3, 5.

155 *Ibid*. 4–5, 9. For further reflections on "philosophizing about God," see Or. 28. 1–4; Or. 31.5.

156 Or. 21.1–2 (trans. Charles Gordon Browne and James Edward Swallow: *Nicene and Post-Nicene Fathers* 2.7 [repr. Grand Rapids: Eerdmans, 1983] 269–270 [altered]).

157 Or. 38.7.

158 *Ibid*. 8.

159 *Ibid*. 11.

160 Ep. 31.

161 Ep. 56. The recipient of this and several other of Gregory's letters is not otherwise known, but the fact that he writes here to a plural audience suggests that she may have belonged to a women's monastic community.

162 Ep. 47.

163 For versions of this phrase, see Or. 4 (*Against Julian*) 1, 23; Or. 7 (*Panegyric on his Brother Caesarius*) 1; Or. 43 (*Panegyric on Basil*) 28; cf. "my philosophy" or "our philosophy," referring to Gregory's personal pattern of life: Or. 3.1; Or. 9.4; Or. 19.1, 4.

164 Or. 8.15; see *ibid*. 6–15 for a description of her way of embodying the classical virtues.

165 Or. 25.1.

166 *Ibid*. 2.

167 *Ibid*. The Cynic philosophers, whose name means "doglike," emphasized their socially critical perspective by cultivating an unkempt appearance and

deliberately flouting social mores. Diogenes and Krates, the founders of the school, were said to have performed sexual acts in the public square.

168 *Ibid.*

169 *Ibid.* 3–4, 7.

170 *Ibid.* 6.

171 Or. 26.3.

172 *Ibid.* 5–6.

173 *Ibid.* 8–9.

174 *Ibid.* 9.

175 See, e.g., I Cor. 13.7; II Cor. 11.21–29.

176 Or. 26.12.

177 Cf. Gen. 16.12 (referring to Ishmael as a "wild ass of a man"); Job 39.5–8.

178 Or. 26.13.

179 For a stimulating comparison of the practices of the early Christian ascetics with those of the pagan philosophers, as presented in biographical material from both traditions, see Anthony Meredith, "Asceticism—Christian and Greek," *Journal of Theological Studies* 27 (1976) 313–332.

180 See, for instance, Ep. 123, written to his friend Bishop Theodore of Tyana during the 380s, in which he begs off Theodore's invitation to return a visit: "I was delighted at your presence here, and I love your company, even though I have laid down the rule for myself, otherwise, to stay at home and philosphize in peace. For I find this is the most profitable of all the things I can do. Since the weather is still stormy and my sickness has not grown any less acute, please be patient with me a little longer, and pray for my health. When the right time comes, I will yield to your entreaties."

181 Ep. 94. Cf. Ep. 194, to Vitalianus, from the same period, in which Gregory congratulates his friend on the marriage of his daughter and hopes that Vitalianus will now be able to devote himself also to the "philosophic life:" "You say that we are lazy; but to speak the truth, we are ill, not lazy. Still, whatever comes from the hand of God is well with us. We have handed over all disturbances to others, and we will enjoy the benefits of philosophy when you withdraw to be with God, and become completely concerned with the things that are above, no longer bound by any other tie." For Gregory to be a philosopher completely, even his distant friends must become philosophers as well.

182 Pierre Hadot remarks that ancient philosophy from the time of the Presocratics, was rooted in "the choice of a certain way of life and existential option which demands from the individual a total change of lifestyle, a conversion of one's entire being, and ultimately a certain desire to be and to live in a certain way. This existential option, in turn, implies a certain vision of the world, and the task of philosophical discourse will therefore be to reveal and rationally justify this existential option, as well as this representation of the world." To enter on such a way of life, to learn through philosophical discourse to analyze and understand its reasons, always required companions. As Hadot puts it, "This choice and decision are never made in solitude. There can never be a philosophy or philosophers outside a group, a community—in a word, a philosophical 'school'" (*What is Ancient Philosophy?* 3).

183 An excerpt from Gregory's first letter to Cledonius (Ep. 101), ascribed to "the blessed Gregory the Theologian," appears in the florilegium of patristic

authorities added to the Address to the Emperor Marcian in the *acta* of the Council of Chalcedon: ACO II, 1, 3.114 [473].14. He is simply referred to in this way (as if by a familiar title) by such later Greek writers as the Emperor Justinian (*Against Origen*: ACO 3.193.2, 26, 35; 194.4; 195.32; *Edict against Origen*: *ibid*. 205.37), Maximus the Confessor (e.g., *Dialogue with Pyrrhus*: PG 91.316 C) and John of Damascus (*On the Orthodox Faith* 3.15).

184 Ed. Xavier Lequeux (CCG 44; Corpus Nazianzenum 11 [Turnhout 2001]) 176.46–51; PG 35.288 C10–14). Gregory the Presbyter claims to have been a priest of Caesaraea in Cappadocia; his dates are uncertain. Lequeux (*ibid*. 15–16) argues from less than overwhelming evidence that he wrote between the mid-sixth and the mid-seventh century.

185 E.g., *Republic* 2 (379a).

186 E.g., *Metaphysics* 1 (983b29); 3 (1000a9); 10 (1071b27).

187 *Metaphysics* 6 (1026a7–33).

188 *Contra Celsum* 2.71 (trans. Henry Chadwick; Cambridge: Cambridge University Press, 1965) 121. Cf. *ibid*. 6.18 and 7.41, where Origen contrasts the "theology" implied in Biblical statements about God with Celsus's favorite passages from Plato or the Greek poets.

189 *Commentary on John* 2.34.205. For Origen's use of the term *theology*, see Henri Crouzel, "θεολογία et mots de même racine chez Origène," in Khoury, Crouzel and Reinhardt (eds), *Lebendinge Überlieferung* (above, n. 2) 83–90.

190 Eusebius, *Church History* 1.1.7; cf. the preface to Book 2 of the same work: "Whatever it was fitting to set forth, as a preface to the history of the Church, concerning the divine identity (θεολογία) of the saving Word and the ancient tradition (ἀρχαιολογία) of the doctrines we teach, and of the ancient character of the evangelical way of life practiced by Christians ... we have explained." For Gregory's use of the now-classical distinction of θεολογία and οἰκονομία, see Or. 38.8 below, pp.112–113 and n. 376.

191 For an important and thorough study of the constantly pastoral and spiritual character of Gregory's theology and of the centrality of θεολογία in his pastoral practice, see Christopher A. Beeley, *Gregory of Nazianzus: Theology, Spirituality and Pastoral Theology* (Dissertation: University of Notre Dame, 2002; New York: Oxford University Press, forthcoming).

192 Or. 20.1.

193 *Ibid*. 4–5; this theme of the need for purification before one engages in theological discourse is developed at greater length in Or. 27, the first of the "Theological Orations."

194 Or. 20.6. For this same description of orthodox theology as the middle path between the extremes of modalistic monotheism and polytheism, see also Or. 18.16; Or. 25.16.

195 Or. 20.10.

196 Or. 20.10–11. In a similar vein, Gregory speaks scornfully in the Fifth Theological Oration of the futility of trying to understand fully, let alone to take literally, the necessarily analogous language used of the relations of the divine Persons: The Holy Spirit, he says, "inasmuch as he proceeds from that source [i.e., the Father], is no creature; and inasmuch as he is not begotten is not Son; and inasmuch as he is between the unbegotten and the begotten is God. And thus escaping the toils of your syllogisms, he has manifested himself as God, stronger than your divisions. What then is 'procession'? You tell me what the unbegottenness of the Father is, and I will explain to you

the physical details of the generation of the Son and the procession of the Spirit, and we shall both be frenzy-stricken for prying into the Mystery of God!" (Or. 31.8: trans. Browne and Swallow: NPNF 2.7.320 [altered]).

197 Although Gregory of Nyssa argues at length against the later "Arian" position on the creaturely status of the Son in his books *Against Eunomius*, his work to give precision to a genuinely Trinitarian understanding of the divine Mystery appears especially in some of his shorter essays: *Against the Greeks, based on Common Notions* (ed. Friedrich Mueller: *Gregorii Nysseni Opera* III/1 [Leiden: Brill, 1958] 19–33); *To Eustathius, on the Holy Trinity* (ibid. 3–16); *To Ablabius, on Why We Do Not Think of Saying 'Three Gods'* (ibid. 37–57); *To Simplicius, on the Faith* (ibid. 61–67).

198 The literature on the classical formation of Trinitarian terminology and conceptuality in the late fourth century, especially by the Cappadocian Fathers, is extensive. A magisterial summary of the origin and classical significance of these terms is provided by André de Halleux, "'Hypostase' et 'personne' dans la formation du dogme trinitaire," *Revue d'histoire ecclésiastique* 79 (1984) 311–369, 623–670 [= *Patrologie et Oecuménisme. Receuil d'études* (Leuven: University Press, 1990) 113–214]. For a study of the Cappadocians' decisive contribution to the formation of Trinitarian dogma, see de Halleux, "Personnalisme ou essentialisme trinitaire chez les Pères cappadociens?" *Revue théologique de Louvain* 17 (1986) 129–155, 265–292 [= *Patrologie et Oecuménisme* 215–269]. For important recent discussions, see John Behr, *The Nicene Faith* 2 (Crestwood, NY: St. Vladimir's, 2004), especially 263–474; and Lewis Ayres, *Nicaea and its Legacy* (Oxford: Oxford University Press, 2004), especially 187–221 (Basil of Caesaraea), 244–251 (Gregory of Nazianzus), and 344–363 (Gregory of Nyssa). Ayres rightly points out (250–251) that there are significant, if subtle, differences of emphasis in the Trinitarian conceptions of the three Cappadocians, but inexplicably gives less attention to Gregory of Nazianzus's theology than to that of the other two.

199 Or. 29.2. The Scriptural reference Gregory makes in the last sentence is to John 15.26, where Jesus says to the disciples at the Last Supper, "When the Advocate comes, whom I shall send to you from the Father, even the Spirit of truth who proceeds from the Father, he will bear witness to me." For Gregory and the later Greek tradition, this verse remains the linguistic norm for conceiving of the origin of the Holy Spirit within the Mystery of God; and of Jesus' role in sending him forth on his saving "mission" in human history.

200 Or. 23.8. McGuckin (262–264) dates this oration to the spring of 380, after Gregory and his congregation had been physically attacked during their Easter celebration by anti-Nicene militants, but before the more elaborate argument of the five "Theological Orations," written later that summer.

201 It is interesting to note that Gregory does not identify the distinguishing hypostatic characteristic of the Spirit here as "proceeding" (ἐκπόρευσις, τὸ ἐκπορεύεσθαι), but "mission." Terminology for the relation of the Spirit to Father and Son is still somewhat fluid at this stage in the history of Trinitarian theology.

202 Matt. 11.27.

203 Cf. I Cor. 13.12. This passage is Or. 25.16. For similar delineations of what is unique about Father, Son, and Holy Spirit within the one divine reality, see Or. 31.9; 39.12.

204　Here it is the Son who is called "the Beginning" (ἀρχή), not because he is the origin of the divine substance but because he is the beginning or cause of all that is not God; see John 1.3: "All things were made through him, and without him was not anything made that was made."

205　I.e., the Holy Spirit, who here is simply said to be "with" the Son in his role as source of creation. Gregory may be thinking of Gen. 1.1–3, where God creates "in the beginning" by his Word, while his Spirit hovers over the unformed waters.

206　Or. 42.15.

207　Or. 25.18–19. Gregory's reference to the Trinity as "dwelling in tents" is clearly meant to evoke both Israel's tabernacle in the desert and the assertion of John 1.14 that the Word, who is God, has "become flesh and pitched his tent among us."

208　Or. 42.24.

209　*Ibid.*, alluding to I Cor. 9.22.

210　See above, p. 9. The title given to Oration 2 varies in the Byzantine manuscripts but is usually some variant of the following: "An Apologetic Discourse of Saint Gregory the Theologian, on Account of his Flight to Pontus and Return from There, because of his Ordination as Presbyter; in which the Subject is: What the Nature of Priesthood is, and What Kind of Person a Bishop Should Be."

211　Chrysostom's treatise in six books is usually dated to the time of his ministry as deacon in Antioch, between 380 and 386.

212　On Gregory's theology of ministry, see Dr. Menn, "Zur Pastoraltheologie Gregors von Nazianz," *Revue internationale de théologie* 12 (1904) 427–440; Andrew Louth, "St. Gregory Nazianzen on Bishops and the Episcopate," in *Vescovi e pastori in epoca Teodosiana* (Studia Ephemeridis Augustinianum 58; Rome: Institutum Patristicum Augustinianum, 1997) 2.81–285; Susanna Elm, "The Diagnostic Gaze: Gregory of Nazianzus' Theory of the Ideal Orthodox Priest in His Oration 6 (*De Pace*) and 2 (*Apologia de Fuga Sua*)," in S. Elm, E. Rebillard and A. Romano (eds), *Orthodoxie, Christianisme, Histoire* (Rome: École française de Rome, 2000) 83–100; Andrea Sterk, *Renouncing the World yet Leading the Church. The Monk-Bishop in Late Antiquity* (Cambridge, MA: Harvard University Press, 2004) 119–140. See also my short article, "Saint Gregory of Nazianzus as Pastor and Theologian," in Michael Welker and Cynthia A. Jarvis (eds), *Loving God with our Minds. The Pastor as Theologian* (Essays in honor of Wallace M. Alston; Grand Rapids: Eerdmans, 2004) 106–119.

213　See Hebr. 4.14–10.25.

214　Rom. 12.1.

215　Ps. 49.14 (LXX).

216　Ps. 50.19 (LXX).

217　Greek: ἀντίτυπον.

218　Or. 2.95.

219　Or. 39.2; cf. 39.14, where he makes it clear that baptism is the core of those Mysteries.

220　Or. 38.6.

221　*Concerning Himself and the Bishops* (*Carm.* 2.1.12) 749–761 (trans. Meehan 72). For similar themes in other poems, cf. *To the Priests of Constantinople, and to the City Itself* (*Carm.* 2.1.10; PG 37.1027A); *To the Bishops* (*Carm.* 2.1.13) 1–4 (PG 37.1227A).

222 *Carm.* 1.2.34.224–229 (PG 37.961–962). John Henry Newman, in his *Verses on Various Occasions*, includes a short poem entitled "The Priestly Office. From St. Gregory Nazianzen," and dated "Oxford, 1834," which touches on some of the same images:

> In service o'er the Mystic Feast I stand;
> I cleanse Thy victim-flock, and bring them near
> In holiest wise, and by a bloodless rite.
> O fire of Love! O gushing Fount of Light!
> (As best I know, who need thy pitying Hand)
> Dread office this, bemired souls to clear
> Of their defilement, and again make bright.

(*Prayers, Verses and Devotions* [San Francisco: Ignatius Press, 1989] 603). I have not been able to find a poem in Gregory's corpus to which this directly corresponds; it may simply be inspired by the general portrait of liturgical priesthood contained in Oration 2 and the poems we have mentioned.

223 Or. 2.78.
224 Or. 2.113.
225 Or. 2.44.
226 In speaking of the ordained ministry as προεδρία or "presidency" here (esp. Or. 2.111), Gregory seems to be referring both to the office of bishop, the single head of a local Church, and to that of presbyter, a member of the body of elders ordained to assist and represent the bishop in his various presidential tasks.
227 Or. 2.35.
228 Lk. 12.42.
229 Or. 2.35. This list of subjects, on which the Christian mind is led by Scripture to speculate, corresponds roughly to the subjects Origen discusses systematically in *On First Principles*: see the preface to that work. Cf. Gregory, Or. 27.10; his *Poemata Arcana* deal with the same subjects in turn, in a form and style modeled on the Homeric Hymns.
230 Or. 2.36–39.
231 I Cor. 2.6.
232 Or. 2.45.
233 II Cor. 2.16.
234 Or. 2.16. Two centuries later, Gregory the Great quotes this phrase at the start of his *Pastoral Rule*: "Ab imperitis ergo pastorale magisterium qua temeritate suscipitur, quando ars est artium regimen animarum." (*Regulae pastoralis liber* 1.1 [*Sources chrétiennes* 381 (Paris: Cerf, 1992) 128]). For the influence of Gregory of Nazianzus's Oration 2, in the Latin translation of Rufinus of Aquileia, on Pope Gregory's work, see the introduction of Bruno Judic, *ibid.* 27–32.
235 Or. 2.16–20.
236 I Peter 3.4.
237 Or. 2.21.
238 *Phaedrus* 246b.
239 See Eph. 3.16–17.
240 Or. 2.22.
241 Phil. 2.7.
242 Cf. Or. 38.13.

243   Cf. Or. 38.12.
244   Or. 2.25–26.
245   Or. 2.28.
246   Or. 2.77.
247   Or. 2.57–68.
248   Or. 2.60, referring to Hab 2.6–19.
249   Or. 2.52–56.
250   Matt. 3.7.
251   Or. 2.71–72.
252   Or. 2.83; see 79–85.
253   *Ibid.* 88–90.
254   Phil. 3.21.
255   Ps. 39.3 (LXX).
256   Rom. 7.23.
257   Or. 2.91.
258   Or. 2.11l; cf. Or. 43.26–27, where he approvingly describes Basil's preparation for the episcopate by first exercising the offices of lector and presbyter.
259   Or. 2.48. Gregory contrasts that with the contemporary practice of recognizing "instant sages," in Or. 2.49.
260   This Greek proverb is already cited by Plato, in *Laches* 178b and *Gorgias* 514e.
261   Or. 2.47.
262   Or. 2.51, quoting—the "Western" text-form—I Cor. 9.22 ("I became all things to all, that I might by all means save some"). The κυβέρνησις to which Gregory refers here, as practiced by the two Apostles, seems in context to make better sense if it is taken to refer to their self-mastery, rather than to their governance of others.
263   Or. 6 (*First Eirenical Oration*).6, alluding to Prov. 9.2 (LXX).
264   "St. Gregory Nazianzen on Bishops and the Episcopate" (see above, n. 205) 282.
265   Ps. 21.11 (LXX).
266   Gregory is referring to the promise he made to God during a storm on his voyage from Alexandria to Athens to continue his studies: see above pp. 5–6; *On his Life* 195–202.
267   Or. 2.77. Gregory alludes to this same ability, to devalue the very eloquence in which he can express his attachment to Christ, in Or.4.5 and 100.
268   Or. 2.102–103.
269   Or. 2.113.
270   Or. 2.103, referring to Jacob's theft of the paternal blessing that belonged by right to his older brother Esau: Gen. 27.1–41.
271   Or. 2.78.
272   Or. 21 (*On the Great Athanasius*).19.
273   PG 35.14. See above, n. 125. On Erasmus's slow process of becoming acquainted with Gregory's work, which was only published piecemeal during his lifetime, see Peter Walter, "Erasmus von Rotterdam und Gregor von Nazianz" (above, n. 2).
274   The collection *Nicene and Post-Nicene Fathers*, series II, volume 7, first published in 1894, includes translations of 24 of Gregory's orations (Or. 1, 2, 3, 7, 8, 12, 16, 18, 21, 27, 28, 29, 30, 31, 33, 34, 37, 38, 39, 40, 41, 42,

43, and 45) and 95 of his letters, by Charles Gordon Browne and James
Edward Swallow. A translation of the two orations against Julian (Or. 4 and
5) by C. W. King was also published in 1888. More recent translations of
Gregory's funeral orations on his brother Caesarius, his sister Gorgonia, his
father, and his friend Basil (Or. 7, 8, 18, and 43) are included in the volume,
Funeral Orations by Saint Gregory Nazianzen and Saint Ambrose by Leo
McCauley, S.J. (Fathers of the Church 22; New York: Catholic University
of America Press, 1953). A new translation of the *Five Theological Orations*
(Or. 27–31) by Lionel Wickham and Frederick Williams, with introduction
and commentary by Frederick W. Norris, appeared under the title *Faith
Gives Fullness to Reasoning: the Five Theological Orations of Gregory Nazianzen*
(Leiden: Brill, 1991); this translation has been republished, along with a
translation of Gregory's two letters to Cledonius on the person of Christ
(Ep. 101–102) and with a briefer introduction and notes by Lionel Wickham
under the title *On God and Christ* (Crestwood, NY: St. Vladimir's, 2002).
Most recently, a translation of all the orations not included in Browne and
Swallow's collection, except the two against Julian, has been published by
Martha Vinson (Fathers of the Church 107; Washington: Catholic University
of America Press, 2003).

Of Gregory's poems, three fairly recent translations of the main autobiographical works exist (II, 1.1; II, 1.11; II, 1.12): by Denis Molaise Meehan
(Fathers of the Church 75; Washington, DC: Catholic University Press,
1987); Caroline White (*Gregory of Nazianzus: Autobiographical Poems*
[Cambridge: Cambridge University Press, 1996], which includes an edition
of the Greek text); and Peter Gilbert (*On God and Man: the Theological
Poetry of Saint Gregory Nazianzen* [Crestwood, NY: St. Vladimir's, 2001],
which includes some other poems as well). An edition of the Greek text of
the *Poemata Arcana*, with English translation and commentary, by Claudio
Moreschini and Donald W. Sykes, was published by Oxford University Press
(Oxford, 1997). John McGuckin has also published poetic English
translations of a selection of Gregory's poems (*St. Gregory Nazianzen: Selected
Poems* [Oxford: SLG Press, 1986]).

2 ORATIONS

1 See Bernardi, *Prédication* 109; McGuckin 166. On Alypius, as a native of
   Iconium, see the commentator Elias of Crete (PG 36.893–894).
2 The text used for this translation is the critical edition of Marie-Ange Calvet-
   Sebasti, *Sources chrétiennes* 405 (Paris: Éditions du Cerf, 1995) 246–299.
3 Gregory begins his oration with an elaborate justification of giving a formal
   encomium or funeral oration for his own sister. Funeral orations were
   traditionally highly elaborate, artificial pieces of epideictic or "show" oratory,
   meant to move the hearers to praise the deceased and to blame his or her
   enemies. They were usually fulsome in their praise of the subject, and drew
   on a traditional stock of themes and techniques, which often bore little
   relationship to the subject's actual life and personality. Gregory, too, intends
   to speak here in high rhetorical style but promises to limit himself strictly to
   what his audience already knows to be true about her life. The fact that the
   subject was his sister reinforces his purpose of honesty and modesty and
   gives added insight and poignancy to his description of her character.

4   Cf. Gorgias, *Eulogy of Helen* 1: "It is an equal sign of failure and foolishness to blame what should be praised, and to praise what should be blamed." It is significant that Gregory here echoes the axiom of Gorgias, the pioneer of the Greek art of rhetoric from the fifth century B.C., taken from a speech intended to justify the memory of the mythical Helen. Although Gregory is speaking of his own sister and is clearly aware of the different obligations such a relationship imposes, the allusion reinforces his self-presentation as a "sophist," a professional artist in persuasive speaking, whose traditional role in classical culture was to speak out in praise of what is good and in censure of what is evil.

5   Gregory attempts in this chapter to protect himself against what seems to be an accepted rule that rhetoricians should not employ their skills in praise of their own families. Again, his argument for breaking custom is that such praise, in his sister's case, is required by truth and justice.

6   In this paragraph, Gregory deftly fits the oration within the genre of funeral discourses, showing how he intends it to fit the traditional mold and how he does not. He expresses his intention to avoid overly decorative speech—itself a fairly frequent claim in funeral orations (cf. Gregory of Nyssa, *Life of Macrina* 1)—and points out that of the usual topics used at the beginning of such a speech, such as homeland, ancestry, and physical appearance, he will confine himself to a brief mention of their parents, Gregory the Elder and Nonna (Chaps. 4–5). Gregory is using the techniques and traditional form of funeral rhetoric to redefine the very nature of his art. His purpose, he emphasizes here, is not simply entertainment or the reinforcement of social relationships, but the moral and spiritual formation of his Christian listeners. The work, in other words, is not simply epideictic oratory but a sermon.

7   Gregory alludes here to the rhetorical practice of avoiding proper names (especially those of living persons) in formal orations of praise and of replacing them with elaborate and allusive paraphrases (see Ep. 197.7). He proceeds here to develop a moving little portrait of his parents, apparently still alive and present as he speaks, in terms of the Biblical story of Abraham and Sarah.

8   Gen. 15.6; Rom. 3.28; etc.

9   Gen. 17.5. Gregory may be alluding here to his father's pastoral efforts among the inhabitants of rural Cappadocia, and of Nonna's assistance.

10   Gregory the Elder had been brought up in a heretical Christian sect called the "hypsistarii," about which we know little, but was converted to orthodox faith through the efforts of Nonna, who came from an impeccably Christian family. Gregory here emphasizes the distinctive role each of them played in bringing others to share their faith.

11   Hebr. 11.9.

12   Gregory plays here with the word παροικέω: a term that literally means "dwell among strangers," live in a place that is not one's true home. Since the New Testament, the cognate noun παροικία, from which our English word *parish* comes, had been used as a kind of technical term for the Christian community as a kind of alien body within secular society. Gregory seems to be referring to his parents' strong sense of themselves as members of the Christian community, despite social connections and a cultural background that would also situate them well in the secular world. He may also be alluding

to his father's pastoral work as bishop of the Church "sojourning" at Nazianzus.

13 Gregory is referring to himself here. According to his poem *On his Life* 80–89, he was born, like Isaac, somewhat late in his parents' marriage, and they offered him to God as a child. Gorgonia was apparently several years older than Gregory, and his brother Caesarius several years younger.

14 Literally, "to share salt."

15 Gregory's will, translated in this volume, reveals that his parents had left their considerable property to him as heir, with the instruction that he would in turn make the poor of the Church of Nazianzus, where his father had long been bishop, the estate's major beneficiary.

16 Normally, the first subjects to be dealt with in a funeral oration were the ancestry and homeland of the person being praised, as Gregory has already noted. As he begins here to describe Gorgonia herself, he begins to sketch out a Christian reinterpretation of these concepts, leading to a new understanding of nobility (εὐγένεια).

17 Gal. 4.26.

18 Hebr. 12.23.

19 Job 1.3.

20 Gregory begins the praise of Gorgonia's virtues by considering her σωφροσύνη (self-control, temperance): one of the classic "cardinal" virtues of Aristotelian ethical theory. Its range of meanings is hard to capture in a single English word: level-headedness, balance, moderation, and a hard-won freedom from enslaving passions are all implied in it. Gregory focuses his treatment of Gorgonia's *sophrosyne* on her success in combining both faithful married life and dedicated chastity.

21 In his treatise *On Virginity*, Gregory of Nyssa takes a different line, arguing that while holiness and the purification of inherited passions are possible in every state of life, virginity is actually the easier and less "dangerous" route; marriage, in his view, was too full of responsibilities and potential sorrows to allow a person to focus one's energies easily on God. One reason for their different approaches may be that Gregory of Nyssa was himself married, while Gregory of Nazianzus was a celibate.

22 In his treatise *On Holy Virginity*, St. Augustine, too, warns of pride as the main pitfall of a life of consecrated virginity. Asceticism, in late antiquity, was seen as the pinnacle of human self-perfection but was therefore seen as likely to lead to self-congratulation.

23 Gregory may also be referring here to the "craft" of the divine Logos or heavenly Reason (cf. Or. 6.14), or to the "skill" taught by Scripture (also λόγος), but the context suggests he is simply talking about the role of human reason in the formation of virtue.

24 I Cor. 11.3; Eph. 5.23.

25 In the prologue to his commentary on the Song of Songs, Origen presented the three Biblical books attributed to Solomon—Proverbs, Ecclesiastes, and the Song of Songs—as containing respectively introductory, intermediate, and advanced teaching on the way in which the soul may advance through wisdom to union with God: see *Comm. In Cant.* Prol. 3.1, 5–16, 21–23. Gregory assumes that conception of these books here.

26 Prov. 7.10–13.

27 Prov. 31.12–24.

28 Gregory chooses to describe his sister's self-control (σωφροσύνη) not on the basis of the description of the virtuous wife in Proverbs 31 but in terms of ascetic withdrawal and internal balance—a portrait not unlike those of the ideal monk or nun sketched by Gregory's pupil Evagrius and by other writers of the emerging desert tradition, a few decades later. Gravity, self-control and the rule of reason guided by Scripture are the core of this vision of virtue.

29 Ps. 140.3.

30 Gregory now turns to two further classical virtues, and finds them also present in Gorgonia's life: prudence (φρόνησις) and reverence or piety (εὐσέβεια).

31 A number of the manuscripts here present a slightly different reading, which could be translated: "remaining within the limits of reverence proper to women." I have followed the text offered by Mme. Sebasti in SChr 405, on the basis of her reasoning given there (see 269, n. 5). A favorite theme in Gregory's works is the danger of being too ready to offer one's opinions on theological subjects, before one is spiritually mature: see Or. 27.3–7.

32 It is not entirely clear to whom Gregory is referring here. He may be alluding to Gorgonia's husband Alypius, who became a Christian under his wife's influence, although there is no other evidence that he was ever ordained bishop ("priest" in the language of the fourth century). A further mystery in the text is Gregory's allusion to "the pair of children consecrated to God," since Gregory's will—our only source for the names of Gorgonia's three daughters—suggests that only one of them, Alypiane, practiced the faith uprightly, in Gregory's view. Elias of Crete, the tenth- or twelfth-century commentator on some of Gregory's works, says in this context that the couple also had two sons who became bishops but who are otherwise unknown (PG 35.802, n.1). If that is so and if Alypius himself had become a bishop before his death, he could well be the "fellow-combatant and teacher" mentioned here. However, it may also be an allusion to their father, the elder Gregory, who was bishop of Nazianzus, two of whose children—Gorgonia and Gregory himself—devoted their lives chiefly to contemplation and ascetical practice. Their other brother, the physician Caesarius, is not described by Gregory as a saint in the same terms.

33 Without naming it as such, Gregory now turns to discuss his sister's generosity toward the poor, an aspect of the classical virtue of great-heartedness or "magnificence" (μεγαλοψυχία) which he will mention at the start of the following paragraph. As he makes clear in his oration on the love of the poor, he also considers this virtue, modeled on Christ, an essential part of Christian "philosophy."

34 Job 31.32.

35 Job 29.15.

36 See Job 29.16.

37 In other words, her husband Alypius survived her. According to Gregory's epitaph for Gorgonia and Alypius, he died soon after his wife:

> Offering to Christ her wealth, her flesh and bone,
> Gorgonia left her spouse alone behind.
> Even this legacy did not last for long:
> Suddenly Christ took noble Alypius, too.
> O doubly blessed pair! Live now anew,

Washed of all stain in his baptismal stream!

(*Palatine Anthology* 8, Epigram 103; *Carmina* II/2.24: PG 38.27).

38 Ps. 111.9 (LXX).
39 Matt. 6.4, 6.
40 Eph. 6.12.
41 Matt. 6.19–21.
42 Literally, "luxury and the unrestrained pleasures of the belly."
43 Dan. 3.39 (LXX).
44 In this list of Gorgonia's increasingly challenging feats of asceticism, Gregory succeeds in portraying her as the equal of the monks and nuns of the desert, even though she continued to live in the domestic world of family, home, and village. Sleeping on the ground, genuflecting frequently in adoration, and spending a large part of the night chanting the Psalms were all acknowledged features of early monastic practice.
45 Gregory continues to describe Gorgonia's ascetical austerity in intense, even exaggerated, terms. Looking unkempt was by now an accepted part of the ascetical character. Regular washing of the body and its clothing, like the use of jewelry and makeup, were considered signs of luxury among Christians of the late fourth century. The paragraph that follows gives us a strikingly concrete portrait of the external practices of the early Christian "philosopher," their effect on the soul in reversing the results of the fall, and their theological roots in the self-emptying of the Son of God.
46 Ps. 125.5 (LXX).
47 This is clearly a reference to baptism, and the "inner adornment" that results.
48 I.e., of the forbidden fruit of the tree of knowledge, in Gen. 3; cf Or. 38.4.
49 Having enumerated Gorgonia's principal virtues, Gregory now moves to the final section of his discourse. At this point in classical funeral orations, one customarily recounted some striking incidents from the deceased person's life and concluded with a description of his or her noble death. Here Gregory will focus on two seemingly miraculous recoveries: one from a serious accident (Chaps. 15–16), one from a dangerous fever (Chaps. 17–18), which he presents as signs of her unshakeable faith in God; he will conclude with a narrative of her holy death.
50 Literally, "her philosophy."
51 Ps. 36.24 (LXX).
52 Gregory seems to be making a veiled reference to the passion and resurrection of Christ here, as the paradigm for Gorgonia's remarkable recovery from her injuries.
53 Hos. 6.2.
54 Gregory is addressing a bishop who seems to have been Gorgonia's pastor: probably Faustinus of Iconium. The incident that follows is another healing, this time from a serious illness, which is apparently less widely known beyond Gorgonia's intimate circle. Gregory sees in it another example of his sister's faith and importunate trust in God.
55 Literally, "the philosophy."
56 Gorgonia seems to have had a private chapel in her house or else to have lived very close to a church where the Eucharist was celebrated.
57 Matt. 13.52.
58 Mark 5.25–29.
59 Lk. 7.37–38.

60 As in the traditional conception of virtue, so in the ideals of rhetorical style, proportion and self-restraint were considered by the Greeks to be the key to excellence and beauty.

61 Phil. 1.23.

62 Here and throughout this passage, Gregory speaks of other people's love for the body and its comforts, and of Gorgonia's love for Christ, in terms of ἔρως, the strong love expressed in physical desire and longing for union.

63 As occasionally happens in Gregory's rhetoric, the thought here is almost too compressed to be clear. He seems to mean that Gorgonia knew of her coming death—and rejoiced at it—both because of her natural intuition and because God gave her foreknowledge of it in a dream, during one of her periods of nightly prayer.

64 Gregory is referring here to Gorgonia's baptism, which apparently she received as an adult, not long before her death. From Gregory's other writings, it is clear that adult baptism was the norm in his day in Cappadocia, even in families of such strong Christian conviction as his own; he opposes such a deferral of baptism strongly, in fact, in Oration 40. He suggests here that while the transformation given in the sacrament is a free gift of God, it was Gorgonia's lifelong dedication to faith and her ascetical seriousness that assured its effectiveness for her salvation; for the same balance of emphasis on grace and practice, sacraments and faith, see Gregory of Nyssa, *Catechetical Discourse* 33–40.

65 Gregory seems to be alluding here to Gen. 2.24 and Matt. 19.5-6, where the Scriptures speak of husband and wife as "one flesh." He has already told us (Chap. 8) how Gorgonia had convinced Alypius, her husband, to join her in her ascetical practices after their children were grown; Alypius's baptism, however, seems to have been deferred along with her own.

66 An important part of any civil or religious festival was a solemn discourse. Gregory depicts Gorgonia's dying words to her household as a kind of festal sermon.

67 Gregory plays here with the Greek verb λύεται, which can mean variously "she died," "she was destroyed," and "she was released."

68 Gregory seems again to be addressing Gorgonia's local bishop, who was apparently both her spiritual director and the one who had baptized her and her husband shortly before her death.

69 This striking phrase, in Greek μνήμης ἐμπύρευμα, seems to be original with Gregory. He uses it again near the start of his encomium on Cyprian of Carthage, Or. 24.3 (SChr 284.42). It later seems to have become proverbial among some Christian writers: see Leontius of Byzantium, Preface to *Contra Nestorianos et Eutychianos* (PG 86.1268B).

70 Ps. 4.9.

71 Here Gregory begins the concluding part of his discourse by addressing Gorgonia directly, for the first time. He seems to have reserved this particularly emotional effect for the end, in keeping with his proclaimed intention of keeping the rhetoric of the oration modest in comparison with secular models.

72 Gregory here mentions, for the first time, his brother Caesarius and his oration in memory of him (Or. 7).

73 For a discussion of the date and context of this oration and of its probable literary dependence on the second of Gregory of Nyssa's homilies on the poor, see the literature cited above, Introduction, n. 57.

74 This translation is based on the text of the Benedictine edition of the eighteenth and nineteenth centuries, reprinted in PG 35.857–909. At the time of this writing, no critical edition has yet appeared.

75 I Cor. 13.13. Gregory begins his reflection on the Christian virtues with the implied question of which virtue is most precious (Chaps. 2–4). For each virtue he discusses, he offers at least one Biblical example, a practice he will continue throughout this oration.

76 Gen. 15.6.

77 Gen. 4.26.

78 See Rom. 9.3.

79 I John 4.8.

80 Eph 2.10.

81 Lk. 22.50f.

82 Is. 42.2.

83 Num 25.7.

84 I Kg 19.14.

85 II Cor. 11.2.

86 Ps. 68.10 (LXX).

87 Gregory is clearly referring to Jesus here but calls him simply "God" in order to underscore the divine mandate to pray.

88 I Cor. 8.25.

89 II Sam. 23.15.17.

90 Apparently an allusion to some apocryphal work on the life of Peter. I have not been able to identify the source.

91 Phil. 2.6

92 Is. 50.6; 53.12; Lk. 22.37.

93 Lk. 19.8.

94 Matt. 19.21.

95 John 14.2.

96 Ps. 88.14 (LXX).

97 Hos. 12.6.

98 Is. 28.17.

99 Rom. 12.15.

100 Is. 10.16–18.

101 Literally: "philosophize."

102 Rom. 12.5.

103 Gregory returns to considering the plight of people suffering from leprosy, which he began in Chapter 6.

104 Gregory suggests here that lepers are forced to leave both their families and village or city life, to live in remote caves—a feature in which the Cappadocian countryside near Caesaraea and Nazianzus abounds. The only other inhabitants of these caves, he seems to suggest, are hermits.

105 The quotation is a somewhat expanded paraphrase of Job 3.11–12 (LXX).

106 A scholion in the manuscripts of the oration explains this rather obscure remark: "In that we do not make any provision for them, we force them to come back to us for help." Then as now, neglect of the homeless does not make them any less present in our streets.

107 Here Gregory makes it clear that the context of his oration is a Church festival; his description of the begging lepers in the dusty heat of summer also suggests the time of year.
108 Job 10.8–11.
109 Eph. 3.15.
110 II Cor. 1.22.
111 John 1.29.
112 I Cor. 8.11.
113 Rom. 6.4; Col 2.12.
114 Rom. 8.17.
115 I Pet. 2.9.
116 Tit. 2.14.
117 Is. 53.4.
118 II Cor. 8.9.
119 II Cor. 5.1.
120 Matt. 18.12.
121 Ezek. 34.4.
122 Literally: "the arrangement of tiny pebbles."
123 Apparently some of these lepers have become blind as a result of the disease.
124 See Phil. 3.8–11.
125 Job 31.40.
126 Luke 12.20.
127 Jer. 9.23.
128 James 3.13.
129 Ps. 83.6 (LXX).
130 Col. 3.1.
131 cf. Gen. 3.15.
132 Ps. 4.3f.
133 Mic 2.9f.
134 John 19.31.
135 Ecclesiastes 11.2 (LXX): "Give a portion to the seven, and indeed to the eight." Gregory apparently takes the number "seven" here to refer to life in this world, created in seven days, and "eight" to refer to the new creation, beginning with God's "eighth day" of resurrection. See Or. 44.5, where he interprets this text in the same way.
136 I Cor. 13.12.
137 Unclear is whether Gregory is here thinking of Peter in his traditional role as heavenly doorkeeper, bearer of "the keys of the Kingdom of heaven" (Matt. 16.19), or alluding to his challenge to the stinginess of Ananias and Saphira in Acts 5.3–5. Gregory may also be thinking of some now-lost passage in one of the early Christian apocrypha concerning Peter.
138 Amos 8.5.
139 Gregory seems to be confusing Amos 6.4–6, which he paraphrases here, with the prophecy of Micah.
140 See Amos 6.4–6.
141 Matt. 5.45.
142 Matt. 19.8.
143 Gregory may be alluding here to the story of Noah's drunkenness, Gen. 9.20–27.
144 Ps. 37.26.

145 Gregory is mistakenly convinced that leprosy is not a communicable disease and that people's fear of contact with those who have contracted it is unfounded.

146 Cf. Ps. 10.14.

147 Inscriptions honoring Apollo under this title have been found in several places in Thessaly.

148 Sirach 1.2.

149 Rom. 11.33.

150 Rom. 11.34.

151 Job 15.8.

152 Hos. 14.10; cf. James 3.13.

153 John 5.19.

154 Rom. 1.21–22.

155 Gregory is playing here with various senses of the Greek word *logos*, which can mean "word," "speech," "order," and—in a Christian context—both "Scripture" and the Word of God who is the second person of the Trinity.

156 Christian ascetics of the fourth century saw voluntary self-emptying, in imitation of Christ, as central to the Christian's pursuit of true wisdom.

157 Luke 16.22–25.

158 Ps. 11.6 (LXX).

159 Ps. 9.35 (LXX).

160 Ps. 9.13 (LXX).

161 Ps. 9.26 (LXX).

162 Ps. 10.5 (LXX).

163 Gregory is here interpreting the Septuagint text of Ps. 10.5, which literally reads: "His eyes gaze on the poor man, and his eyelids examine the sons of men."

164 Prov. 17.5.

165 Prov. 22.2.

166 Prov. 19.17 (LXX).

167 Prov. 15.27 (LXX); Hebr. 16.6.

168 Is. 1.18.

169 Is. 1.18; Ps. 50.7 (LXX). In the Old Testament, the skin of a leper is several times said to be "white as snow": e.g., Ex. 4.6; Num. 12.10; II Kg. 5.27.

170 The Greek text in PG here reads literally "no infection of significance;" this may be simply a mistake in the manuscripts used or in the printed text, or it may be a rhetorical reversal by Gregory himself.

171 Luke 10.30.

172 Ps. 37.6 (LXX).

173 Gregory is unusually compressed and allusive here. His meaning seems to be: heal your own wounds by tending the wounds of the poor (or: by Christ's wounds), regain your likeness to him by acting like him (or: by his having become like you), and most of all, heal your own greater defects by what are inevitably lesser acts of goodness. However, he leaves it to the hearer to fill in all the details of these moving phrases.

174 Ps. 39.3 (LXX).

175 Matt. 9.22.

176 John 5.14.

177 Matt. 5.7.

178 Ps. 40.1 (LXX).

179 Ps. 111.5 (LXX).
180 Ps. 36.26 (LXX).
181 Prov. 3.28; cf. Luke 11.7.
182 Is. 58.7.
183 Rom. 12.8.
184 Gregory may again be referring here, in passing, to the religious festival that seems to provide the context of his sermon.
185 Is. 58.6.
186 Again, Gregory takes pains to interpret what seems to be an odd phrase in the Septuagint translation of Isaiah, suggesting moral or psychological explanations for both the "fetter" mentioned in the text and the "selectiveness" (literally, "selection" or "appointment").
187 Is. 58.8.
188 John 12.6.
189 Gal. 2.8–10.
190 Matt. 19.21.
191 See Matt. 25.31–46.
192 Hos. 6.6; cf. Matt. 9.13.
193 Dan. 3.40.
194 See Lk. 16.9.
195 See Justin Mossay, introduction to his edition: *Sources chrétiennes* 270 (Paris: Cerf, 1980) 50–51, following Sinko, Gallay and Bernardi in dating it to the spring of 380; for the earlier date, cf. McGuckin 243–248.
196 For details, see Mossay, SChr 270.42–44.
197 Even the titles given in various manuscripts of the work suggest this: some call it "the first work on theology," while several others label it as a "sketch" (σχεδιασθείς). One manuscript labels it "the first oration delivered in Constantinople."
198 This translation is made from the critical edition by Justin Mossay and Guy Lafontaine in *Sources Chrétiennes* 270, 56–84.
199 Jer. 9.1.
200 These sentences, from "for nothing" to here, appear also in Gregory's Oration 2.7. Like many ancient rhetoricians (and Baroque musicians), he was not averse to using phrases and even whole passages from earlier works, when he considered them effective and suitable to a new context; for another doublet, see Chapter 4 below.
201 Here as elsewhere, Gregory uses "philosophy" to mean the Christian pursuit of divine wisdom through ascetical practice and the contemplative study of Scripture.
202 Note that Gregory is speaking, here and throughout the oration, of the requirements both for studying and speaking about God's reality and for holding episcopal office in the Church. Presumably, he considers the requirements similar because the bishop must always be, in some sense, a teacher of the true faith, whereas the theologian always speaks with some responsibility to and for the believing community.
203 Ex. 24.9–12.
204 Ex. 19.3–25.
205 Hebrew, "Uzzah," the son of Abinadab.
206 I Sam. 2.12 17, 22–36; 4.10–18.
207 II Sam. 6.2–8.

208 Rom. 12.1.
209 This paragraph, up to the end of Chapter 4, reappears almost verbatim as Chapter 9 of Or. 39, "On the Holy Lights."
210 Jud. 13.22.
211 Luke 5.8.
212 Matt. 8.8.
213 Just as the centurion was a middle-rank officer in charge of a company of about a hundred soldiers, so the "ordinary sinner" is still under the influence of Satan, "the prince of this world" (John 12.31; for Gregory's term, κοσμοκράτωρ, cf. Ephesians 6.12), and in turn may exercise a negative influence on many others.
214 Gregory is here punning on the word "fool" (μωρός): as a number of variant spellings in the Greek manuscript tradition of the oration suggest, he and many of his copyists may have assumed the etymology of "sycamore" to be σῦκον, "fig," plus μωρῶν, "foolish ones"—"a fool's fig." In climbing up the sycamore tree, Zacchaeus would thus be exemplifying the asceticism that overcomes his earth-bound lowliness and foolishness before God.
215 Luke 19.1–10.
216 Prov. 20.2.
217 I Kg. 3.12; II Chron. 1.11–12.
218 Gal. 2.10.
219 Literally, "hypostases."
220 To attribute "madness" to Arius and his mid-fourth-century followers who had argued that the Son (and in later developments of the same tradition, the Spirit) were different in being from God, was a commonplace in anti-Arian polemics of the fourth century: see, for example, Athanasius, *De sententia Dionysii* 1; *Life of Antony* 68; Epiphanius, *Panarion* 69.11; 73.1; and see Gregory Nazianzen, Or. 2.37; 25.8; 43.30. It was also a commonplace in Patristic writing, from the fourth century on, to depict official orthodoxy as a mean between two extremes. See my article, "Boethius's Theological Tracts and Early Byzantine Scholasticism," *Mediaeval Studies* 46 (1984) 158–191.
221 Greek: οὐσίαι.
222 Gregory is here referring to the more extreme anti-Nicene theology of the later Arians, represented by Aetius and Eunomius in the 350s and 360s; they insisted that since the defining characteristic of God may be identified in God's being "unbegotten" or without origin, the very notion of a "begotten Son" suggests that the Son is, by definition, substantially something other than God.
223 Gregory uses the word πρόσωπον here; for a discussion of the origin and developing significance of this terminology for the distinct identities of Father, Son, and Spirit, see above, pp. 45–48.
224 Literally, "he says."
225 Gregory here introduces the notion of "passivity" or "passibility" (πάθος), long familiar in the Greek philosophy of the human person. It means not simply "passion," in the sense of strong emotion valorized by nineteenth-century romanticism, but a kind of experience over which human freedom is not in complete control—an experience we "suffer" or "undergo" rather than initiate through our own choosing. In this sense, "passion" in ancient thought is lack of freedom. The imagined opponents are suggesting that being begotten or generated is an example of such "passivity" and therefore

cannot be proper to one who is literally God. Gregory will argue, in return, that the act of creation, too, as we humans understand it, involves the passivity of the thought process, which depends on sensory experience for its origin, as well as the circumstances of time and place. His point is that just as we must ascribe creativity to God in a way free of these human limitations, so God's generating must be understood analogously to our own and without being thought to involve our limitations.

226   Literally, "he says."

227   Ps. 148.5 (LXX).

228   Hebr. 7.10; Gen. 19.34.

229   Gregory obviously shares the ancient assumption that the apparent movement of sun and moon, planets, and stars was explained by the rotation of a series of concentric, transparent spheres around the earth.

230   Ps. 8.4.

231   For Gregory, being a "theologian" means being a person who can speak truthfully and intelligibly about the reality of God on the basis of direct personal knowledge. Here as elsewhere in his writings, notably in his *First Theological Oration* (Or. 27), he develops the notion that knowing God sufficiently well to be able to speak adequately of the divine Mystery requires a long process of moral purification and spiritual growth; in its full sense, it is an eschatological gift, the heart of beatitude. In the context of Gregory's conception of theology, the great danger is "rashness:" trying to rush the process of purification and growth or to replace them by purely human dialectical skills.

232   Gregory reflects here a terminology that was already becoming canonized for describing stages of the spiritual life: one begins with the "practical" aspect (πρᾶξις, πρακτική), by learning to recognize and subdue the passions or "passivities," the weaknesses and drives that enslave the soul from within, using vocal prayer, moral self-examination, and ascetical practices. Only after one has reached a fairly high degree of self-mastery and inner peace can one move gradually on through the "contemplation of nature" (θεωρία φυσική: affectionate meditation on the created world as a mirror of God) to a more exalted, less controllable, contemplative participation in the life of the unknowable God.

233   See II Cor. 12.1–4.

234   I Cor. 13.12.

235   I Cor. 13.12.

236   This translation is based on the critical edition of Justin Mossay and Guy Lafontaine, *Sources chrétiennes* 284 (Paris: Éditions du Cerf, 1981) 224–272.

237   I Cor. 15.31. The overriding metaphor of the oration is that of a trial: Gregory suggests he and his congregation have each been called before a tribunal to account for their actions during the last few months.

238   Deut. 7.6.

239   The strait of Euripus, which separates the island of Euboea from the Greek mainland, was known for its treacherous, constantly shifting tides and currents.

240   See Gen. 29.20. Gregory is quoting the text somewhat loosely; it reads: "So Jacob served seven years for Rachel, and they seemed to him but a few days because of the love he had for her."

241 Gregory's French translator (S Chr 284.229) suggests this may be a reference to Pliny the Younger, Ep. 20: "Desire for all things is weak, when they are easily obtainable." Gregory may have come to know this simply as a proverb, however, as no evidence suggests that he knew Latin literature directly.

242 See Lk. 15.3–7.

243 See Acts 20.29–30.

244 John 10.1.

245 Ezek. 22.25 (LXX).

246 Gregory is using the language of John 10.1–2 to refer to Maximus's treachery.

247 Gregory seems still to be talking about Maximus, who adopted the style of a Cynic philosopher. The title "Cynic" meant "doglike."

248 See Job 5.7 (LXX).

249 Gregory alludes here to Maximus's claim to be a philosopher, one whose life is devoted to training himself and others to practice virtue. He also seems to be suggesting that others—local dissidents, or the Church of Alexandria— have "set the dogs" upon the faithful flock in Constantinople.

250 See Ps. 94.6 (LXX).

251 Gregory is referring, here and in the previous sentence to Ezek 34.2–4.

252 II Cor. 11.29 (the end of which Gregory quotes loosely).

253 II Cor. 12.14.

254 Gen. 31.40.

255 Gen. 30.31–43. Gregory turns again to the story of Jacob and Laban for an image of his own career as a shepherd.

256 Greek: περὶ θεολογίας. The goal of the Christian philosopher's ascetical practice is to be able to think and speak correctly of God, insofar as that is possible for mortals in this life. See Orations 27–28 for further development of the same thought.

257 See Matt. 25.18–25.

258 Matt. 6.3.

259 Matt. 5.16.

260 Matt. 7.20.

261 See I Cor. 14.25.

262 James 2.20.

263 Eph. 5.6.

264 See I Cor. 9.11; Matt. 13.4–12, 30.

265 Matt. 13.8.

266 Mark 4.20.

267 Gen. 26.13.

268 Ps. 83.8 (LXX).

269 Ps. 83.6 (LXX).

270 I Tim. 5.10.

271 Literally: "so that it might turn out this way for me."

272 I Cor. 9.15.

273 I Cor. 9. 16. Here, as throughout the previous paragraph, Gregory borrows heavily from Paul to describe his own attitude to his ministry and to present himself as another apostle. As in Oration 2, Paul is Gregory's main Biblical model for ministry.

274 Gregory here picks up the thread of thought he had dropped a few sentences earlier. The whole sequence of this paragraph is quite convoluted, suggesting spontaneous reflection rather than ordered exposition. Occasional outbursts

of such seemingly improvised, in fact highly cultivated speech was a characteristic feature of the rhetorical style of the "second Sophistic" school.

275 Matt. 25.40.

276 Hebr. 4.15.

277 See Matt. 25.40, 45.

278 Lk. 16.19–31.

279 Is. 66.18.

280 Is. 40.10.

281 Gregory seems to be echoing a saying attributed to Jesus in many ancient sources, although not in the canonical Gospels: "Be good money-changers." See Joachim Jeremias, *Unknown Sayings of Jesus* (London: SPCK, 1958) 89–93; for a full list of ancient sources referring to the saying, see Alfred Resch, *Agrapha. Aussercanonische Schriftfragmente gesammelt und untersucht* (Texte und Untersuchungen 15.3–4; Leipzig, 1906) 111–112.

282 John 6.18.

283 Ps. 68.2 (LXX).

284 Ps. 68.15 (LXX).

285 Ps. 68.3 (LXX).

286 See I Cor. 10.4, and possibly Matt. 16.18.

287 Commentators point out that this same plant is mentioned by the Latin poet Horace in *Odes* 4.4.57–60.

288 See Eph. 6.14–16.

289 Gregory now begins a description of the behavior of the true philosopher, which runs through Chapter 12, a section drawing on Hellenistic rhetorical commonplaces about different types of character, and tailored to fit the details of Gregory's own career. The point is that whatever his circumstances in life, the philosopher makes use of them to give himself in service to God and to his fellow human beings.

290 Here, as in the previous sentence, Gregory seems to be talking ironically of family inheritance: the genetic "stuff" that underlies aristocratic good looks.

291 Gregory is referring to hereditary titles, which are handed on by the process of physical begetting that is naturally inseparable from sexual desire.

292 Gregory comments ironically on the ranks and titles bestowed on his contemporaries by the imperial court.

293 Ps. 44.3 (LXX).

294 Rom. 7.22; Eph 3.16.

295 See Matt. 6.26.

296 I Kg. 17.14–16. Elijah is represented here as "feeding" the widow, by causing her oil and flour supply to remain miraculously undiminished for "many days."

297 I Kg. 17.4; Ps. 109.8 (LXX). The significance of this Biblical gesture, mentioned in the Psalm, is unclear.

298 See II Cor. 11.27.

299 Job 24.8 (LXX).

300 Matt. 5.39.

301 John 8.48.

302 Gen. 16.12. Gregory seems to be conflating this reference to Ishmael with the following allusions to Job 39.

303 Job 39.7 (LXX, Hebrew: "the shouts of the driver"); cf. 39.5.

304 Job 39.9 (LXX; Hebrew: "a wild-ox"). The full verse, in the LXX, reads: "Will the unicorn be willing to serve you, or the sheep by your manger?"

305 Job 39.9; cf. 39.10.

306 Prov. 5.23 (LXX).

307 Gregory here describes the "philosopher" in terms proper to the angels, or even to God and to Christ. He may also be echoing Paul—for him, the original "Christian philosopher"—in II Cor. 4.8–12; 6.4–10.

308 I Cor. 7.40.

309 In listing the possible ways in which his enemies can attack his reputation, Gregory inverts the standard list of *topoi* by which a classical rhetorician, in an encomium for some illustrious person, would normally seek to praise him: his education, his affluence, his distinguished homeland, his physical vigor and good looks. For each of these things, what Gregory seems to lack is actually the key to the genuine "philosophical" qualities he seeks to boast of.

310 Prov. 1.7; Ps. 110.11 (LXX).

311 Eccl. 12.13. In the LXX, the verb is in the passive: "the end of the argument, everything, has been heard…"

312 Gregory moves from the poverty of his dress to his desire to depart from the "clothing" of the body altogether, to put away "this perishable nature" and "put on immortality" (see I Cor. 15.53–54).

313 Hebr. 13.14.

314 See John 4.32.

315 Here, in an aside, Gregory turns to address Maximus directly.

316 A somewhat elliptical sentence. Gregory may be suggesting that his own rhetorical skill allows him to imagine, and even partially to verbalize, what is in the minds of his enemies, or he may be referring to the ability of his enemies to discredit his motives.

317 Gregory seems here to be referring to his earlier, rather theatrical resistance to the pleas of the Nicene congregation in Constantinople that he agree to be their bishop, early in 381. See Or. 36.2; *De vita sua* 1273–1277; 1305–1335; 1371–1395.

318 Presumably the name "Christian," linking the disciple with the glorified Christ: see Acts 11.26; Phil. 2.9.

319 Gregory is speaking of ecclesiastical rank in terms of relative positions within a liturgical assembly.

320 See Matt. 25.32–33. Gregory skillfully contrasts his contemporaries' jockeying for a position in the liturgical assembly with the position assigned by Christ the judge at the end of time.

321 John 3.10.

322 Hebr. 10.8.

323 Ps. 42.4 (LXX). Significantly, Gregory has added the word "spiritual" to the Septuagint text of this Psalm-verse.

324 Gregory seems to be alluding to the story of Icarus, who strapped on wax wings made by his father, Daedalus, in order to be able to fly; Icarus crashed to his death, because in his arrogance he flew too close to the sun. Gregory hints that he has never made use of the financial resources available to him as bishop of the imperial capital, because he realizes how unreliable such human means of influence are.

325 See John 12.6; 13.29.

326 See II Kings 4.8–10. Here as elsewhere, Gregory depicts himself as a Biblical prophet.

327 Ps. 37.12 (LXX).

328 *Ibid.*; cf. Mk. 15.40 par.

329 Matt. 26.31. Here Gregory identifies his own plight with that of Jesus, abandoned by all his friends at the time of his passion.

330 Matt. 26.69–75. Gregory's ironic reference to Peter may be an allusion to the betrayal of his interests by Peter, bishop of Alexandria, who, while offering support to his leadership of the Nicene community in Constantinople, was apparently scheming to promote his own candidate, Maximus the Cynic. His reference in the start of the next paragraph, however, to opposition "in the East and in the West" seems to suggest that he is really speaking here of a lack of support by Pope Damasus of Rome.

331 Ps. 26.3 (LXX).

332 Here Gregory rhetorically addresses those who would install Maximus in his place as bishop of the Nicene community in Constantinople, thus further dividing the divided Christians of the capital.

333 Gregory's language here suggests passages in the Greek Pentateuch (e.g., Lev. 26.34; Num. 4.20).

334 Maximus and his party continued to appeal for support, in a manipulative way, to Peter of Alexandria, Ambrose of Milan, and Damasus of Rome, even after Gregory had retired from the see of Constantinople.

335 Hosea 13.9.

336 Characteristically, Gregory turns to the holy Trinity at the end of his oration: here precisely as the divine mystery of unity in distinction, of harmony that becomes all the more perfect in the variety of its members.

337 Greek: ἰδιότητες—a word denoting the particular characteristics that mark off an individual or hypostasis.

338 Eph. 4.6.

339 In this phrase, Gregory seems to be speaking of the equality of the persons with each other.

340 Here, Gregory speaks of the possibility of full human knowledge of God with his characteristic blend of caution and hope: in this life it is not possible, but in the life to come, he often hints, a unitive, affective "grasp" of God's full reality may be the reward of faithful seeking. See Or. 27.

341 See the discussion of the date of these orations, with a summary of earlier scholarship on the question, by Claudio Moreschini, *Sources chrétiennes* 358 (Paris: Cerf, 1990) 16–22; also above, p. 22.

342 McGuckin 336–337.

343 This translation is based on the critical text by Claudio Moreschini, in *Sources chrétiennes* 358, 104–148.

344 Psalm 95.1 (LXX).

345 Psalm 95.11 (LXX).

346 I John 1.1.

347 Apoc. 1.17; 2.8.

348 Ex. 13.21.

349 See Is. 9.2. The word ἐπίγνωσις, in the New Testament and early Christian writers, suggests not merely knowledge but the recognition of the truth of things that unites the mind to them—in this case, to God.

350 II Cor. 5.17.

351 II Cor. 3.6.
352 Ps. 46.1 (LXX).
353 Is. 9.5 (LXX; Hebrew Is. 9.6).
354 Matt. 3.3.
355 Hebr. 13.8.
356 See I Cor. 1.23.
357 Gregory frequently characterizes the Arian party in the capital—in his view, "heretics" *par excellence*—as playing clever games with words and encouraging ordinary Christians to speak about divine mysteries they do not understand: see Or. 27.1–3; Or. 28.11. Cf. Gregory of Nyssa, *Sermon on the Divinity of the Son and the Holy Spirit, and on Abraham* (GNO X/3, 120.15–121.14).
358 In Greek, "Theophany" (Θεοφάνεια).
359 Gregory's point is that there is no rational explanation we can give in words for the origin of the Son from the Father; rationality and language all owe their origin to God and so cannot be used to give account of God's being. If that were possible, it would imply that God's being conforms to some prior standards of explanation, which would thus be logically and metaphysically prior to God himself.
360 See Eph. 4.22–24.
361 See I Cor. 15.22.
362 See Gal. 2.19; Rom. 6.4; Col 2.12; Eph. 2.6. To the familiar list of Pauline expressions referring to the Christian's share in Christ's death and resurrection, Gregory adds the detail that we must also be "born" with him.
363 Rom. 5.20.
364 Rom. 13.13.
365 Gregory may be alluding here to the Jewish way of celebrating the feast of Tabernacles by constructing canopies of leaves to shelter outdoor banquets.
366 In this paragraph, Gregory uses themes and images familiar from the contemporary practice of moral rhetoric to satirize the uncaring self-indulgence of his wealthy contemporaries. For similar passages, see Or. 14.16–17; Or. 36.12; *Carmina* I, 2.28 (PG 37.856–883); cf. Gregory of Nyssa, Sermon *On Beneficence* (= *On Loving the Poor* I; GNO IX/1, 105).
367 Reading πόμποις for κόμποις, "boasts," which appears in the *Sources Chretiennes* edition of the oration (SC 358.112).
368 Gregory here plays with the various meanings of the Greek word λόγος: "word," in its ordinary as well as in its Christian sense; "speech," as a faculty and as an activity; "reason;" "order" or structure. Because they worship the Word who has become flesh, Christians celebrate most properly by behaving reasonably, by ordering their behavior, and by "luxuriating" in Christian discourse such as Gregory's.
369 As he often does, Gregory presents himself here both as a skilled artisan of speech, preparing an intellectual and religious feast for his hearers, and also as a social outsider in the sophisticated and wealthy capital. Even this oration on the birth of Christ is, at the same time, a carefully crafted presentation of the preacher's own persona. Inspired by Gregory, later preachers borrowed this metaphor of oratory as a banquet set by the preacher before his congregation on a great feast of faith; see, for example, Leontius Presbyter, Sermon 14 (on the Transfiguration) 1 (CCG 17.443.20–434.28); Andrew of Crete, Sermon 2 on the Dormition (PG 97.1084C).

370   Here Gregory begins an extended reflection on the qualities of the Divine
       being, drawn from familiar principles of Greek philosophy (especially in the
       Platonic and Stoic tradition) yet frequently spiced with Biblical allusions
       (Chaps. 7–10). As he will himself admit, near the end of sec. 10, this may
       strike his hearers as a needless digression in a homily on the birth of Christ,
       but it forms the necessary theological and rhetorical backdrop for his later
       emphasis on the "strangeness" of the Christian message that God has humbled
       himself to share fully in our human condition, in order to save us from sin
       and death.

371   Ex. 3.14.

372   Literally: "not from what belongs to him, but from what surrounds him".

373   Greek: ἡγεμονικόν, a term used by the Stoics for reason as the proper
       controlling faculty of our conscious mind, our emotions and drives, and our
       body.

374   Cf. I Cor. 13.12: "then [at the time of our fulfillment] I shall know, even as
       I am known." As in a number of other passages in his orations, Gregory here
       speaks of the final goal of the life of faith and holiness as the divinization of
       the human person, but he speaks of it with express diffidence as a hope that
       risks being thought rash and absurd by trained philosophical minds. Cf. Or.
       14.23; Or. 23.11; Or. 30.21. See also Jules Gross, *The Divinization of the
       Christian according to the Greek Fathers* (trans. Paul Onica; Anaheim, CA: A
       and C Press, 2002) 193–197.

375   With tantalizing brevity, Gregory here reflects on what "eternity" (αἰών, τὸ
       αἰώνιον) means when applied to God. In the present passage, he describes
       it as a kind of succession experienced by beings who are not subject to the
       limits of the space and time we know on earth: not "measured," yet still
       involving "motion" (κίνημα) and an "interval" or a "before and after"
       (διάστημα). He seems here to be speaking of the dimension properly
       experienced by limited beings who are not corporeal in the way that we are:
       pure spirits and divinized humans—a dimension we apply, somewhat
       improperly, to God. For Gregory has already told us, at the beginning of
       sec. 7, that God is without "before" or "after," that God simply holds all
       being together in himself. For a discussion of this distinction of God's timeless
       being from both time as we know it and this "eternity" or "sempiternity,"
       see Brooks Otis, "Cappadocian Thought as a Coherent System," *Dumbarton
       Oaks Papers* 12 (1958) 95–124; "Gregory of Nyssa and the Cappadocian
       Conception of Time," *Studia Patristica* 14 (TU 117; Berlin: Akademieverlag,
       1976) 327–357.

376   Literally: "Our present subject is not speech about God (θεολογία) but his
       saving plan (οἰκονομία)." It is important to notice that, having said this,
       Gregory immediately goes on to speak about the Trinity; for him, talking
       about God as Father, Son, and Holy Spirit is proper to a discussion of God's
       saving action in created history, whereas θεολογία is a more abstract,
       philosophical consideration of the nature of the Divine in itself.

377   Is. 6.2–3, the origin of the *Trisagion* hymn chanted in ancient Eucharistic
       liturgies.

378   As is typical in ancient rhetoric, Gregory neglects to tell us exactly who this
       predecessor is. A marginal note in one of the manuscripts containing this
       Oration (Coislin 51) identifies him as St. Athanasius, perhaps on the basis
       of the Pseudo-Athanasian work *On the Incarnation and against the Arians* 10

(PG 26.1000 B). It could also refer to Basil of Caesaraea, *Contra Eunomium* 3.3.

379 Gregory seems to be speaking of the "first creation," pure intelligences, which most closely resemble Father, Son, and Holy Spirit, if still in a limited way.

380 In speaking of the highest order of creation, which he identifies as bodiless intelligences, Gregory is sensitive to the philosophical difficulty of accounting for their fall from God, as he tends to see the root of sin in the disordered effect of bodily existence on the mind. However, he is persuaded by Scripture to identify the origins of a fall from grace with such spirits and to see in them the force leading human creatures to fall as well. For similar difficulties in explaining the Biblical idea of fallen angels, see Origen, *On First Principles* 1.4; 2.9.

381 Latin: *Lucifer*. Cf. Is. 14.12–15.

382 This phrase seems to be an allusion to Ps. 18.4–5 (LXX): "There is no speech, nor are there words; their voices are not heard; yet their sound goes out through all the earth, and their words to the end of the world."

383 This sentence, along with the one before it, deftly summarizes Origen's explanation of the theological meaning and purpose of human fleshly embodiment. It is a temporary state assigned to souls in response to a previous sin to allow them a condition in which they might recognize their alienation from God and be healed through instruction.

384 Gregory's interpretation of Chapters 2 and 3 of Genesis here is character-istically enigmatic and allusive but suggests a reading of the story of the fall in terms of a Promethean desire for self-directed knowledge, an unwillingness on the part of humanity to accept God's revelation of the fullness of truth on God's timetable. The "seeds" mentioned here seem, in the context of the following interpretation, to be not simply the seeds of plants but the seeds of eternal ideas, "seed-structures of intelligibility" (σπερματικοὶ λόγοι), implanted by the Creator in the material cosmos.

385 See Gregory of Nyssa, *Catechetical Oration* 8.

386 A central feature of Gregory's understanding of salvation in Christ is that it is above all the gift of life—new, immortal life; a share in God's own life—and that God the Son communicates this life to humanity first of all by sharing fully in every aspect of our natural being. See also the famous passage in his Letter 101, to Cledonius, 32, 50–62 (S Chr. 208.50, 58–64).

387 Although the terminology of "mixture" (μίξις, κρᾶσις), well-known already from Stoic physics, would come to be regarded as dangerous by the defenders of a two-nature Christology in the debates of the fifth century, Gregory uses it frequently to express the integral unity of God and a human being in the incarnate Word.

388 Following Origen (*De Principiis* 2.6.5; 2.8.2) and anticipating Augustine (e.g., *De fide et symbolo* 4.10; Ep. 137.8, 11; *In Joh. Ev. Tract.* 47.10–13), Gregory insists that it is the rational soul of Jesus that is the point of contact between the transcendent, uncircumscribed Word of God and his "coarse" material body. So for each of us, it is the soul that is capable of receiving the Holy Spirit and mingling with God and the soul that communicates to the body the divine life that will reach its material perfection in the resurrection.

389 II Cor. 8.9.

390 Phil. 2.7.

391 Eph. 3.19; Col. 2.9.

392   The "first communication (κοινωνία)" to which Gregory alludes is clearly the kinship between the human creature and God established by our being made in his image and likeness: a communication of knowledge and love, of life and immortality; after this kinship and likeness were lost by sin, God has established a still more wonderful communication by making our complete human nature his own, in order to restore and perfect the original likeness. Compare Newman's lines in *The Dream of Gerontius*:

> O wisest love! That flesh and blood
> Which did in Adam fail,
> Should strive afresh against their foe,
> Should strive and should prevail;
>
> And that a higher gift than grace
> Should flesh and blood refine,
> God's presence and his very self,
> And essence all divine.

393   Gal. 2.21.

394   Hos. 4.13 (LXX).

395   Gregory uses the Gospel image of the shepherd in search of the wandering sheep (Lk. 15.4–6; John 10.11–17) as the framework for a summary narrative of Jesus' work of salvation; he suggests at the end that the goal of the journey of the saved is to join the angels who had never fallen.

396   Here Gregory offers a similar soteriological interpretation of Jesus' parable of the woman searching for a lost coin (Lk. 15.8–10).

397   John 1.4–9; 5.35. The lamp, of course, is John the Baptist.

398   John 1.1, 23.

399   John 3.29.

400   Luke 1.17.

401   John 1.31–33.

402   See Luke 14.11; 18.14.

403   See Deut. 22.4; Matt. 12.11.

404   Gregory's tenth-century commentator, Basil "Minimus," justly remarks on this passage, "The discourse is almost overstuffed with lofty ideas and rhetorical connections here." (Thomas S. Schmidt [ed.], *Comm. In Or. 38*: CCG 46.98, ll. 8–9.)

405   Rom. 4.25; I Cor. 11.23.

406   Gal. 2.20; Eph. 5.2, 25. Gregory is dealing here with the complicated issue of the relationship of the divine and human wills in Christ and whether his obedience to the Father, as well as the Father's initiative in sending him to death and raising him from the dead, should be taken to imply (as the Arian tradition had argued) that the Son is himself less than fully God.

407   Acts 17.31; Rom. 4.24.

408   Mark 16.19.

409   Mark 16.9.

410   Acts 1.9; John 20.17. Gregory here contrasts the use of both the passive and the active voice in New Testament references to the resurrection and ascension of Jesus. These were things that happened to him, as a human being, but also things that he, as Son of God, did by his own divine power.

411 "Blended in" with, or "broken off" from, God. Gregory is here speaking about the implications for Trinitarian doctrine of how one interprets the various words and actions of Jesus: If one simply emphasizes the Word's divinity, one is tempted to deny any real and permanent distinction between Father and Son (and, implicitly, Holy Spirit), whereas if one simply considers Christ's humanity and finitude, one is led to separate the Son from the divine essence.

412 It is a standard feature of Gregory's Trinitarian theology that numbering the three Persons in God does not imply that they are divided in their substance but only that some abiding distinction must be observed within the divine substance.

413 John 8.48.

414 Gregory is alluding to the challenging statement by some of Jesus' opponents in John 8.48, "Are we not right in saying that you are a Samaritan, and have a demon?" Perhaps he wants to suggest that the second suggestion is simply too blasphemous even to quote.

415 So John 5.18: the Jews wanted to kill Jesus, because "by calling God his Father, he was claiming equality with God."

416 Mark 1.24; cf. 1.34.

417 Gregory now begins a vivid summary narrative of the events of Jesus' later life, the further details of the "economy" or planned work of salvation that began in his Incarnation, celebrated on this feast. He presents these events as things his hearers will "see" and "experience" for themselves: presumably in the ensuing celebrations of the liturgical year, as well as in their further reading of Scripture.

418 John 1.29.

419 Matt. 4.23.

420 Gregory likes to give the impression that his Arian opponents are among the audience, if only as a device for adding to his discourse the vividness of actual confrontation..

421 Luke 1.41.

422 II Sam. 6.14.

423 Gregory plays with the paradoxical image of a manger meant to feed animals as the place where the Word-become-flesh is laid before us. The Greek word λόγος, of course, means both the faculty of reason and the word or speech that communicates reason's content. Here ἄλογοι, brute and irrational beasts, such as humans became after the fall, are restored to their original ability to know God by the presence of God's incarnate Word as a living human being.

424 Is. 1.3.

425 Gregory repeats this sentence and the one following, now in the past tense, in Oration 39.14, which seems to have been delivered in the festival liturgy immediately after the present one. As we have seen, he was not at all averse to echoing a resonant phrase or image from earlier works!

426 Ps. 23.7, 9 (LXX). Gregory is alluding, of course, to the Psalm that seems to have been used, even in his day, in the liturgy of the feast of the Ascension of the Lord: "Lift up your heads, O gates! And be lifted up, O ancient doors! That the King of glory may come in …"

427 See Oration 30.21, where Gregory urges his hearers to "walk through" all the Scriptural titles of Christ by contemplating them. The same image of

walking is applied to their reflective participation in the feasts of the liturgical year.

428 Here and in the sentences that follow, Gregory may be hinting at his own struggles with political and ecclesiastical opponents in Constantinople; the passage may well show traces of redaction later in the 380s.

429 I.e., the "taste" of the tree of knowledge, discussed above in section 12.

430 See above, pp. 22, 109 f. For a thoughtful analysis of the significance of this oration within Gregory's changing political and ecclesiastical situation early in 381, see Heinrich Dörrie, "Die Epiphanias-Predigt des Gregor von Nazianz (Hom. 39) und ihre Geistesgeschichtliche Bedeutung," Patrick Granfield and Josef A. Jungmann (eds), *Kyriakon. Festschrift Johannes Quasten* 1 (Münster: Aschendorff, 1970) 409–423.

431 The text used for this translation is the edition of Claudio Moreschini, published with translation and notes by Paul Gallay, in *Sources Chrétiennes* 358.150–197.

432 John 1.9.

433 John 8.12.

434 Ps. 33.6 (LXX).

435 Or simply: "born again". For the same ambiguity, see John 3.3–4.

436 John 1.5.

437 Compare the narration of Gregory of Nyssa regarding the deceit and defeat of Satan in his attack on Christ, whom he thought was simply the perfect human creature, never realizing he was the Son of God: *Catechetical Oration* 23–24.

438 Hebr. 9.13.

439 Gregory here takes the familiar position of Christian apologists, that the rituals and religious stories of pagan religion—defended as the outward form of deeper truths about ultimate reality in the thought of fourth-century Neoplatonists, such as Porphyry and Iamblichus—were really the work of demons, deforming the reality of God's presence in the world in order to deceive gullible minds.

440 Gregory is satirizing the mysteries connected with the birth and childhood of Zeus. The story is that when his father Kronos learned from an oracle that one of his sons would dethrone him, he set out to eat them all, but his wife Rhea, hoping to protect the newborn Zeus, gave his father a stone to eat instead and sent the baby to Crete, where he was protected by a group of warriors called *Kuretoi*. Later rituals of noisy, armed dancing were meant to recall their actions to prevent Kronos from noticing the crying infant.

441 The Corybantes were an orgiastic cult who were centered in Phrygia in central Asia Minor and worshipped Rhea, the mother of the Gods, with ecstatic rites that included extended dancing and self-mutilation with small knives.

442 Gregory is referring, in typically compressed fashion, to the story passed on in the popular Eleusinian Mysteries, a cult of mainland Greece connected with the annual cycle of vegetation and the cultivation of grain. Demeter, the goddess who ruled the world of the dead, came to the earth in search of Kore (= maiden), her kidnapped daughter. She meets Celeus, king of Attica, and teaches his son Triptolemos how to plant and harvest corn. Both the rituals of initiation and the narrative accompanying them in this religious sect were to be held in strictest secrecy by initiates.

443 This refers to the cult of Dionysus, originally centered in Thebes in north-central Greece. Dionysus was thought to have both male and female qualities; the rites worshipping him emphasized both drunkenness and sexual license. His mother, Semele, was supposed to have been struck by a thunderbolt sent by Zeus, her deserted lover.

444 Aphrodite was the Greek goddess of sexual attraction; she was supposed to have been generated from the sea's foam, when Kronos cut off the genitals of Uranus and threw them into the ocean. Her worship, like that of other Greek deities associated with fertility and sexuality, involved dances in which phallic totems were carried.

445 Euripedes' play, *Iphigeneia in Tauris*, tells of a temple of Artemis in Tauris, in the Crimea, in which traveling strangers are sacrificed to the goddess.

446 The Spartans were said to have honored Artemis Orthia by a ritual of adult initiation, by which boys gathered in her sanctuary whipped each other until they bled.

447 According to myth, Tantalus made a meal for some visiting gods by carving up and roasting his son Pelops.

448 These are all traditional pagan oracles. Hecate, goddess of the night, was thought to cause people to see ghosts and terrifying apparitions. Trophonius was associated with an underground cave in Boeotia, north of Athens, where people could receive oracular answers to their questions after performing rites of purification and being shown symbolic images. The oracle of Zeus at Dodona, a temple near Ephesus in Asia Minor known for the significant rustlings of its sacred oak, and that of Delphi, where a priestess answered questions while seated on a three-legged stool, were celebrated places for consultation. Water from the spring of Castalia, on the slopes of Mount Parnassus in Greece, was thought to inspire poets in their own form of prophetic vision.

449 Later Christian apologetic writings, in fact, from the sixth century, did put into the mouth of the pagan oracles prophecies that they would someday give way to the truth spoken by Christ: see my article, "Apollo as a Chalcedonian," *Traditio* 50 (1995) 31–54, with the text of one such Christian "oracle" and references to others.

450 The Magi, priests of Persian Zoroastrianism, like the officiants in some ancient Roman sacrifices, professed to be able to read the future from the entrails of the animals they were sacrificing. They were also known for their interest in astrology: cf. the story of the Magi who came to visit the newborn Christ, in Matthew 2.1–12.

451 It was a commonly accepted notion that the Thracians were the first mortals to worship the gods; one of the Greek words for cult, *threskeia*, was supposed (by a false etymology) to be derived from Thrace, a region in northern Greece.

452 Orpheus, the musician whose lyre playing is supposed to have charmed all nature, was especially venerated in Thrace. The Orphic mysteries were the source of much of Plato's religious thought, especially its promise of immortality and cycles of rebirth.

453 Initiation into the mysteries of Mithras, a sun god from Persia, which included a bath in bull's blood, was said to be so strenuous that initiates sometimes died in the process. It was a favorite cult with soldiers in the Roman army, thought to prove one's virility.

454 Osiris, according to Egyptian myth, was cut into pieces by his brother, Typho; his wife Isis was forced to search for the fragments of his body and reassemble them.

455 The people of Mendes, also in Egypt, worshipped a god in the form of a goat.

456 Apis was a sacred calf, venerated at Memphis.

457 The Nile was revered almost as a god in Egypt, because the prosperity of the land's agriculture depended so heavily on its annual floods.

458 Rom. 3.23.

459 Rom. 1.27.

460 See Psalm 113.13–14 (LXX).

461 Here again, as in Or. 38.11–13, Gregory prefaces his proclamation of the Mystery of human redemption and transformation in Christ, revealed in his baptism, with a brief but dramatic summary of the story of humanity's fall and of the fall of the angels that led to the assault of the serpent on Adam and Eve.

462 Literally, "a jealous and human-hating nature."

463 See Hebr. 9.14.

464 Gregory's word is "philosophize."

465 Prov. 4.7.

466 Prov. 9.10: "The fear of the Lord is the beginning of wisdom"; see also Ps. 110.10 (LXX); Sirach 1.16.

467 Here Gregory turns to what will be the central theme of the Oration: the purification and illumination of the inner person by God, which is most perfectly accomplished by baptism into Christ.

468 Chapter 9 of this Oration corresponds, almost verbatim, with a large portion of Chapter 4 of Oration 20, *On Theology, and the Appointment of Bishops.*

469 Ex. 34.30–35.

470 Jud. 13.22.

471 Lk. 5.8.

472 Matt. 14.28–29.

473 Acts 9.1–18.

474 Matt. 8.5–10.

475 Matt. 8.8.

476 Col. 3.5.

477 Phil. 3.21.

478 Lk. 19.9; see 19.2–10, the story of Zacchaeus.

479 Matt. 12.44.

480 For the significance of the word used here, ἐπίγνωσις, see Or. 38, n. 9.

481 Matt. 12.44–45; cf. Is. 11.2, where the prophet enumerates seven positive "spirits" that the Spirit of the Lord will send upon the coming "shoot from Jesse."

482 Matt 12.45.

483 Prov. 4.23 (LXX).

484 Ps. 83.6 (LXX).

485 Jer. 4.3.

486 Hos. 10.12.

487 Literally, "the theatre." Gregory continues to preach in the metaphor of a pagan festival, invoking the semi-ritual context of a public theatre.

488 Literally, "let us philosophize."

489 Ps. 86.7 (LXX): "The dwelling-place of all who rejoice is in you."

490 Gregory seems to be referring to Or. 38, *On the Theophany*, which he has already quoted at some length: another circumstantial reason for supposing that that sermon forms a trilogy with the present one and Or. 40, *On Baptism*.

491 As in most of his Orations, Gregory does not miss the chance to speak in a summary way about the Trinitarian understanding of the one God, which for him remained the central, characteristic point of Christian doctrine. For the origins and significance of his Trinitarian terminology, see above, pp. 45–49; for a close analysis of Gregory's carefully worded argument here and its significance in the light of the issues to be faced at the coming Council of Constantinople, see Dörrie (above, n. 430).

492 I Cor. 8.6.

493 This third phrase, about the Holy Spirit, is Gregory's addition to the Pauline formula, added in the context of the development of the articulated view of God as Trinity that characterized Cappadocian theology.

494 Gregory may be alluding here to Basil's extended argument, in his treatise *On the Holy Spirit*: that there are a variety of prepositions by which one can express the relationship of the three Persons in an orthodox way, depending on tradition and context. If the Persons were in fact different in their being, presumably these expressions of relationship would be more fixed.

495 Rom. 11.36.

496 One of the great debates in the years around 380 was the precise character of the Holy Spirit. Gregory insisted with increasing clarity that the Spirit is both a distinctive hypostasis within the divine Triad, characterized by the Biblical word "procession," and that he is fully God, "of the same substance" as both Father and Son. He expresses that position unambiguously here, unlike his more cautious friend Basil. (See also Letter 58: below, pp. 165–166).

497 Literally, "unmovable."

498 See Ps. 71.19 (LXX); Is. 6.3.

499 Literally: "honored by the hand and the image of God": Gen. 1.26–27.

500 Ps. 67.34 (LXX).

501 This sentence, another of Gregory's memorable characterizations of the Christian Mystery, is often quoted in the florilegia of the fifth-century councils and later Patristic works on the person of Christ.

502 Literally, "the sophist of wickedness." The Sophists were professional experts on argument and persuasion and had the reputation of often being careless about truth.

503 Gen. 3.5.

504 Cf. again Gregory of Nyssa, *Catechetical Oration* 23–24.

505 As in the last chapters of Or. 38, Gregory presents liturgical commemoration of the events of Christ's birth as a kind of dramatic participation: the faithful, with all creatures, actually enter into the events whose story is again being narrated to them.

506 This lovely sentence is also an echo from Oration 38.17, delivered probably on the previous day.

507 John 1.11.

508 A typically compressed sentence. Gregory is playing on John 1.11: "He came to his own, and those who were his own did not receive him …" The human

race presumably is the "stranger" who originally had belonged to Christ and to whom his present visit, unrecognized as a child born in an obscure stable, restores the glory of original creation.

509 Always conscious of being an ascetic and a visitor from rural Cappadocia in the Empire's capital, Gregory now presents his evangelical activity, centered on the episode of Jesus' baptism, in the image of John, the desert-dweller, preaching by the Jordan.

510 Note the rhetorical parallel to Or. 38.1.

511 Gregory here echoes a thought he emphasizes in several other Orations, particularly in the First Theological Oration (Or. 27): that "talking about God" (θεολογία) is dangerous unless one is first morally and ascetically purified and intellectually mature.

512 Prov. 26.11; II Pet. 2.22.

513 I.e., to think lowly thoughts. This caution seems to be a veiled criticism of rebellious and scheming clerics in the Church, perhaps Maximus the Cynic and his supporters.

514 I.e., to proclaim the Gospel at the time of spiritual and bodily maturity. As Gregory will develop at length in Or. 40, he is deeply opposed to the prevailing custom among lay people of deferring baptism until late in life out of a desire to avoid the restrictions being a full communicant in the Church might impose on a worldly lifestyle. His strictures here, however, are against those who want to become preachers and teachers in the Church before they have taken the time to grow wise.

515 A familiar Greek proverb: see Cratinus, frag. 33; Aristotle, *Nicomachean Ethics* 1098 a18.

516 See Rom. 6.4: "We were buried therefore with him by baptism into death, so that as Christ was raised from the dead by the glory of the Father, we too might walk in newness of life." The theology of this chapter in Romans provides Gregory with his central understanding of the effect of baptism.

517 Matt. 3.14. Gregory vividly depicts the scene of Jesus' baptism here, relying mainly on Matthew's narrative.

518 See John 5.35 and Mal .3.20.

519 See Matt. 3.3.

520 John 3.29.

521 Matt. 11.11.

522 Col. 1.15.

523 Matt. 3.14.

524 Matt. 3.15.

525 Matt. 3.12.

526 Matt. 3.10–12.

527 Matt. 3.10.

528 Matt. 10.34; cf. Hebr. 4.12.

529 Matt. 10.35.

530 Mark 1.7.

531 Matt. 11.9.

532 Matt. 3.16.

533 Mark 1.10.

534 Gen. 3.24.

535 Gen. 8.11.

536 Dan 2.45.

537 Job 41.1.
538 Job 41.26 (LXX).
539 John 1.29.
540 Matt. 13.46.
541 Ps. 71.6 (LXX).
542 Cf. Phil. 2.7–8.
543 Gregory may be alluding to Moses' opening a stream of water from a rock for his people in Ex. 17.6, because he goes on to say that their crossing of the Red Sea, a more common type of baptism, was "before this."
544 I Cor. 10.1–2.
545 I Cor. 10.3.
546 See John 6.32–33, 53–58.
547 See John 3.5.
548 Again, Gregory makes a point of emphasizing the full divinity of the Spirit, equal to that of Father and Son.
549 Ps. 6.7.
550 Ps. 37.6 (LXX).
551 Ps. 37.7 (LXX).
552 II Chron 33.12–16; the apocryphal "Prayer of Manasseh," expressing the repentance of the converted king, is the twelfth of the "Odes" included in the Septuagint after the Psalter and used in the Greek liturgy.
553 Jonah 3.5–10.
554 Luke 18.13–14.
555 Matt. 15.22–27.
556 Hebr 5.2.
557 Matt. 7.2.
558 Gregory turns to criticize the Novatianist sect, who denied the possibility of repentance and readmission to the Church's communion for those who had committed serious sins after baptism and were generally considered overly rigorous on moral questions. Novatus, a Carthaginian deacon from the mid-third century, moved to Rome and became a colleague of the priest Novatianus in the leadership of the sect. Gregory seems to be confusing their names here. The sect had a long life and was apparently still active in Asia Minor and Constantinople at the end of the fourth century. Gregory is suggesting here that the general unwillingness of young adults in Asia Minor to be baptized, out of fear that they might later "sow their wild oats" and be incapable then of reconciliation with the Church through the "baptism of tears," has its roots in Novatianist rigorism.
559 Matt. 8.17, quoting Is. 53.4, but not in the LXX version.
560 Luke 5.32.
561 Hosea 6.6; cf. Matt. 9.13; 12.7.
562 Matt. 18.22.
563 Gregory may be alluding to Psalm 50 (LXX; Hebr. Ps. 51), a "prophetic" work like all the Psalms, which is said in its title to be David's prayer of repentance after he was confronted with his crime in seducing Bathsheba and having her husband Uriah killed in battle.
564 John 21.15–17.
565 See I Cor. 5.1.
566 II Cor. 2.7.
567 I Tim 5.14.

568 Cf. II Cor. 12.2–4.
569 Gregory seems to be alluding to different ranks or degrees of penitent or else to different locations in the Church where penitents were expected to stand during the liturgy.
570 Ps. 33.4 (LXX).
571 Cf. Is. 65.5.
572 Gregory alludes here to the likelihood of universal salvation or *apokatastasis*, which he seems to have cautiously espoused. See also Orations 3.7. and 40.36.
573 Is. 1.16.
574 Is. 1.18; cf. Ps. 50.7 (LXX).
575 See Psalms 5.7; 54.24; 58.3; 138.19 (LXX).
576 Is. 1.18.
577 Phil. 2.15.
578 Gregory here coins a new word, φωταγωγία, to parallel μυσταγωγία: "leading others into light," as one would conduct them through an initiation in a mystery cult.
579 For this Church, which was constructed under the emperor Anastasius (491–518) and stood near the basilica of the Holy Apostles, see Janin, *Géographie ecclésiastique* 29–30.
580 See Jean Bernardi, *Sources chrétiennes* 384 (Paris: Cerf, 1992) 7–17, who sees it as an entirely fictive composition; McGuckin, 361–367, is more willing to see the work as at least based on one or more real farewell addresses given in Constantinople. Several of Gregory's poems parallel the content and dramatic situation of this address in much briefer form, especially *Carmen* 2.1.16, "A Dream of the Church of the Anastasia, which He Built in Constantinople" (PG 37.1254–1261). See also *Carmina* 2.1.5–9 (PG 37.1022–1026). After returning to Cappadocia, Gregory clearly spent a good deal of time and creative effort visualizing his final words in the capital.
581 The text of Oration 42 translated here is that of Bernardi, *Sources chrétiennes* 384, 48–114.
582 Is. 52.7; cf Rom. 10.15. The opening words of the address clearly suggest that Gregory is speaking to his fellow bishops.
583 Mingling his address to his "fellow shepherds" with an allusion to the parable of the lost sheep in Matt. 18.10–14, Gregory plays on the words ἐπιστρέψητε, "turn back" or "rescue from wandering," and ἐπισκέψησθε, "watch over," "care for:" the verb from which the title "bishop" (ἐπίσκοπος) is derived. By giving pastoral care to their fellow bishop, himself always an "exile" in Constantinople, the bishops gathered for the Council of 381 are carrying out the task modeled for them by the Good Shepherd.
584 Gregory presents his resignation from episcopal office at Constantinople in accord with the judgment of his fellow bishops gathered in council as a return to the solitary ascetic life he has always craved, led by the prompting of the Holy Spirit. Having been, in his own view, an exile and stranger during his time in the capital as Nicene bishop, he now returns "home" to the "philosophic" exile in which he will no longer feel himself an alien.
585 Gal 2.2. In this oration as in many other works, Gregory tends to take Paul as his model for ministry.
586 I Cor. 14.32.
587 Gal. 2.2.

588 Literally, "our apologia."

589 I Thes. 2.19.

590 Gregory now suggests that his own Church is present along with his fellow bishops. In a dazzling array of Biblical allusions and quotations, he alludes to the condition of the Nicene community in Constantinople when he arrived to provide it with pastoral care, its suffering at the hands of the opponents of Nicene theology, its struggle to remain orthodox, and its present vindication. This dense tissue of images summarizing the recent history of his congregation with hardly any direct narration of the events themselves continues through the end of Chapter 9—a *tour de force* of indirect, yet highly dramatic, scene painting.

591 Hebr. 11.38.

592 Jer. 27.17 (LXX).

593 Gregory suggests a comparison between his Nicene community and the captive Jerusalem portrayed in the book of Lamentations and hints that his own turbulent experiences as pastor have put him in the same pitiable state.

594 Cf. Ezek. 34.6.

595 Gregory seems to be suggesting that even the accession of the orthodox Theodosius as Emperor and his presence in the capital, as well as the presence there of bishops from throughout the Greek Christian world, has not put the anti-Nicene party completely out of circulation.

596 Ex. 10.21.

597 Is. 63.16. Using powerful verses from the Prophets, Gregory here reproaches God for seeming to abandon those who have defended Trinitarian orthodoxy.

598 Is. 26.13.

599 Jer. 12.1.

600 Is. 63.19.

601 cf. Deut. 4.23, 31; II Kg. 17.38; Jer. 27.5 (LXX). Here and throughout this part of the Oration, Gregory mingles Scriptural quotations and informal allusions to the Bible with phrases of his own that have a generally Old Testament ring but do not come from any Biblical text.

602 Cf. Dan. 3.33 (LXX); Is. 26.17. The "beloved one," presumably, is Christ.

603 Gregory is alluding to Arian theology in broad and rather facile terms. The main theme of that theology since the time of Arius himself was to insist that the Word or Son of God must be a creature, because begotten of the unbegotten Father—even though, as Arius and his associates had insisted, he was "not like one of the creatures" (*Confession of Faith, to Alexander of Alexandria*).

604 Gregory here speaks of the "apostate" Emperor Julian in the figure of the persecuting king Nebuchadnezzar (LXX: Nabuchodonosor), in the Book of Daniel.

605 Jer 28.34 (LXX), a verse that refers explicitly to Nebuchadnezzar. In the Septuagint, the text reads, "… he seized (κατέλαβεν) me as insubstantial darkness." Gregory reads, "… he covered (ἐκάλυψε) me," either correcting a puzzling reading of LXX or citing a lost variant of it.

606 Ps. 93.17 (LXX).

607 Literally, "if just blood had not been shed for the sake of unholy blood." Gregory seems to mean Julian met his death because he had revived and patronized the unholy practice of pagan sacrifice. Julian was killed in battle on an expedition against the Persians in June 363. Although the ancient

sources are uncertain whether he was felled by an enemy arrow or by an arrow shot by one of his own soldiers, Gregory hints that he accepts the latter theory of "friendly fire."

608   Ps. 93.17 (LXX).

609   A reference to Valens (364–378), younger brother of the Western emperor Valentinian I (364–375) and Julian's successor as Eastern emperor. Valens also was a baptized Christian but a member of the "Homoean" Arian party, who rejected the theology of Nicaea, increasingly being accepted during his reign as the standard of orthodoxy. Valens tried to impose religious uniformity on the Christian Churches of the East by political and legal measures but was strongly resisted by Nicene bishops, especially Basil of Caesaraea. Gregory arrived at Constantinople to take over the pastoral care of the Nicene Christians just at the end of Valens's reign.

610   Cf. Joel 1.20 (LXX):"Fire has consumed the loveliness of the desert."

611   Joel 1.4 (LXX).

612   Ps. 65.12 (LXX).

613   cf. Ps. 128.6-8 (LXX).

614   Cf. Matt. 6.6.

615   cf. Hos. 9.10 (LXX).

616   Is. 30.17.

617   I Sam. 2.7.

618   I Sam. 2.6.

619   cf. Amos 5.8.

620   Gregory is probably thinking of the story of Elijah in I Kg. 18.

621   Ex. 3.7.

622   Deut 3.14; 4.34; 5.15; 6.21; 7.8, 19; 11.2; 26.8; 29.3; Ps. 135.12 (LXX); etc.

623   Ps. 76.21 (LXX).

624   Bar 2.29. With an unusual word (Greek: βόμβησις), Gregory seems to be suggesting that the change in his Church's fortune has caused a good deal of "buzz" in other parts of the world.

625   Cf. Ps. 79.9–12 (LXX).

626   cf. Ezek. 37.7–10.

627   Ps. 65.7 (LXX).

628   Ps. 72.20 (LXX).

629   Job 9.26.

630   Zach. 11.2.

631   Ps. 9.19 (LXX).

632   Hab. 3.14 (LXX).

633   Another allusion to Arian doctrine.

634   Is. 54.2 (LXX; altered).

635   cf. Is. 54.8 (LXX).

636   In Gregory's appropriation of the prophetic promises, the fidelity of God's people is measured, above all, by the norm of right faith in God as Trinity.

637   I Sam. 2.30.

638   Deut. 32.21. Gregory implies that the change in fortunes of the divided Christian communities in Constantinople will provoke the anti-Nicenes to jealousy.

639   Cf Deut. 32.34.

640 Literally, "carefully arranged pebbles." Gregory raises a caution here against the new ambitions of the Nicene Church in Constantinople to re-establish its wealth and power.

641 Matt. 18.20: taking "one or two" as added together to make three!

642 Cf. Eph. 2.19. Gregory again hints at his own "foreign" status in the capital.

643 Jud. 7.4–7.

644 Gen. 14.11–16. The account in Genesis mentions that Abraham defeated the Canaanite kings with a force of 318 household servants: the same number as that traditionally given for the bishops assembled at Nicaea!

645 Is. 10.22.

646 cf. I Kg. 19.18.

647 cf. Gen. 13.16; Acts 9.15.

648 cf. I Cor. 8.6.

649 Jer. 23.24.

650 Is. 66.1. See below, n. 654.

651 Is. 1.12 (LXX).

652 Is. 26.6.

653 Is. 57.13.

654 cf. I Sam. 5–6.

655 cf. Hos. 4.6. In the preceding two chapters, Gregory has pieced together from Old Testament texts and echoes a speech of God reminiscent of the divine oracles given to Israel but clearly tailored to the situation in Constantinople in 380–381, as the anti-Nicene community, which has been given official status and patronage under Valens, is forced by the new emperor Theodosius to hand over property and leadership to the Nicenes, led until now by Gregory.

656 Is. 62.10 Gregory seems to be alluding to the move of the Nicene congregation from its temporary quarters in the Anastasia to the official "temple," the church of the Holy Apostles, as well as the imperial basilica of Hagia Sophia (i.e., Holy Wisdom, a designation for the eternal Word of God), next to the palace. Both Holy Apostles and the Hagia Sophia had been built in the time of Constantine; after being destroyed by fire in the great Nika riots of 532, the latter was replaced under the patronage of Justinian by the present monumental church, consecrated in 538.

657 Is. 62.10.

658 Is. 57.14.

659 Gal. 4.26.

660 Rom. 1.6.

661 Tit. 2.14.

662 I Pet. 2.9.

663 cf. Ps. 64.10–11 (LXX).

664 cf. Apoc. 4.5.

665 cf. Matt. 13.32.

666 Gregory asks us now to picture him presenting to the bishops assembled in council his faithful congregation, who now constitute the orthodox community of Constantinople. This imagined gesture is central to Gregory's apologia for his own stewardship.

667 II Cor. 6.10.

668 Literally: "the eye of the world."

669 Cf. Is. 60.4.

670 Is. 28.1 (LXX).
671 Presumably the Council of bishops which has gathered in Constantinople and which Gregory presents himself as addressing here.
672 Cf. II Cor. 3.6; John 6.63.
673 Here Gregory plays again with the word λόγος, which can mean both "reason" and "word" or "speech" and which is embodied in the Word of God.
674 I.e., the congregation in Constantinople. See the beginning of Chap. 11.
675 II Cor. 11.17.
676 Gregory may be referring to Maximus the Cynic, who even during and after the Council of Constantinople continued his campaign to succeed Gregory in the see of Constantinople.
677 As he frequently does in his Orations, Gregory claims a special relationship to the Holy Spirit, whose full status as a divine Person he has championed. He may be referring to the Spirit's enlivening work through his ministry of preaching and baptism or to the Spirit's ability to give him energy despite illness and advancing age.
678 In his struggle with the anti-Nicenes and now in his efforts to establish the divine personhood of the Holy Spirit, Gregory's constant aim has been to promote Trinitarian orthodoxy.
679 Matt. 5.5, 9.
680 Greek: εὔλογος, which could also be translated "eloquent." Being "reasonable" in every respect is, for Gregory, an essential part of serving the divine Logos.
681 Gregory now begins a somewhat extended exposition of Trinitarian orthodoxy, which will occupy him through Chapter 18. Although some reflection on the Trinity usually finds its way into most of his sermons, he clearly feels it is essential to offer an ample summary of the doctrine here, in the context of his accounting for his ministry to his fellow bishops and to the Nicene faithful.
682 Literally, "philosophize".
683 Literally, "making use of some management (οἰκονομία) concerning the Word." See Letter 58, where Gregory tells of his attempts to excuse Basil's diplomatic policy of "managing" his language about the divinity of the Holy Spirit, to avoid causing disunity in the Church.
684 Cf. II Tim. 4.7.
685 Another reference to the theological position of Eunomius, Aetius, and their radical "Arian" followers; see above, n. 220. As we have already seen, opposition to this kind of theology was a driving force in the development of classical Trinitarian doctrine by the three Cappadocian Fathers.
686 A familiar figure for virtuous, purposeful moderation among early Christian writers, probably inspired by Num 20.17: "We will go along the King's Highway; we will not turn aside to the right hand or to the left…"
687 Gregory seems to mean that baptism, which initiates a person into the life of the community of grace, both includes the direct, verbal invocation of the Persons of the Trinity and, through sacramental action, immerses the person initiated into a new, living relationship with each and all of them, making him or her a child of the Father, alongside the Son, by the gift of the Spirit.
688 Greek: οὐσίας. How to translate the language of *ousia* (substance) and *hypostasis* (concrete individual), *physis* (nature) and *prosopon* (persona), into

languages other than Greek has caused difficulties since the time of the Cappadocians themselves: witness Augustine's discussion in *De Trinitate* 5.1–11 and 7.7–11. Because *hypostasis* was sometimes translated into Latin as *substantia,* it seems clearest to use Augustine's own newly coined word, "essence" (*essentia*), to capture the central meaning of *ousia*: it refers to generic or universal reality, what something is understood to *be* (which, in the Platonist world, was genuine reality), not to the concrete, individual reality designated by a proper name.

689 Greek: πρόσωπα. It is important to remember that when ancient writers, Greek or Latin, used this term, they were thinking not of the "person" as understood in the modern West—defined principally in terms of freedom, self-consciousness, and relationships to other conscious persons—but of an acting human individual perceived "from outside," such as a character in a play or a subject of legal rights: a human individual with a definable role and a history ascertainable by others. See above, pp. 45–46.

690 Greek: τριπόσωπον, which could also be translated as "three-faced." Gregory's point here, however, seems to be that God is not a triad of separate individuals on the model of a family or a committee.

691 This is, of course, a contradiction of one of Arius's central theses: that if the Son is "of God," generated by the Father in order to be the Mediator of creation and salvation, the Son must himself be a creature who had a beginning, and cannot be divine in the full sense in which the Father, who begot him, is divine. Here Gregory implies a certain hesitation to speak of human salvation in terms of "divinization."

692 This, applied to the Son or Word of God, was the best-known and most shocking slogan associated with Arius and his associates in the controversy leading to the Council of Nicaea in 325. Convinced that the Son was a creature delegated by God to carry out the work of creation and redemption, Arius insisted on drawing the explicit conclusion that the Son had a beginning, like all creatures, and so cannot be thought of as eternal in the way that God is.

693 The being of creatures, in other words, which begins in time, is a participation in the being of God the creator; only God has being properly in himself without depending on a prior cause, because only God eternally *is*.

694 cf. Deut. 23.4.

695 Having rejected the classical position of Arius and his immediate followers, Gregory now addresses the arguments of the so-called neo-Arians, the followers of Eunomius and Aetius, which drew their force from a highly developed theory of linguistic signification and from a continual emphasis on logic.

696 Gregory is doubtless referring to his five "theological orations" (Or. 27–31), which together form his own most extended treatment of Trinitarian theology and its Biblical foundations and are the Greek tradition's classical expression of this central, summary doctrine of Christian faith. Orations 29 and 30, particularly, deal with the scriptural passages central to the fourth-century Trinitarian controversies.

697 Gregory seems here to be cautioning the assembled bishops against moving too quickly to produce some new official formulation of Trinitarian faith or trying to deal exhaustively with contested Scriptural texts in the Trinitarian debate. He seems rather to be urging them to spend time listening to the

voices of the tradition and to the best contemporary theologians; the best strategy in all problem solving, he implies, is: first learn, then teach! On the question of whether or not the Council of 381 did produce a creedal formula, see above, n. 109.

698   For the first time in this oration, Gregory addresses his audience by the general title "gentlemen" (ὦ ἄνδρες), a title familiar from classical oratory and the title by which Socrates addresses the Athenian jury in Plato's *Apology*. For the first time since Chapter 2, he also here refers to his discourse as an "apology." He further suggests he is giving this address in response to the bishops' invitation.

699   cf. I Sam. 12.3–5.

700   I.e., to work completely without expectation of reward.

701   Literally, "of states of mind no less than of the limits of the earth." In the ecclesiastical struggles of 380–381, which the bishops gathered at Constantinople were commissioned by the Emperor Theodosius to resolve, Pope Damasus of Rome had not only given his support to the strongly Nicene party of Paulinus in the long-divided Church of Antioch (see below, n. 732) but was sympathetic to those who argued that Gregory had not been canonically installed in the see of Constantinople.

702   Gregory skillfully uses the image of excited fans at a sporting event as a metaphor for the competitiveness that so often seems to drive ecclesiastical and political conflict.

703   Gregory likes to present himself, in his poetry and letters and even here, as an uncompromising loner.

704   Probably Democritus of Abdera (born c.460 B.C.), the first Greek philosopher to describe the material universe as made up of atomic particles. He was known as "the laughing philosopher," according to Diogenes Laertius 9.36.

705   Acts 2.13.

706   Gregory represents the faithful of his own party in Constantinople as criticizing him for being too weak in pressing for their advantage, now that imperial policy favors the supporters of Nicaea.

707   Around 370, the Emperor Valens—who supported the "homoean" opponents of the Nicene theology—ordered his notoriously heavy-handed praetorian prefect, Modestus, to arrest and execute eighty pro-Nicene clerics who had come to visit him at the imperial residence at Nicomedia, complaining of persecution. According to the fifth-century historian Socrates (*Church History* 4.16), the prefect had them put on board a ship and taken out into the Gulf of Astakeia, the arm of the sea of Marmara leading to Nicomedia; there, at Modestus's instructions, the crew set the ship afire before abandoning it themselves in a lifeboat. Gregory also refers to this incident in Or. 25.10, Or. 33.4, and Or. 43.46. For an incident in which Gregory's friend Basil of Caesaraea calmly defied the same prefect, see Gregory's Oration 43 (Panegyric on Basil) 48–51; Sozomen, *Church History* 6.16.

708   The Greek word, πολυάνδρια, could also mean "common burying-places," but this is harder to imagine.

709   Gregory is using the term here purely to designate the dignity of age. The term *Patriarch* was not used for senior bishops until the mid-fifth century.

710   In a decree of April 22, 376, the emperor Gratian (Valens's Western colleague) ordered that the churches of heretical Christians be confiscated. Theodosius,

Valens's successor in the East, decreed in February, 380, that the creed of Nicaea be held normative for Christian faith. Apparently anti-Nicenes in Constantinople continued to hold on to their property after these decrees.

711 In the eighteen months in which Gregory exercised power as bishop of Constantinople, he apparently refused to take any punitive measures against the anti-Nicene Christians who had formerly been the dominant Christian group in the capital.

712 Had Gregory been criticized for not spending enough on the renovation of church buildings for the return of the Nicene party?

713 Gregory adopts a satirical tone, either to depict the disappointed expectations of his backers that he play the part of a great ecclesiastical figure or to deflate criticisms that he has lived in too high a style by reducing them to absurdity.

714 This remark, intended to be a criticism of the atmosphere in the capital, reveals a tension at the heart of Gregory's own career and self-understanding. His rhetoric, always exercised with exquisite care in his surviving work, remained for him a way of carrying out a ministry to and in the Church.

715 Literally: "not pure officiants at sacrifice, but strong presiders."

716 I Cor. 9.22.

717 Gen. 22.8.

718 After Gregory's resignation from office, the bishops at the Council, along with the Emperor Theodosius, considered a number of possible successors and chose in the end a "dark horse": a civil servant named Nectarius, a "mild, virtuous and excellent man" (Sozomen) of senatorial rank from Tarsus in Cilicia, who at that time had not yet been baptized. He seems to have been originally the candidate of the bishops from the Antiochene region and was first sponsored by his own bishop, the distinguished exegete Diodore of Tarsus. By the time of his ordination, however—which he received still clothed in the white robe of a neophyte—his election seems to have been regarded as an inspired choice. See Socrates, *Church History* 5.8; Sozomen, *Church History* 7.8.

719 Gregory seems to be referring to the elaborate ceremonial of speechmaking that attended the retirement of major public figures. Someone representing the body responsible for electing or confirming him in office would make a valedictory oration (προπεμπτήριος λόγος: literally, a "speech sending him on the way"), after which the person retiring would respond with a farewell oration (συντακτήριος λόγος). Gregory here speaks of both as constituting a formal occasion yet to come. The present oration seems all the more likely, then, to be a retrospective summary of his sentiments on leaving office rather than an actual speech to the assembled bishops of the Council. In the remaining paragraphs, however, he anticipates that farewell in words filled with vivid images, tender memories, and noble emotion, and also with a touch of bitterness.

720 The "Chapel of the Resurrection," in which the Nicene Christians had assembled, until Theodosius recognized them as the official Christian body and allowed them to use the other Churches of the city; see above, Introduction, n. 77.

721 cf. Jos. 15.8; II Sam. 5.6–9. Gregory seems here to be addressing the Church of Holy Wisdom (Hagia Sophia), the Constantinian basilica adjoining the imperial palace, where the bishops met in Council in 381.

722 cf. I Cor. 15.10.

723 The Church of the Holy Apostles, built by Constantine to house the relics of the Twelve, became not only his burial place but the cathedral Church of Constantinople.

724 Cf. II Cor. 12.7–9.

725 Probably a reference to the suffragan bishops who formed the Church of Constantinople's resident synod.

726 I.e., monks. In ancient Israel, the Nazirites were men and women who made a special vow to separate themselves from the body of the community for a fixed period of time, to pursue a special degree of holiness by observing a higher level of ritual purity, abstaining from wine, and letting their hair grow; see Num. 6.1–20. Here Gregory turns to the various aspects of institutionalized Church life that realized its common vocation to sanctity.

727 Clearly a special reference to his cousin Theodosia, who has offered him hospitality, along with his congregation, during his stormy tenure in the capital.

728 Like most ancient orators, Gregory did not read his orations from a prepared text but spoke from memory; stenographers would have copied down his words, which he would later have edited into their present written form. He suggests here that some of those writing down his sermons were not official notaries but simply people who wanted to make copies for themselves.

729 Like his successor John Chrysostom, Gregory is not averse to criticizing court officials for their questionable morality and orthodoxy. He suggests here that many of the imperial staff remained sympathetic to the anti-Nicenes, even after the arrival of Theodosius.

730 Probably Demophilus, the Homoean Arian bishop whom Gregory replaced when Theodosius took possession of the capital in February 380. See Socrates 5.7; Sozomen 7.5.

731 Rom. 10.2.

732 The first issue that the Council of 381 was called to resolve was the long-standing schism in the Church of Antioch, in which two (at times three) rival bishops led dissident groups within the city. Historically, Gregory, the other Cappadocian Fathers, and most of the bishops of Asia Minor supported Melitius, a moderate who was willing to make peace with the Homoean Arians; the Churches of Alexandria and the Latin West supported the more uncompromising Nicene Paulinus. Meletius was the first president of the Council but died a few weeks after the sessions began, and Gregory was forced briefly to take the chair.

733 I Tim. 6.20. To the end of the oration, Gregory continues to represent himself in the persona of Paul, the faithful, itinerant, and persecuted Apostle.

734 Cf. Col. 4. 18, the closing verse of that epistle: "Remember my chains. Grace be with you." During the Easter celebrations of 379, Gregory's first Easter in Constantinople, a crowd of monks from the rival faction forced their way into the Anastasia and began pelting him and the congregation with stones. See his references in Carm. 2.1.12.103; 2.1.15.11; 2.1.30.125; 2.1.33.12; and Ep. 77. See also McGuckin 257. Gregory's allusion to the event here, at the very close of his Oration, with clear echoes of Paul (cf. Acts 14.19, where Paul is stoned at Lystra), adds to the tone of bitter irony that has increasingly characterized Chaps. 26 and 27. His "farewell" ends in quiet, Biblical anger.

735 Basil of Caesaraea, Homily 23 (PG 31.589–600). Cf. the later *Life of Saint Daniel the Stylite* 45 (ed. Hippolyte Delehaye, *Analecta Bollandiana* 32 [1913]

162), which informs us that the feast of St. Mamas in September was celebrated with a vigil.

736   The text of Oration 44 has not yet appeared in a critical edition. For this translation, we have used the text of PG 36.608–621.

737   τὰ ἐγκαίνια, the Greek word translated here by "feast of renewal," has a number of related meanings, on which Gregory plays skillfully throughout this homily. Derived from the adjective "new," it can mean "inauguration" or "dedication" and is the normal Greek word used in the Septuagint and the New Testament for the Jewish feast of Hanukkah, which commemorated the rededication of the Temple in Jerusalem by Judas Maccabaeus in 167, after its desecration by the Greek Seleucid emperors (I Macc. 4.36–59; II Macc. 10.5; cf. John 10.22). It can also refer to the annual commemoration or anniversary of such an inaugural event. More broadly, it has the meaning of restoration or renovation and is used by Gregory here with the whole range of its possible significations.

738   Is. 41.1.

739   The opening sentences of the Oration up to this point form the first *sticheron* of the Greek Orthodox vesper service for the consecration of a church: see Εὐχολόγιον τὸ μέγα (Athens, 1992) 294.

740   Jer. 1.18.

741   Ps. 149.1.

742   Here also, the word translated as "was dedicated," ἐγκαινίζεται, is from the same root but refers to the consecration of the tabernacle rather than to its annual commemoration.

743   Ex. 31.1–11; 35.30–36.7; 40.17–33.

744   Once again, the Greek word is ἐγκαινίζεται: here in the sense of "establish newly."

745   I Sam. 16.13.

746   II Sam. 5.1–5.

747   John 10.22.

748   John 2.19; Mk. 14.58.

749   In some manuscripts, "be called back."

750   Ps. 50.10 (LXX).

751   Gregory never misses the opportunity to emphasize that the God of whom he speaks is a Trinity of persons.

752   Gregory's point here seems to be to emphasize the difference between the eternal, uncreated light, which is God, and the created light we know in the universe. Whereas God simply gives of his light, enabling creatures to know and be known, the created light is both the condition for seeing objects and a visible thing in itself—so it "takes what it gives," namely the experience of seeing.

753   See Ps. 18.1–3 (LXX).

754   See Gen. 1.1–5. Gregory here reflects the Biblical understanding of God's creation as being first of all an act of bringing life-giving order out of primeval chaos.

755   See Gen. 1.14–18, where the creation of the two "great lights" in the heavens (the sun and the moon) takes place only on the fourth day. Both the sun and the moon are occasionally referred to as "the eye of the heavens" in Greek literature: see Pindar, *Olymp.* 3.20; Aeschylus, *Septem contra Thebas* 390 [moon]; Secundus of Athens, *Sententia* 5 [sun].

756   See Gen. 1.26–27; 2.7, 21–22.

757   See Gen. 1.28; 2.19–20.

758   See Rom. 5.12. Nicetas explains Gregory's understanding of the "original" immortality of the human race in this passage as follows: "The human person was not created as actually mortal, nor as immortal; but being in a middle position between God and materiality, he was in the position that if he obeyed the divine command he would be united to God and given a share in immortality; but if he broke the law, he would be made liable to death, passible rather than free from suffering, mortal rather than immortal." (PG 127.1419 A) Gregory differs here from Athanasius, *On the Incarnation* 3, who suggests that the human creature is mortal like all animals but originally was given immortality and the image of God as a "second gift" beyond his nature; however, his position closely resembles that of Gregory of Nyssa, *Catechetical Oration* 8, who describes human bodily death as a gift—not part of God's original design—given humanity after the fall to put a limit on sin and the misery it causes. Cf. the second-century apologist, Theophilus of Antioch, *Ad Autolycum* 2.24, 27, for a position similar to that proposed by Nicetas.

759   The Greek text here, τῷ σὰρξ παγῆναι, is uncertain; a possible alternative is τῷ σαρκοφαγῆναι, "he endured the poverty *of having his flesh eaten*," suggesting a reference to John 6.53–56, or to Jesus' burial (in a "sarcophagus").

760   II Cor. 8.9.

761   I.e., Easter Sunday, eight days earlier than the present feast.

762   Gregory depicts the dedicatory feast as pointing to the continuing renewal, in the Church, of the Mystery of Christ's death and resurrection reflected in the sacrifice of martyrdom.

763   Ecclesiastes 11.2. Gregory takes this as referring to the present age and to the new age or "restoration" (ἀποκατάστασις) yet to come, of which the "Eighth Day" is a familiar symbol in Patristic literature. See also Or. 14.22, where he interprets this verse from Ecclesiastes in the same sense.

764   Psalms 6 and 12 (LXX: 11) bear the inscription, "according to the eighth" (Hebrew: *'al ha-shminith*; LXX: ὑπέρ τῆς ὀγδόης). This may be a reference to musical performance (e.g., in the eighth mode) but was taken by many of the Fathers as a hint that the psalms were intended to refer to the Eighth Day, the coming Kingdom of God. See especially Gregory of Nyssa, *Homily on the Sixth Psalm* (GNO V, 187–193). See my essay, which includes a translation of this homily: "Training for 'The Good Ascent': Gregory of Nyssa's Homily on the Sixth Psalm," in Paul M. Blowers, Angela Russell Christman, David G. Hunter, and Robin Darling Young, *In Dominico Eloquio— In Lordly Eloquence: Essays in Patristic Exegesis in Honor of Robert Louis Wilken* (Grand Rapids: Eerdmans, 2002) 185–218.

765   Psalm 29 (LXX).

766   Eph. 2.20–21.

767   Eph. 4.22.

768   The second sentence of this paragraph ("So be renewed … flee from them"), with the addition of a sentence from par. 8 ("This is the way a human person is renewed, this is how the Day of Renewal should be honored") form the second *sticheron* of Greek Orthodox vespers for the consecration of a Church (Εὐχολόγιον 294).

769   Gen. 3.6.

770   Gregory's words here are somewhat enigmatic, but his thought seems to be: Even God's desire to save humanity, and the "costly remedy" of Jesus' death

and resurrection, are of little avail for those who continue to be dominated by their own sensual desires.

771   The Greek word φθόνος, on which Gregory is playing here, means both "ill-will" or "malice" and "envy." His point seems to be that one must be on one's guard against this feeling, because it lies at the root of humanity's fall: The evil spirit, out of envy against the first human pair, led them to believe that God begrudged them the status that would be theirs through knowing good and evil, and so led them into the disobedience that destroyed them; see Gen. 3.1–5.

772   Gregory is referring here to the practice of consecrated, celibate men and women living together in informal monastic communities, a source of occasional scandal in the Eastern Churches: see, for instance, John Chrysostom's homily against the practice (PG 48.513–532). Their sexual relationship, Gregory goes on to say, may be symbolic rather than physical, "through the air" rather than through the body, but it seems to him nonetheless an abandonment of the liberty of real chastity. See the comments of Nicetas on the passage (PG 127.1426C–1427 A).

773   Reading ἐπικόπτετω, "let it cut short," instead of Migne's ἐπικύπτετω, "let it lean towards," which makes less sense here.

774   Deut. 16.16.

775   II Cor. 5.17.

776   Ps. 76.11 (LXX).

777   II Cor. 5.17.

778   Gregory begins here a series of exhortations, contrasting his hearers' behavior on the day before his sermon with their present display of reverence and also with the "new person" they are called to be "tomorrow" in Christ. The annual feast commemorating the dedication of St. Mamas's shrine, at the end of the Paschal octave, may well have been preceded by several days of public festival; hence his references to the theatre, to riotous behavior, and to fine clothing and good food. The ideal Gregory holds up for the future, in place of self-indulgent reveling, is that of the ascetic life: the life of a Christian "philosopher."

779   Cf. I Kg. 18.21: Elijah's taunt to the prophets of Baal, "How long will you go limping with two different opinions," trying to combine faith in the God of Israel with faith in Baal.

780   Gregory plays here on the words οἰκονομεῖν, "manage a household," a metaphor meaning "adapt to the situation at hand," and οἰκοδομεῖν, "build a house."

781   Another word-play: This time Gregory contrasts θεατρικός, "stage actor," with θεωρητικός, "contemplative."

782   Is. 65.17; 66.22; II Pet. 3.13; Rev. 21.1.

783   The small sailing ships of the ancient Mediterranean normally did not sail in the winter months because of the frequency of winter storms. Gregory here is referring to the spring launching, in which a ship would be rowed out of its winter harbor into open water, where the sails would be raised. The boatswain's orders and rhythmic calls to the oarsmen may have occasionally been salted with profanity, but Gregory assures us here in this generally sunny passage that such was the exception rather than the rule.

784   Gregory seems to be confusing dolphins with whales.

785   As he concludes his sermon by reflecting on this season of religious and natural renewal, Gregory finally turns to the martyr Mamas. A central part

of the celebration of the dedication of his shrine seems to have been an open-air procession with the saint's relics.

786　Nicetas of Heraclea (PG 127.1434 A), as we mentioned in the introduction, suggests that Basil may have been present at this occasion, and that Gregory— with tongue in cheek—wanted to make sure his friend did not suspect him of wanting to appropriate the relics or the patronage of Caesaraea's martyr for his own little Church of Sasima. For the theme of "grudging" or envy in Gregory's narrative of the fall and salvation, see above, n. 771.

787　The sources for the life of St. Mamas are highly legendary and give little historically reliable information on his life. Most of them depict him as a shepherd, who, like Orpheus, lived in extraordinary harmony with wild animals. On the detail of his being fed by the milk of deer, for example, see the medieval Latin *Passio sancti Mammetis* 8 (ed. Hippolyte Delehaye, *Analecta Bollandiana* 58 [1940] 131).

788　I.e., Caesaraea.

789　Again, Gregory seems to be alluding to the presence of other bishops (perhaps including Basil) in the congregation listening to his oratory.

3　POEMS

1　In the absence of a critical edition, I have used the Greek texts in PG 37.

2　Above, p. 26.

3　Among those who consider it as dubiously authentic are R. Keydell, "Die Unechtheit der Gregor von Nazianz zugeschriebenen Exhortatio ad Virgines," *Byzantinische Zeitschrift* 43 (1950) 334–337, who questions it because it seems to share an "accentual" rather than a quantitative meter with the longer "Exhortation to Virgins" (*Carm.* 1.2.3), which Keydell rejects on thematic as well as literary grounds; and H. M. Werhahn, "Dubia und Spuria unter den Gedichten Gregors von Nazianz," *Studia Patristica* 7 (Texte und Untersuchungen 92; Berlin: Akademieverlag, 1966) 337–347, who follows Keydell. On the other hand, it is included by Wilhelm von Christ and Matthaios Paranikas in their important *Anthologia Graeca Carminum Christianorum* (Leipzig: Teubner, 1871) 29. In fact, the meter of this poem is probably not to be taken as accentual or popular meter (parallel to Augustine's *Psalmus contra Partem Donati*) but as a "hemiamb" or iambic dimeter catalectic, a fairly unusual classical meter.

4　Carmina II, 1 (*Poemata de seipso*) 39 (PG 37.1329–1336). This reflective monolog is written in the meter of dramatic monolog and dialog: iambic trimeter. For a recent discussion of the poem, see Cecilia Milovanovich-Barham, "Gregory of Nazianzus: Ars Poetica. *In suos versus*: Carmen 2.1.39," *Journal of Early Christian Studies* 5 (1997) 497–510.

5　Reading οὕτω for PG οὔτε. The text as published in the Patrologia Graeca would have to be translated: "they measure the work of others by their own measurements, / not even showing this [i.e., their own measurements] greater / honor than godly labors."

　　This seems to make little sense and suggests an emendation such as we have proposed.

6　By the fourth century, a "Sophist" was a professional grammarian, a teacher of classical language and literature. Gregory seems to be suggesting that one result of his own classical education (largely at the hands of pagan professors) was to motivate him to claim their cultural role for Christians. Hence his "lion-hearted gratitude"—a fierce and consuming recognition of the importance of literary studies.

7   Gregory's words take on a polemical tone in the section that follows. Unclear is just who his critic or critics are, although Gregory paints them as unsuccessful would-be poets themselves.

8   This is a proverbial phrase roughly equivalent to our frequent English allusion to the difficulty of comparing apples with oranges. Gregory uses it in several other poems, sometimes along with a similar, more specifically Biblical version: "The waters of Marah (see Ex. 15.23) are far from the waters of Siloam (see John 9.7)": see *On his own Life* (Carm. II, 1, 11) 1240; *On himself and on bishops* (Carm. II, 1, 12) 662. The line may have its origin in classical tragedy and is included by modern editors of the fragments of the Greek tragedians as no. 560 of the "anonymous" quotations (*adespota*): see Richard Kennicht and Bruno Snell (eds), *Tragicorum Graecorum Fragmenta* 2 (Göttingen: Vandenhoeck und Ruprecht, 1981) 154, with further references to its use by ancient and medieval authors. According to one Greek commentary on Gregory, it was first spoken—perhaps in one of the tragedies—by Telephus, son of Heracles and king of Mysia, the region northeast of Troy on the Hellespont; Greek ships on the way to Troy, the story goes, had landed on his coast, and he pointed out that Troy was in fact in Phrygia, a different province further to the south (see Kennicht and Snell, *ibid.* for details). Gregory is at least aware of the saying's classical echoes.

9   Carmina I, 1 (*Poemata dogmatica*) 30 (PG 37.508–510). This poem is written in the Anacreontic meter, which our translation attempts to replicate.

10 Carmina I, 1 (*Poemata dogmatica*) 33 (PG 37.514). This hymn is written in dactylic hexameter.

11 Carmina I, 1 (*Poemata dogmatica*) 32 (PG 37.511–514). This hymn is written in iambic dimeter catalectic, which we have tried to reproduce here.

12 Carmina I, 1 (*Poemata dogmatica*) 35 (PG 37.517). The original is written in dactylic hexameter.

13 Carmina I, 1 (*Poemata dogmatica*) 37 (PG 37.520–521). This prayer is written originally in dactylic hexameter.

14 Carmina II, 1 (*Poemata de seipso*) 3 (PG 37.1020–1021). This prayer is written in iambic trimeter, the usual meter of dialog passages in Greek drama, which we have used here. The prayer may be meant to reflect Gregory's hope at the time of his move to Constantinople in the autumn of 379. Inevitably, it summons up associations with Newman's celebrated poem, "The Pillar of the Cloud" (or: "Lead, Kindly Light").

15 See Ex. 17.8–13. Gregory now conceives of his journey in terms of Moses' trek across the desert at the head of his people.

16 Gregory seems to allude to the practice of beginning a journey by making the sign of the cross with one's hands, perhaps to ward off evil spirits.

17 Carmina II, 1 (*Poemata de seipso*) 74 (PG 37.1421–1422). This autobiographical prayer is written in iambic trimeter, which we have adopted here.

18 Carmina II, 1 (*Poemata de seipso*) 24-26 (PG 37.1284–1286). All three of these prayers, which clearly form a set, are written in the "conversational" iambic trimeter.

19 Carmina II, 1 (*Poemata de seipso*) 22 (PG 37.1281–1282). This prayer is written in dactylic hexameter.

4 LETTERS

1 There is some uncertainty about the addressee of this letter. Two manuscripts contain the marginal notation, "not to Gregory of Nyssa, but to some other Gregory, with the same name;" another has the note, "in another manuscript it is written Andronicus." Most of the manuscripts, however, identify the addressee as Gregory, the brother of Basil who later became bishop of Nyssa. The date of the letter must be after Christmas 362, when Gregory of Nazianzus was ordained a priest, and before 371, when Basil's brother Gregory was made bishop of Nyssa. It probably comes from the mid-360s and reflects the situation of educated Christians in the decade after the Emperor Julian's decree of 362, prohibiting Christians from teaching literature or philosophy in publicly supported schools. The Cappadocians continued to struggle with the tension felt in their culture between being a good Hellene and being a good Christian. The text translated here is that edited by Paul Gallay, *Saint Grégoire de Nazianze. Lettres I* (Paris: Les Belles Lettres, 1964) 16–18.

2 Gregory the addressee has chosen the public role of being a teacher of rhetoric, rather than a junior member of the clergy: a lector whose role was to proclaim and perhaps even interpret Scripture. Here Gregory of Nazianzus, himself highly skilled in the literary art, pretends that he is adopting a foreign style in his use of paradox and other features of the Second Sophistic style.

3 Euripides, *The Phoenician Women* 531–532.

4 Literally, "wisest one" (σοφώτατε), suggesting that Gregory of Nyssa is an accomplished σοφιστής or teacher of rhetoric.

5 An allusion to Hesiod, *Works and Days* 629, where the poet advises sailors to hang their rudders over the fireplace in winter to allow the wood to dry and harden. Gregory uses the same image in his letter 235 to Adamantius.

6 Cp. Rom. 14.7–8.

7 A quotation from the end of the *Third Letter* attributed to Pythagoras: *Epistolographi Graeci* (ed. Hercher) 603.

8 Euripides, *The Phoenician Women* 1446.

9 See Hesiod, *Works and Days* 293–295.

10 This letter was written towards the end of 368. Gregory's brother Caesarius, a physician by training, has entered the imperial civil service and is now financial administrator of the province of Bithynia in northwestern Asia Minor. After a severe earthquake there in October of that year (see Socrates, Church History 4.16), Gregory writes him this letter, speaking of the positive value that can be providentially hidden in adversity. The Greek text translated here is that of Gallay 1.28–29.

11 This phrase, which Gregory also uses in Oration 17.5, does not appear in either of the Letters of Peter in the New Testament or in any known apocryphal work. A marginal note in one of the manuscripts of this letter attributes it to "the so-called *Teaching of Peter*," a work now lost.

12 Gregory gently apologizes for making his letter not simply a general piece of moral advice but an exhortation aimed directly at the civil servant Caesarius.

13 Philagrius, who had studied in Alexandria with Gregory's younger brother, Caesarius, and was a friend of the family, lived in Mataza, another small

town in Cappadocia, and received several letters from Gregory (Letters 30–36, 87, 92). A highly cultivated man like Gregory and Caesarius, he was a teacher (Letter 32), and Gregory considered him a "philosopher" in the full range of the term's meanings. Apparently he suffered from a chronic illness that severely limited his activities. In this letter, from the end of 369, Gregory shares his own feelings in the days shortly after the death of Caesarius and thanks Philagrius for stirring up his own happy memories of his brother by writing to him. The Greek text translated here is that of Gallay 1.37–38.

14 Gregory is referring to his own memories of growing up with Caesarius, stirred up by a letter from his brother's friend.

15 *Iliad* 3.175.

16 The Greek text translated here is that of Gallay 1.38–39.

17 *Phaedo* 81a.

18 Gregory here alludes to Plato's famous pun, found in *Gorgias* 493a and *Cratylus* 400c, which likens the body (σῶμα) to a tomb (σῆμα) for the soul.

19 This letter, dating from the spring of 372, is Gregory's angry, even bitter, reply to several letters from Basil (no longer extant), which apparently sharply criticized him for failing to support Basil in his struggles to promote the faith of Nicaea. For the historical circumstances of his appointment as bishop of what he considered to be the insignificant hamlet of Sasima, see above, pp. 10–12. Gregory, who always recoiled from Church politics and even from public ministry, has fled to solitude after his episcopal ordination and in fact never took up residence in Sasima. In this letter, he responds to Basil's reproach of neglecting his duty to their friendship and to the Church. The Greek text translated here is that of Gallay 1.61–63.

20 Gregory suggests here that their opponents are criticizing both himself and Basil; the charges he mentions in the next sentence clearly refer to Basil's way of treating him.

21 Paul Gallay, the French translator, has noticed a play on words here: καταβάλλειν, "strike down," can also mean "pay a debt." Gregory is asking Basil to pay the debt of friendship by disabusing their critics of the suspicion that he has only been playing on Gregory's own ambition for Church office.

22 When Basil first approached Gregory with the proposal of ordaining him bishop, Gregory apparently refused him indignantly, then later somewhat half-heartedly agreed. He now suggests that his first reaction represented his real feelings about Church politics.

23 Gregory likes to portray himself as sickly and thus lacking in the power to resist the strong persuasion of others.

24 A reference to Exodus 17.8–13. In the mountains of Cappadocia, Gregory suggests, Anthimus will engage both in ecclesial sheep stealing and in territorial encroachment.

25 Gregory ironically suggests that Sasima, a peasant village far from his home, is really of no pastoral significance for the Church, however pastoral it may be in the agricultural sense.

26 Gregory may be alluding ironically here to Basil's championing of the activity of the Holy Spirit as that of a divine and sanctifying person.

27 This letter, probably written after 384, during Gregory's years of productive retirement, is addressed to Nicoboulus the Younger, the teenaged son of Gregory's nephew by marriage, Nicoboulus. The elder Nicoboulus, who came from a wealthy and well-connected Cappadocian family, had married Gregory's

niece Alypiane, daughter of his sister Gorgonia and her husband Alypius, and had been a military officer in Julian's Persian campaign of 352–353. Their son, to whom Gregory wrote this and Letters 52–55, had received early training as a stenographer and was then taken on as a pupil by Gregory's friend, the respected rhetorician Eudoxius (see Letter 174). He was apparently not a very talented or very ambitious young man but was close to his great-uncle Gregory nonetheless. Here Gregory, apparently in response to a request, makes some succinct remarks to this rhetorician-in-training about the art of writing letters. The text translated here is that of Gallay 1.66–68.

28   The Greek word here is χρεία: literally, "necessity" or "use." In the Greek rhetorical tradition, a *chreia* was a useful saying or maxim often accompanied by an illustrative anecdote. Handbooks of *chreiai* had been assembled by the classical rhetoricians for use in oratory. Gregory is talking here about the proportions of a good letter, as determined by the demands of the subject, but the term *chreia* situates his discussion squarely in the world of the rhetorical art.

29   An allusion to the lyric poet Callimachus, *Aitia*, Oxyrhyncus 2079.18: "Do not measure verbal eloquence with the Persian cord, but judge with skill." The metaphor seems to suggest exaggerated precision. Callimachus uses the word σοφία, literally "wisdom," as his term for rhetorical sophistication; a grammarian or rhetorician was usually called a *sophist* (σοφιστής).

30   A cubit was the distance from the tip of one's middle finger to one's elbow; the standard was an adult arm, so that "a child's cubit" is a deficient measure. To "measure with a child's cubit," therefore, is to say less than is needed.

31   Gregory's images have somewhat run away from him here. He seems to be talking about imprecision or impressionism in writing, comparing it to a drawing in which the lines are so vague as to need to be completed by guesswork on the part of the beholder.

32   Gregory seems to be alluding to a proverbial phrase here, but its origin is unknown.

33   Genuine purple dye, in the ancient world, was made from Mediterranean mollusks, and the process of producing it was costly and labor-intensive. Hence, purple wool was the most expensive kind and was used in normal fabrics only for decorative embroidery.

34   These stylistic features of artistic speech, which Gregory himself uses lavishly in his orations, he considers forced and precious in a letter. Good epistolary style cultivates a tone of intimacy and informality while remaining thoroughly controlled.

35   This letter, a well-known example of Gregory's ability to annoy his politically astute but imperious friend Basil (see Letter 59), was probably written in 372 or 373, as debate over the status of the Holy Spirit as a distinct person within the Mystery of God became intense in Asia Minor. The letter illustrates how risky a theological step it was, in the third quarter of the fourth century, to affirm the full, substantial divinity of the Spirit. Even though a consensus was forming among Christian leaders that the Nicene term "consubstantial" was the only way to safeguard an orthodox understanding of the Savior's divine status, it apparently still seemed daring to extend that notion to the Spirit sent by the Son into the Church. Basil's reluctance to exacerbate divisions by using such language is clear in his treatise *On the Holy Spirit*, which probably emerged from discussions held at about the time of this letter and was put in final form in 375; there he makes the divine status of

the Spirit clear but avoids calling him "God" or "consubstantial with the Father." The same caution is reflected even in the creed of the Council of Constantinople of 381, despite Gregory of Nazianzus's open advocacy of a more forthright affirmation of the Spirit's full and personal share in the being of God. The subject of the letter is not so much the divinity of the Holy Spirit as it is the perennial tension between forthrightness and diplomacy in public theological debate. We do not have Basil's immediate response, but Gregory's Letter 59, his reply to Basil's reply, makes it clear that "my letter has caused you pain," despite all his care here to explain the incident in a positive way. The text translated here is that of Gallay 1.73–77.

36   Apparently a monk or cleric.

37   In Num. 16, the Levites Dathan and Abiram, along with Korah, son of Izhar, challenge Moses' authority and accuse him of leading them out of a secure life in Egypt and exalting himself and Aaron for self-serving reasons. At God's command, Moses orders the people to keep away from the rebellious Levites, and the earth opens to swallow them up, along with their households. Gregory claims to have made this severe comparison with Basil's monastic or clerical critic.

38   St. Eupsychius was put to death in Caesaraea during the reign of the Emperor Julian, some ten years before the events narrated in the present letter; see Sozomen 5.11.

39   Here being "a philosopher" seems to mean engaging in speculation about God rather than living the ascetical life.

40   Probably the anti-Nicene party supported by the Emperor, who remain eager to reject any affirmation of substantial equality between both the Son and the Spirit and the eternal God. For Basil to affirm openly the full and equal divinity of the Holy Spirit, Gregory suggests, would be to risk putting weapons in their hands.

41   Caesaraea.

42   Gregory's word here, οἰκονομεῖσθαι, originally meant the management of a household but came to be used in ecclesiastical circles for the prudent adaptation of doctrine and canonical practice to the particular needs of time and place. The question always is how much adaptation can take place without abandonment of central tradition. Basil's extant response to the incident (Basil, Letter 71) suggests he was stung by Gregory's suggestion that he had compromised the essentials of the Church's faith by failing to speak out clearly for the full divinity of the Holy Spirit.

43   The text translated here is that of Gallay 1.93–94.

44   It is usually accepted that Basil died on January 1, 379. Gregory here responds to an announcement of the news by Basil's younger brother, Gregory of Nyssa. Gregory is apparently still in Seleucia, a city in the mountains south of Cappadocia, to which he had retired for his health in 375. Gregory's letter combines features of a philosophical "consolation" with a personal letter of condolence to a respected friend; Gregory of Nyssa's philosophical way of life is presented here as his shield against debilitating grief.

45   I.e., Basil.

46   This anguished letter can be dated either to the year 380, when Gregory is acting as unofficial bishop of the Nicene community in Constantinople, or to the early years of his retirement back in Cappadocia, around 381–382, when he seems to have been extraordinarily conscious of his misfortunes.

Although earlier editions of the Greek text give "Eudoxius" as its addressee, the manuscripts clearly indicate that it is rather Philagrius: presumably the same person as the addressee of Letters 30–36, 87, and 92. This Philagrius was an educated Christian, a teacher, and a friend of Gregory's brother Caesarius; he lived in Mataza, a town in Cappadocia. The text translated here is from Gallay 1.103.

47   This letter, written after Gregory's retirement from Constantinople, is addressed to an otherwise unknown person, probably also the addressee of Letter 226. The letter shows Gregory's characteristic blend of ironic wit and self-pity as he reflects on the extent to which his life has changed. The text translated here is that of Gallay 1.111.

48   Eudoxius was the son of a well-educated Cappadocian friend of Gregory's, who was also called Eudoxius: the addressee of Letter 80 and mentioned also in Letters 37 and 38. The younger Eudoxius, to whom Gregory's Letters 174–180 are addressed, was a teacher of rhetoric, probably still in his mid-twenties and at the beginning of his career; he had taken on Gregory's grand-nephew Nicoboulus the younger as his somewhat recalcitrant pupil. Although he had once recommended Eudoxius to the celebrated rhetorician and philosopher Themistius as a possible protégé, Gregory here notes Eudoxius's natural penchant towards the contemplative life and in this letter urges him to devote his energies above all to the practice of a Christian "philosophy." The letter was probably written around 383 during Gregory's retirement. The Greek text translated here is in Gallay 2 (Paris: Les Belles Lettres, 1967) 66–69.

49   For the proverb, see Sirach 4.32; the second allusion is to an epigram that appears also in the *Palatine Anthology* 9.537.

50   *Phaedo* 66b–68b.

51   Gregory is alluding to a character in Aristophanes's *Knights*. This section is an ironic portrait of the role of the professional rhetor in the late fourth century, a profession Augustine considered to be the systematic production of lies for commercial and political advantage.

52   Gregory alludes to the typical exercises used by rhetoricians to train their pupils in eloquence: writing and delivering speeches to characters of classical mythology.

53   Or. possibly: "the Word [of God];" Greek: τὸν λόγον. Ambiguity is almost inevitable with this multipurpose word, but Gregory's urging, a few lines later, to "give wings to your reason" seems to suggest he is thinking of a highly cerebral form of ascetic withdrawal.

54   An echo, perhaps, of Plato, *Phaedrus* 247a: the gods "mount to the summit of the heavenly vault."

5 GREGORY'S WILL

1   Edward Champlin, *Final Judgments. Duty and Emotion in Roman Wills, 200 B.C.–A.D. 250* (Berkeley, CA: University of California Presss, 1991) 29, n. 1., quoted by Raymond van Dam, "Self-Representation in the Will of Gregory Nazianzus," *Journal of Theological Studies* 46 (1995) 127, n. 32.

2   See François Martroye, "Le Testament de Saint Grégoire de Nazianze," *Mémoires de la Société nationale des Antiquaires de France* 76 (1924) 229–230.

3   Van Dam 132–142.

4   See Turner (above, Introduction, n. 112) 169; Braun (above, *ibid.*) 473.

5   For the dating of Cledonius's arrival in Nazianzus, see Marie-Madeleine Hauser-Meury, *Prosopographie zu den Schriften Gregors von Nazianz* (Bonn: Hanstein, 1960) 54. Gregory addressed two celebrated letters to him (Epistles 101 and 102) in 382 or 383 on the threat to orthodoxy and Church order being posed by the Apollinarian movement in Asia Minor and Syria.

6   The text translated here is found in PG 37.389–396.

7   This is the traditional Roman way of giving the official date: December 31, 381. Even in the early Empire, years were legally dated by the name of the consuls, although their function at this time was largely ceremonial: a reward for faithful service in lower bureaucratic offices. For "Flavius Syagrius," the text of the *Patrologia Graeca* has "Flavius Evagrius," but this is clearly an error of either an early copyist or the printer, as these two consuls are well attested for 381. For their careers, see A.H.M. Jones, J.R. Martindale and J. Morris, *Prosopography of the Later Roman Empire* I (Cambridge: Cambridge University Press, 1971) 288 [Eucherius] and 802 [Syagrius]. For a discussion of the problems of the date and circumstances of Gregory's will, see above, pp. 170–171. See also François Martroye, "Le Testament de Saint Grégoire de Nazianze," *Mémoires de la Société Nationale des Antiquaires de France* 76 (1924) 219–263; Raymond Van Dam, "Self-Representation in the Will of Gregory of Nazianzus," *Journal of Theological Studies* 46 (1995) 118–148.

8   It is significant that Gregory designates the Church of Nazianzus the beneficiary of his will rather than the Church of Sasima, of which he is still canonically bishop, or the members or institutions of his former flock in Constantinople. He goes on to indicate that this bequest carries out the wishes of his parents, from whom he had inherited most of his property in the first place.

9   Literally: "who was born of my household" (τὸν ἐκ τῆς οἰκίας μου γενόμενον); this was a technical equivalent to οἰκογενῦ, suggesting that a slave was born to slaves already part of the household of the owner, rather than being purchased. See Marie-Madeleine Hauser-Meury, *Prosopographie zu den Schriften Gregors von Nazianz* (Bonn: Hanstein, 1960) 78, n. 142; 98).

10   The main point in the act of making a will under Roman law was to name a single person as heir and to specify the conditions under which he or she would be required to receive the property of the testator. As he has no direct descendants, Gregory names the monk and deacon Gregory, an old retainer of his family and apparently the manager of his estates, as his heir and as executor of his will.

11   A legacy (*legatum*) under Roman law was a deduction from the estate for the benefit of some designated person or persons; it could be made only in writing and had to be specified in the will after the heir was named. The heir, who was also the will's executor, was legally responsible for paying such a legacy to the person designated. A *fideicommissum* was originally a formal request, made orally or in writing by the testator, that the heir should use some part of the estate for the benefit of a third party but without legally

binding force; in late antiquity, however, the difference between these two forms of legacy was practically nil, and the Code of the Emperor Justinian, in the sixth century, while retaining the two terms, made them more or less identical. See Max Kaser (trans. Rolf Dannenbring), *Roman Private Law* (Pretoria: University of South Africa, 1980) 330–387, esp. 376–384.

12 The Latin term, which Gregory's Greek will reproduces here, is *peculia*: A *peculium* was a sum of money given by a father to his son or by a master to a slave or freedman as a kind of investment. The recipient was to use the sum to set up a business or carry on some kind of trade; he was free to administer it as he saw fit and to make use of its profits, although it remained the property of the donor, who was legally responsible for debts and liabilities up to the limit of the sum invested. Gregory is ordering that these monetary investments should remain undisturbed after his death and implies that they should be considered the property of his former slaves, for all practical purposes. See Kaser-Dannenbring, 86, 246–247, 308–309.

13 Apparently Gregory's parents had purchased the property of their villa, Karbala, from the family possessions of this Rheginus.

14 Gold coins were the most stable form of currency in the ancient world. Fifty years before Gregory's will, Constantine had established the gold *solidus* as a standard of monetary value; in the fourth century, soldiers were usually paid a wage of four *solidi* a year and were apparently able to live adequately on this income. This was the one unit of currency whose value remained relatively stable in the late Roman Empire. See A. H. M. Jones, *The Later Roman Empire* (Oxford: Blackwell, 1964) 1.438, 444–445. Gregory's bequest of fifty *solidi* to his heir and administrator is clearly a generous gift.

15 Literally: "freely," "in a way befitting a free-born person."

16 Besides direct manumission, a slave could be legally freed by stipulation in the master's will (see Kaser-Dannenberg 89–91). Here Gregory confers liberty on two slaves whom he has not yet freed during his lifetime.

17 A notary was a copyist or stenographer; most were slaves or freed slaves.

18 Gregory here refers to Alypiane, the daughter of his sister Gorgonia, as his "daughter," along with her sisters Eugenia and Nonna. Alypiane was married to Nicoboulus (see Ep. 12) and mother of the younger Nicoboulus and two other sons. See also Epp. 195 and 196, and Or. 8, n. 32. She may be the niece Gregory mentions in Ep. 186, to Nectarius.

19 We have no further information on what aspect of his two nieces' lives Gregory found objectionable.

20 The word used here, βουρικάλιον, is very rare. Some lexica suggest it is a misspelling of βουριχάλλιον, which seems to mean "ox-cart." It seems more likely that it is a Greek equivalent of the Latin *burricus*, a post-classical term for a small horse or pony (cf. Spanish *burro*).

21 Meletius seems to be the husband of one of Gregory's nieces, presumably either Eugenia or Nonna, who have just been mentioned unfavorably by their uncle.

22 Probably Aspenzinsus, a site about 25 km. due south of Arianzus. See Friedrich Hild and Marcell Restle, *Kappadokien (Kappadokia, Charsianon, Sebasteia und Lykandos)* (= Tabula Imperii Byzantini 2; Vienna: Verlag der Österreichischen Akademie der Wissenschaften, 1981) 154.

23 This Euphemius may the same person as the addressee of Ep. 103 and was possibly a relative. Other persons named Euphemius are addressed in Epp. 83 and 230.

24 Probably the same as Genedala, 3 km. northwest of Karbala and 10 km. south of Nazianzus. See Hild and Restle 198.

25 Amphilochius, bishop of Iconium in south central Asia Minor, was Gregory's first cousin, himself a notable theologian.

26 Gregory here is referring to Evagrius Ponticus, a younger friend and supporter of all the Cappadocian Fathers. Evagrius has acted as his deacon in Constantinople and has risen to considerable prominence at court; he would, in the years after Gregory's retirement, undergo a conversion and withdraw to monastic life, first at Bethlehem and later in the Egyptian desert at Scetis. There he would produce important and influential works on the ascetic life and other theological themes and be one of the fourth century's main representatives of the Origenist school.

27 The Greek word here, σιγιλιῶνα, is otherwise unknown. In form and accent, it seems to be a noun in the accusative case. The *Acta Sanctorum* (Maii 2.412, notes p and q) suggests it may be derived from the rare late Latin word *singillio*, which seems to mean a garment made of a single thickness of cloth. Martroye (261–262) understands it as an adjective modifying "cloaks" and suggests that it may mean they were embroidered with figures (*sigilla*). It may possibly be an otherwise unknown Greek word for a seal or signet ring (*sigillum*), although Gregory's other bequests seem all to be either clothing or gold coins. See also Van Dam 147, n. 107.

28 Gregory is here simply stipulating that if some formal defect should later be found in this document to prevent its legal validity as a will, it should at least be regarded as an informal but authentic expression of his desires, morally binding on his heir. A *codicillus* under Roman law was a written expression of the testator's desire to have the heir carry out a *fideicommissum* (see above, n. 11).

29 Here the text of Gregory's will is concluded. There follow his formal signature and those of seven witnesses, the normal number required by Roman law in late antiquity. See Kaser-Dannenbring 346.

30 See note 25 above.

31 Optimus was bishop of Antioch in Pisidia, an important city in Asia Minor southwest of Cappadocia. In the Greek list of signatories to the canons of Constantinople I, he is erroneously listed as "Optisius," but the Syriac list gives his name as "Optimus:" see Turner (above, Introduction, n. 112) 169; Braun (above, *ibid.*) 473. Cf. Theodoret, *Church History* 4.27, and Socrates, *Church History* 5.8, who mention Optimus of Antioch as a leading campaigner for orthodoxy at the time of Constantinople. According to Socrates, 7.36, he had previously been bishop of Agdamia in Phrygia—an example of a bishop who (unlike Gregory) had been allowed to move from one see to another.

32 Hyde was a small city in the province of Lycaonia, a short distance southwest of Nazianzus.

33 Probably Apameia in Pisidia, also southwest of Nazianzus, rather than the larger city of that name, Apameia on the Orontes in Syria, south of Antioch. Of all the bishops who witnessed Gregory's will, Theodulus is the only who does not appear on the list of bishops who attended the Council of

Constantinople in the early summer of 381. The Church of Apameia in Pisidia is represented among the signatories of the Council by the presbyter Auxanon (Turner 169; Braun 473).

34 A city in Lycaonia, south central Asia Minor. In the Greek and Syriac lists of bishops at Constantinople, Hilarius appears as "Ilyrius:" Turner 169; Braun 473.

35 Adrianople in Pisidia, west central Asia Minor, also called Thymbrium. In the Greek list of bishops at Constantinople, Themistius appears as "Themistus:" Turner 169; in the Syriac list, "Themistuns," which is probably a mistake for "Themistus:" Braun 473.

36 No date is given for the copy of the will that serves as the basis of the published text, but the fact that John, a notary of the Church at Nazianzus, refers to Gregory as "holy" or "saint" and uses his title "the Theologian" suggests that it was made at least some years after his death, perhaps in order to confirm the use being made of his legacy at the beginning of the fifth century, in accordance with his wishes.

BIBLIOGRAPHY

TEXTS, COMMENTARIES, AND TRANSLATIONS

No complete critical edition of the Greek text of Gregory Nazianzen's works is yet available. The most comprehensive collection is the eighteenth-century Benedictine edition (Paris, 1778), which was completed by Caillau in his edition of 1840 and republished by Jacques-Paul Migne as *Patrologia Graeca* 35–38. The state of the texts in this edition is uneven in quality, and the identification and classification of the poems, especially, needs considerable correction. Many works have, however, appeared in modern editions.

Orations

Critical editions of Gregory's orations with French translations and extensive introductions continue to be published in the series *Sources chrétiennes*; to date, the following have appeared:

Or. 1–3 (ed. Jean Bernardi; S Chr 247 [1978]);
Or. 4–5 (ed. Jean Bernardi; S Chr 309 [1983]);
Or. 6–12 (ed. Marie-Ange Calvet-Sebasti; S Chr 406 [1995]);
Or. 20–23 (ed. Justin Mossay; S Chr 270 [1980]);
Or. 24–26 (ed. Justin Mossay; S Chr 284 [1981]);
Or. 27–31 (ed. Paul Gallay and Maurice Jourjon; S Chr 250 [1978]);
Or. 32–37 (ed. Claudio Moreschini; S Chr 318 [1985]);
Or. 38–41 (ed. Claudio Moreschini; S Chr 358 [1990])
Or. 42–43 (ed. Jean Bernardi; S Chr 384 [1992]).

Letters

A critical edition of Gregory's letters by Paul Gallay has appeared, in several forms:

Gregor von Nazianz. Briefe (*Griechische Christliche Schriftsteller* 53 [Berlin, 1969].

Grégoire de Nazianze. Lettres (Collection Budé; 2 vols.; Paris, 1964 and 1967), with French translation, introduction and notes.

Grégoire de Nazianze. Lettres théologiques (with Maurice Jourjon; Sources chrétiennes 208 [1974]), Epp. 101–102 and 202, with French translation, introduction and notes.

Poetry

Although preliminary studies of the manuscripts of Gregory's poetry continue, critical editions that have been prepared reproduce some of Gregory's longer or more famous poems:

Poemata Arcana (ed. Claudio Moreschini, trans. and commentary Donald F. Sykes: Oxford, 1996).

Autobiographical poems (*Carmina* II, 1, 1–11; ed. André Tuilier and Guillaume Bady, with translation and commentary by Jean Bernardi: *Grégoire de Nazianze, Oeuvres Poétiques* I, 1; Paris: Les Belles Lettres, 2004). This is the first volume of a projected critical edition of all Gregory's poems.

De Vita Sua (ed. Christoph Jungck, with German translation, introduction and commentary; Heidelberg: Carl Winter, 1974).

Σύγκρισις βιῶν (*Comparison of Life-styles*) (ed. Heinz Martin Werhahn; Wiesbaden, 1953).

On Virtue (*Carmina* I, 2.10; ed. Carmelo Crimi and Manfred Kertsch: *Sulla Virtù*; Pisa: Edizioni ETS, 1995).

To Olympias (*Carmina* II, 2.6; ed. Lucia Bacci: *Ad Olympiade*; Pisa: Edizioni ETS, 1996).

English Translations

The collection *Nicene and Post-Nicene Fathers*, series II, volume 7, first published in 1894, includes translations of 24 of Gregory's orations (Or. 1, 2, 3, 7, 8, 12, 16, 18, 21, 27, 28, 29, 30, 31, 33, 34, 37, 38, 39, 40, 41, 42, 43, and 45) and 95 of his letters, by Charles Gordon Browne and James Edward Swallow. A translation of the two orations against Julian (Or. 4 and

5), by C. W. King, was also published in 1888. More recent translations of Gregory's funeral orations on his brother Caesarius, his sister Gorgonia, his father, and his friend Basil (Or. 7, 8, 18, and 43) are included in the volume, *Funeral Orations by Saint Gregory Nazianzen and Saint Ambrose* by Leo McCauley, SJ (Fathers of the Church 22; New York: Catholic University of America Press, 1953). A new translation of the *Five Theological Orations* (Or. 27–31) by Lionel Wickham and Frederick Williams, with an extensive theological introduction and commentary by Frederick W. Norris, appeared under the title *Faith Gives Fullness to Reasoning: the Five Theological Orations of Gregory Nazianzen* (Leiden: Brill, 1991); this translation has been republished, along with a translation of Gregory's two letters to Cledonius on the person of Christ (Ep. 101–102) and with briefer introduction and notes by Lionel Wickham, under the title *On God and Christ* (Crestwood, NY: St. Vladimir's, 2002). Most recently, a translation of all the orations not included in Browne and Swallow's collection, except the two against Julian, has been published by Martha Vinson (Fathers of the Church 107; Washington, DC: Catholic University of America Press, 2003).

Of Gregory's poems, there are three fairly recent translations of the main autobiographical works (II, 1.1; II, 1.11; II, 1.12): by Denis Molaise Meehan, in prose (Fathers of the Church 75; Washington, DC: Catholic University Press, 1987); by Carolinne White (*Gregory of Nazianzus: Autobiographical Poems* [Cambridge: Cambridge University Press, 1996], which includes an edition of the Greek text); and by Peter Gilbert (*On God and Man: the Theological Poetry of Saint Gregory Nazianzen* [Crestwood, NY: St. Vladimir's, 2001], which includes some other poems as well). John McGuckin has also published poetic English translations of a selection of Gregory's poems (*St. Gregory Nazianzen: Selected Poems* [Oxford: SLG Press, 1986]).

Ancient commentaries and vita

Since the late fifth century, scholars and theologians have put together commentaries on the texts of Gregory of Nazianzus because of their classical literary quality and theological depth. For a discussion of all the known commentaries, see Joannes Sajdak, *Historia Critica Scholiastarum et Commentatorum Gregorii Nazianzeni* (Cracow: sumptibus Academiae Litterarum, 1904); Friedhelm Lefherz, *Studien zu Gregor von Nazianz. Mythologie, Überlieferung, Scholiasten* (Diss. Bonn, 1958); for a discussion of the scholia, or marginal comments, on his Orations, especially the sixth-century Alexandrian tradition of commentary, see Jennifer Nimmo Smith, "The Early Scholia on the Sermons of Gregory of Nazianzus," in Bernard Coulie (ed.), *Studia Nazianzenica* 1 (CCG 41; Corpus Nazianzenum 8 [Turnhout, 2000]) 69–146.

Some of these commentaries have been published, wholly or in part, and more are being edited. These include:

Pseudo-Nonnos [probably sixth century], Commentaries on Orations 4, 5, 39, and 43: edition of Greek original, with Syriac and Armenian versions (ed. Jennifer Nimmo Smith, Sebastian Brock, Bernard Coulie; Corpus Christianorum, Series Graeca 27 [Corpus Nazianzenum 2]; 1992); Georgian version, ed Thamar Otkhmezuri (Corpus Christianorum, Series Graeca 50 [Corpus Nazianzenum 16], 2002); English translation of the Greek original by Jennifer Nimmo Smith, under the title, *A Christian's Guide to Greek Culture* (Liverpool: Liverpool University Press, 2001). [The commentary explains classical names and allusions in the orations, probably for use in schools.]

Cosmas of Jerusalem [eighth century], Commentary on the Poems: critical edition based on a twelfth-century Vatican manuscript, with introduction and notes, by Giuseppe Lozza (Naples: D'Auria, 2000). [This commentary is essentially an explanation of Biblical and classical names alluded to in the poems.]

Basil "Minimus" [tenth century]: commented on all but three of the orations and Letters 101, 102, and 243, both from a stylistic and from a theological and philosophical perspective, partly summarizing the work of previous commentators. The commentaries on Orations 4, 5, 8, and 25 are published in PG 36.1073–1204. The commentary on Oration 38 has recently been published in a critical edition with French translation by Thomas Schmidt: Corpus Christianorum, Series Graeca 46: Corpus Nazianzenum 13.

Nicetas of Heraclea [c. 1030–c.1100]: commented extensively, from a theological and liturgical perspective, on the 16 orations then read as part of the monastic office. His commentaries on Orations 1 and 11 are published in PG 36.944–984; on Orations 38–44, in PG 127.1177–1480.

Michael Psellos [eleventh century]: although he left no complete commentary on any of Gregory's works, he wrote many essays explaining particular passages of the orations, especially from a philosophical point of view: see P. Gautier (ed.), *Michael Psellus, Theologica* I (Leipzig: Teubner, 1989); L. G. Westerink and J. M. Duffy (eds.), *Michael Psellus, Theologica* II (Leipzig: Teubner, 2002).

Elias, Metropolitan of Crete [fl. 1120–1130]: commented on 27 orations and 2 letters completely. A partial Greek text of the commentaries on 19 of the Orations, edited by Albert Jahn [1858], is found in PG 36.759–898; a Latin translation of these passages, by Joannes Leunclavius, was previously included in his Basel edition of Gregory's works (1571), 2–393.

The *Life of Gregory Nazianzen* by Gregory, Presbyter of Caesaraea, dating probably from the late sixth or early seventh century, has now been critically edited by Xavier Lequeux: CCG 44 (Corpus Nazianzenum 11; Turnhout, 2001). An earlier edition appears in PG 35.243–304.

Secondary works

Cultural and Literary Context

Anderson, Graham, *Second Sophistic: a Cultural Phenomenon in the Roman Empire* (London: Routledge, 1993).

Athanassiadi-Fowden, Polymnia, *Julian and Hellenism: an Intellectual Biography* (Oxford: Clarendon Press, 1981).

Bowersock, Glen, *Greek Sophists in the Roman Empire* (Oxford: Clarendon Press, 1969).

—— *Julian the Apostate* (Cambridge, MA: Harvard University Press, 1978).

Brown, Peter, *Power and Persuasion in Late Antiquity: Towards a Christian Empire* (Madison, WI: University of Wisconsin Press, 1992).

Browning, Robert, *The Emperor Julian* (Berkeley, CA: University of California Press, 1976).

Cameron, Averil M., *Christianity and the Rhetoric of Empire: the Development of Christian Discourse* (Berkeley, CA: University of California Press, 1991).

Hadot, Pierre, *What Is Ancient Philosophy?* (Cambridge, MA: Harvard University Press, 2002).

Heath, Malcolm, *Menander: a Rhetor in Context* (Oxford: Oxford University Press, 2004) [arguing that the traditional understanding of "Second Sophistic" rhetoric, based on Philostratus's portrait, is one-sided].

Kaster, Robert A., *Guardians of Language: the Grammarian and Society in Late Antiquity* (Berkeley, CA: University of California Press, 1988). [The most extensive modern study of the role and work of grammarians in late antiquity, including a prosopography of known grammarians who worked between 250 and 565 A.D.]

Kennedy, George, *The Art of Persuasion in Greece* (Princeton, NJ: Princeton University Press, 1963).

—— *Greek Rhetoric under the Christian Emperors* (Princeton, NJ: Princeton University Press, 1983).

—— *Classical Rhetoric and its Christian and Secular Tradition from Ancient to Modern Times* (Chapel Hill, NC: University of North Carolina Press, 1999).

Misch, Georg, *A History of Autobiography in Antiquity* (revised from first German edition, 1907, and translated in collaboration with the author; Cambridge, MA: Harvard University Press, 1951).

Murdoch, Adrian, *The Last Pagan. Julian the Apostate and the Death of the Ancient World* (Stroud: Sutton, 2003).

Russell, Donald A., *Greek Declamation* (Cambridge: Cambridge University Press, 1983).

Van Dam, Raymond, *Kingdom of Snow. Roman Rule and Greek Culture in Cappadocia* (Philadelphia, PA: University of Pennsylvania Press, 2002).

—— *Becoming Christian. The Conversion of Roman Cappadocia* (Philadelphia, PA: University of Pennsylvania Press, 2003).

—— *Families and Friends in Late Roman Cappadocia* (Philadelphia, PA: University of Pennsylvania Press, 2003).

Whitmarsh, Tim, " 'Greece is the World': Exile and Identity in the Second Sophistic," in Simon Goldhill (ed.), *Being Greek under Rome: Cultural Identity, the Second Sophistic, and the Development of Empire* (Cambridge: Cambridge University Press, 2001) 269–305.

Williams, Stephen and Gerard Friell, *Theodosius: the Empire at Bay* (London: Batsford, 1994).

Fourth-century theology

Ayres, Lewis, *Nicaea and its Legacy. An Approach to Fourth-Century Trinitarian Theology* (Oxford: Oxford University Press, 2004). [An important new study of the controversies leading up to Nicaea, and the process of its reception.]

Behr, John, *The Nicene Faith* (2 vols.; Crestwood, NY: St. Vladimir's, 2004–2005). [A study of the theological reception of Nicene theology in the fourth century; the second part of a projected longer series on the development of early theology.]

Hanson, Richard P. C., *The Search for the Christian Doctrine of God. The Arian Controversy 318–381 A.D.* (Edinburgh: T. and T. Clark, 1988). [A detailed survey of the debate over Arius and Nicaea; rather cranky interpretations of some figures.]

Prestige, G. L., *God in Patristic Thought* (London: SPCK, 1952). [A classic survey of the developing Patristic understanding of God, with a chapter on the Cappadocian contribution.]

The Cappadocian fathers

Bernardi, Jean, *La Prédication des Pères Cappadociens. Le Prédicateur et son auditoire* (Paris: Presses Univesitaires de France, 1970). [Thorough analysis of all sermons of the three great Cappadocians, with conjectures on chronology.]

Holman, Susan R., *The Hungry are Dying. Beggars and Bishops in Roman Cappadocia* (New York: Oxford University Press, 2001). [A study of the preaching of the three Cappadocians on social justice, against the background of late antique attitudes towards poverty and disease.]

Meredith, Anthony, *The Cappadocians* (Crestwood, NY: St. Vladimir's, 1995).

Pelikan, Jaroslav, *Christianity and Classical Culture. The Metamorphosis of Natural Theology in the Christian Encounter with Hellenism* (New Haven, CT: Yale, 1995). [A study of the theology of the three Cappadocian Fathers as a reshaping of earlier Greek ideas about God.]

Rousseau, Philip, *Basil of Caesaraea.* (Berkeley, CA: University of California Press, 1994). [The most recent full-length biography of Basil.]

Gregory of Nazianzus

Beck, Hans-Georg, *Rede als Kunstwerk und Bekenntnis: Gregor von Nazianz* (Munich: Sitzungsberichte der Bayerischen Akademie der Wissenschaften, philosophisch-historische Klasse 1977/4).

Bernardi, Jean, *Saint Grégoire de Nazianze. Le Théologien et son temps (330-390)* (Paris: Cerf, 1995). [A readable biography.]

Coulie, Bernard, *Les Richesses dans l'oeuvre de S. Grégoire de Nazianze. Étude littéraire et historique* (Louvain-la-Neuve: Université catholique de Louvain, 1985).

Dörrie, H., "Die Epiphanias-Predigt des Gregor von Nazianz (Hom. 39) und ihre geistesgeschichtliche Bedeutung," P. Granfield and J. A. Jungmann (eds.), *Kyriakon. Festschrift Johannes Quasten* I (Münster: Aschendorff, 1970) 409–423.

Ellverson, Anna-Stina, *The Dual Nature of Man. A Study in the Theological Anthropology of Gregory of Nazianzus* (Stockholm: Acta Universitatis Uppsaliensis, 1981).

Gallay, Paul, *Langue et style de S. Grégoire de Nazianze dans sa correspondance* (Paris, 1933). [Gallay later edited Gregory's letters.]

—— *La Vie de saint Grégoire de Nazianze* (Lyon/Paris: Vitte, 1943). [A detailed and careful study of Gregory's career and works; very influential on modern scholarship.]

Gómez-Villegas, Nicanor, *Gregorio de Nazianzo en Constantinopla. Ortodoxia, heterodoxia y regimen teodosiano en una capital cristiana* (Madrid: Consejo superior de investigaciones científicas, 2000). [A thoughtful, well-informed study of Gregory in the cultural context of his time.]

Guignet, Marcel, *S. Grégoire de Nazianze et la rhétorique* (Paris: Picard, 1911).

Hauser-Meury, Marie-Madeleine, *Prosopographie zu den Schriften Gregors von Nazianz* (Bonn: Hanstein, 1960). [An indispensable collection of the available information on all the persons mentioned in Gregory's works; dated in places.]

Keenan, Sr. Mary Emily, "St. Gregory of Nazianzus and Early Byzantine Medicine," *Bulletin of the History of Medicine* 9 (1941) 8–30.

McGuckin, John, *Saint Gregory of Nazianzus. An Intellectual Biography* (Crestwood, NY: St. Vladimir's, 2001). [The fullest and most recent study of Gregory's life. Learned, detailed, sometimes speculative, always thoughtful and readable. Contains an exhaustive bibliography.]

Milovanović, Čelica, "Sailing to *Sophistopolis*: Gregory of Nazianzus and Greek Declamation," *Journal of Early Christian Studies* 13 (2005) 187–232. [A rhetorical analysis of the structure of several of Gregory's orations, showing the influence of forensic as well as epideictic oratory on his work.]

Moreschini, Claudio, "Influenza di Origene su Gregorio Nazianzeno," *Atti e Memorie dell'Accademia Toacana di scienze e lettere La Colombaria* 44 (1979) 35–57.

—— *Filosofia e letteratura in Gregorio Nazianzeno* (Milan: Università Cattolica, 1997).

—— "Nuove considerazioni sull' Origenismo di Gregorio Nazianzeno," in Mario Gerardi and Marcello Marin (eds.), *Origene e l'Alessandrinismo Cappadoce (III – IV secolo)* (Quaderni di 'Vetera Christianorum' 28; Bari: Edipuglia, 2002) 207–218.

Moreschini, Claudio and Giovanni Menestrina (eds), *Gregorio Nazianzeno teologo e scrittore* (Trento: Istituto di Scienze Religoise in Trento, 1992). [An important collection of articles on Gregory as a literary and theological figure.]

Mossay, Justin, "Perspectives eschatologiques de S. Grégoire de Nazianze," *Questions liturgiques et paroissales* 45 (1964)

—— *La mort et l'au-delà dans S. Grégoire de Nazianze* (Leuven: Publications universitaires de Louvain, 1966). [The most complete study of Gregory's eschatological thought.]

Pellegrino, Michele, La Poesia di S. Gregorio Nazianzeno (Milan: Università Cattolica, 1932).

Pinault, Henri, Le Platonisme de S. Grégoire de Nazianze: Essai sur les relations du Christianisme et de l'Hellénisme dans son oeuvre théologique (La-Roche-sur-Yon: Romain, 1925). [A thorough investigation of the influence of the Greek philosophical tradition on Gregory's thought; balanced and comprehensive.]

Plagnieux, Jean, *Saint Grégoire de Nazianze théologien* (Paris: Éditions Franciscaines, 1948). [Still the most complete and balanced systematic survey of Gregory's theological ideas.]

Radford Ruether, Rosemary, *Gregory of Nazianzus: Rhetor and Philosopher* (Oxford: Clarendon Press, 1969). [Concise, useful overview of Gregory's life and the role of the rhetorical tradition in his writings.]

Smolak, Kurt, "Interpretatorische Bemerkungen zum Hymnus πρὸς Θεόν des Gregor von Nazianz," *Studi classici in onore di Quintino Cataudella* 2 (Catania: Università di Catania, 1972) 425–448.

Špidlík, Tomas, *Grégoire de Nazianze. Introduction à l'étude de sa doctrine spirituelle* (Orientalia Christiana Analecta 189; Rome: Pontificio Istituto Orientale, 1971). [An important survey of Gregory's spirituality.]

Szymusiak, Jan, *Éléments de théologie de l'homme selon S. Grégoire de Nazianze* (Rome: Diss. Gregoriana, 1963).

—— "Pour une chronologie des discours de S. Grégoire de Nazianze," *Vigiliae christianae* 20 (1966) 183–189 [on the chronology of the orations given in Constantinople].

Trisoglio, Francesco, *Gregorio di Nazianzo il teologo* (Milan: Università Cattolica, 1996). [A brief, straightforward survey of Gregory's life, personality, ideas and literary style.]

Winslow, Donald F., *The Dynamics of Salvation. A Study in Gregory of Nazianzus* (Cambridge, MA: Philadelphia Patristics Foundation, 1979). [A thoughtful study of Gregory's soteriology in the Orations.]

INDEX

eBooks – at www.eBookstore.tandf.co.uk

A library at your fingertips!

eBooks are electronic versions of printed books. You can store them on your PC/laptop or browse them online.

They have advantages for anyone needing rapid access to a wide variety of published, copyright information.

eBooks can help your research by enabling you to bookmark chapters, annotate text and use instant searches to find specific words or phrases. Several eBook files would fit on even a small laptop or PDA.

NEW: Save money by eSubscribing: cheap, online access to any eBook for as long as you need it.

Annual subscription packages

We now offer special low-cost bulk subscriptions to packages of eBooks in certain subject areas. These are available to libraries or to individuals.

For more information please contact webmaster.ebooks@tandf.co.uk

We're continually developing the eBook concept, so keep up to date by visiting the website.

www.eBookstore.tandf.co.uk